Language and Thought in Normal
and Handicapped Children

Cognitive Development

This series presents the work of an outstanding group of scientists working together at the Medical Research Council's Cognitive Development Unit who, in spite of diverse backgrounds, have evolved a common approach to the fundamental issues of cognitive developmental psychology. This is nativist rather than empiricist, focusing on the dynamics of change rather than on stages. Covering a range of topics from early infancy onwards, the series will collectively make up a major, new, coherent position.

Autism   *Uta Frith*

Language and Thought in Normal and Handicapped
Children   *Richard F. Cromer*

Language and Thought in Normal and Handicapped Children

Richard F. Cromer

Basil Blackwell

'Developmental Strategies for Language' © Academic Press Ltd 1976

Richard F. Cromer is hereby identified as author of this work in accordance
with Section 77 of the Copyright, Designs and Patents Act 1988.

First published 1991

Basil Blackwell Ltd
108 Cowley Road, Oxford, OX4 1JF, UK

Basil Blackwell, Inc.
3 Cambridge Center
Cambridge, Massachusetts 02142, USA

British Library Cataloguing in Publication Data

A CIP catalogue record for this book is available from the British
Library

Library of Congress Cataloging in Publication Data

Cromer, Richard F.
Language and thought in normal and handicapped children/Richard F.
Cromer
p. cm. — (Cognitive development)
Includes bibliographical references and index.
ISBN 0–631–14526–5 — ISBN 0–631–14527–3 (Pbk.)
1. Language acquisition. 2. Handicapped children—Language.
I. Title. II. Series: Cognitive development (Oxford, England)
P118.C685 1991
401'.93—dc20
90–45700
CIP

Typeset in 10 on 12 pt Plantin
by Wearside Tradespools, Fulwell, Sunderland
Printed in Great Britain by T.J. Press Ltd, Padstow Cornwall

Contents

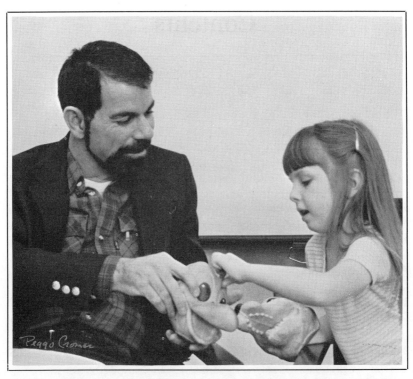

Richard Cromer testing a child on the wolf-and-duck experiment
(photograph by Peggo Cromer)

Foreword

Rick Cromer and I had our best time together in 1968 when he wrote his thesis (287 pages) in a twenty-four day marathon. He came to Harvard as a graduate student in 1962 which was the first year of the Adam-and-Eve project, and for some years he accompanied Ursula Bellugi in her visits to Adam and on alternate weeks, Colin Fraser on his visits to Eve.

Rick was 'wonderful with the children'. What does that mean? It means he did not 'come at them' with torrents of motherese but was a quiet, warm presence prepared to speak if spoken to, play if needed as a playmate, and . . . always an observer on whom nothing was lost. It also means, perhaps just because he was not himself a parent, that he never lost his sense of evidence, never attributed to the children competencies that were his rather than theirs. Developmental psycholinguists usually write as if there were no such thing as a specific talent for research in this field, but there is, and Richard Cromer had it, in spades.

After six graduate school years that he has described (Cromer, 1988) as 'enjoyable', Rick realized early in 1968 that his eligibility for teaching assistantships was nearly at an end, that it was time to face life. So he sequestered himself in William James Hall for twenty-four days and nights and produced 'The Development of Temporal Reference during the Acquisition of Language'. He says I kept the pace, producing comments on what he wrote, and I do remember feeling winded as well as exhilarated. Rick had been interested all along in the development of the concept of time in early childhood and about two-thirds of the thesis is devoted to the analysis of relevant utterances from Adam, but that is not the part of the thesis that I most admired then and remember best today. There was also an experiment with seventeen pre-school children that was, and is, just beautiful.

From the analysis of Adam's speech, it appeared that between four years and four-and-a-half . . . Adam developed the ability to take leave of his own position in a temporal series, to stand outside that series and speak with reference to positions other than his own. Rick called this 'decentering in time', and he invented a way to study it systematically in young children by taking advantage of their familiarity with the convention of left-to-right linear representation of time in comic strips.

Zoo Story

Once upon a time there was a little boy who lived in a house in the city. One day he went out walking. He went to see the zoo. There he saw a lion in a cage. Then he saw a tall giraffe. Later he saw an elephant lifting a big pole. Then he ran home and told his mother all he had seen. (1968, p. 182)

The story tells of a string of seven events and, for each event, there is a corresponding picture. Taking advantage of another cartoon convention – the speaking bubble – the experimenter asks the child: 'In which picture can the little boy say "I see a lion"?' That would be picture 4. In which: 'I'm gonna go out walking?' (1). In which: 'I saw a tall giraffe?' (6 or 7). In which: 'I will see a lion?' (1, 2, or 3). The ingenuity of the method is wonderful and the possibilities great. In which picture could the boy say: 'I will have seen a lion?' (1, 2, or 3).

In the dissertation, Richard Cromer made his first published statement of the relation between language acquisition and cognitive development. 'Approaches which do not take developing cognitive abilities into account cannot hope to explain these otherwise mysterious phenomena. Language acquisition is a complicated procedure and simple models will not suffice . . . We must also look at cognitive processes and their development and at the ways such processes direct language acquisition if we are to acquire new insights into that acquisition process'. (1968, p. 220). In 1968, this was a radical and liberating position, but it was not Richard Cromer's last word on the subject.

In 1974, we have the full-dress statement of the 'cognition hypothesis' which was given this name deliberately so as to create a wording-parallel with its near-opposite, the 'Whorfian hypothesis'. Richard Cromer, as an undergraduate at Tulane University, had concentrated in cultureal anthropology and when he arrived at Harvard in 1962 was inclined to Whorfian views. By 1974, then, he had come a long intellectual journey. It is the special genius of the 1974 formulation to locate the cognition hypothesis with reference to three coordinates: Whorf, Piaget, and Chomsky. The genius is dramaturgical as well as intellectual, and it has excited many imaginations and inspired much research.

Last Sunday (7 October, 1990), I read chapter 2 of the present book and I felt closer to Rick than I have at any time since the twenty-four day

marathon in 1968. Chapter 2 is the last word we shall have from him on
the cognition hypothesis: 'It has been increasingly popular to speculate
about whether there are modular components of human knowledge.
"Language" has often figured prominently in these speculations, but the
different advocates of this position often disagree about what a module
includes. Does modularity apply only to the core syntax? ... Or is
modularity broader even than syntax itself?' (see below, p. 135).

The statement is important because Rick made it – after some twenty-
two years of grappling with the issues. But you do not need to know that
twenty-two years went into the statement to appreciate its weight. You
need only read the critical review that precedes it; it is the most
penetrating, complete, and fair-minded discussion of research on language
and thought ever written. And the concluding statement on modularity,
preserving the intellectual style of a lifetime, is not really a statement, but
a question. Of course, Rick knew that his last words on the great subject
that engrossed him for much of his lifetime would not be the last words
ever written on that subject.

It is not because of his conclusions that I felt close to Rick's mind in
reading chapter 2; it is because of the way he evaluates the evidence; in
considerable part it is because of what he writes in the notes. The
language-and-thought research relevant to the Whorfian hypothesis is
research I know well, or so I thought. But Rick found important sources I
missed, either because they are very recent or because they are more
out-of-the-way than I went. But for the most part, we have written about
the same work: Brown and Lenneberg (1954), Berlin and Kay (1969),
Heider (1972) on colour and codability; Carroll and Casagrande (1958) on
object classification; Bloom (1981) and Au (1983) on counterfactual
conditionals. For the most part, what he read, I have read; where he went,
I have been. But Rick has done a better job, seen implications I missed,
uncovered flaws I overlooked. Any embarrassment at being improved
upon was swamped, last Sunday, by a sense of mutual participation.
Because, you see, it is very often the case that what Rick explicitly
describes and pursues, I noticed and then refrained from pursuing,
whether from fatigue or the wish to believe or insufficient imagination.
Allow me one example.

The famous study by Berlin and Kay (1969) on basic colours, their
universality and evolution, is in part based on the mapping of focal colours
by informants for twenty genetically diverse languages. The two investigators expanded the scope of their study to a total of ninety-eight languages
by drawing upon anthropological descriptions, many dating from the late
nineteenth or early twentieth century, of colour lexicons in the various
languages. I have always felt uneasy about this part of the Berlin and Kay

study. In the absence of colour chips and acetate mapping sheets, how would an anthropologist have decided on the translations of the local terms and how could Berlin and Kay have known what to make of these translations? The ground is soft here. What I did in a 1976 review, and also later, was test the ground with one foot and then draw back – feeling that one must trust some things in a research report and also being taken with the authors' ultimate conclusions. Rick was more energetic and even-handed and he plunged forward and, in this case, turned up so many problems that he says he wonders whether the study's 'conclusions are simply unwarranted' (chapter 2, note 6).

Again and again, reading chapter 2 last Sunday, I followed his reasoning with complete understanding, felt suspense as he approached his conclusion, and then experienced elation as he flew ahead of where things were to establish a new conclusion or a more powerful synthesis – dimly sensed in the past perhaps, but only now made clear. I relished with him the pleasure of overcoming inconsistencies and seeing how things really go. And as I read, I subvocally said: 'Good for you, Rick! Bravo! Well done!' As if he were once again just twenty-three.

Roger Brown,
14 October, 1990
Cambridge, Massachusetts

Preface

Richard F. Cromer was born on 26 November 1940 and died on 14 June 1990 in the midst of a life devoted to research on language and thought. A PhD of Harvard, he wrote his thesis, 'The Development of Temporal Reference during the Acquisition of Language', under Roger Brown. With Ursula Bellugi, Colin Fraser and others he was part of Roger Brown's team which reported the first ever cases of the *development of language* from the new Chomskian perspective that revolutionized linguistics. These cases have become classics under the names of Adam and Eve. He was also a member of Jerry Bruner's team studying with novel and ingenious methods the performance of young children on conservation tasks. These studies have had enormous impact on our understanding of the *development of thought*. Rick made London his permanent home in 1968, when he was asked by Neil O'Connor to join the newly formed Medical Research Council Developmental Psychology Unit. He became a founder member of the MRC Cognitive Development Unit, which was formed by John Morton in 1982, and he worked there for the remainder of his career.

For as long as colleagues and friends have known him, Rick worked on the age-old question of the relationship between language and thought. Although he challenged established views and published extensively on the subject, these writings were dispersed in various journal articles and book chapters. Rick was also much in demand as a speaker at international conferences, where he was able constantly to update and communicate his views. Eventually Philip Carpenter of Basil Blackwell persuaded him to bring these different writings together in a book.

Richard Cromer's first major position paper on language and thought appeared in 1974, subtitled 'The Cognition Hypothesis'. It attracted a lot

This preface was jointly written by Uta Frith, Annette Karmiloff-Smith, Sigrid Lipka and John Morton.

of attention and generated much new research throughout developmental psycholinguistics. It is reprinted here as chapter 1. In the late 1980s, on the basis of his own research and a detailed examination of the extensive literature published on the topic from the 1970s onward, Rick began a major reanalysis of the relationship between language and thought. He managed to finish this task just a few weeks before he died. Only minor editing changes were made, on the basis of comments by Uta Frith, Annette Karmiloff-Smith, Sigrid Lipka, John Morton and Neil O'Connor. This new, hitherto unpublished work forms chapter 2 of this book. The reprinted essays have been minimally edited to avoid gross repetitions.

An interest in the relation between language and thought throughout the course of development was accompanied by a focus on the relation of language and thought inside a single experimental situation. Rick placed great emphasis on the role of strategy in language tasks. In fact, he made others see the concept of 'strategy' in language acquisition in a totally new light. This formed the topic of an important publication in 1976, which is reprinted here as chapter 3. Five years later Rick's work led to another major reconceptualization of the problem, in a paper published here as chapter 4. In this, as in other work, Rick analyses the specific tasks faced by children during language acquisition, tasks which differ in important ways from those a child deals with in other areas of cognitive development. Finally, chapter 5, which was first published in 1978, is a discussion of developmental aphasia which critically examines the range of current theories of aphasia and looks at the relation of language and thought in abnormal development.

For those of us who read Richard Cromer's work when it was first published, the rereading is refreshing, and the new writing exciting and provocative. For those who are unfamiliar with the clarity of his thinking, this entire volume will illustrate a field of inquiry boldly delineated and carefully explored. Rick inspired many students to do work in the area. He gave them unstinting help and will be remembered by many as one of the most outstanding teachers in his field. Very little escaped his painstaking scrutiny. Through his own high critical standards he helped to raise the standard of work in psycholinguistics in general. With this volume the effect will be seen to reach into the future. Rick had a special talent for presenting even the smallest of relevant details from various fields without ever losing sight of the general perspectives. In fact, he enjoyed creating these perspectives and organizing into a coherent picture what would otherwise have remained disjointed and amorphous research scattered about the literature.

He was a true scholar in every sense of the term. His wide collection of others' books and articles was a valuable reference source generously shared with colleagues and students alike. For many years Rick ran a fortnightly Friday-evening psycholinguistics group which was regularly and enthusiastically attended by researchers and lecturers from almost every college in London.

It is difficult to know whom Rick would have wished to acknowledge in a preface to his book, but it is clear from his writing whose work he admired and was influenced by. To be sure, he would have wanted to pay tribute to many years of discussions with his colleagues, teachers and students, and above all his many friends. Certainly he would have wanted to thank all his colleagues at the Developmental Psychology Unit and at the Cognitive Development Unit, particularly his research officers, Hilary Johnson and Sigrid Lipka, for their contributions to his work. And to Sigrid Rick would surely have proffered special thanks for being able to rely on her during the final months of his life, when she went well beyond the call of duty in her editorial dedication to the preparation of this book.

Certainly, too, Rick would have wished to place on record his indebtedness to Lorenzo Vivaldini for his constant encouragement, confidence and support over many years and particularly during the months of his illness.

One of Rick's most well-known projects was the wolf-and-duck experiment on children's understanding of 'easy to please'/'eager to please'. Richard Cromer was not easy to please intellectually; he questioned every theory in detail. But he was always eager to understand. We have lost a dedicated scholar. But by this book we have gained an invaluable contribution to developmental psycholinguistics.

Acknowledgements

On behalf of the author the publishers thank the following for permission to reprint or reproduce copyright material.

Penguin Books Ltd for the text of chapter 1; Academic Press Ltd for the text of chapters 3 and 5 and the line drawings on pp. 76, 77, 79, 80, the first two originally executed by Clare Wake and all four first published in Cromer (1983); University Park Press Inc. for the text of chapter 4; Scientific American Books Inc. for the table on p. 62, first published in Cole and Cole (1989); Lawrence Erlbaum Associates Inc. for the table on pp. 133–4, to be published in H. Tager-Flusberg (ed.), *Constraints on Language Acquisition: studies of atypical children*; and Peggo Cromer for the photograph of the author.

1

The Development of Language and Cognition: the Cognition Hypothesis

That was when I learned that words are no good; that words don't ever fit even what they are trying to say at . . . .

William Faulkner, *As I Lay Dying*

That thought might be possible without language does not strike most people as an unreasonable idea. In fact, some artists claim that they cannot express themselves in a purely verbal medium. Even writers, whose life work immerses them in the very task of arranging words and sentences to convey meaning, often complain that their thoughts 'will not enter words'. It may come as a surprise, then, to find that the predominating view of psychologists over the last half century has been precisely the opposite: namely, that thought is dependent upon language and not possible without it. How can such a state of affairs be? What has brought about an adherence to a view which seems to go against our intuition?

Before tracing the intellectual currents which influenced the adoption of this view, it may be well to note that psychologists have not always believed that language is necessary for thought. According to William James, thinking would tend to make use of the kind of 'mind-stuff' which is easiest for the purpose. In his famous textbook *The Principles of Psychology* (1890) he asserted that words, whether uttered or unexpressed, are the handiest mental elements we have, and thus would be the material

This chapter (copyright © Richard F. Cromer, 1974) was first published in Brian Foss (ed.), *New Perspectives in Child Development* (Harmondsworth, Middx: Penguin, 1974), pp. 184–252. It is reprinted here by kind permission of Penguin Books Ltd.

usually used for thinking. However, he also noted that the deaf and dumb can weave their tactile and visual images into 'a system of thought quite as effective and rational as that of a word-user'. To support this claim, James quoted at length an extract of reminiscences of childhood by a Mr Ballard, a deaf-mute who was an instructor in the National College at Washington. For our purposes, a few excerpts will suffice:

> I could convey my thoughts and feelings to my parents and brothers by natural signs or pantomime, and I could understand what they said to me by the same medium; our intercourse being, however, confined to the daily routine of home affairs and hardly going beyond the circle of my own observation. . . .
>
> My father adopted a course which he thought would, in some measure, compensate me the loss of my hearing. It was that of taking me with him when business required him to ride abroad; and he took me more frequently than he did my brothers; giving, as the reason for his apparent partiality, that they could acquire information through the ear, while I depended solely upon my eye for acquaintance with affairs of the outside world. . . .
>
> It was during those delightful rides, some two or three years before my initiation into the rudiments of written language, that I began to ask myself the question: *How came the world into being?* When this question occurred to my mind, I set myself to thinking it over a long time. My curiosity was awakened as to what was the origin of human life in its first appearance upon the earth, and of vegetable life as well, and also the cause of the existence of the earth, sun, moon and stars. . . .
>
> I have no recollection of what it was that first suggested to me the question as to the origin of things. I had before this time gained ideas of the descent from parent to child, of the propagation of animals, and of the production of plants from seeds. . . .
>
> I think I was five years old when I began to understand the descent from parent to child and the propagation of animals. I was nearly eleven years old when I entered the Institution where I was educated; and I remember distinctly that it was at least two years before this time that I began to ask myself the question as to the origin of the universe.*

We will see, further on, that evidence of thinking by the deaf in controlled, experimental situations has been used as support by more recent exponents of the view that thinking is independent of language. But, before we leave William James, it is worth noting one more short passage from his argument (1890, repr. 1950, pp. 269–70) that thinking is

---

* This passage is excerpted from a longer version quoted by William James and attributed by him to Samuel Porter, 'Is thought possible without language?', *Princeton Review*, 57th year (Jan. 1881 ?), pp. 108–12.

not dependent on language, for this idea is only currently becoming acceptable again, and James has been able to render it in words more ably than most others:

> Let *A* be some experience from which a number of thinkers start. Let *Z* be the practical conclusion rationally inferable from it. One gets to the conclusion by one line, another by another; one follows a course of English,

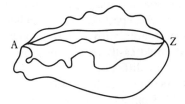

> another of German, verbal imagery. With one, visual images predominate; with another tactile. Some trains are tinged with emotions, others not; some are very abridged, synthetic and rapid, others hesitating and broken into many steps. But when the penultimate terms of all the trains, however differing *inter se*, finally shoot into the same conclusion, we say and rightly say, that all the thinkers have had substantially the same thought. It would probably astound each of them beyond measure to be let into his neighbour's mind and to find how different the scenery there was from that in his own.

A view directly contrary to this arose in the 1920s and 1930s, primarily through the writings of two men – Edward Sapir, an anthropologist and linguist, and Benjamin Lee Whorf, who was a fire-prevention engineer for an insurance company but who spent his non-business hours working in linguistics. The new viewpoint, which became known as the Sapir–Whorf hypothesis, basically asserted that the commonly held notion that all human beings possess a common logical structure and think in similar ways was incorrect. Indeed, the Sapir–Whorf hypothesis claims that individuals are not even able to observe the world in the same way. Rather, they are constrained to certain modes of interpretation by the language they speak. The grammar of one's language leads one to different types of observations and different evaluations of external experience. As Whorf (1952) put it,

> We cut up and organize the spread and flow of events as we do largely because, through our mother tongue, we are parties to an agreement to do so, not because nature itself is segmented in exactly that way for all to see. Languages differ not only in how they build their sentences but in how they break down nature to secure the elements to put in those sentences. . . .

Whorf claimed, for example, that European languages (which he lumped together as SAE or Standard Average European), treat 'time' as an objective entity, as if time were a ribbon with equal spaces marked off, presumably because of the use of past, present and what can be called the future tense. The Hopi Indian language of North America, however, gets along without tenses for its verbs, and it has no words, grammatical forms, constructions or expressions that refer directly to what we call 'time'. Consequently, the Hopi speaker's conception of 'time', or more precisely 'duration', is very different from that of SAE speakers. Whorf believed that, while Hopi speakers would have trouble with concepts such as simultaneity, which we find easy, they would easily be able to deal with concepts of relativity, which we often find difficult. Whorf (1958) has indeed noted several ways language affects our scientific views.

If all this seems a bit abstruse, a passage from Sapir (1949) will perhaps serve to clarify the claim that the Sapir–Whorf hypothesis makes:

> when we observe an object of the type that we call a 'stone' moving through space towards the earth, we involuntarily analyse the phenomenon into two concrete notions, that of a stone and that of an act of falling, and, relating these two notions to each other by certain formal methods proper to English, we declare that 'the stone falls'. We assume, naïvely enough, that this is about the only analysis that can be properly made.
>
> [However], in German and in French we are compelled to assign 'stone' to a gender category – perhaps the Freudians can tell us why this object is masculine in the one language, feminine in the other; in Chippewa we cannot express ourselves without bringing in the apparently irrelevant fact that a stone is an inanimate object. If we find gender beside the point, the Russians may wonder why we consider it necessary to specify in every case whether a stone, or any other object for that matter, is conceived in a definite or an indefinite manner, why the difference between 'the stone' and 'a stone' matters. 'Stone falls' is good enough for Lenin, as it was good enough for Cicero. And if we find barbarous the neglect of the distinction as to definiteness, the Kwakiutl Indian of British Columbia may sympathize with us but wonder why we do not go a step further and indicate in some way whether the stone is visible or invisible to the speaker at the moment of speaking, and whether it is nearest to the speaker, the person addressed, or some third party. 'That would no doubt sound fine in Kwakiutl, but we are too busy!' And yet we insist on expressing the singularity of the falling object, where the Kwakiutl Indian, differing from the Chippewa, can generalize and make a statement which would apply equally well to one or several stones. Moreover, he need not specify the time of the fall. The Chinese get on with a minimum of explicit formal statement and content themselves with a frugal 'stone fall'.

These differences of analysis, one may object, are merely formal; they do not invalidate the necessity of the fundamental concrete analysis of the situation into 'stone' and what the stone does, which in this case is 'fall'. But this necessity, which we feel so strongly, is an illusion. In the Nootka language the combined impression of a stone falling is quite differently analysed. The stone need not be specifically referred to, but a single word, a verb form, may be used which is in practice not essentially more ambiguous than our English sentence. This verb form consists of two main elements, the first indicating general movement or position of a stone or stonelike object, while the second refers to downward direction. We can get some hint of the feeling of the Nootka word if we assume the existence of an intransitive verb 'to stone', referring to the position or movement of a stonelike object. Then our sentence may be reassembled into something like 'It stones down.' In this type of expression the thing-quality of the stone is implied in the generalized verbal element 'to stone', while the specific kind of motion which is given us in experience when a stone falls is conceived as separable into a generalized notion of the movement of a class of objects and a more specific one of direction. In other words, while Nootka has no difficulty whatever in describing the fall of a stone, it has no verb that truly corresponds to our 'fall'.

It would be possible to go on indefinitely with such examples of incommensurable analyses of experience in different languages. (pp. 157–9)

Various aspects of the language we speak, then, and of which we are normally unaware, restrict the way we view the world and the ways we are able to think. This is what is meant by the 'strong' form of the Sapir–Whorf hypothesis. However, it is interesting to note that we can translate concepts expressed in one language into another, although the expression of those concepts may be more tortured – we may have to use long phrases where the original language uses a single word. And certainly, even if our language is resistant to the concept of relativity, we can come to grasp its meaning by attending lectures or reading on the subject. (It is also interesting to note in this regard that Einstein was somewhat of a slow child and acquired language rather late; he claims that language did not play much part in his thought processes.) Roger Brown (1956), in an essay on the relation between language and thought, offered a suggestion which somewhat undermines the extreme position of linguistic determinism. Brown noted that languages differ in their 'codability' of certain concepts, and he reasoned that codability of a concept would affect the 'availability' of that concept to the speakers of that language. He thus held that languages do not *determine* thinking, but only that they *predispose* people to think in particular ways. A number of experiments using memory for variously coloured discs examined this 'weak' form of the Sapir–Whorf hypothesis. Brown and Lenneberg (1954) forced subjects to place greater emphasis on verbal cues when remembering colours they had seen by two methods. In one, they increased the delay interval between the time the colours were first seen and the time when an array was presented from which the subject had to choose the remembered colours. In the second method, they merely increased the number of colours to be remembered. When the subjects' reliance on verbal memory was increased in these ways, Brown and Lenneberg found that the colour was more easily and accurately picked out of a large array the more codable it was in language. Lenneberg and Roberts (1956) examined the memory for colours by Zuni- and English-speakers. The Zuni language has only a single term for yellows and oranges, and, as predicted, Zuni-speakers had difficulty with these colours and often confused them, a mistake English-speakers rarely made; and the number of errors made by bilingual Zuni–English-speakers was midway between monolingual Zuni and monolingual English subjects' error scores. A review of these results is found in Brown and Lenneberg (1958). The same type of task has also been approached using a concept of communication accuracy instead of codability (Lantz and Stefflre, 1964), and there is a full discussion in Miller and McNeill (1969).

There are several good reviews of the Sapir–Whorf hypothesis (e.g. Henle, 1958; Hoijer, 1954; Slobin 1971b), and Adams (1972) has republished a number of interesting readings on language and thought. The writings of both Sapir and Whorf used to be difficult to obtain, but many of them are now more readily available. Sapir's writings have been collected by Mandelbaum (1949, 1961), and Whorf's essays have been brought together by Carroll (1956).

It is clear that the common-sense notion that thought is independent of language, and that thinking runs its own course, indeed encountering difficulty when it must be put into words, is severely challenged by the Sapir–Whorf hypothesis whether in its strong or weak form. But there was a second intellectual current, one which stirred directly in the mainstream of psychological theory, which has played a major part in inducing most psychologists to adopt the view that language determines thought. We can label this influence the 'behaviourist' tradition. By 'behaviourist' we will mean here a conjunction of intellectual trends the most important of which, for our purposes, are the empiricist theory of mind, the emphasis on objective, publicly observable events, and the associationistic theory of the connection of ideas. These trends which affected the study of psychology at the end of the nineteenth century are discussed and put into historical perspective by George Miller in his introductory text *Psychology: the Science of Mental Life* (1962a). The infant's mind was believed to be a blank slate upon which experience inscribed its lessons. The only events which could be observed were those impinging from outside the organism, and the possibility of internal organization of these events was discounted as being unscientific speculation. The outside events were analysed in terms of their elements and these were seen to combine by the laws of association. At this point we should note that, as far as the issue of the relationship between thought and language is concerned, there was no necessity to equate the two. When the two are equated, however, it is easier to conceptualize language as the determiner of thought since speech units are observable phenomena which impinge on the child, who is seen as essentially passive. This view has certain consequences for a theory of language acquisition, and these will be discussed in more detail further on. The consequence for the thought–language controversy is simply that in the behaviourist view speech units are heard and imitated by the child, acquired through the process of selective reinforcement, and thereby become the means of thought. One did not have to hypothesize any unobservable events in thinking. The extreme position was put forward by John B. Watson, the founder of American behaviourism, in 1912. He held that all thought processes are really motor habits which would be observable as movements in the larynx during so-called 'silent' thought. This is in some sense an ironic claim by Watson since at the time he made it instruments sufficiently precise to measure these movements were not available, and their existence was based on speculation. Nevertheless, movements of the larynx have since been recorded during silent thought. But whether they *are* thought or are even necessary for thought is another matter. Experiments using the drug curare leave no doubt that movements of the larynx are not necessary for thought processes to occur. A dose of d-Tubocurarine chloride two and a half times that necessary for complete respiratory paralysis and adequate for complete skeletal muscular paralysis was given intravenously to a subject. He was, of course, kept breathing by artificial means. While in this state, with the speech musculature completely immobilized, the individual was still capable of thought and was later able to report his thoughts and perceptions (Smith et al., 1947). Lenneberg's demonstration (1962, 1964) that a child unable to speak due to congenital anarthria (impairment of the speech organs) was nevertheless able to understand language propositions and concepts, as well as the common observation of the ability of the deaf to think (see Furth, 1966, for experimental support of such observations), would seem to indicate that this extreme view is unwarranted. It is easy to see, however, the reasons why a less extreme theory is appealing. Thoughts and their acquisition are difficult to observe, but speech units and the acquisition of productive language are scientifically observable and quantitatively measurable. Any kind of thinking which appears to be more elaborated than could be explained by the mere acquisition of immediate motor habits can be seen in the same theoretical framework as these habits, if words serve as a mediating influence but are themselves acquired as habits.

There has been a good deal of study of language serving a mediating function in thought and in the development of children's concepts (see for example Kendler, 1963; Spiker, 1963). The question which is of central concern to us, however, is not whether verbal materials can facilitate performance on some tasks, but whether certain cognitive abilities are actually dependent on language. It was thought at one time that cross-modal transfer between different sensory modalities was limited to human beings and that, therefore, language served as the device which mediated between differing modalities. Hermelin and O'Connor (1964) found, however, that normal, subnormal and autistic children showed crossmodal transfer from vision to touch. As these groups differed markedly in their verbal ability, but not in their capacity to transfer from one modality to another, Hermelin and O'Connor rejected the view that crossmodal effects were due to verbal coding. Looking at the effects of language from the other way round, O'Connor and Hermelin (1971) found in another experiment that normal, subnormal and deaf children were unable to transfer a touch discrimination to another modality even though most subjects could verbalize the solution. In other words, these results indicate that verbal coding and crossmodal transfer are independent processes. Furthermore, the initial assumption on which the importance of language was based, i.e. that other animals, because they lack language, are unable to transfer information from one modality to another, seems to be unwarranted, and some crossmodal transfer has, in fact, been demonstrated in other species (Davenport and Rogers, 1970; see also studies reported by Koehler, 1972).

A strong claim for the importance of language in higher thinking processes was made in 1956 in the Soviet Union by A. R. Luria and F. I. Yudovich. They separated a pair of identical twins who were retarded in their language and mental development in order to force them to communicate with others. The ensuing improvement in their mental abilities was attributed to the improvement in their language. However, whether such a causal relationship can be asserted between the two processes, as Luria and Yudovich have done, is questionable. Indeed, Luria and Yudovich report that special speech training for one of the twins, while accelerating the conscious application of speech, nevertheless played only a subsidiary role in intellectual improvement, since both twins made great gains.

A more extended version of the importance of language in thinking has been proposed by Bernstein (1961). He has claimed that children from working-class backgrounds have a restricted language code while children from middle-class homes possess an elaborated code. Bernstein asserts that, since the relationship between potential and developed intelligence is mediated through the language system, the lack of an elaborated code by the working-class child prevents him from developing his intellectual faculties to their fullest capacity. There are a number of problems in such a view, particularly in the assessment of intelligence itself in groups from differing backgrounds. But even the basic assumption that working-class children possess a less elaborated code than middle-class children has come under criticism (Houston, 1970). It is probably true to say that, while Bernstein's proposal concerning the relation between language and cognition is an interesting one, the direction of causation is still undetermined. If Bernstein's ideas on language are interpreted in the sense that certain linguistic abilities in an individual (regardless of what social group he belongs to) are facilitative of particular forms of thought, one is still left with the question of whether that individual's intellectual capabilities in fact provided the ability necessary to master those linguistic forms. It is this question – whether language precedes cognition or whether cognition precedes language – which will be the central concern of this chapter, but we will be looking at the problem in terms of the young child first acquiring his native language.

What has been characterized as the behaviourist tradition in psychology has been shown to influence the view that language precedes thought because of its emphasis on the empiricist theory of mind and its beliefs concerning the mechanisms by which knowledge, including language, is acquired. As has been pointed out, the behaviourist viewpoint does not exclude the possibility of cognition prior to language, but the application of behaviourist principles to the study of the acquisition of language has led most adherents of that position to conceptualize language acquisition in a vacuum, with the organism passively being exposed to the language about him, being reinforced for his imitations (which occur first to those items which are most frequent in the language behaviour about him) and thus slowly approximating the language spoken in his community. Probably the clearest and strongest expression of this view was by Skinner (1957), although others had expressed similar positions (e.g. Mowrer, 1954). As is now well known by students in the field, the linguist Noam Chomsky (1959) wrote a devastating criticism of the stimulus–response, learning-theory view expressed by Skinner.

There are many psychologists who still adhere strongly to the Skinnerian viewpoint on the acquisition of language, and there are many others whose thinking is still coloured by an overriding interest in processes such as frequency, imitation, reinforcement and generalization as explanatory principles in the child's acquisition of his native language. There is increasing evidence, however, that such principles, while possibly important in explaining some aspects of language-learning, are nevertheless by themselves inadequate to account for the linguistic changes occurring in children acquiring language. It is beyond the scope of this chapter to review the arguments and the evidence against these stimulus–response principles, although some of the findings concerning cognitive processes preceding and in some cases directing language acquisition, which will be discussed further on, also serve as warnings against a too-simplistic view of the language-acquisition process. The reader who is interested in both the theoretical reasoning and the empirical evidence against stimulus–response theories of language acquisition can find excellent reviews by Bellugi (1967, 1971), Bever, Fodor and Weksel (1965a, 1965b), Brown, Cazden and Bellugi-Klima (1969), Ervin-Tripp (1966), McNeill (1966, 1970a, 1970b), Miller and McNeill (1969), Sachs (1971), Slobin (1971a) and Vetter and Howell (1971).

One of the main points of contention has centred on the problem of what exactly the child brings with him to the language-acquisition task if he is not an empty organism with a 'blank slate'. Chomsky's viewpoint (1962, 1965, 1966, 1968) is that the child has, innately, a number of formal and substantive linguistic mechanisms which are part of his 'language-acquisition device' (LAD). These mechanisms are, of course, universal since they are innate, and they provide schemata which are applied to the particular language to which the child is exposed. McNeill has attempted to describe several possible innate features. He claims, for example, that the basic grammatical relations are innately part of the child's grammatical competence (McNeill, 1966, 1970a, 1970b). He has also asserted that the grammatical category 'noun' is a strong linguistic universal and that this category is based on a strictly linguistic ability as a necessary cause (1970c). The claim, then, by this school of thinking, is that language has its own specific roots which are observable in the linguistic universals which can be recorded in children's language acquisition everywhere in the world regardless of the particular language being acquired. Some loose writing has occasionally seemed to indicate that what was being claimed was the illogical view that, because these features are found universally, they are innate. However, the actual claim is that certain linguistic features are innate and can, therefore, be observed universally.

This theory has been subjected to severe criticism by adherents of the empiricist theory of mind. And there are others less committed to the 'blank slate' theory who nevertheless are distrustful of assuming any processes as innate since such suppositions, in the past, have sometimes served as cloaks to cover the ignorance of the details of particular developmental phenomena. Theories of innate analysers and inborn organizational properties are, however, more acceptable today than they used to be. For example, advocates of innate organization of perception have found support in the discovery of specific perceptual receptors in the cortex of the cat for horizontal and vertical orientation (Hubel and Wiesel, 1962). The prospect of discovering similar 'real entities' for language functions, however, is slim – and the necessity to do so logically dubious in any case. The argument between those linguists and psycholinguists who posit the existence of innate language functions, and psychologists who refuse to consider the possibility of any 'innate ideas', seems destined to continue for some time. The notion that language has its own roots has, however, been attacked by a second group who have little in common with the behaviourist school of thought in psychology as sketched earlier. This new attack on the Chomskian position has come from Piagetian psychologists in Geneva, who claim that language reflects thought, i.e. that language is, in fact, structured by thought.

It would be impossible to summarize succinctly Piaget's view of development. There are a number of good reviews of Piagetian theory, however (e.g. Flavell, 1963; Furth, 1969), and Piaget himself has published some excellent overviews of his theory (Piaget, 1970a, 1970b; Piaget and Inhelder, 1969b). The point to note for our purposes is that in the Piagetian view of development the child for his first two years of life has represented the world to himself through sensorimotor actions, and his 'pre-linguistic thought' (for we can call it that from the Piagetian point of view) is characterized by sensorimotor intelligence. According to Piaget, the accomplishments of this period include a number of striking cognitive attainments – for example, the achievement of object permanence, imitation of actions seen sometime previously, the anticipations of the future position of an object before its movement, etc.

The Piagetian view on language is a very complex one. Piaget notes that, when language begins, it obviously plays a major part in the person's representation of the world and in the interiorization of action into thought. But he also points out that language is only one factor of the symbolic function as a whole – other factors being deferred imitation, mental imagery, symbolic games, drawing and the like.

When the symbolic or semiotic function begins to be operative, it has the advantage of being able to detach thought from action. It therefore has several important effects on sensorimotor thought. Piaget notes, for example, that language, in particular, allows for three developments: a speeding-up of representation over that possible by sensorimotor representation, an ability to transcend immediate space and time, and the ability to represent a number of elements simultaneously rather than by means of successive, step-by-step thought. The semiotic function, then, detaches thought from action, and language plays a particularly important role in this formative process (see Piaget and Inhelder, 1969b). But the main point for us is the claim that language builds on and affects a number of cognitive abilities which have already arisen in the sensorimotor period.

What about thought in the more traditional sense? Even though it may be true that there are a number of cognitive structures which are built up during the first two years of life which have little relationship to language, what about the kind of thinking which has been characterized by Piaget as operational thinking, which arises at about the age of seven years? Surely, it could be argued, this type of more elaborated thought is dependent on language, especially in view of the importance which Piaget has attributed to language in freeing representation from its reliance on immediate action. Indeed, it has been claimed by some (e.g. Bruner, 1964) that language transforms experience by lifting it to a new plane of symbolic manipulation. According to this view, language frees the individual from the immediate perceptual qualities of a situation (as in the traditional conservation experiment where water transferred from one of two identical beakers to a taller but thinner one is thought by the younger child to change in amount and become 'more') and enables him to give correct adult-like answers in such situations. But Piaget denies that language is responsible for the new logical structures which define the stage of 'operational thinking' (see for example Inhelder and Piaget, 1964, p. 282). Further, he cites evidence (Piaget, 1970a, 1970b; Piaget and Inhelder, 1969b) that the deaf are as capable of operational thinking as those who have language, although the particular studies he mentions show the deaf to be greatly delayed in the emergence of operational thought. Furth (1966) has conducted a number of studies of the development of thought in the deaf using Piagetian techniques. Although his results are also ambiguous in that operational thinking is somewhat delayed as compared to non-impaired children, he too concludes that language does not appear to be necessary for operatory functioning. Piaget contrasts the studies of the deaf with studies of the blind. The deaf have complete sensorimotor schemes but lack language, while the blind are in full possession of normal language but are impaired in their sensorimotor experiences. Yet, while the deaf are said not to be deficient in the development of their operational thinking, the blind (on evidence by Hatwell, 1966) are said to be severely delayed in the emergence of operational thought. Piaget claims that this comparison especially well illustrates that language is not the source of operational thinking. The actual evidence on which this claim is made is very shaky in that the experimental studies showed a considerable delay in the emergence of operational thinking in the deaf, which was, however, attributed by the experimenters to other factors. Furthermore, further evidence (Cromer, 1973) indicates that the blind may not be delayed in the emergence of operational structures, as had previously been suggested. Nevertheless, the claim that operational thinking precedes particular linguistic changes finds support in the study of non-handicapped children. We will see later on, for example, revealing experimental evidence by Sinclair on this point.

Finally, there is the period of formal operations which arise at adolescence according to the Piagetian school. Formal operations are manifested in propositional thinking. That is, these operations consist of a combinatorial system which allows the construction of hypothetical possibilities, so that the individual is enabled to envisage all the possible relationships which could hold true in a set of data. Is it possible that at least this type of thinking is dependent on language and the elaboration of verbal categories? Those who have studied thinking by the deaf seem to feel that this is a real possibility. Furth and Youniss in a review of their studies (1971) assert,

> Whereas language is never a sufficient or necessary condition of operatory functioning, the evidence from our work with linguistically deficient persons indicates that it may have, at best, an indirect facilitating effect for concrete operations, but can have a direct facilitating effect on certain formal operations precisely because of the close relation between formal operations and symbolic functioning. (p. 64)

Piaget also notes that the propositional operations are closely related to 'a precise and flexible manipulation of language' but warns that it would be a mistake to assume that the only advances at that stage are those marked by an advance in language. Indeed, Piaget conceives the formal operational structures which allow formal thinking in a way which goes quite beyond a mere linguistic ability to manipulate propositions, and he makes this clear in his writings on that topic (see Inhelder and Piaget, 1958, chs 16 and 17). I think one would not be far wrong in characterizing Piaget's position by saying that language may possibly be necessary for the propositional manipulations of formal thought but that language itself is not a *sufficient* condition for that type of thinking. Indeed, it is difficult to see in what way the language of the individual at the stage of formal operational thought significantly differs from that of the individual who has not yet attained this stage of thinking, except in the use he makes of his linguistic structures.

It would appear then that, in Piaget's view, at all stages of thought, the later as well as the earlier, it is cognition which affects language and not the reverse. It is in this context that Piaget, though supporting much of what Chomsky has to say, finds fault with him. Chomsky does not make any specific claims about the relation between language and thought, and it is not here that the controversy between Piaget and Chomsky lies. Rather, Piaget takes issue with the Chomskian view that certain linguistic mechanisms are innate. Piaget claims,

> Chomsky goes so far as to say that the kernel of reason on which the grammar of language is constructed is innate, that it is not constructed through the actions of the infant as I have described but is hereditary and innate (1970a, p. 47)

and

> Chomsky's transformational structures are facilitated by the previous operation of the sensori-motor schemes, and thus . . . their origin is neither an innate neurophysiological program (as Chomsky himself would have it) nor in an operant or other conditioning 'learning' process [as Chomsky (1959) has shown conclusively]. (1970b, p. 711)

In the next section, we will return to some evidence which Piaget offers on this.

Up to this point, an attempt has been made to sketch in a bit of the more recent historical background of the positions psychologists have held on the issue of the relation between language and thought. We have seen that psychologists did not always oppose the view that thought and cognitive processes preceded language. We then reviewed two contributions to the opposite point of view – the Sapir–Whorf hypothesis, which directly asserted the formative role of language, and the behaviourist tradition in psychology, which has significantly influenced the types of experimentation and observation carried out by psychologists. I have purposely left one significant figure, Vygotsky, for the conclusion. We have also seen two more recent contributions to the controversy. The Chomskian linguistic position has emphasized the independence of the origins of language and maintained that these linguistic roots are innate. This view has met with opposition by the Piagetian psychologists, who, though not at all in the behaviourist tradition, reject the nativist assumption of inborn linguistic mechanisms and argue instead that cognitive properties which are built up through interaction with the environment precede language and directly influence its acquisition.

The remainder of this article will be based on experimental evidence bearing on these issues. In the next section we will examine the evidence for cognition preceding language. The studies will be subdivided into three subsections, which will deal with the effects of cognitive factors on babbling and first words, the acquisition of grammar, and later acquisitions. We must also note, however, that there is a good deal of evidence to support the linguists' claims that language has its own roots. There will, therefore, follow a section concerned with the evidence that language progresses according to its own developmental rules and is not wholly dependent on cognition. Finally, we will put forward two forms of a 'cognition hypothesis' and take a measure of the distance we have covered.

Evidence for Cognition Preceding Language

Cognitive effects on babbling and first words

One can observe the influence of behaviourist psychology, as outlined earlier, in the way psychologists have until recently theorized about the babbling of the very young infant and his later acquisition of words. It has often been observed that the infant, in one stage of his babbling, produces all of the sounds which are available to all of the world's languages and only in later childhood narrows his repertoire so that it includes only those sounds which are present in the language he hears about him. Indeed, it is very difficult at later ages even to produce certain sounds of foreign languages, but we are assured that we easily did so during our initial babbling stage. The processes by which the narrowing occurs are said to be a combination of imitation and differential reinforcement. According to this view, the child in his babbling occasionally stumbles across sounds which are similar to those occurring in the adult speech around him. It was hypothesized by some that when the child does this, the adult reinforces the child by attention of some kind, such as smiling. Thus the child tries to imitate the sounds around him and makes successively closer approximations to them. A slightly different version of this type of theory was that the child finds the production of the sounds reinforcing itself, rather than requiring some adult reinforcement directly, and the reason this sound production is reinforcing is due to association with adult comforting, attention and the like. In either case, the important principles for phonological acquisition were thought to be imitation and reinforcement. It is somewhat ironic that this learning-theory view of the acquisition of phonology has often paid so little attention to the empirically observable facts. Linguists, looking far more closely at the child's phonological acquisitions, have come to a very different point of view.

The linguistic position is that the child does not imitate sounds; instead, he produces them according to a systematic set of phonological rules. In 1941, Roman Jakobson put forward a theory concerning the features of sounds used in language. This was not translated into English until 1968. Basically, his theory is that the infant discriminates features of sounds which are represented by phonological contrasts such as vocalic/non-vocalic, voiced/voiceless, nasal/oral, grave/acute, etc. The child seems first to dichotomize all sounds on the basis of one feature, and he thus begins making sound-distinctions with that single contrast. Later, he adds features to his system and by this means he progressively separates sounds until all of those in the language have been identified on the basis of the distinguishing features. The features are rules which act across particular sounds. For example, when the child acquires the contrast voiced/voiceless, he creates not one but a number of distinctions based on the voicing feature – for example /g/ versus /k/, /b/ versus /p/, /d/ versus /t/, and /v/ versus /f/. It is also said that these contrast rules appear in the child's productions in a constant order, and that this order will correspond to the number of languages in the world which contain the particular feature. The details of theories of this type can be found in Chomsky and Halle (1968), Jakobson (1968), Jakobson and Halle (1956) and Jakobson, Fant and Halle (1952). Good short introductory summaries of the linguistic position are available by David Palermo in his chapter on language acquisition in Reese and Lipsitt (1970), and by Kaplan and Kaplan (1971). Ervin-Tripp (1966) has examined the data from several diary studies of language acquisition by individual children in terms of the distinctive features, and Neil Smith (1973) has made a longitudinal study of phonological acquisition in this light. In these, there is strong evidence for the acquisition of phonology according to a set of rules like those described. In general, there is a rough correspondence with Jakobson's predictions, but there are individual variations as well.

The identification of the full set of phonological rules by linguists is not complete, but the evidence nevertheless indicates that imitation as traditionally conceived does not appear to be the process whereby the infant acquires the sounds of his language. Lenneberg, Rebelsky and Nichols (1965) have found that vocalizations of children born to deaf parents do not differ from those of babies born to hearing parents in the first three months of life. Thus, at least in early vocalization, the types of sounds made are identical. This is not surprising, and it is really the later stages of babbling which are crucial for an imitation theory. Barbara Dodd (1972) has made a study of infant vocalizations at the peak of their babbling period (age 9–12 months). Against a baseline of the sounds each individual infant was already producing, she compared the sounds produced after a period of concentrated vocal stimulation. This stimulation by an adult included sounds not found in the child's babbling during the base period. Dodd found that with purely vocal stimulation there was no imitation of the adult, and indeed not even an increase in the amount of babbling by the infant. In a group which received both social and vocal stimulation, however, the infant increased his *amount* of vocalization. But, there was no increase in the range of the *types* of sounds made. Thus, imitation was not produced even in situations which combined social and concentrated vocal stimulation, although the *amount* of babbling was increased.

There is the further consideration, too, that, at least for receptive language competence, the child need never have imitated sounds made by adults. Lenneberg's study mentioned earlier (1962, 1964) indicated that children with impaired speech apparatus are able to acquire language and understand linguistic propositions. But, even among non-impaired children normally acquiring productive speech, the notion of imitation in the traditional sense is now disputed. As we have seen, modern linguistic theory holds that the child progresses through a series of contrastive phonological features by which he analyses the sounds he hears, and he produces his own sounds in accordance with those rules. Neil Smith (1971, 1973) reports an amusing observation which shows how the young child's application of particular phonetic rules in fact prevents him from being able to imitate accurately certain words, even when it can be shown that he has the ability to do so. When the child, playing an imitation game, was asked to say *puddle* he replied *puggle* since his phonological rules at that stage required him to replace /t/ or /d/ before syllabic /l/ with a velar sound, e.g. /g/ or /k/. But, when the same child was asked to say *puzzle*, he then replied *puddle*, since his rules require the replacement of non-continuant sonorants by /d/ or its allophones.

The fact that children universally apply the same type of phonological feature analysis to the sounds they hear would seem to indicate that the phonological aspects of language are not acquired from external sources in the way usually hypothesized by psychologists (imitation and reinforcement). At the same time, however, the application of these features universally would be strong evidence that at least some aspects of language obey their own developmental laws, and this is a question to which we will return in the next major section. But what is interesting for our purposes here is an idea put forward by Eleanor and George Kaplan (1971) that *meaning* also affects the acquisition of early sounds. Before looking at their proposal, however, let us look at the possibility of 'meaning' in the very first cries of the newborn infant.

It has been proposed that infant cries contain a set of differentiated messages. Lind (1965) has edited a number of studies of the crying sounds of the newborn infant, and Wolff (1969) has demonstrated that these different cries communicate distinct messages. Derek Ricks (1972) has carried out a very interesting study on communicative aspects of the cries of normal children of 8–12 months of age and the cries of autistic children of age 3–5 years. Under controlled conditions, Ricks elicited four types of messages: a requesting sound, a frustrated sound, a greeting sound, and a sound expressing pleased surprise (e.g. a novel and exciting event). This was done by setting up actual situations which stimulated the child to produce the appropriate 'message'. The cries were recorded on tape and, in addition to the English children, the cries of Italian and Spanish children in the four situations were also recorded. In the experiment, six parents of normal children and six of autistic children each listened to the tape-recorded sounds of four babies each giving the four cries in the situations just noted. Thus, each parent had 16 cries to identify. The four babies that the parents of normal children heard included their own baby, one non-English baby and two infants randomly selected from the other normal English babies. The four children that the parents of autistic children listened to included their own autistic child, one non-autistic subnormal child and two other autistic children randomly selected from the other autistic children. The task of the parents was fourfold: they had to identify and label all four sounds for each of the four children; they had to identify their own child; the parents of normal children had to identify the non-English child while the parents of autistic children had to identify the non-autistic child; finally, the parents heard the request cries of six babies and had to pick out their own child from amongst these. The results were that the parents of normal children could identify the messages, but to their surprise were not able to pick out their own child. Furthermore, these parents correctly identified the messages of the cries of the non-English babies but were not able to pick out which child was non-English. The parents of autistic children, on the other hand, could only identify the messages of their own child or of a non-autistic child, and they could easily recognize which child was their own. In other words, it appears that, while autistic children do not use the vocabulary of intonated signals of normal children and instead have their own distinctive cries, the cries of normal children show a marked similarity converging on the same message, and these signals seem to be independent of language background. This would again be evidence of universal phonological laws, but here these are tied to a function of communicating specific meanings.

Kaplan and Kaplan (1971) propose that the child's semantic system develops out of the early distinctions present in his communication system. They feel that with adequate data one will be able to identify a set of semantic features and chart the developmental order of their emergence. For example, when the infant makes the early distinction between human and non-human sounds, the Kaplans suggest the feature '±human' has become operative. When the infant differentiates himself from others, as observable in the effect of delayed auditory feedback on crying (i.e. indicating that the infant can distinguish between his own voice and other sounds), he is credited with the feature '±ego'. As the child develops his knowledge of object properties he adds such features as '±existence' and '±presence'. Other later acquisitions would include '±agent', and '±past' and the like. These semantic features would place constraints on the child's language acquisition. Although the Kaplans have formulated this theory with reference to the infant's first sounds, it would be possible to extend a similar kind of analysis to grammatical acquisitions at later ages.

On the acquisition of first words, Ricks (1972) has conducted an experiment which has a bearing on the issue of imitation and acquisition. He first made the interesting observation that the child's first words were of two major types. Between 11 and 18 months, the infant begins to produce a number of early words which have either loose referents or are used in babble without any referents at all. Furthermore, they are imitated when spoken by the adult to the child. These first utterances include words like *dada* and *mama* and Ricks calls them 'dada words'. However, at some point, a second type of word appears and this type is used concurrently with the 'dada words'. This second type, which he calls 'label words', has an interesting set of characteristics which separates them clearly from 'dada words'. For example:

1 The 'label words' are not found in the babbling as the 'dada words' are.
2 The 'label word' occurs only in the context with the stimulus for which it is a label, and is used by the child only when related to that particular stimulus or event.
3 When the 'label word' is repeated, it is not modified by the child to resemble a more conventional term. Indeed, Ricks points out that the parents often begin using the child's term in context so that it is the parental language which is modified!
4 Once utilized, a 'label word' frequently generalizes to other objects, e.g. *bow wow* used for a dog soon becomes used for any four-legged animal.
5 The child always expresses the 'label words' with a great deal of excitement and zeal.
6 Mention of a 'label word' usually captures the child's attention and alerts him to look for the object to which, to him, it refers.

7   Mention of a 'label word' by the parent produces very ready repetition by the child.

   In an imitation experiment, infants heard three tapes, each played on different days. On each tape, the words were spoken by the child's mother, his father and by two adults, unknown to the child, one male and one female. One tape was made up of a 'dada word' of the individual child, and each adult uttered it five times at 10-second intervals. A second tape consisted of one of the child's own 'label words'. The third tape had the adults uttering a meaningless combination such as *dibby* which the child was capable of uttering, but as far as could be ascertained had never actually uttered. Thus, each child was presented with one of the types of words 20 times on each tape (each of four adults uttering it five times) for a total of 80 times during the day (each tape was played four times during the day). The child's imitations were carefully recorded, and the results showed that, although there was some imitation of all three word types, it was fairly low for the meaningless words; 'dada words' were moderately imitated, but 'label words' elicited by far the greatest number of imitations. In other words, the child seems to imitate mainly the sounds which he already spontaneously applies to the world about him. He also shows some moderate imitation of words which he already uses but which do not constitute a label which he, in some sense, invented. Meaningless but phonetically possible combinations are imitated practically not at all. It would appear, then, that the child does not *learn* words, but that he *invents* them for the things he wants to communicate. Furthermore, imitation does not appear to be a mechanism of acquisition. This does not mean that these inventions are totally independent of the language he hears about him; they are closely related to it, but are nevertheless independent of it in important respects, the most important appearing to be the creativity which he brings to bear on the acquisition process, and this creativity has to do with the communication of concepts which he is cognitively able to handle.
   In fact, just prior to the time when the child begins to utter his first multi-word combinations, are the words he utters merely labels at all? There is some evidence that they may not be. Many investigators have noticed that the words young children utter are more like complete sentences or thoughts, and these early words have been called 'mot-phrases', 'sentence words', or 'holophrases'. For example, in 1927, Grace de Laguna noted that the proper names uttered by a child were not used by him simply to designate or label that individual; rather they were used to make all sorts of comments about that person or even about objects and events connected with him. The child might, for example, point at a pair

of slippers and say 'Papa'. More recently, McNeill (1970a, 1970b) has argued that holophrastic speech is evidence that children possess basic grammatical relations. That is, he claims that, since most of the utterances express predication (i.e. they are *comments* on the situation in which the speech occurs), the basic grammatical relations such as subject, predicate, verb, object, modifier and head are being honoured in this earliest speech. There is some dispute over whether these one-word utterances should be considered grammatical (see for example Bloom, 1970), but the fact that they express such relations as predication, direct- and indirect-object relationships, and modification indicates that children are able to express meaning from the onset of language acquisition. In other words, the child does not arrive at a meaning of these relationships because he has learned linguistic categories which then restructure his thinking; instead, he brings certain meanings to the task of language acquisition, and these affect even his very first words. But the child's intellectual accomplishments are not complete at this time. Do continuing developments in cognition affect language acquisition at later stages?

Cognitive effects on grammar

In a theoretical paper on the cognitive bases of language-learning, Macnamara (1972) has claimed that the child cannot discover many syntactic structures without the aid of meaning. He proposes a specific theory of acquisition in which children determine the referents for main lexical items in sentences that they hear and then use their knowledge of these referents to decide what the semantic meaning of the structures intended by the speaker must be. In other words, once the child is able to determine the meaning of particular words, he will be able to work out the intended meaning of a speaker's utterances using them on the basis of what he knows about the world. Whether this particular theory is true can only be determined by evidence from language-acquisition studies. We will see further on that there is some evidence that when children acquire a new cognitive category they acquire both the syntactic structures for it and associated lexical items simultaneously – and that would seem to be at odds with the particular mechanism of acquisition which Macnamara proposes. Nevertheless, in a more general sense Macnamara's proposal that acquisition is dependent on cognitive prerequisites is an intriguing one.

In a review of language-acquisition studies, Susan Ervin-Tripp (1971) has suggested that language could never be learned unless the meanings were obvious to the child when he heard sentences expressing them. If this is true, she argues, then the study of the categories, features and relations available to children at the very outset of language acquisition is crucially important in the explanation and prediction of language-learning. In addition, if one could establish a developmental order of cognitive growth, then one would be better able to account for developments within language. And one would also be able to specify which properties of input are incomprehensible to children due to limitations of their cognitive development at particular stages. One is reminded here of the developmental theories of the Piagetian psychologists whose claims have already been dealt with in a general way. It will be recalled that, when language acquisition begins, the foundations of sensorimotor thought have already been laid. This in itself is of very great interest, for, if language has its own independent developmental laws, why does it appear only at the close of the sensorimotor period?

Hermine Sinclair, a linguist working in the Piagetian framework, believes that the child begins to acquire language only at the conclusion of the sensorimotor period because language is dependent on some of the intellectual accomplishments of that period. Not until then has the child reached a stage where he is an active person distinct from the objects he acts upon. This allows a differentiation between himself and others and therefore calls for communication. After about 18 months of age, there is evidence that the child can achieve problem solutions cognitively, i.e. prior to carrying out actions. In other words, it is inferred from behavioural observations that the child of about 18 months comes to possess the ability to represent reality mentally. Such representation includes the ability to recapitulate actions in the past and to anticipate actions in the future. It should be especially noted that this representation is said initially to occur in non-verbal form. Piaget's example of his daughter's use of motor representation at the age of 1 year 4 months is often cited. A small chain was placed in a matchbox, the opening of which was made so small that little Lucienne could not retrieve it by poking her finger into the box as she had been doing previously. After manipulating the box, she suddenly stopped, opened and shut her mouth several times more and more widely, and then immediately pushed the box open to retrieve the chain. Piaget interpreted this as evidence of motor symbolism, in which could be seen the beginnings of anticipatory thought.

Sinclair (1971) notes a number of sensorimotor schemes which she feels can account for corresponding linguistic abilities observed in language acquisition. The child's ability to order things both spatially and temporally would have its linguistic equivalent in concatenation of linguistic elements. The child's ability to classify in action (i.e. to use a whole category of objects for the same action, or to apply a whole category of action schemes to one object) has, as its linguistic counterpart, categorization of linguistic elements into the major categories like noun phrase and verb phrase. The ability to relate objects and actions to one another provides the underpinnings for the functional grammatical relations such as 'subject of' and 'object of'. The ability to embed action schemes into one another allows a linguistic recursive property such that phrase-markers can be inserted into other phrase-markers. These serve as examples, then, of the types of sensorimotor abilities which have been achieved when the symbolic function begins to make possible the acquisition of language, and these schemes account for the ability to acquire particular aspects of that linguistic system. In Sinclair's words, 'The child possesses a set of coordinations of action schemes which can be shown to have certain structural properties which will make it possible for him to start comprehending and producing language' (1971, p. 127). The linguist John Lyons, who incidentally has written a short book which serves as an excellent introduction to Chomsky's ideas (see Lyons, 1970), makes much the same point as Sinclair:

> By the time the child arrives at the age of eighteen months or so, he is already in possession of the ability to distinguish 'things' and 'properties' in the 'situations' in which he is learning and uses language. And this ability seems to me quite adequate as a basis for the learning of the principal deep structure relationship between lexical items (the subject–predicate relationship), provided that the child is presented with a sufficient amount of 'primary linguistic data' in real 'situations' of language use. (Lyons, 1966, p. 131)

There seems to be a growing interest on the part of linguists and psychologists in the possibility of underlying meanings which affect the surface structures of language. Fillmore (1968), for example, has put forward a case theory of grammar in which underlying meanings play a primary role. McCawley (1968) has suggested a directly semantic deep structure. Schlesinger (1971a, 1971b) has proposed a theory taking into account the speaker's intentions and these are based on cognitive capacities. Sinclair's Piagetian analysis, in a sense, goes somewhat further than these since it incorporates not only the idea of cognitive principles underlying language acquisition but also specifies some *developmental* features of these cognitive abilities. Her analysis of the sensorimotor schemes and their relationship to particular linguistic abilities may be very useful, and the sensorimotor schemes may indeed eventually be shown to be *necessary* to make language acquisition possible, but we are entitled to ask whether such structures are *sufficient* to account for human linguistic abilities. This question will be put off until later, however, as it is the topic of the next major section; and it will be our task now to examine instead the available evidence that supports the view that cognitive properties precede grammatical distinctions.

For several years, Roger Brown and his associates at Harvard University have been carrying out a detailed study of the acquisition of language by three children. Basically, the research workers recorded the child's utterances in his natural home situation for two hours at fortnightly intervals. Any adult speech was also recorded; this was usually speech by the mother. Pertinent situational cues were also noted. Detailed descriptions of the study itself and analyses of various parts of the linguistic data have been reported in several papers (Brown and Bellugi, 1964; Brown and Fraser, 1964; Brown and Hanlon, 1970; Brown, Cazden and Bellugi-Klima, 1969; Brown, Fraser and Bellugi, 1964). Most of these papers are reprinted in Brown (1970b). These reports deal almost entirely with purely linguistic changes occurring as the child acquires language. Later Brown (1973) turned his attention to the semantic or meaning aspects of the child's utterances.

In looking at the children's utterances at Stage I of their language acquisition (a stage defined not by age but by a comparable mean utterance length in the three children ranging from approximately 1½ to 2 morphemes, and thus constituting a very early stage in multi-word constructions), Brown noted that for all three children the verb was initially in an unmarked form, i.e. it did not have any inflectional endings. Nevertheless, such a verb was understood by the parents in one of four ways, depending not only on the utterance itself but on the situational context in which the utterance occurred. One of these was the *imperative,* as in 'Get book.' A second meaning which was communicated at this stage was reference to the *past,* as for example, in 'Book drop' where the book had just dropped. A third meaning ascribed to the child was that of *intention or prediction,* as in 'Mommy read' in a context where Mommy was about to read to the child. Finally, there was the expression of *present temporary duration* as in 'Fish swim' where the context would call for an adult utterance using a progressive, such as 'The fish is swimming.' Brown reports that after Stage I the children gradually learned to modify the generic verb in three ways. They began marking the past, with *-ed* or an irregular allomorph, producing such utterances as 'It dropped' and 'It fell', with the time range at first limited to a very immediate past. Another way they modified the verb was to use it in conjunction with a semi-auxiliary or catenative such as *gonna, wanna* and *hafta.* Although it was not possible to judge when the use of these was necessary, Brown notes that their meaning can be mainly characterized by intentionality or imminence, a kind of immediate future of the child's intentions or of actions about to occur (e.g. 'I wanna go', 'It's gonna fall'). A third modification was that the child began to use a primitive progressive form, i.e. he used -*ing* endings on the verb but without an auxiliary. It is startling to note that these first three operations that children perform on the verb just after Stage I encode three of the four semantic intentions attributed by adults to the child (past, intention or prediction, and present temporary duration) when he was only using the unmarked, generic form of the verb at the earlier stage. The fourth semantic intention, the imperative, has no specific grammatical marker in English, but Brown notes that the children began to use 'Please' at this time along with the other three markers. It would appear, then, that the first grammatical distinctions the child makes with verbs in his utterances after Stage I are those which encode the types of *meaning* he had been credited with expressing just prior to the acquisition of his new linguistic abilities.

Brown also traced the development of prepositions, but found that in the earliest stages only two were used with a great enough frequency to yield analysable data. These were the prepositions *in* and *on*. When Brown listed all occurrences of these along with the nouns with which they were used by the children, a semantic principle motivating their differential use was revealed. The nouns used with *in* were objects which could contain other objects, i.e. they were objects having cavities or containing internal spaces, such as *bag, box* and *briefcase*. The nouns used with *on* were all objects which had flat surfaces which could support other objects, such as *floor, shelf* and *table*. In addition, one of the children had a meaning for *in* which was used to denote intermingling, and was used in such utterances as 'in my hair' and 'in the snow'. The parents of these children were similarly using *in* and *on* to denote the same spatial locations, but, interestingly, they were also using them in phrases with abstract non-spatial forms (as in '*in* phrases with abstract non-spatial forms'). Yet the children, while exposed to these, did not give evidence of using them in this abstract way (except in the case of a few idiomatic expressions). Although there is not a careful study of the spatial relations children use at their first stages in speech, it is clear that they are able to express the spatial concepts encoded by *in* and *on* before they acquire any prepositions. In particular situational contexts, phrases like 'put box' can be reliably interpreted by adult observers as encoding *in*; and 'pot stove' uttered while pointing to a pot on the stove will be interpreted as encoding *on*.

The prepositions *in* and *on* used to encode spatial relations are locatives whose meaning can be described in terms of simple topological notions. This is not true of all locatives. There are some, like *in front of, below* and *beside*, in which dimensional space notions (Euclidean) are prominent. There is also a third type which encodes more complex spatial notions, as in *along* and *through*. Parisi and Antinucci (1970) predicted an order of acquisition of these three types of locatives based on the Piagetian order of the development of spatial notions, an order beginning with topological space and only later encoding Euclidian spatial concepts (see Piaget and Inhelder, 1956). The study they report, while not longitudinal, showed that Italian children had least trouble with words indicating simple topological concepts, slightly more trouble with locatives concerned with Euclidian space, and most trouble with terms encoding complex spatial notions. Comparing this study on the acquisition of locative prepositions with Brown's study of *in* and *on*, it is interesting that Brown's children, at the very earliest stages of language acquisition, seem to have acquired only the prepositions which refer to the cognitively simplest spatial relations – those to do with topological relations. And other studies also seem to indicate that children are expressing these relations in their two-word utterances, even before they have acquired the particular prepositions which encode them.

Brown also studied the acquisition of the possessive inflection, the *'s* in 'Adam*'s* bike', for example. Using a criterion of 90 per cent use in contexts where this inflection was obligatory, he found that the children did not fully control this inflection until after what he called Stage III, based on a mean utterance length above $2\frac{1}{2}$ morphemes. What is interesting, however, is that the child has been indicating possession quite clearly before this time – that is, he has been doing so before acquiring the grammatical inflection. Thus, the child has made many constructions like 'Adam chair' in contexts where possession is indicated. That these are not rote-learned seems indicated when, for example, the child said 'Fraser coffee' the first time Colin Fraser was ever served coffee by the mother. Brown gives other evidence that the concept involved in possession preceded its grammatical marking. One day Eve went round pointing and appropriately saying 'That Eve nose', 'That Mommy nose right there', 'That Papa nose right there.' Bloom (1970) also presents evidence from three other children acquiring language which clearly shows that they possess the genitive relation (concept of possession) well before they ever begin to use the grammatical inflection proper for its linguistic expression. Brown reports several other observations on the acquisition of semantic categories and their relation to the grammatical features which encode them, and those who are interested in this topic should consult his work (1973), as it is a most comprehensive examination of the relation between particular concepts and their grammatical expression during the acquisition of language.

Both Bloom (1970) and McNeill and McNeill (1968) have studied the growth of the concept of negation, and, as it happens, in children acquiring very different languages – English and Japanese. Bloom's study of three unrelated children in America paid particular attention to the situational contexts of the children's utterances and thus focused on meaning. One part of her study was concerned with the syntactic development of negation. She identified negative utterances in two ways: all utterances containing a negative element such as *no, no more, not, don't*, etc., signalling negative intent were analysed, as well as all utterances in which a negative intent was expressed by such means as shaking the head, pushing the object away or refusing to follow a direction, even though no negative element was expressed. From the contexts of the utterances, Bloom found that three basic types of negation were occurring: non-existence, rejection and denial. Non-existence, as the term indicates, was used by the child in situations where the referent was non-existent. For example, when the child uttered 'no pocket' while handling a piece of clothing where there was no pocket, the category 'non-existence' was scored. Rejection seemed indicated when the child used actions which appeared to be rejecting in nature – such as pushing away the rejected object. Bloom gives an example of this category which illustrates the kinds of cues the researcher can use in determining the meaning of an utterance. While being given a bath, the child said 'no dirty soap', and, as he did so, pushed away the soap which was being offered. The researcher did not rely on the evidence of the pushing motion alone, however, but noted both the existence of the soap and the fact that it was dirty. The utterance of 'no dirty soap', in context then, was not being used to indicate that there was no soap, nor that there was no *dirty* soap. Therefore, through a combination of cues – the pushing-away, the fact that a dirty piece of soap was present – the utterance could be reasonably classified as an instance of rejection. In this manner, Bloom was able to categorize many of the children's utterances. The third type of negation, denial, asserted that some predication was not the case. If we say 'That's not an apple' when someone has said that it is, we are using this third type of negation.

Bloom noted a fairly constant developmental order of the syntactic expression of the three types of negation. For all three children, non-existence was the first category to be syntactically elaborated, usually with the words *no more* as in 'no more lights', 'no more people'. Rejection was the next category to emerge, and the children mainly came to use *don't* in contexts where this meaning seemed called for; examples include 'I don't need pants off', 'don't eat it'. Denial was the last meaning to appear and it came to be marked mainly by the use of *not*, as in 'that not lollipop' and 'it's not cold out'. The developmental order – non-existence, rejection, denial – was constant in the syntactic development across the three unrelated children. But Bloom's study was concerned solely with the emergence of *syntactic* negative reference and not with negative reference itself. It is not clear in her report whether the child was able to refer to other types of negation at earlier stages with the non-syntactically elaborated *no*. We are told, for example, that, when syntactic expression was limited to non-existence, the child's use of rejection and denial was limited to the single word *no*, and this would seem to imply that all negative meanings might have been available from the very beginning. However, this may be a misinterpretation, since each new category emerged, as we will see, with the simplest forms for expressing it. It may be that the non-elaborated *no* was only being used to indicate rejection and denial sometime *after* non-existence was being *syntactically* expressed.

McNeill and McNeill (1968) had a somewhat easier time as they were studying the development of negation in Japanese, where the different meanings are expressed by different vocabulary items. Their analysis of the acquisition of negative meaning is made in terms of three binary dimensions labelled existence/truth, external/internal, and entailment/ non-entailment. The McNeills' examples of each category, however, make it possible to translate their terminology into that used by Bloom, and I will use that latter terminology in order to facilitate comparison. According to the McNeills, *nai* (adj.) is used to express non-existence. An example would be, 'There's not an apple here.' *Nai* (aux.) indicates falsity of statements, or what we will call denial$_1$, a simple form of denial. The example given by the McNeills is the utterance 'That's not an apple' when someone pointing to a pear claimed it was an apple. What they call 'internal desire or lack of it', which we will call 'rejection', is indicated by *iya* and would be used in contexts similar to 'No, I don't want an apple.' Finally, the form *iiya* is said to be used in a contrastive sense, as in 'No, I didn't have an apple; I had a pear.' This is called 'entailment' in that its use indicates that one alternative is false while the other is true; we will call this denial$_2$ for it is a more complex type of denial.

The McNeills report the emergence of these negative items in a Japanese child. At the earliest stage (27 months), no semantic contrasts are observable, although *nai* (adj.) is used from the beginning and always where called for – that is, in situations of non-existence. At this stage *iya* is also used, but inconsistently, in that it is often replaced by *nai* (adj.). During the next stage, at 29 months, the child begins to use *iya*, but always in contexts calling for *nai* (aux.) and *iiya*. McNeill and McNeill interpret this as evidence that the child is really using a shortened form of *iiya*, for the contexts are always those where denial is called for. At the third stage (31 months), the child has acquired the real *iya*, and its replacement by *nai* (adj.) ceases. The child is now credited with the external/internal dimension – that is, he is now able to express rejection.

But the long form, *iiya*, and *nai* (aux.) are still being used as synonyms. Finally, at 32 months, the child begins to distinguish *nai* (aux.) from *iiya* and is said to have acquired the entailment/non-entailment dimension. The order of acquisition for the Japanese child, then, is said to be non-existence, denial$_1$, rejection and finally denial$_2$. This closely parallels Bloom's findings for English-speaking children, where the order of emergence was non-existence, rejection and denial. The only difference is the insertion of the category denial$_1$ into the developmental order found by Bloom. I find it very difficult to specify contexts where denial$_1$ and denial$_2$ are differentiable. It is, of course, impossible to check the reliability of coding, but it may be that what Bloom has called 'denial' occurs in situations that the McNeills would have labelled denial$_2$, where a closer distinction is called for in Japanese. And, if we look at some of Bloom's examples of 'non-existence', we may perhaps begin to question the validity of her coding of that category. There are, for example, many instances of the use of *can't* listed under non-existence – such utterances as 'I can't put this here', 'I can't get out', 'I can't fix it', and 'I can't reach it.' There are also several entries using other lexical items: 'This don't fit in', 'I didn't make dirty', etc. I wonder if other investigators would have listed all of these as instances of non-existence, even if they had all the contextual material available on which to base their decision. Many of these seem to me not to be examples of non-existence, but a kind of denial, although, as I have said, I would find it difficult to separate the two types of denial in most real-life situations. In any case, there is a close parallelism in the emergence of the types of negation in the two unrelated studies in two unrelated languages, and I suspect that the parallelism might be closer if the data of both studies were examined together using explicit and reliable coding procedures.

It is interesting that Bloom's children slowly began to use particular lexical items to express the different kinds of negation. Adult English certainly does not impose this differentiation. All three children, it will be recalled, came to express non-existence mainly by the use of *no more*, rejection by *don't*, and denial by *not*. But, as Bloom notes, the important point is that the progressive differentiation in the forms by which negation was expressed was directly related to the three semantic categories, and she cited further evidence that the process did not occur the other way round, i.e. that it did not happen that children acquired new forms like *don't* or *not* which caused the emergence of new negative categories. The crucial evidence is that, when children first began to use a new type of negative reference such as rejection or denial, they did so by using a primitive structure that previously had expressed the earlier-acquired concept, non-existence. For example, non-existence had originally been expressed by *no more*. But, as this category began to develop, it was expressed by other syntactic forms such as *don't* and *can't*. When rejection first began to be expressed, the original *no more* was used. And, as rejection developed as a category and began being expressed in several ways, as, for example, by adding *don't* as an operator, denial emerged using the primitive *no more*. In other words, all three children used the primitive form *no more* to express newer functions. The form used for non-existence developed and was expressed through the use of more complex forms. Thus, learning to express new semantic categories of negation did not require the learning of new structures at that time. Furthermore, it was not the case that new linguistic forms were used productively by the children before they understood the cognitive notions these forms expressed. Rather, new and more complex structures for particular categories developed only after these categories had been expressed with simpler, familiar structures. There was strong evidence in Bloom's data, then, that cognitive categories of negation developed before the acquisition of linguistic forms to refer to them. And, as we have seen, the emergence of these categories may follow a similar developmental order in children acquiring strikingly different languages.

I once made a study of the development of time concepts during the acquisition of language by two of the children in Roger Brown's study (Cromer, 1968). Some of the findings are of interest in that they indicate that the understanding of certain temporal notions precedes the acquisition of linguistic forms proper for their expression. A short review of the findings in four categories which bear on this point follows – the expression of the order of events in time, a category called 'unactuals', another called 'relevance', and finally the expression of timeless events.

The two children studied were Adam and Sarah and their speech was examined from 2 years 3 months to 5 years 5 months in the case of Sarah, and from 2 years 3 months to 6 years 2 months for Adam. As the two children had similar mean utterance lengths at similar chronological ages, only the ages and the order of development will interest us here. The speech protocols of the children were made from fortnightly recording sessions in the home, but, in order to study the changes, only the protocols from approximately 4-month intervals were examined. Each utterance was scored for its intended reference using situational and contextual cues.

One of the scoring categories was 'point in time' with each reference to past, present or future being noted. Some utterances referred to more than one point in time. At the earliest ages almost all utterances with relations between two points in time preserved the occurring order of events, and it was not until after 4 years in Adam and 4 years 2 months in Sarah that the children began to reverse these relations occasionally. An average of about

8 per cent of relations no longer preserved real order after these ages. Now, what is interesting is that the ability to reverse the order of events in time did not arise with new linguistic forms such as the acquisition of particular conjunctions. The kinds of reversals being referred to here are not the type wherein two significant events are reversed in descriptive retelling – an ability which arises even later, as we will see in the next section. Rather, these points in time often refer to single events only, as expressed in natural conversation. They are not even noticeable to most observers unless a careful scoring is made. Some examples will make this clear. The following are drawn from the records and illustrate reversals in temporal order:

D'you know the light went off?	present–past
I like everything I liked.	present–past
Look what I found.	immediate future–past
Wanna see what I coloured?	immediate future–past

These sentences may seem like any others and the observer feels certain he has heard similar utterances by the child at earlier ages. In fact he *has* heard similar utterances – except that until age 4, they have retained temporal order. Compare these with utterances retaining temporal order:

Can I put it on his chest so it be a button?	future–later future
I hope he won't bother you.	present–future

And that is the important point. Most of the reversals use linguistic forms which were available to the child at an earlier age.

Related to this ability to reverse temporal relations is the use made of two words, *before* and *after*. In order to retain the actual order of events, *after* must come at the beginning of an utterance while *before* must be inserted in the middle, as in

After X, (then) Y
X before Y

To reverse order, however, just the opposite placement of the two terms is necessary, as in

Y after X
Before Y, X

In the two children whose temporal reference was being charted longitudinally, these two terms were rarely used. Indeed, Sarah never used either of them to relate two points in time in the protocols studied. Adam made his first use of one of the words at 4 years 6 months, but in a way which retained the actual order of events. Only after age 4 years 10 months did he make use of a reversed order. These terms are specifically focused on time relations and it is interesting that they should arise rather late in the child's language acquisition. The Clarks (see Clark, 1970; Clark and Clark, 1968) have made careful studies of the use of these terms by young children and have found that 3½-year-olds retain the actual order of events in time in their spontaneous speech. They have also found in a memory experiment that children were better able to remember the sense of sentences which retained temporal order. They also noted that, in the children's preference for response mode, syntactic considerations played a part and sentences were preferred which had the subordinate clause in second position. Thus, transformational complexity has an influence which must be considered. Nevertheless, in utterances of equal syntactic complexity, children before age 4 tend to use only those in which the actual order of events in time is maintained.

Statements of a hypothetical nature are based on an ability to move one's viewpoint about in time. A true hypothetical, as defined here, means the predication of a future event on another event which is also in the future – the hypothesized event being slightly later than the event on which it depends. For example, in 'If it rains, I will take my umbrella', the possibility of rain is taken as a future event which, if it occurs, will result in the even later event of taking the umbrella. This is, however, only one type of 'unactual' or 'unactualized' event. There are other types which make a different use of time reference. For example, in counterfactual statements such as 'If you had telephoned, I would have come to your aid', a possibility in past time is noted which did not, in fact, occur. Hypothetical and counterfactual statements therefore require complex cognitive abilities which include the ability to refer to 'possibilities' as well as the ability to change one's vantage point in a time sequence.

It may be that a primitive type of 'possibility' is to be found in the ability to pretend. In Adam and Sarah, pretending was present in some of the earliest protocols; it was expressed by such utterances as

Dis could be a . . .* his house
Dis could be the mother
Dis'll be the blanket

---

* In the child utterances given as examples, three points (. . .) indicates a pause.

It was almost a year and a half later that 'possibility' was first expressed, for, although there was a single utterance by Adam at 3 years 2 months which seemed to indicate 'possibility' ('Maybe it's can . . . go dis way'), it was only after 4 years 6 months that 'possibility' emerged as a category in regular use, as in

> Someping might come out my pocket
> I bet I could play it
> Think cows would like this?
> We can do all three (where context indicated 'possibility' and not 'ability')

And it was only at this age, 4 years 6 months, that hypotheticals began to appear in regular use. Examples include

> If you keep on going, it's gonna get bigger on this side and bigger on
>   that side, right?
> What you think would happen if I put a stick?
> Don't tear it again or I turn you into a puppet.

There are two points of interest here. First, the expression of hypotheticalness does not depend on the acquisition of some new linguistic form. It is expressible, for example, by the use of *if* in a subordinate clause or by the use of *or* as a conjunction. Second, the child has had the ability to make statements of the same linguistic type at an earlier age, but he has done so only when they make a different kind of reference. At 4 years and after, Adam began making use of utterances the meaning of which can be called 'uncertainty of conditions':

> Maybe that's my Daddy
> In case you're hungry, I got grain
> See if the flowers would like to watch me

In these utterances, the speaker is asking for a determination of facts or conditions, the nature of which is unclear to him. Some linguistic forms were available to the child which could have been used to express hypotheticalness, but they were not used with that meaning until several months later, after age 4 years 6 months. Sarah's use of hypotheticals was very limited but the pattern was the same. She evidenced an early use of pretending and a somewhat later acquisition of possibility and hypotheticalness (4 years 10 months).

Slobin (1966) has made a similar observation on children acquiring Russian as their native language. He points out that, grammatically speaking, the hypothetical is exceedingly simple. Its emergence, however, in Russian-speaking children is quite late. Slobin concludes that it is the semantic and not the grammatical aspect which is difficult for the child.

The third category from which there is some evidence that particular cognitive abilities precede their normal (adult-like) linguistic expression is that of 'relevance'. Use of 'relevance' indicates that the speaker is noting the importance of a referred-to event to the time indicated by his utterance. For example, a statement like 'The lamp fell' tells us nothing about the current state of the lamp; it may still be in the fallen position or it may have been righted some time ago. However, when we say 'The lamp has fallen', the use of the perfect tense would appear to indicate that the lamp is still in a fallen position at the time of the utterance or is in a state effected by the fall. In other words, the state of the lamp or the consequence engendered by its falling is relevant to the utterance we are making. Linguists have often referred to the function of the perfect tense as being one of 'current relevance' of a past event. It is possible to extend the term, however, to include not only the relevance of some event in the past, but also the relevance of future events on current behaviour. We will only consider here the more usual meaning of 'relevance'.

There are two approaches one can take in studying relevance from the past: one can trace the development of the perfect tenses in the children or one can trace the cognitive development of relevance, i.e. the development of the ability to use this type of reference regardless of the linguistic devices used to express it. Looking first at the use of the perfect tense by Adam and Sarah, one immediately found that its use was rare. In Adam's record the first meaningful use of the perfect occurred at 4 years 6 months. But Sarah never once used the perfect tense through 5 years 5 months in the protocols examined. The reason for the late emergence of the perfect tense is difficult to understand. To illustrate the elements of the perfect tense, let us examine the sentence 'I have seen it.' The essential features include the use of *have* as an auxiliary verb with the main verb consisting of the past participle, *seen*. In many cases the past participle is the same as the past tense of the verb, as with *tell* becoming *told* and *have told*. But there are a number of common verbs which have a distinct past participle, as in *see*, *saw* and *have seen*. In linguistic terminology, the formation of the perfect depends on the grammatical feature *have -en*, which requires a rule of affix movement. Now, what is interesting in all this is that both Adam and Sarah possessed all of the necessary elements for the production of the perfect tense at a much earlier age. Both were using *have* as a type of auxiliary ('have to') from 2 years 11 months. At that time they had a sufficient 'production-span capacity' to produce the perfect tense. It is also noteworthy that the *be -ing* involving affix movement and other grammatical characteristics like *have -en* were occurring before the age of 3. The children also possessed, at an early age, some specific past participles like *seen* and *gone*. Adam and Sarah, then, possessed all the necessary elements and the capacity to produce utterances of a sufficient length to combine them at a very early age. Furthermore, an analysis of the utterances of the parents revealed that they were using the perfect tense (although with a somewhat lower frequency than other grammatical forms). So both Adam and Sarah were being exposed to this grammatical feature. It is thus very difficult to see why the children were not producing the perfect tense at an earlier age – difficult, that is, until the *meaning* of the perfect tense is examined. And, when the data are analysed from that point of view, it becomes apparent that the ability to use the perfect tense properly rests on a late-developing ability to consider the relevance of another time to the time of the utterance. Although it is exceedingly difficult to specify the speaker's intention, there are nevertheless situations in which relevance is important. If there is a point in the child's development before which he ignores a relation between a past event and the present, but after which he begins to relate the two, then we may have found the reason for the late emergence of the perfect tense. In Adam, in the language samples between the ages of 2 years 3 months and 4 years, there were no attempts to make such a relation. But at 4 years there was one utterance which appears to be the first use of the category of relevance. It was at 4 years 6 months that Adam first used the perfect tense, but at that time and shortly thereafter he made several utterances which included the notion of relevance, even though in many of these he employed other linguistic forms which were available at a much younger age:

> Hey, what else you bring the pyjamas for?
> How come you didn't bring your car today?
> This one is the mostest tight you ever saw
> You finished me lots of rings

The data from Sarah are even more striking for she never used the perfect tense in the speech samples which were analysed. Nevertheless, regular use of the notion of relevance began at age 4 years 6 months. Sarah did not use the perfect tense, but instead seems to have developed uses of *now* and *yet* to refer to the relation of past time to the present. For example, to an adult question as to the state she was in, Sarah replied, 'Now, hit myself' (='I just hit myself' or 'I have just hit myself'). Other utterances at 4 years 6 months, like 'You didn't peek yet?' and 'Did ya peek yet?' may not seem strange until the context is noted:

ADULT. When are you gonna let us peek?
SARAH. When I'm finished.
Did ya peek yet? (=relevance expressible either by 'Did you peek?' or 'Have you peeked?')

Again, what is interesting is that, although Sarah had the components to produce utterances like these at an earlier age, she did not use them to indicate relevance before 4 years 6 months. A similar conclusion can be drawn from the early use of past participles in both children. An examination of their use indicates that they were not instances of the perfect tense from which the auxiliary *have* was merely dropped. Rather, no early uses of the past participle by either child ever referred to relevance. Examples include

Kitty gone
All done
Light broken

It would appear, then, that the reason why children were not producing the perfect tense at an early age was that they were not making reference to what the perfect tense usually expresses. Once they did begin to communicate this meaning, they did so by using various linguistic forms which had been at their disposal (e.g. using *now* and *yet* appended to utterances about the past). And it was only then that they began in addition to acquire the perfect tense.

One final temporal category we will consider is that of 'timeless utterances'. Something rather special is intended by this term. It is not meant to refer to descriptions, definitions, or even to 'states' of persons. While these may often be thought to be timeless, they are, in fact, from a behavioural point of view, usually rooted in the present. Thus, if the child points to a toy and says 'It's red', he is really describing or making reference to something which is phenomenally present. Something very different occurs, however, when the child develops the cognitive ability to take some action or event which normally occurs at some point in time, and lifts it out of any particular situation and so imbues it with a timeless quality. An example of this 'true timelessness' would be Adam's utterance 'Playing a banjo is good exercise for your thumb.' Although the playing of the banjo could have taken place in the past, or might be occurring at the time of the utterance, or might even take place in the future, the central idea of the statement is specifically concerned with none of these, or rather with all of these. The action of playing a banjo has been removed from a time sequence. This is what is meant when an utterance is classified as 'timeless'.

Timeless references seem to develop slowly out of a type of description which I have designated as 'timeless characterizing descriptions'. Such descriptions go beyond the 'present time' of the utterance in that they describe what something 'does' or what something is 'for' even though the object or event referred to is present when the utterance is made. In the speech samples from both Adam and Sarah the most primitive form of timeless characterizing descriptions is found at 3 years 2 months. These include

Tiny car for what?
Dat push it?
De wheels turn?
A marble bag for what?
What are dose for?

In nearly all instances at 3 years 2 months, timeless characterizing descriptions ask a question concerning how something works or what it does. In a sense, none of them really takes an action out of a timed context except in so far as an explanation is asked for. However, at about 4 years timeless characterizing descriptions have advanced from being used merely to seek explanations to include descriptions of actions:

Dis goes up
Is that how you do it?
It's something that you eat

And it is also at 4 years in Adam and 4 years 2 months in Sarah that true timeless references begin to be used. Some examples of utterances expressing this ability to take something out of a timed context are

I save dem
I never have no cookies
I keep falling down
I have a good time at school
I always lose things when I move
Paul blames everything on his own self

So far, the development of four types of reference has been traced in the utterances of two children in the Roger Brown study. For all of these, our attention has been focused on the meaning of each utterance taken in its entirety. However, there is another fact which is rather startling. All of the speech protocols were searched for any *words* which had something to do with time. This search revealed that the children began spontaneously to use time words of a particular reference type only when they had begun to make reference to that category in their complete utterances. Thus, the words *always*, *sometimes* and *never* were not used by the children until they had begun to express timelessness at ages 4 years and 4 years 2 months. It is rather startling that in the two unrelated children the emergence not only of temporal categories expressed by these words, but the very words used, should parallel one another so closely. Similarly, words related to relevance, in that they look forward or backward in time from the time of the utterance, only appeared once the children were cognitively able to make reference to that category. For example, it was not until Adam was 4 that he began to use the phrase *about to*. His first use of the word *remember* (if one can consider it a type of looking back into the past from the present) also occurred at that time. And it will be recalled that it was at 4 that Adam had first begun to be able to use the category 'relevance'. More complex words related to that category appeared at even later ages: *until* (4 years 10 months), *yet* (5 years 2 months) and *just* as in 'You just messed mine' (5 years 6 months). Similarly, Sarah's first use of lexical items bearing on the category of relevance was at 4 years 2 months, when she began using *remember* and *just*. At 4 years 6 months she began to use *yet* in the interesting way discussed earlier.

The emergence of words referring to specific types of time reference only when that reference has begun to be expressed by the child, often in utterances not necessarily using time words at all, was found not only for the categories mentioned here, but for a number of other categories as well, e.g. expressions of duration and speed. Such evidence is damaging for a theory of language acquisition which holds that the child imitates the words he hears around him and thus builds up a series of categories through language. But there is even more direct evidence that cognition precedes language and indeed determines its acquisition. Robbins Burling (1959) studied the acquisition of language by his bilingual son, who, for a time, beginning at 1 year 4 months, was brought up speaking both English and Garo. Garo is a language of the Tibeto-Burman group spoken in an area of India where Burling lived while making a two-year anthropological study. He noticed that in some cases his son 'simultaneously learned English and Garo words with approximately the same meanings, as though once his understanding reached the point of being able to grasp a concept he was able to use the appropriate words in both languages'. For example, when he suddenly grasped the meaning of colour terms, he was able to use the English and Garo words simultaneously. Similarly, when he began to use words indicating time such as *last night* and *yesterday morning*, he also began using the corresponding Garo terms. This would appear to be evidence that cognitive categories affect the acquisition of language rather than the other way round.

Returning to the data from Adam and Sarah, we can attempt an overview of the development of the four categories. Below are listed the ages (in years and months) at which each of the categories first emerged in regular use by the two children.

	Adam	*Sarah*
Reversals	4;0	4;2
Hypotheticals	4;6	4;10
Relevance	4;0	4;6
Timeless utterances	4;0	4;2

It is striking that these features emerge at approximately the same time, and some two years after the language-acquisition process has begun. And this is only a partial list. Several more temporal features not discussed here were also found to emerge sometime after the age of 4 or $4\frac{1}{2}$ years (Cromer, 1968). It may be that there is some common factor in these time categories – some cognitive ability which becomes active and permits the expression of several new types of temporal reference. What these new types of reference seem to have in common appears to be an ability to free oneself from the immediate situation or from the actual order of events in time. It is as if the child is now able to 'decentre' his viewpoint as a speaker so as to approach a temporal sequence in other than real sequential order. This would be a basis for the reversals which emerge at this age. The freedom from the actual order of events in time would permit the child to place himself at other perspectives and thus to consider events which are contingent on future possibilities – the definition of hypotheticals. In addition, this ability to consider time from other viewpoints might also constitute the cognitive ability necessary for considering the relevance of other times to the time of the utterance. And this ability to stand outside the actual order of events in time is indeed essential to the very notion of utterances which have been defined as 'timeless'.

But whether the advances at this age are considered together in the framework of a new cognitive ability to decentre from one's own immediate viewpoint as regards the flow of time, or whether each of the new achievements is seen as being due to specific new cognitive attainments, the evidence is strong that changes in cognition precede the acquisition of new linguistic forms which are normally used by adults to express them. Such a view would go a long way towards explaining some otherwise mysterious phenomena. For example, before certain particular cognitive changes occur, the child is exposed to many types of linguistic behaviour, which include both structures (e.g. the perfect tense) and lexical items (e.g. whole categories of time words) which he does not make a part of his spontaneous speech and which, indeed, he rarely imitates.

Furthermore, the structures he does use are limited only to particular types of reference. After particular cognitive changes have occurred, however, the child not only begins to use the forms he has at his disposal to express new ideas and relationships, but he rapidly acquires new forms of expression which he lacked until that time. It may even be that the developing cognitive abilities stimulate the child into an active search for or a heightened awareness of particular forms and structures used by adult speakers to express the newly understood relationships. Language acquisition may not be the passive process of merely imitating the adults in the environment as was once supposed. In his very earliest utterances the infant is imposing his structure on the language he hears. But what about acquisitions at later ages when the basic linguistic structures have been mainly acquired? Do cognitive processes assert an influence even then? It is to some evidence concerning cognitive effects at later ages which we will now turn our attention.

Evidence from later language acquisition

The relevant work on the relation between cognitive structures and language acquisition at later ages comes from the Piagetian school of thought. It will be recalled that the Piagetian view is that language is not the source of the operations of thought but is itself structured by those operations. Hermina Sinclair-de-Zwart (1969) carried out an investigation of the verbal abilities of children at different levels on the standard Piagetian conservation task. Conservation studies require the child to indicate whether an amount of water remains the same when poured into different vessels. Young children (about 4 or 5 years) believe that the amount changes with the shape of the container, and that, for example, if water from a standard beaker is poured into a tall narrow container, the latter receptacle will have 'more'. Older children, who have achieved conservation, compensate the dimensions. They say that the amount of water has remained the same and often justify their answer by pointing out that while the level of the water is higher, the new container is also narrower so that what has been gained in height has been lost in width. Piaget claims that this compensation is of central importance for it shows that the child has achieved a stage of operational thinking which is based on certain structural developments which underlie thought processes. Such a view has been challenged, however. Bruner, Olver and Greenfield (1966) have claimed, for example, that young children are perceptually seduced by the height of the liquid. Conservation is achieved, according to this view, through the mediation of the symbolic properties of language, which eventually override the apparent (perceptual) differences in amount. There is here, then, a direct confrontation between those who hold that thought structures language and those who feel that language processes in some cases aid thought.

From a linguistic point of view, there are at least three things to note in the child's speech *vis-à-vis* conservation: (1) the child's use of comparatives as opposed to absolute terminology in describing materials differing in two dimensions, (2) his use of differentiated instead of undifferentiated terms, and (3) the types of sentences he uses to co-ordinate the two dimensions. Sinclair-de-Zwart directly studied these processes by having the children carry out tasks of the type 'Find a pencil that is longer but thinner' (comprehension), and having them describe the differences between materials differing in two dimensions, as with two pencils, a short thick one and a long thin one (production). The children, after undertaking the conservation test, were then divided into three groups: those totally lacking conservation, those at an intermediate stage and those who had achieved conservation. Sinclair-de-Zwart reports that all three groups performed about equally well in the comprehension task. But she reports differences between conservers and total non-conservers on the verbal-production task. For convenience I have attempted to arrange the figures she reports into table 1.1. These results by themselves do not provide sufficient grounds on which to base a definite judgement as to the relation between language and operational thought. All one has is a correlation

Table 1.1 *Sinclair-de-Zwart's results on the language used by conservers and non-conservers*

	Non-conservers	Conservers
percentage using comparatives to describe plasticine (continuous quantity)	10[a]	70
percentage using comparatives to describe marbles (discontinuous quantity)	20	100
percentage using differentiated terms for different dimensions	25[b]	100
percentage using two sentences co-ordinating two dimensions	10[c]	80

[a] Sinclair-de-Zwart reports that 90 per cent of the non-conserving children used absolute terms, e.g. 'one has a lot and the other has a little'.

[b] 75 per cent used undifferentiated terms giving one word for both dimensions, e.g. using 'small' for both shortness and thinness.

[c] 90 per cent of the non-conserving children described only one dimension or used four separate sentences. Sentences co-ordinating the two dimensions would be, for example, 'This is tall but it's thin; this is short but it's wide.'

between conservation ability and the spontaneous use of complex structures and differentiated terminology. But whether new linguistic structures and terminology *cause* operational thought to come about, or whether the new thought structures make it easier for the child to use more advanced language patterns, cannot be determined on the basis of these figures. For the non-conservers, for example, any percentage which is greater than zero could be interpreted as evidence that some children are acquiring language structures which will later make conservation possible. But these same figures could also be interpreted as evidence that some non-conserving children have the more complex linguistic structures without these giving rise to conservation and operational thinking. It is this latter interpretation that Sinclair-de-Zwart adheres to, and she carried out a second series of experiments to support her view.

An attempt was made to teach the non-conservers the more advanced language, i.e. differentiated terminology, comparative terms and co-ordinated structures to describe differences in two dimensions. Sinclair-de-Zwart found that differentiated terminology (e.g. *short* instead of *little* and *thin* instead of *little*) was easy to teach. Comparative terms like *more* and *less* were more difficult to teach to non-conservers, and co-ordinated sentence structures the most difficult of all. However, even the children who successfully learned these expressions rarely advanced on the conservation test. Only about 10 per cent of these language-taught children acquired conservation. However, many of the children who remained non-conservers began to notice and make reference to the differing dimensions. Sinclair-de-Zwart concluded that verbal training may lead children to pay attention to important features in the conservation task, but such language training does not of itself lead to conservation and operational thinking.

Finally, there are two studies on the relation of productive language ability to another aspect of operational thought, reversibility. Inhelder (1969) reports a study of seriation ability that she and Sinclair undertook. The ability to seriate a number of sticks of increasing size is made possible, like conservation, by the thought structures which are available to the child once he has achieved the stage of operational thinking. It is said that the child is unable to put the sticks into an order of increasing or decreasing size and to insert new sticks into their proper place in the series until he is able to conceptualize a particular stick as being at the same time both longer than some sticks and shorter than others in the series. It was found that verbal descriptions of the materials paralleled the stages on this task. Youngest children used only two descriptive terms, *long* and *short*, to describe successive pairs of sticks. Slightly older children used three descriptive terms. But, at the stage which precedes operational solution, children were able to use comparatives. They described the sticks once again using only two terms, but one of these was in a comparative form. Thus, they would give as their verbal description statements like 'short, longer, longer, longer . . .'. But what is significant is that when they were asked to describe the series a second time beginning at the other end they were unable to do so. The children seemed unable to describe a stick they had just called 'longer' 'shorter'. Thus the lack of reversibility would seem to extend to the verbal descriptions as well.

Somewhat related to this is a study by Ferreiro and Sinclair (1971) on the inability of children who have not yet reached the Piagetian stage of operational thinking to reverse linguistically the order of two events in time. This notion has some striking similarities to the inability to reverse temporal viewpoints at an earlier age which has previously been discussed. Ferreiro and Sinclair presented the child with some actions carried out on dolls in front of him. One of the child's tasks was to describe the actions but he was made to talk about the second action first. For example, in one situation, first a girl doll washed a boy doll and then the boy doll went upstairs. In their inverse-order description, the youngest children (about $4\frac{1}{2}$ years) did one of two things. Some simply repeated their original description which retained temporal order and thereby did not comply with the instruction to begin with the second action: 'She cleaned him and then he went up.' Other children at this age complied with the instructions, but did not supply any temporal indicators, as in 'He went upstairs and she washed him.'

At the next stage, children about $5\frac{1}{2}$ years always complied with the instructions to begin their verbal description with the second event, but they were incapable of using correctly the temporal indicators necessary to describe the actual order. Some found it impossible, saying, 'The boy . . . the boy . . . No. You've got to start with the girl.' Other children attempted various solutions to the problem. Some simply inverted the order in their description: 'The boy went to the top of the stairs and afterwards the girl cleaned him.' Others attempted the curious solution of inverting the *action*: 'He goes downstairs again and the girl washes his arms.' Still others inverted the actors and the events so that the action performed in the second event was attributed to the actor in the first: 'The boy goes and washes her face and then it's her that goes upstairs.' Yet other solutions consisted of attributing a neutral action to the actor in the second event: 'The boy came, she washed his face and then he left.' At this stage, a series of questions about the order of events revealed that the children knew perfectly well which event had occurred first and which had come second. But they were unable to code this reversibility linguistically. Ferreiro and Sinclair conclude that the child at this stage is unable to make a correct inverse description because his 'syntactic transformations are not yet integrated into a system which permits the conservation of the entire semantic content'. This aspect of the linguistic transformational system only becomes possible when the child has attained the stage of operational thinking, for the structures necessary for reversibility are not available until that stage of thought is reached.

Not a great deal of work has been done with older children on the relation between meaning and thought on the one hand and the acquisition of language on the other, partly because it had often been assumed that most aspects of language acquisition were complete well before the age of 5 years. But, with increased attention now being given to structures which are not acquired until 10 or 11 years of age in some cases (see for example Chomsky, 1969; Cromer, 1970a, 1972a; Kessel, 1970), we can look forward perhaps to new experimental studies on this complex topic.

The cognitive hypothesis

Near the beginning of this review, it was noted how psychologists used, for the most part, to favour the view that language structures the thought processes. It may be recalled that the Sapir–Whorf hypothesis, in its strong form, claimed that the way we view the world, the way we process and understand reality, is almost totally determined by the language we speak. With increasing research on language acquisition, however, the pendulum has begun to swing in the other direction. We have seen that in his very first words the child is not merely imitating the language he hears about him; he is creating a set of categories to make reference to particular relations. Piagetian theorists have argued that the child begins his language-acquisition process only when the cognitive processes of the sensorimotor stage have been completed. At slightly later ages, evidence has been quoted which seems to indicate that each new acquisition is made possible only through particular cognitive advances. We have seen how the earliest operations of verbs code only a specific set of cognitive meanings. We have also seen that the acquisition of prepositions depends on the advancing understanding of spatial relationships. In addition, we have noted the differentiation and addition of different types of negation as the child grows older. We have seen that a number of grammatical relationships are lacking until the child is cognitively able to free his viewpoint from an egocentric point in the flow of time. Evidence has also been reviewed that even more advanced linguistic techniques must await particular cognitive developments such as those formulated in the Piagetian stage of operational thinking. It would appear, then, that a position directly the reverse of that put forward by the Sapir–Whorf hypothesis is indicated, and we can call this the 'cognitive hypothesis'.

To parallel Whorf's wording of the hypothesis of linguistic determinism (see p. 3), the cognitive hypothesis might possibly be phrased like this: we are able to use the linguistic structures that we do largely because through our cognitive abilities we are enabled to do so, not because language itself exists for all merely to imitate. Cognitive processes differ not only at different ages but in how they enable the individual to break down the language that he hears to secure the elements which he can understand and produce.

The evidence adduced so far has been in support of the cognitive hypothesis. But it must also be noted that this is only part of the story. There are linguistic structures, including some which are found at the very earliest ages as well as others which appear later, whose acquisition seems to be little related to the maturing cognitive processes. We will, therefore, turn now to a very brief review of a few ideas and studies which seem to indicate that some aspects of language development operate relatively independently of more general cognitive abilities.

The Independent Development of Language

One of the advocates of the cognitive hypothesis, Sinclair-de-Zwart (1969), made the claim that developing cognitive processes are necessary in order to acquire language. She put forward the view that the reason language acquisition does not begin until about the age of 1½–2 years is due specifically to the need for the processes of sensorimotor intelligence to be complete, and indeed she bases much of her attack on Chomsky's view of innate linguistic mechanisms on this time lag between the first manifestations of practical intelligence during that period and the first verbal productions. There may be other reasons for that time lag, but, even if Sinclair-de-Zwart's view is accepted, it is possible to speculate, as mentioned earlier, whether those cognitive processes, even if necessary, are nevertheless sufficient to account for the language-acquisition process. This same question has been posed in a different context.

Roger Brown (1970a) examined the first 'sentences' of a chimpanzee and compared them to the first utterances of the children he was studying. The chimpanzee, Washoe, was raised by Allen and Beatrice Gardner (Gardner and Gardner, 1969) and was taught the sign language used by the deaf in North America. By 3 years of age, Washoe was able to acquire a certain amount of communication ability. Whether that ability constituted a grammar is still open to doubt. McNeill, in a personal communication, speculated that Washoe might have a single rule of an evolutionarily primitive grammar: increase the number of signs used in proportion to the subjective importance of the message. In practice, this might mean, for example, that the chimpanzee, wanting the door opened to go outside, would sign 'open'. With a small degree of emphasis, she might sign 'you open'. With greater emphasis she might sign 'hurry open you out go' and so on. In all these, although the signs might have a meaning on a one-to-one basis, there would be no evidence for a real grammar beyond the rule of adding more signs to indicate greater emphasis. The order in which Washoe produced the signs did not itself seem to carry a grammatical meaning. And Roger Brown notes that this is in sharp contrast to the children he was studying. The children indicated various grammatical meanings through the use of definite word orders. In the data, violations of order were exceedingly rare. For Washoe, at 3 years of age, there was no evidence that order played any part in the communication process, and without this, or without some evidence of differential marking of meaning in some way, one is not yet able to infer that Washoe possesses a grammar.

Now, Brown also notes that the kinds of meanings expressed by the children in their first sentences appear to be extensions of sensorimotor intelligence. He reasons that, if these meanings truly are extensions of sensorimotor intelligence, then they are probably universal but not innate, as they would be built up through sensorimotor experience. Furthermore, these meanings would not be limited to man but might operate in animals as well. And in view of the fact that, at least to age 3, the chimpanzee still gave no positive evidence of a grammar in her signing, Brown carefully points out: 'Grammatical relations are defined in purely formal terms, and while they may, in early child speech, be more or less perfectly coordinated with the semantic rules, the two are not the same' (p. 222). In other words, the possession of sensorimotor intelligence would still not explain the *expression* of that intelligence in language. That early grammar expresses the meanings which sensorimotor intelligence makes possible does not in itself solve the mystery of how these meanings are conveyed by a grammar. So Washoe, in spite of possessing sensorimotor intelligence, might never necessarily acquire a grammatical language.

David Premack (1969) has also made an attempt to teach a type of language to a chimpanzee (see pp. 202–3). Premack does not make the claim, however, that the chimpanzee has or can be taught a grammatical system in the same sense as a human being, although he speculates on the possibility of the existence of grammars of varying degrees of weakness in the feeble-minded and in animals (Premack and Schwartz, 1966). He concludes instead that the functions of language are not uniquely human. If by this we can take the meaning that some aspects of the deep structure of human language may be unique but that this is not true of the semantics, then this would appear to be similar to Roger Brown's tentative conclusion that animals may have, for example, sensorimotor intelligence, but lack the uniquely human ability for expressing that intelligence in grammatical structures.

But why might it be important that this distinction be kept clear? Some linguists have already proposed that semantics and deep structure be equated (Fillmore, 1968; McCawley, 1968) or that surface structures be generated directly from a semantic base (Schlesinger, 1971a, 1971b), and in terms of descriptive adequacy it is difficult to choose between these types of grammars and the Chomskian model with specifically linguistic deep structures (Chomsky, 1965). One possibility is that a Chomskian analysis may prove to be the more useful one for studying certain types of language disorders. With this in mind, another interesting study may be usefully cited. Mrs Jenny Hughes, under the direction of Neil O'Connor at the Medical Research Council unit, studied the communication ability of children who were classified as receptive aphasics. These children, though of normal intelligence, as measured on non-verbal tests, seem to be unable to acquire language in spite of intensive efforts to achieve this. Hughes used essentially the same materials with the children as Premack did with Sarah, the chimpanzee. She reports (Hughes, 1972) that the aphasic children rapidly acquired all of the functions taught: names for objects, verbs like *give* and *point to*, direct and indirect objects, negation, modifiers and questions. That these children were able to acquire these functions rapidly in twice-weekly half-hour sessions in less than 10 weeks shows that their ability to understand and even communicate such functions is not impaired. We do not know why aphasic children are unable to acquire language. Probably there are multiple reasons and these may vary from individual to individual. But is it possible that in some of these children there is some impairment to a specifically linguistic mechanism which Chomsky claims is innate in human individuals? It may, then, be useful not to discard the distinction between semantic meanings and deep structure, for, as the few studies of other species and of aphasic children show us, one may have all sorts of cognitive abilities and semantic meanings while lacking the means to communicate these in a truly grammatical language.

There are other reasons why certain properties of language appear to be independent of cognition. During normal language acquisition in unimpaired children, various stages can be observed while the child is acquiring particular linguistic structures, and these stages do not appear to be related to a growth in 'meaning'. Earlier, the work of Lois Bloom (1970) and of McNeill and McNeill (1968) on negation was discussed. Ursula Bellugi (1967) based her doctoral dissertation on the development of negation by the children of the Roger Brown study. In following the means by which negation was expressed, she found a series of structural stages. At first, the child simply attached a negative morpheme such as *no* or *not* to the beginning of an utterance, so as to produce sentences like 'no wipe finger' and 'not fit'. In the second stage, the negative appeared in five unrelated grammatical settings, and there were still no transformations. For example, in addition to the 'direct print-out of the base', as in 'no Rusty hat', some negatives were used with demonstrative pronouns (e.g. 'that no fish school'), some had the element *why not* prefixed to negative sentences (e.g. 'why not cracker can't talk?'), and others made use of *don't* and *can't* either in demonstrative sentences (e.g. 'I don't sit on Cromer coffee') or in imperatives (e.g. 'Don't eat daisy'). In the third stage, there were seven types of negative structures. The direct print-out of the base had disappeared. Auxiliary transformations had begun in which the negative was truly attached to the auxiliary verb, and thus sentences like 'Why not cracker can't talk?' disappeared, i.e. *don't* and *can't* were treated as transformed from a negative element and an auxiliary instead of being used as vocabulary items with negative meaning.

Bloom (1970) claimed that in her own study, by paying attention to the semantic correlates of the negative sentences, she was able to study the syntax of negation more deeply. Although the negative sentences produced by the children she studied matched the surface features that Bellugi found, Bloom was able to specify some structures as making particular kinds of negative reference. As was noted earlier, rejection came to be mainly signalled by *don't*, and denial by *not*. Non-existence, the developmentally earliest form, was mainly signalled by *no* plus an element and by *can't*. It would appear here, then, that the structure used is determined by meaning. However, Bloom noted that, as each new category was acquired, it was expressed by a form which was already being used to convey the earlier meaning. Thus, non-existence, the first concept of negation to be expressed grammatically, became the grammatically most complex form, while reference to rejection and denial were made with simpler forms initially used to indicate non-existence. If, to express the meaning of non-existence, the child comes to use more and more complex techniques over time, these new structures cannot be being acquired due to advances in 'meaning'.

It is possible that there are other cognitive constraints than 'meaning'. For example, there may be limitations due to what the child at a particular age can process. Or there may be a limitation on the number of elements he can produce in a single utterance. Bloom (1970) has made a very convincing case for a cognitive limitation on production. She postulates a 'reduction transformation' in order to account for the differences between the underlying structure necessary for the assumed semantic interpretation and the reduced surface structure which the child actually produced. The evidence which she used to support this position consisted of sequential utterances of the child which exhibited both the expansion of some elements and deletion of others, in conjunction with semantic interpretation. For example, in the child's sequence of utterances

Raisin there
Buy more grocery store
Raisins
Buy more grocery store
Raisin ə grocery store

it becomes apparent that, whenever the subject of the sentence was expressed, either the verb, the object, the adverbial phrase, or more than one of these was omitted. This means that the child has organized the linguistic categories in a hierarchical structure and this accounts for the ability of the child to add categories without increasing sentence length, i.e. by deleting some categories when other categories either occurred or were expanded. Bloom claims that such an interpretation is supported by the semantic interpretation of the situation. For example, take the following set of utterances which one of the children, Kathryn, produced:

Kathryn under bridge
Kathryn ə make ə under ə bridge
Make ə more under bridge
Make ə car under bridge

Only by assuming that the child is employing a reduction transformation can one account for the relationship between *Kathryn* and *bridge* in the first utterance of the set, for in the observed situation in which the utterance was produced Kathryn was not under the bridge.

It is also interesting to note that the production limitation is not on sentence length as such. Bloom believes it to be rather a cognitive limitation in handling structured complexity. That is, it appears that the number of syntactic operations within a sentence increases the 'cognitive weight' of the sentence. But what determines which categories are eliminated? Bloom suggests that the cognitive limitation interacts with linguistic constraints in some as yet unspecified manner. She notes, for example, that it was often a more recently acquired form which was most likely to be deleted by the children.

But there are still other linguistic progressions which appear to depend neither on changes in meaning nor on changes in cognitive complexity or the growth of the cognitive capacities of the child. For example, Ursula Bellugi also studied the development of 'self-reference' during the acquisition of pronominalization or the formation of pronouns by the child (Bellugi-Klima, 1969; Bellugi, 1971). She found that there was a progression through several stages. At the earliest stage, the child used his own name in all positions, as the mother did about half the time. During this stage he was making utterances like

> Adam home
> Adam go hill
> Like Adam book shelf
> Pick Adam up

In the second stage, he began to substitute the pronoun *I* for his name if it occurred in the first position in the sentence, and occasionally produced both together:

> I like drink it
> I making coffee
> I Adam driving
> I Adam do that

And at the same stage he was substituting *me* for his name if it occurred other than in the first position in the sentence (with the exception of vocatives and greetings). This strategy produced some adult-like sentences:

> One for me
> Wake me up
> Why laughing at me?

But it also produced a regular pattern of errors:

> Why me spilled it?
> What me doing?

At the third stage, the rules changed and the child now produced *I* if his name served a nominative function in the sentence, and he produced *me* if it served an object function in the sentence:

That what I do
Can I put them on when I go outside?
You watch me be busy
You want me help you?

That is, the child's pronouns no longer depended on sentence position but on grammatical function.

There are even further stages in the process having to do with reflexives like *myself*, but this is enough to illustrate the point. A number of things can be noted. First of all, no strict theory of imitation could account for these findings. Instead, the child is clearly developing his grammar in a systematic and regular manner. The set of rules that he has at a particular time produce a regular set of errors when judged against adult grammar (e.g. 'Why me spilled it?', 'What me doing?', etc., at the second stage). It is therefore clear that his grammatical system has characteristics which are not shared by the adult model. The series of stages show that these systems change over time. But, most important for our present argument, the developments are not solely based on meaning or reference. Throughout, the meaning has remained the same – reference to self. It is also difficult to see how cognitive constraints could have played a part except inasmuch as later rules sometimes result in simplification. But, while such simplification may reduce cognitive strain, the child must have had the capacity to produce the cognitively more cumbersome utterances at a time just prior to the application of any simplifying rule. Cognitive constraints and their progressive easing would not appear to play a role in the acquisition of this and many other linguistic structures. Especially difficult to explain in terms of either meaning or the progressive easing of cognitive constraints would be the many structures mentioned earlier, which are acquired rather late – sometime between 5 and 12 years of age (see for example Chomsky, 1969).

We have already touched on some of the findings of Roger Brown in an earlier section having to do with cognition preceding language (Brown, 1973). It may be recalled, for example, that he cited evidence that the three earliest operations on verbs encoded the earliest semantic meanings attributed to the child. But Brown was not looking solely for the way semantics affected acquisition. In his study, he subjected the data to three analyses: semantic complexity, grammatical complexity and the frequency of the use of particular forms by the parents of the three children. He specifically looked at the development of 14 early morphemes in these terms. The morphemes whose grammatical acquisition he followed included the *-ing* of the present progressive, regular (*-ed*) and irregular past tense, regular and irregular third-person singular, plurals, possessives, the prepositions *in* and *on*, the articles *a* and *the*, and the copula and auxiliary *be*. There was a high degree of correlation between the respective orders of acquisition of these grammatical elements by the three children. Furthermore, there was a high degree of correlation among the parents in the frequency of use of these morphemes. But there was no meaningful correlation between the order of acquisition by the children and the frequency of use by the parents. It appears that the frequency with which a form is used, though similar in these adults, has little effect on the order of acquisition by the children.

But the order of acquisition across the children was very similar. Brown compared this order both to the degree of semantic complexity (the more complex defined as containing elements of the less complex) and to the order of grammatical complexity (based on the transformational grammar of Jacobs and Rosenbaum, 1968). And his findings indicated that both of these notions about equally well predicted the order of acquisition. There was evidence that transformational complexity was a determinant of the order of acquisition, but the evidence was alternatively interpretable as demonstrating that semantic complexity was a determinant of the order of acquisition. Since both semantic and grammatical complexity seem to be confounded in the acquisition of these 14 morphemes, it would appear difficult to render a judgement on their differential effects. However, a very ingenious solution has been offered by Dan Slobin (1973).

After reviewing data to support the argument that there are cognitive prerequisites for the development of grammar, Slobin notes that at some point formal linguistic complexity also plays a role in acquisition. For example, children learning Finnish lack yes/no questions at an age when children learning other languages have acquired them. The reason these are lacking in the Finnish children appears to be that yes/no questions are a particularly complex form in Finnish. They are not formed by the use of a rising intonation but by adding a question particle to the word and moving that word to the front of the sentence. Similarly, we know that very young children are able to understand and use plural forms. But Slobin reports that in Egyptian Arabic the complete set of plurals is not acquired until nearly 15 years of age! Again, it happens that this is an especially complex grammatical form in Arabic. There are many special irregular forms; there are differences depending on whether a counted or collected noun is used; and things numbering 3–10 take the plural, while 11 or more take the singular.

Slobin's suggestion as to a way to study the differential grammatical complexities of language is to make use of bilingual children. If the bilingual child acquires new expressions in both languages at the same time, then the formal devices in the two languages are similar in complexity. We have already quoted an example of this by Burling (1959), whose child was brought up speaking both English and Garo. And Slobin quotes some examples from children simultaneously acquiring Russian and Georgian. If the new expressions are acquired at different times, however, then a difference in formal complexity would be suggested. Slobin gives an example of a bilingual child acquiring both Serbo-Croat and Hungarian. Hungarian has a number of case endings for expressing spatial locations. The child had acquired these in Hungarian but at the same time had practically no locative expressions in Serbo-Croat. And the locative expressions in Serbo-Croat appear to be grammatically more complex in that they require both a locative preposition before the noun in addition to case endings attached to the noun.

Aside from the semantic generalities across children learning different languages, it is also possible to judge from the situational context when a child possesses particular meanings even though these are not yet being expressed grammatically. The whole study of intended reference discussed in an earlier section was devoted to showing how cognition preceded language acquisition. What we are emphasizing now is that grammatical structure has its own complexities which often resist acquisition once the child is attempting to express particular meanings. Another example which makes this clear is taken from Bloom's work (1970). She found that one and the same expression could be fulfilling different grammatical functions if meaning was taken into account. For example, the utterance 'Mommy sock' was interpretable as expressing a subject–object relation where the mother was putting the child's sock on the child; but the same utterance, 'Mommy sock' was interpreted as expressing the genitive relation (possession) when the child was picking up a sock belonging to Mommy. The possessive was meaningfully used before the child acquired the *'s* in order to produce utterances like 'Mommy's sock'.

We can see then, that cognitive development and linguistic development do not necessarily proceed together. The child, once he has the cognitive ability to understand certain relationships, will attempt to express these in language. As Slobin has pointed out, sometimes the linguistic means of expression for the new concept will be easily accessible, as with the Hungarian locative, and sometimes grammatical complexity will make the form inaccessible, as with the Arabic plural. Thus cognition can make certain understandings available, but there may be linguistic constraints.

The cognitive hypothesis: weak form

Earlier, in a discussion of the Sapir–Whorf hypothesis which held that language structured thought, we noted that some theorists had moved away from the extreme position and advocated what was called the 'weak form' of the Sapir–Whorf hypothesis. This weak form held that, while language did not wholly determine thought, it influenced thinking because of the categories made available by the language. Easy codability of a concept by a language made that concept easily available and thus more likely to be used in thinking. We have seen that there is accumulating evidence instead that it is cognition which determines language acquisition, but we have also seen that language has its own influences quite apart from meaning. Some linguistic changes, while not being solely determined by meaning, await other types of cognitive change due to their complexity. But there were still other structures whose late acquisition or changes over time seemed due neither to meaning nor to purely cognitive developments which eased particular cognitive constraints.

It would appear, then, that the cognitive hypothesis must also be modified. The 'weak form' of the cognitive hypothesis would hold that we are able to understand and productively to use particular linguistic structures only when our cognitive abilities enable us to do so. Our cognitive abilities at different stages of development make certain meanings *available* for expression. But, in addition, we must also possess certain specifically linguistic capabilities in order to come to express these meanings in language, and these linguistic capabilities may indeed be lacking in other species or in certain pathological conditions. Though language development depends on cognition, language has its own specific sources.

That indeed is really the same as the position put forward in 1934 by the Russian psychologist Vygotsky. In his classic work, *Thought and Language*, Vygotsky held that thought and speech have different genetic roots and that these two processes develop along different lines and independently of each other. The two processes are clearly distinct and can be observed in a pre-linguistic phase in the development of thought and in a pre-intellectual phase in the development of speech. It appears that much of what is being discovered during the current vogue of psycholinguistic research supports Vygotsky's view. Who knows – perhaps both Piaget and Chomsky are right!

2

The Cognition Hypothesis of Language Acquisition?

The cognition hypothesis of language acquisition seems too obviously true. In one of its forms, in which it is claimed that there are cognitive prerequisites for what one can *express* in language, it would appear impossible that things should be otherwise. But is this in fact the case? – a question that will be posed more directly at the end of this chapter. For now let us suppose that the cognition hypothesis is obvious; from a historical perspective we might then ask whether it was apparently so obvious even at the time it was first put forward (Cromer, 1968). In fact, at that time, the view that we must 'look at cognitive processes and their development, and at the ways such processes direct language acquisition' (Cromer, 1968, p. 220) was neither an obvious nor an accepted one. The cognition hypothesis of language acquisition arose out of a specific background at a particular time. The behaviourist tradition had been emphasizing general learning principles that were claimed to be adequate for explaining the child's acquisition of language – principles in which representations of concepts themselves played no part. Under the later influence of the Chomskian revolution in linguistics, most psychologists interested in language began to concentrate on the acquisition of linguistic structure (e.g. Braine, 1963b). Studies were even made of the acquisition of artificial languages without semantic content (Braine, 1963a), and it was not until several years later that researchers began to argue that the acquisition of such artificial languages was facilitated when the language reflected properties of a reference field (Moeser and Bregman, 1972; Moeser and Olson, 1974; see also Bloom, 1971, for criticisms of Braine's notion of pivot grammar). Piaget's theories were not generally known, and his specific views on language development were not available in English until 1969 (Piaget and Inhelder, 1969a; Sinclair-de-Zwart, 1969). Thus, in the late 1960s there was very little emphasis on or interest in any notion of conceptual underpinnings for language acquisition. One exception to this was to be found in the work of Slobin (1966), which claimed that some aspects of language acquisition depend on developing conceptual ability. Basically, however, it was not until Lois Bloom's important and influential book appeared in 1970 that child-language researchers began to take seriously the notion that the developing thought processes of the child might play a crucial part in language acquisition itself.

Chapter 1, originally published in 1974, was a summary of the evidence that had begun to accumulate in favour of a cognition hypothesis of language acquisition. It drew on Slobin's claims, my own thesis work from 1968 on specific acquisitions by the children of the Roger Brown longitudinal study, Bloom's data, and the arguments made by the Genevan psychologists. The purpose of the present chapter is to examine the claims for the cognition hypothesis of language acquisition and to see whether they still hold with the same force that they appeared to do, or whether there are reasons for questioning the adequacy of the cognition-hypothesis formulation. The first thing to be noted is that most of the original evidence has held up with time, one possible exception being some dispute over the interpretation of the perfect-tense data.[1] Changes in the basic hypothesis, however, follow from new evidence and from finer definitions of what is meant by 'language' and what is meant by 'cognition'. Chapter 5 seeks to break down 'language' into its component subsystems and inquires into the usefulness of such a breakdown, especially in regard to disordered language populations. A differentiation of the various aspects of 'cognition' is begun in this chapter, and developed in chapter 4 as one of the reconceptualizations of language acquisition. The present chapter will be primarily devoted to new lines of evidence that bear on the cognition hypothesis of language acquisition, some of which may even bring that hypothesis into question.

Recent Studies Supportive of the Cognition Hypothesis

Some aspects of 'cognition'

In 1976, in a review of the cognition hypothesis in terms of its implications for child-language disorders, I drew a distinction between two aspects of cognition:

> There are really two separate issues involved when one talks about cognitive processes underlying language. First, there are the thoughts, intentions, and

meanings themselves, which can be called 'cognitions'. . . . Second [is] a related type of notion, which goes to a 'deeper level', so to speak, and emphasizes the underpinnings of these thoughts or cognitions. . . . These mechanisms can be termed 'cognitive structures'. . . . Piagetian theory is essentially concerned with these cognitive structures and the ways in which various 'cognitive operations' result in particular cognitions at different developmental stages. The Piagetian view is that cognitive structures and operations make language acquisition possible. (Cromer, 1976a, pp. 289–90)

In the famous debate between Piaget and Chomsky (Piattelli-Palmarini, 1980) this distinction was similarly raised. Everyone seemed to agree that the attainment of concepts preceded their encoding in language. The debate then centred on whether sensorimotor *mechanisms* were necessary and sufficient to account for language acquisition or whether language-specific properties, probably innate, need to be hypothesized.

Studies of concepts and their relation to language

Let us begin by examining the putative 'truism' that the possession of particular concepts necessarily precedes their encoding in language. While this may be true, there are at least three positions with which this view can be contrasted. In one, the child begins to use new forms or lexical items, perhaps by mere imitation, and thereby slowly comes to understand what they encode through their repetitive use in particular situations. A second view sees the child as attaining primitive concepts during development which then affect and are affected by the language in which they are encoded (cf. the position of Gopnik and Meltzoff outlined later in this chapter). A third view credits the child with already possessing a variety of primitive concepts or at least conceptual possibilities. Those that are specifically encoded in the language that the child is acquiring are retained and developed (cf. Bowerman's position, also reviewed below). These positions are similar to or extensions of Whorfian views in which concepts are determined or at least influenced by language. It is against the background of these competing possibilities that the review of studies purporting to support the cognition hypothesis (in terms of concepts) should be viewed.

Siegel (1978) stated the principle of the language and thought studies very clearly: 'Evidence for the independence of language and thought in the young child comes from studies that have examined the sequence of development of a particular concept and those linguistic abilities that are assumed to be analogous to this concept' (p. 48). She felt that, in general, such studies had given positive evidence that concepts develop prior to the language related to them. In her own studies, for example, Siegel reinforced children for selecting the larger or the smaller of a group of dots (the magnitude task), and for selecting from four choices the one with the same number of dots as a sample (the equivalence task). A language task examined the child's understanding of the words *big*, *little* and *same* when applied to objects. Forty-five three-year-olds and 57 four-year-olds were tested. Some children, of course, fail both the concept and the language tasks, while, at the other extreme, there are children who succeed at both tasks. Interest, however, centres on the children who fail one type of task but succeed at the other. While not definitive, a pattern in which some children succeed at the concept task but fail the language task would look to be supportive of the cognition hypothesis, especially if this were accompanied by findings that no children succeed at the language task if they fail the concept task. By contrast, if children fail the concept task but succeed at the language task, this would be crucial evidence against a cognition hypothesis. The pattern on Siegel's equivalence tasks was supportive of the cognition hypothesis: 90 of the 102 children either succeeded at both tasks or failed both tasks and thus provide no evidence one way or the other; but of the remaining 12 children all succeeded at the concept task while failing the language task – no child showed the pattern of succeeding at the language task while failing the concept task. Results on magnitude were nearly as good: 62 children either succeeded at or failed both tasks, and of the 40 children who succeeded at only one task 37 succeeded at the concept task while failing the language task, and only three showed the reverse pattern. Siegel concluded that children's concepts exist independently of and prior to even the simplest language used to refer to those concepts. This may not be an unreasonable conclusion in view of the data – but what of those three children who understood language about magnitude, but failed tasks examining the associated concepts? Especially in testing children, one is aware of problems of attention, motivation, fatigue and other factors that affect performance. The results of these three children may represent nothing more than the variance in performance to be expected when testing large numbers of children. On the other hand, even one child who truly shows this pattern in a manner that cannot be explained away is important evidence against the notion that the cognitive attainments are necessary prerequisites for the associated language attainments. We simply do not know whether the performance of the three non-congruent children is a fluke or whether it is crucial evidence against the theory.

In recent years a good deal of Piagetian-inspired research has examined the relation between emerging concepts and language. Piaget had written mainly in general terms about the attainment of full sensorimotor competence. Later researchers have further specified children's conceptual attainments during the sensorimotor period and related these to language measures. Smolak and Levine (1984) studied 40 children who were 1–3 years of age. In this study, children were given a number of cognitive tasks to perform and their language was also assessed. Piaget had argued that non-linguistic, conceptual representation is a precursor of 'representational language', i.e. language that is used to refer to past events and absent objects. Smolak and Levine examined the development of object permanence and its relation to representational language. If the Piagetian view is correct, success at tasks involving invisible displacements should predate representational language. Object permanence was assessed through the administration of a graded series of invisible-displacement tasks. These ranged from the easiest, a single invisible displacement involving the use of a single screen, through intermediate tasks involving a single displacement with three screens, to the most difficult – tasks involving multiple displacements with multiple screens. Language was assessed during special play sessions which included a special interview designed to elicit references to past events and absent objects. Of the 40 children, 34 possessed representational language, and all of them had successfully completed at least the intermediate multiscreen single-invisible-displacement task. By contrast, none of the six children who had not yet attained that level of cognitive ability gave any evidence of using representational language referring to past events or absent objects. The Smolak and Levine study suggests, then, that the child must attain a particular stage of object-concept development before the use of particular kinds of representational language can occur.[2]

McCune-Nicolich (1981) had made a similar claim that particular stages of object-concept development must be attained before particular language uses would be found in the child. However, she was critical of earlier studies that had focused on 'object words', some of which had shown only low correlations between language and sensorimotor measures. McCune-Nicolich therefore studied 'relational words', which, she argued, develop and exist apart from specific contents. That is, relational words encode consistent relational meanings regardless of the objects involved. Thus, she argued, a word like *more* that encodes the notion of recurrence does so whether another cookie is requested after one has been eaten, a second shoe is observed, or the child requests additional tickling. Since the use of such relational words is seen as being based on the operative knowledge attained at the end of the sensorimotor period, McCune-Nicolich predicted that such words should only appear after the attainment of sensorimotor knowledge. Entry into Stage 6 of sensorimotor intelligence was defined as the capacity to solve a single invisible displacement on at least two trials. Furthermore, since this intelligence is a universal aspect of cognition, the same categories of meaning should be observed in all children regardless of the varying lexical items used to encode them.

In her longitudinal study, McCune-Nicolich observed five girls who were aged 1 year 2 months to 1 year 6 months at the outset of the study. They were seen monthly in their homes for a 30-minute play session for a period of 7–11 months. The prediction was that relational words would not be acquired by the child until *late* in Stage 6, and the criterion for having attained this level of competence was immediate solution of random invisible displacements using three screens. McCune-Nicolich's observations revealed that each child began to use 8–10 relational word forms at some point during this period of single-word use. But, contrary to her prediction and to earlier studies, some of the children had begun to use a number of these relational words prior to the attainment of late-stage-6 sensorimotor competence. However, since all of the children were observed to have attained early Stage 6 competence by the first observational session, McCune-Nicolich concluded that the operative sensorimotor knowledge of *early* Stage 6 appears to be a sufficient cognitive foundation for the use of relational words.

More important than the precise point of emergence of relational words during Stage 6 development, however, is their pattern of emergence. In fact, the onset of their use was found to be fairly abrupt. For example, McCune-Nicolich reported that for each child more than half of the relational words first appeared within a one-month span. Furthermore, there was no consistent order of emergence for particular words or meanings. Instead, the relational words tended to enter the child's lexicon as a group. What such results seem to show is that a certain level of cognitive development is necessary before the child can begin to use relational words. When that level of cognitive ability has been attained, a number of relational words begin to be used regardless of their specific content.

The McCune-Nicolich study is perhaps a good example of empirical research results being in conflict with previous Piagetian predictions concerning the emergence of particular language abilities. Corrigan (1979) had earlier reviewed the research evidence on the cognitive correlates of early language and found many conflicting results. Language was found in some studies to be occurring before the attainment of those substages of sensorimotor intelligence that Piagetians had argued were prerequisite. In her perceptive discussion, Corrigan focused criticism on the particular measures used, on variations in task factors and administration, and on the fact that different criteria were used for assignment of behaviour to particular cognitive stages. In other words, the relations observed by various experimenters depend crucially on how the cognitive-stage level of the child is operationalized. Furthermore, Corrigan argued that, since development is gradual rather than abrupt, one cannot make broad predictions about what should occur at the Stage-6 level of sensorimotor development. Instead, one must specify precisely what cognitive tasks the child can perform and relate these to particular aspects of language.

In her own research, Corrigan (1978) had used an object-permanence scale consisting of 21 tasks. In an 18-month longitudinal study of three children, Corrigan found that two semantic categories – non-existence and recurrence – were not meaningfully expressed by the children until they had attained the cognitive ability to perform correctly on the most difficult object-permanence item, task 21. Note that this finding is in conflict with McCune-Nicolich's observations, cited earlier, that relational words, regardless of specific content, emerge together in the *early* part of Stage 6. How might this apparent conflict in results be resolved?

Tomasello and Farrar (1984) have claimed that the semantic content of the child's early words should be related to specific developments in cognitive ability. They suggested that McCune-Nicolich failed to make a distinction between relational words that signify visible displacements of objects (e.g. *up* and *move*) and those that signify invisible displacements (e.g. *gone, all gone*). Furthermore, they argued that, since 'this is precisely the distinction between stage 5 and stage 6 object permanence behaviours, . . . it should be reflected in the cognitive structures underlying the child's early words' (p. 480). In other words, their view is that, contrary to McCune-Nicolich's predictions concerning relational words in general, those relational words requiring only the understanding of visible displacements are based on Stage 5 object-permanence attainment and should begin to appear in the child's language at that time. By contrast, those relational words requiring the knowledge of invisible displacements should not appear until Stage 6 of the sensorimotor period. In this context, it can be suggested that Corrigan's 'non-existence' category and perhaps most instances of her 'recurrence' category involve 'invisible displacements', and it is therefore not surprising that words encoding these concepts were not used by the children in her study until late-Stage-6 attainment. Table 2.1 gives details of the substages of the sensorimotor period to illustrate the differences in conceptual attainment.

In the Tomasello and Farrar study, six 12-month-old children were observed weekly for a period of six months. All were initially in Stage 5 of object-permanence development. During the weekly visits, language samples were obtained, and these were supplemented by diary records of the child's vocabulary kept by the mother. The child was only credited

Table 2.1 *Sensorimotor substages and the development of object permanence*

Substage	Age range (months)	Characteristics of sensorimotor substage	Developments in object permanence
1	$0-1\frac{1}{2}$	Reflex schemas exercised	Infant does not search for objects that have been removed from sight
2	$1\frac{1}{2}-4$	Primary circular reactions; repeated actions that are pleasurable	Infant does not search for objects that have been removed from sight
3	4–8	Secondary circular reactions; dawning awareness of relation of own actions to environment; extended actions that produce pleasant sensations	Infant will reach for partially hidden object but stops if it disappears
4	8–12	Co-ordination of secondary circular reactions; earliest form of problem-solving	Infant will search for a completely hidden object; the infant keeps searching the original location of the object even if it is moved to another location in full view of the infant
5	12–18	Tertiary circular reactions; deliberate variation of problem-solving means; experimentation in order to see what the consequences will be	Infant will search for an object after seeing it moved but not if the object is secretly moved
6	18–24	Beginnings of symbolic representation; invention of new means of problem solving through symbolic combinations	Infant will search for a hidden object, certain that it exists somewhere

Source: Cole and Cole (1989).

with understanding a particular relational word when productive use was demonstrated in more than one context. Whether a word referred to a visible or an invisible displacement was decided by examining the particular contexts in which the word occurred. Cognitive attainment was examined through testing carried out at monthly intervals and consisted of modified versions of the object-permanence and means–ends subscales of the Uzgiris–Hunt infant-assessment scale.

The results revealed that the children first began to use a variety of present-relational words during Stage 5 object permanence – which requires the attainment of understanding visible displacements but not invisible displacements. Depending on which of two different criteria Tomasello and Farrar used, either five of the six children or all six children used present-relational words during Stage 5. These included the use of *thank you* to refer to the transfer of objects, *uh-oh* in situations in which the child fell down or dropped or spilled something, *bye* in situations in which people who were in spatial proximity to the child began to move away, and *hi* to greet people within the visual field. Tomasello and Farrar note that words like *bye* and *hi* were never used by any child at this stage to refer to objects or persons already gone or to the existence or transformation of objects or persons outside the child's perceptual field. The children never used any words to refer to absent objects. Absent-relational words first appeared during Stage 6; they were not used by any child in Stage 5. These words included *gone* for objects that were initially present and then disappeared, *find* and *more* for objects that were initially absent and then appeared, and *all gone* for objects that were initially absent and remained absent – as when a cup was found to be empty. Tomasello and Farrar concluded that 'stage 5 object permanence does not suffice for the use of absent-relational words. These do not appear until stage 6, when children come to have an understanding of invisible-object transformations' (1984, p. 486).

There is an additional finding reported by Tomasello and Farrar that appears to be of special importance since it gives evidence of considerable specificity between conceptual development and language development. They noted that one of the children in their study used an absent-relational word while still in Stage 5 means–ends development. This child was, of course, at the Stage 6 level on object-permanence tasks. Such a finding would appear to support what Corrigan (1979) called a skill-specific model of development. That is, in the present context, the child's abilities in language would reflect specific conceptual developments; such a view would be at odds with the older Piagetian position, which saw the child as having common cognitive structures across varying domains at particular substages of development. In the present view, one does not find a Stage 5 or Stage 6 child, but a child who may have a mixture of abilities dependent on the specific tasks examined. These in turn will be related to specific developments in language. Findings in two studies by Gopnik and Meltzoff give support to this view.

In the first study (Gopnik and Meltzoff, 1986a), 30 18-month-old children underwent cognitive testing, and the results were examined in relation to their use of particular words. The cognitive tasks explored the child's competence on both object-concept and means–ends relations as adapted from the Uzgiris–Hunt infant psychological development scale. Word use was based on questionnaires describing the words Gopnik and Meltzoff were interested in; these were completed by the mothers. The child was credited with having acquired a word only if it was used appropriately in three different contexts. In addition, the experimenter recorded whether the child used either disappearance or success/failure words appropriately during the recording session in the lab, and children were scored as having acquired the word if they used it appropriately during the recording session. It is important to note that scoring was based on the assumed *meanings* of the child's words in context and not merely on the forms of the words themselves. Thus, words like *there*, *uh-oh* and *no* were only scored as instances of success/failure words when used in conjunction with success or failure of the child's 'plans' – as in the child uttering *there* at the completion of building a block tower, or saying *uh-oh* when the tower toppled over while being built. Similarly, words like *gone* and *all gone* were only scored as instances of disappearance if they actually encoded the concept in context.

Gopnik and Meltzoff's results showed a relation between success at particular cognitive tasks and the use of particular words relevant to those tasks. Children who were most advanced on the object-concept tasks were the ones most likely to use disappearance words, while those children who were most advanced in solving the difficult means–ends problems were more likely to use success/failure words. This was reflected in the increase in the percentages of children using those word types as a function of three levels of attainment on the associated cognitive task. Significantly, there was little relation between the use of disappearance words and perform-ance on the means–ends tasks, or between use of success/failure words and performance on the object-concept tasks. As Gopnik and Meltzoff put it when they first reported these results, 'These results suggest specific relationships between *particular* linguistic attainments and *particular* cognitive skills. The use of disappearance words is closely related to progress in object-permanence, but not so closely related to progress in means–ends ability. Similarly, the use of success/failure words is more closely related to means–ends abilities than to object-permanence skills' (1984, p. 13).

In their second study, a longitudinal study reported in the same paper, Gopnik and Meltzoff (1986a) followed for several months the progress of 19 children who were initially 13–19 months old. During the period of study, cognitive skills were investigated approximately every three weeks, using the same methods as in the cross-sectional study just noted. The children's language was assessed by questionnaires and observations as in the first study. Results are reported for varying levels of object-concept and means–ends attainment. One of the more striking findings concerned the gaps between the first uses of particular word types and the associated and non-associated cognitive attainments. For example, it was found that the gap between the first use of disappearance words and the first solution of the more advanced object-permanence task (task 14 of the Uzgiris–Hunt scales) was on average 28 days, but the gap between that same first use of a disappearance word and the first solution of the more advanced means–ends tasks (tasks 10–12 on the Uzgiris–Hunt scales) was 65 days. The difference between these gaps – 28 days versus 65 days – was statistically significant. Similarly, the gap between the first use of a success/failure word and the first solution to the advanced object tasks was on average only 14 days, but the gap between the first use of success/failure words and the advanced means–ends-permanence task was 56 days. This difference – 14 days versus 56 days – was also statistically significant. Here, then, as in the cross-sectional study, there is evidence of a connection between the acquisition of disappearance words and the solution of object-concept tasks, and of a connection between the acquisition of success/failure words and the use of insight to solve complex means–ends problems. More significantly, the results showed a dissociation between these two developments, underlining the specificity in the relation between cognitive development and language acquisition.

If there is evidence of a connection between the acquisition of specific word types and particular cognitive attainments, the important question then becomes, what is the direction of that relationship? The Gopnik and Meltzoff data as regards this issue are somewhat complicated. As noted earlier, there were varying levels of attainment within Stage 6 on both object-concept and means–ends tasks. The gaps and dissociations just discussed were between the first use of particular word types and the *more advanced* level of attainment on the associated cognitive tasks. However, if one considers the *earliest* signs of attainment of these cognitive abilities (task 13 in the object-permanence scale and task 9 in the means–ends scale), the findings look rather different. Gopnik and Meltzoff report that, when only these earlier levels are considered, the cognitive tasks were generally solved before the related word types were acquired. For example, only two of the 19 children had acquired a disappearance word before having solved the earliest object-permanence task. Furthermore, children generally solved the cognitive task a considerable time before first using a disappearance word. In fact, the average gap in time between these two developments was about 43 days. The findings for means–ends development were similar. Only one child used a success/failure word before having solved means–ends task 9. The time gap between cognitive and language attainments was also large, the mean being 57 days. One interpretation of these data is that they are strongly supportive of the cognition hypothesis in that a particular level of concept attainment is achieved well before the associated word types begin to be used. This assumes, of course, that the observation of an occasional child showing a reversed order of acquisition, as noted above, is due to problems inherent in testing and/or to the fact that the observation was not continuous (gaps of two or three weeks between observations, etc.). One must always keep in mind, however, that even one case of a *truly* reversed order of acquisition would undermine the notion that particular conceptual developments are *necessary* for the associated word types to be acquired. In the Gopnik and Meltzoff observations, we are again left with the problem of how to interpret those rare cases that go against the overwhelming majority of observations.

In any case, Gopnik and Meltzoff (1986a) focus their attention on the later conceptual attainments. It was observed that, at the *more advanced* levels of attainment, language developments and the related cognitive developments could occur in either order. On 11 occasions the child solved the cognitive task before first using the associated term, as would be consistent with a cognition hypothesis; but on eight occasions the child used the relevant word before solving the related cognitive task. In the remaining 19 cases, the children first achieved the cognitive-task solution and first used words encoding the related concepts in the very same session. This pattern of results was interpreted by Gopnik and Meltzoff as evidence that concepts and language develop together. In other words, it is not the case that concepts develop before words, or that words develop before concepts; rather, there exist transitional periods during which conceptual ability and language develop concurrently, 'with each area of development influencing and facilitating the other' (p. 1051). In the interaction between these two domains, language is seen as a contributing cause rather than as a simple consequence of cognitive development. This position will be considered in more detail in a later section on the influence of language on conceptual development. Here, however, it is worth mentioning a somewhat different view that would be consonant with the Gopnik and Meltzoff data just noted.

The alternative interpretation claims that there develop underlying capacities that are common to both linguistic and non-linguistic domains.

This very strictly Piagetian view was proposed by Bates (1979) to account for the relationship that she observed between the development of gesture and the development of language. It differs from Piaget in scope in that, whereas Piaget concentrated on broad stages of development, Bates proposed 'local homologies' or 'skill-specific' parallels. As regards the development of language and cognition, this homology model would claim that a developing underlying capacity could manifest itself either in cognitive tasks or in language, and that either of these could emerge first in observed development.

Tomasello and Farrar (1986) contrasted Bates's homology model with their own prerequisites model, which emphasizes the primacy of cognition at least at early stages of cognitive development. Furthermore, they subjected the two views to an interesting experimental test. The attempt was made to teach new words to children who were in either Stage 5 or Stage 6 of object-permanence development. Three types of words were used: some referred to physical objects, some to the visible movement of objects, and some to the invisible movement of objects. Children in Stage 6 should be able to learn all three word types. However, for children in Stage 5 the two models make contrasting predictions. If the prerequisites model is the more accurate, then Stage 5 children, while being able to learn object and visible-movement words, should be unable to learn words for invisible movements. On the other hand, according to the reasoning of Tomasello and Farrar, the homology model should predict some success by Stage 5 children on invisible-movement words – i.e. some Stage 5 children should be able to learn invisible-movement words before entering Stage 6. Presumably this latter prediction is based on the claim that in previous research the reason why the cognitive-stage development has been observed to emerge before the corresponding words is due to some sort of performance factors associated with the use of language. If the learning conditions are appropriate, and Stage 5 children can acquire words encoding objects and visible displacements, then some of them should also be able to acquire invisible-displacement words. While this reasoning may not be entirely convincing, the finding that Stage 5 children do not acquire specific predicted word types would act as support for the cognitive-prerequisites model.

Tomasello and Farrar tested 23 middle-class children, aged 1 year 2 months to 1 year 9 months, all of whom were producing some language (mostly single words). On the basis of a cognitive pre-test, seven of the children (mean age 15.9 months) were found to be in Stage 5, and 16 (mean age 17.2 months) in Stage 6 of object permanence. Children were trained to learn the names of two unfamiliar objects chosen such that these names matched the child's individual phonological capabilities. Training took the form of the utterance 'This is a ———.' For visible- and invisible-displacement terms, the nonsense words *deke* and *dop* were used (counterbalanced across the children) in the utterances 'Watch the *x* deke' or 'Watch the *x* dop' while either spinning the object on the floor (visible movement) or hiding the object (invisible movement). The child's learning was measured by an elicited production task ('What is this?', 'What happened?', 'What's the *x* doing?') and a comprehension task (picking the object out of a group of four objects and carrying out commands such as 'Can you make the *x* dop? Make it dop'). In addition, observations were noted of the child spontaneously using any of the words during the session.

Results supported the cognitive-prerequisites view. On the comprehension measure, Stage 6 children learned all three word types equally well. By contrast, Stage 5 children, while comprehending the object and visible-movement words equally well, showed very poor performance on the invisible-displacement word. Tomasello and Farrar also report the results for individual children. Of the 16 Stage 6 children, 14 comprehended the object word, 13 the visible-movement word and 13 the invisible-movement word. Of the seven Stage 5 children, however, four comprehended the object word, three the visible-movement word, but none the invisible-movement word.

Word *production* by the children was very rare, and spontaneous and elicited productions were combined; a single use of either type was used as criterion for production. Of the 16 Stage 6 children, 13 produced an object word, 12 produced a visible-movement word, and 11 produced an invisible-movement word. Of the seven Stage 5 children, three produced an object word, two produced a visible-movement word, and only one an invisible-movement word (Tomasello and Farrar report that this child was one of the two Stage 5 children who passed the single invisible-displacement task – as opposed to the series of invisible displacements used as criterion for Stage 6 ability).

Overall, considering both comprehension and production together, the results show that either one or no Stage 5 child was able to learn an invisible-movement word. Since these same Stage 5 children nevertheless learned object and visible-movement words, Tomasello and Farrar concluded that these results are strong evidence for the cognitive-prerequisites model.

The Tomasello and Farrar study is interesting for another reason. It is one of the few studies to attempt an experimental intervention with an outcome that can either confirm or falsify specific predictions guided by theoretical considerations. It may be that other techniques could be developed that would move this field of study beyond the observational and correlational methods usually used. One can think of other intervention methods that might be useful for shedding light on theoretical considerations. For example, Wishart and Bower (1985) have reported that early exposure to visual tracking tasks substantially accelerated object-concept development. In their longitudinal study, 24 infants were studied from 12 weeks of age until they achieved Piaget's Stage 6 of object-concept development some nine months later. The infants were exposed weekly to tracking tasks from the onset of the study (12 weeks of age). Reaching tasks were begun during the week when the infant first demonstrated the ability to reach and touch a dangling object within two minutes of its presentation. After this, both tracking and reaching tasks were given in each weekly session. Wishart and Bower report that the infants in their study attained Piaget's Stage 5 by 5–6 months of age, and Stage 6 by 11–13 months of age. If these represent true conceptual attainments, then the first words of these children should include word types (e.g. words for invisible movements) that are not observed in the early words of control children who have not yet attained Stage 6 in their normal unaccelerated development. I am not aware of any research that has attempted to study the language development in children of supposedly accelerated cognitive development, but it may be a technique worth pursuing.

As has been seen, recent studies of the relation between language and cognitive development have become increasingly more detailed in their analysis of particular cognitive attainments and their expression in language. Furthermore, a great many of these studies have been undertaken within a Piagetian framework in which attention has been focused on various sensorimotor developments. However, it should be noted that not all of the research studying the effects of cognitive growth on language has been based on Piagetian concepts. It is perhaps worth mentioning a few examples of recent research examining aspects of development that are not tied to the achievement of the object concept or to the completion of the sensorimotor stage.

Levine and Carey (1982), for example, studied the relation between the development of the concept of front–back orientation and the acquisition of comprehension of the words *front* and *back*. Their initial hypothesis, opposite to a cognition-hypothesis view, was that in some cases learning a new word may precede and influence concept acquisition. 36 children ranging in age from 2 years 1 month to 3 years 3 months were tested. Two non-linguistic tasks were used to evaluate the children's concept of front–back orientation. In a 'parade task', the child had to line up nine toy objects with their fronts facing in the line of motion of a parade. In the 'canonical encounter' task, the child had to place each of nine objects in an orientation in which the object could 'talk to' a doll held by the experimenter. For linguistic understanding, the children's knowledge of the words *front* and *back* was assessed by having them point to the fronts and backs of toy objects and to the front and back of themselves and the experimenter.

Three children failed all the tasks. The remaining 33 children succeeded in at least one of the concept tasks, scoring at least eight out of nine correct object placements on either the parade or canonical-encounter task. (In fact, 30 of these 33 children obtained a score of at least seven out of nine correct on *both* tasks.) By contrast, results on the linguistic task were much poorer. Only five children made no errors. Another 20 children scored in the range of 40–80 per cent correct, and there were eight children who scored in the range of 0–30 per cent correct. In other words, whereas the 33 children performed at about the same high level on non-linguistic tasks assessing their concept of front–back orientation, their scores for linguistic knowledge of *front* and *back* ranged from extremely low (eight children) to perfect (five children). Conversely, none of the children succeeded on the linguistic tasks while failing on the concept tasks. The results suggest, then, that, contrary to the hypothesis with which Levine and Carey (1982) began, acquisition of the concept 'front–back orientation' precedes acquisition of the words *front* and *back*.

Johnston (1985) has recently summarized similar data from her own PhD work (Johnston, 1979) on children's use of *in front of* and *in back of* [American English] in relation to their understanding of the various spatial notions that comprise the meanings of those terms, e.g. proximity, order and projective relations.[3] Testing 33 children of between 2 years 7 months and $4\frac{1}{2}$ years of age, she found that spatial notions and prepositional uses emerged in parallel. Furthermore, while children who used these prepositions verbally in particular senses could solve non-verbal spatial problems requiring the application of the pertinent spatial notions, the reverse was not the case, thus supporting the notion of temporal priority of conceptual achievement. There were remarkably few disconfirming children. Indeed, the number of children who used a preposition in a sense on which they failed the concept task was usually only one, and, in one case, two. Johnston concluded that specific uses of spatial terms appears to follow the acquisition of related non-verbal concepts. (As noted earlier, one must interpret the one or two disconfirming children with caution.)

Another recent experiment purports to show that conceptual knowledge precedes linguistic encoding. Halpern, Corrigan and Aviezer (1981) studied two differing concepts often encoded by the word *under*. In type 1, space is visible due to the structure of one of the objects referred to, as in 'a boat under a bridge'. By contrast, in type 2, the space is not perceivable and must be mentally created, as in 'a flat block under another flat block'. Halpern et al. hypothesized that, since type 1 is conceptually easier than type 2, it would develop earlier in language comprehension and production. They observed that in English the terms *under* and *underneath* may encode this distinction; however, they also noted that these terms are not necessarily distinguished by English-speakers. By contrast, Hebrew has only one spatial preposition for both types of *under*. Halpern et al. therefore studied the acquisition of the two concepts of *under* and the associated acquisition of their linguistic encoding by Hebrew-speaking children.

Seventy-five Hebrew-speaking Israeli children were tested. They ranged in age from 1 year 2 months to $2\frac{1}{2}$ years. The children had to construct representations of the various types of *under* with bridges or blocks either by copying the experimenter's completed model or by imitating the experimenter's actual observed process of construction. Language comprehension was tested through the use of toy animals and objects which the child had to place in response to the experimenter's instructions. Language-production tasks required the child to tell the experimenter where to place these same objects, and also to answer questions about the relationships depicted in six pictures. Overall, the results lent support to the notion that cognitive ability, as gauged by the construction task, developed prior to the corresponding linguistic counterpart. These results can be usefully examined in some detail.

For the first type of *under*, 36 children failed both the construction and the language tasks and so nothing can be learned from them as regards the relation between thought and language. Of the remaining 39 children, 19 succeeded at the construction task but failed both the language-comprehension and language-production tasks. One might say that these children have the concept but have not yet mastered its encoding in language. A further 19 succeeded at the construction task and at one or both of the language tasks. These two latter patterns are consistent with a cognition-hypothesis interpretation in that such children not only possess the concept but have partially or totally mastered its linguistic encoding. Only one child demonstrated language ability on type-1 *under* but failed the cognitive construction task. Results for the second type of *under* were similar, but these were based on fewer instances since most children scored poorly on all measures. In fact, 62 of the 75 children failed both the construction and language tasks. What are of interest, then, are the patterns of results shown by the remaining 13 'intermediate' children. Five succeeded at the construction task but at neither language task; four succeeded on the construction and one or both of the language measures; and only four demonstrated either comprehension or production of type-2 *under* while failing the cognitive construction task. Halpern et al. interpret these results as supporting the hypothesis that the ability to perform the cognitive construction task develops prior to the ability to perform its linguistic counterpart. At first glance this may appear a reasonable conclusion, but one is worried by the counterexamples of a few of the 'intermediate' children.

To repeat, in evaluating the evidence concerning which is prior, the cognitive ability or the linguistic form, one must concentrate on those 'intermediate' cases where only one of the abilities is present. Children who either fail all of the tasks or, conversely, show both cognitive and linguistic ability as adults would do, give no information about the relation between language and cognition during development. Looking at just the 'intermediate' children in the Halpern et al. study, then, 30 of 31 children succeeded at the cognitive construction task while failing to evidence either linguistic comprehension or production ability, or both, for the first type of *under*. Only one child's performance (3.2 per cent) goes against prediction by showing a pattern of failing the cognitive task while succeeding at both comprehension and production in language. But on the second type of *under* the results are not so supportive of the cognition hypothesis. Of 12 'intermediate' children, eight succeeded at the cognitive construction task while failing on one or both of the language measures – a pattern consistent with the cognition hypothesis. But the performance of four children (33.3 per cent of the crucial 'intermediate' children) went against the cognition hypothesis, since they failed the cognitive construction task while succeeding on one or both of the language measures. Evidence like this, even from a small number of cases, is important since it can be interpreted as a challenge to the notion that conceptual development is *necessary*, in all cases, for linguistic development to occur. I will return to this important issue of necessity later in this chapter.

So far, most of what has been reviewed appears to support the cognition hypothesis of language acquisition; the acquisition of particular conceptual abilities usually precedes the acquisition of the particular linguistic terms with which they are associated. But we have already seen some hints of a different viewpoint as found in some interpretations of the Gopnik and Meltzoff and of the Halpern et al. results. Before turning more directly to positions that are in direct conflict with the 'obvious' view that concepts must be developed before they can be encoded in language, the evidence for the cognition hypothesis from the study of more basic cognitive operations and mechanisms will be considered.

Cognitive mechanisms and their relation to language

Piaget's original conceptions concerning the relation of cognitive development and language have been discussed in chapter 1 (pp. 11–14, 22–3, 40). Under one interpretation, it is thought to be the achievement of a particular stage of mental organization that makes possible the acquisition of particular language abilities. This is certainly what Piaget seemed to argue. For example, it was claimed that language acquisition could only begin when the achievement of sensorimotor intelligence was complete. Piaget's position, as found most recently in the published account of the Piaget–Chomsky debate (Piattelli-Palmarini, 1980), can be characterized as claiming that sensorimotor intelligence is both necessary and sufficient to account for the beginnings of language acquisition. By contrast, Inhelder (1980) in the same debate took the view that sensorimotor intelligence was merely necessary for structured language acquisition to begin, a view to which Chomsky claimed he had no objection. Piaget's position rules out the necessity to postulate anything specifically linguistic (and possibly innate). Inhelder's view, however, is compatible with the weak form of the cognition hypothesis found in chapter 1, wherein cognitive attainments must be supplemented by specifically linguistic abilities in order for language acquisition to occur. Note, however, that in both views it is the achievement of an overall mental structure that accounts for some aspects of progress in language acquisition.

A different interpretation might question these conclusions in one of two ways. First, it may be that the overall cognitive-stage level is too broad a notion to give predictive validity. One needs to specify precisely the attainments of particular sub-skills and to see their relationship to specific linguistic attainments. Attempts to do this at the level of *conceptual* acquisition were discussed in the previous section of this chapter. Second, it may even be that no such overall organizational structure exists – i.e. that there is no such thing as an achieved sensorimotor intelligence or an operational level, or that, at most, these are merely convenient fictions for general descriptive purposes. If this is so, then again one can only study the relationship between language and the component sub-skills that these overall structures were thought to comprise. But under all these interpretations – Piaget's overall stage notions and those that, by contrast, focus on the specific sub-skills – the purpose is to examine the part played in language acquisition by processes and mechanisms, not conceptual content. Unfortunately, these processes and mechanisms are not well defined, and there is little empirical work on them or on their relation to language acquisition.

However, outside of the Piagetian framework a large literature exists on a number of such mechanisms that may be relevant to language acquisition and language-processing. These include memory, or more specifically auditory storage; auditory processing mechanisms; specifically phonological processing mechanisms; sequencing abilities; and hierarchical planning mechanisms. Much of our knowledge of the importance of these mechanisms comes from studies of language-disordered groups whose linguistic impairments are thought possibly to be caused by deficits in one or another of these more basic cognitive mechanisms. A discussion of these mechanisms in relation to dysphasic children will be found in chapter 5. Here, only one such mechanism and its impairment – a hierarchical planning disability – will be discussed as an example of how particular underlying cognitive abilities may be necessary for language.

Behaviour takes place in time and consequently evidences a sequential ordering of its elements. It can be argued, however, that thoughts and intentions are not themselves temporally ordered and that to produce behaviour a central planning mechanism is necessary in order to convert them into events that occur in real time. This is what is referred to here as a 'hierarchical planning ability'. For many years, the attempt to account for serial activities relied on notions of associative chains in which the performance of each element of the series was seen as providing the excitation of the next. In a now-classic paper, Lashley (1951) challenged the validity of explaining serially ordered behaviour on the basis of processes themselves thought to be serially ordered. He claimed that associative-chain theories were inadequate to account for the structure of sequences of actions such as speech, language and rhythmic activity. Purely sequential theories of language, for example, overlook the essential structure of sentences. Since Chomsky (1957), most modern linguistic analyses, regardless of specific competing details, have viewed language in hierarchically structured terms. Miller and Chomsky (1963) demonstrated that it is impossible to account adequately for the *processes* by which sentences are understood or produced in terms of associative linkages between words or even between categories of words. Similarly, it has been claimed that rhythmic activity cannot be adequately conceptualized merely as periodic, repetitive sequences. Martin (1972) has argued that viewing the sequential elements of a rhythmic series solely in terms of the successive beats overlooks their structured internal organization. Instead, the series of elements is a structured ensemble comprising hierarchically structured units in which the change of any one element alters the interrelations of all the elements. Therefore, altering one unit in a rhythm does not merely change the relationship between adjacent beats; rather, the perceived overall rhythmic structure is changed.

It had been noted that some severely dysphasic children not only lack language but have an almost uniformly poor sense of rhythm (Griffiths, 1972; Lea, 1975, 1980), and this is true whether such rhythms are presented auditorily or are conveyed to the fingertips by means of a vibrating disc (Kracke, 1975). On the basis of this and other clues, I entertained the hypothesis that such children suffer from a hierarchical planning disability, and that such a disability effectively prevents them from acquiring language (Cromer, 1978a, reprinted here as chapter 5). Details of severely dysphasic children and their specific disabilities will be found in chapter 5. For our purposes here, the claim is that the mechanism that is responsible for the hierarchical planning ability is a cognitive prerequisite for the acquisition of language. To examine this mechanism and its impairment more directly, an experiment was conducted on severely dysphasic, deaf, and normally hearing children (Cromer, 1983).

In examining such an ability or its impairment, it is important to note that individuals may fail a task for a variety of reasons. Failure by itself tells us very little. In a study in which one is predicting failure on a hierarchical task, it is especially important to exclude those reasons for failure that have nothing to do with the hypothesized impairment. What is needed, then, is a task which the child can perform adequately when the defective ability is not required for its execution, but which the child will fail if that ability is involved. For this reason, a task was chosen that can be performed in two ways – either sequentially or in a manner requiring a hierarchical planning ability. The task used in the experiment was based on that used with developmentally normal children by Greenfield and Schneider (1977). In their study, children were given construction straws and asked to build a flat, tree-structured mobile to match a flat, two-dimensional model that was placed in front of them. In my own 1983 study, children had to copy a two-dimensional drawing of that model (see figure 2.1) and to build a replica of the three-dimensional model itself (see figure 2.2). The execution of these tasks can be characterized in two different ways. A serial (or chaining) strategy consists of starting at the bottom of one side, working sequentially up the figure, across the mid-line, and down the other side. By contrast, a method requiring hierarchical planning consists of operating on the model in terms of its subunits – for example, by beginning at the superordinate connecting level and drawing or building the subunits by alternating from one side to the other. The children were allowed to draw (and later to construct) the model by whatever method they wished. When the model was completed, the experimenter required the child to copy (or build) the same model again but by a method opposite to the one that had been spontaneously used, the new method being non-verbally demonstrated by the experimen-

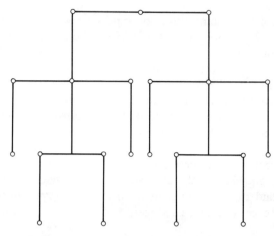

Figure 2.1   *The line drawing the children were asked to copy. Source*: Cromer (1983)

ter. Since these tasks were modelled on those originally designed by Greenfield and Schneider, it is important to point out a theoretical difference in their use. Greenfield and Schneider claim that their construction task represents a direct expression of hierarchical language structures in active, constructional terms (cf. Bates's homology model mentioned earlier). No such claim is made in my paper (1983). There is no reason to believe that the tree structures used by linguists to represent linguistic structures in any way resemble the processes used in language production. Rather, the cognitive-prerequisites hypothesis that I put forward was that some central planning mechanism – specifically a hierarchical planning ability – underlies a number of skills, including rhythmic ability and the ability to process complex linguistic structures. If this hierarchical planning mechanism is impaired, then any skills dependent on that mechanism will also be affected. It was known that this special group of severely dysphasic children perform poorly on language and on rhythmic tasks. If part of the reason for their poor performance is a defective hierarchical planning ability, then they should also perform poorly on non-verbal tasks that require the use of such an ability. Notice that, by contrast, unless the lack of oral language is somehow responsible for the hierarchical planning deficit, then profoundly deaf children should show no such deficits on these tasks and should perform like age-matched normally hearing and speaking children.

The group of severely receptively dysphasic children that was of primary interest consisted of children suffering from 'acquired aphasia with convulsive disorder'. Only five children fully fitted the relevant

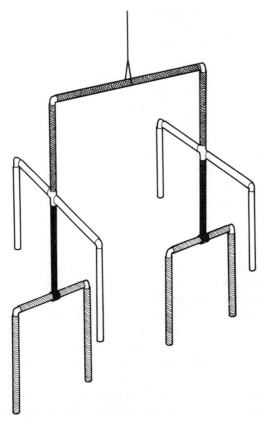

Figure 2.2 *An illustration of the three-dimensional straw model the children were asked to construct. Source: Cromer (1983)*

criteria. However, a further seven children from the same residential school were included who were described as being 'expressive aphasics'. Many of these children had also been found to have rhythmic processing deficits (Kracke, 1975; Lea, 1975). Thus, the entire group consisted of 12 dysphasic children whose ages ranged from 8 years 5 months to 16 years 4 months. A group of 12 congenitally profoundly deaf children and a group of 12 normally hearing children, matched on chronological age to the 12 dysphasic children, were also tested. A quantitative analysis based on the highest score of the two attempts by each child showed that, on both the copying (drawing) task and on the construction task, the scores of the dysphasic children were significantly poorer than those of the profoundly deaf and normally hearing groups; the latter two groups did not differ from each other.

The drawings and constructions were also rated in terms of whether the child's attempt was basically serial, hierarchical, or mixed. Five of the 12 dysphasic children (three of the five receptive dysphasics and two of the seven expressive dysphasics) were never able to copy or to build the figure hierarchically. By contrast, all 12 of the normally hearing children and 11 of the 12 deaf children were able to do at least one task hierarchically. It should be noted that it was not the task itself that was difficult for the dysphasic children. When doing the tasks spontaneously, they could complete them, but they chose to draw and construct the model serially. When shown the hierarchical method, some of these children could not complete the task at all. Figure 2.3 shows the results achieved by a receptive-dysphasic child, and figure 2.4 those of an expressive-dysphasic child. In each case, the top drawing is what the child produced spontaneously, using the serial method, and the bottom drawing represents the same child's attempt at using the hierarchical method. As can be seen, the serial copies are faithful representations; by contrast, when using the hierarchical method, neither child was able to make a complete or reasonably faithful copy of the model at all. Similarly, in the construction task, some dysphasic children who were able to construct the figure spontaneously using the serial method proved unable to do so by the hierarchical method: either they could not complete the task or they constructed figures that were bizarre and did not resemble the model.

If this demonstrated association between a hierarchical planning disability and disabilities in language and rhythm is truly causal, then this would be an example of the cognition hypothesis; underlying cognitive mechanisms are a prerequisite for language acquisition. It should be noted that this hypothesis does not merely concern performance factors but is directly relevant to underlying linguistic competence. That is, cognitive limitations can determine the level of grammar attained by the child. This is compatible with similar ideas put forward for *normal, unimpaired* children acquiring language. That is, it has been argued that cognitive limitations in younger (less mature) normal children prevent them from being able to interact with data that are crucial for grammatical change. For example, in recent linguistic theories that view some aspects of language acquisition in terms of setting and changing particular 'parameters' certain parameters remain fixed to particular values until the maturation of cognitive mechanisms makes it possible for the child to experience linguistic data that would act to reset those parameters. (See the discussion of the 'triggering problem' in Borer and Wexler, 1987,

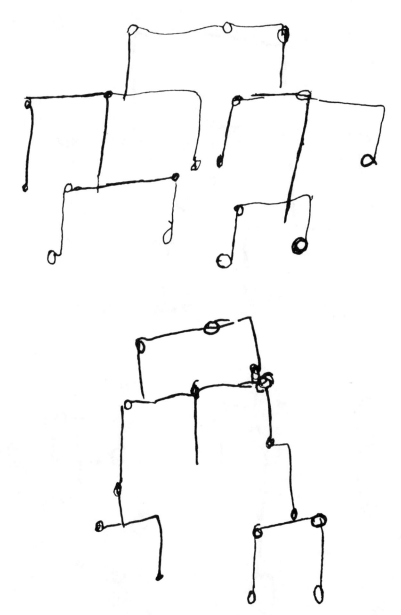

Figure 2.3 *Top: spontaneous copy of the line drawing done serially by a receptive-dysphasic child. Bottom: Attempt by the same child to copy the same figure using the hierarchical method. Source: Cromer (1983)*

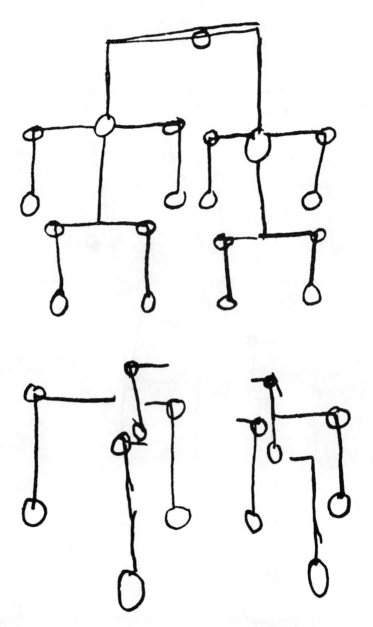

Figure 2.4   *Top: spontaneous copy of the line drawing done serially by an expressive-dysphasic child. Bottom: Attempt by the same child to copy the same figure using the hierarchical method. Source*: Cromer (1983)

though they put forward a different and more specifically linguistic view of the maturational component.)

A 'Whorfian' Position on the Relation between Language and Thought

The notion that one must possess particular cognitive mechanisms, or that such mechanisms must have reached a particular level of maturation and development in order for language acquisition to proceed, might at first seem rather obvious. Indeed, it appears at least as obvious as the idea that one must possess concepts before those concepts can be encoded in language. The first part of this chapter has been primarily devoted to setting out recent experimental evidence of the effects of the development of particular concepts on the acquisition of language. However, it is possible to challenge these conclusions. Later in this chapter some data on language acquisition in some unusual children will be reviewed – data that may cast some doubt on how *necessary* some cognitive 'prerequisites' may be. In this section, however, the same issue will be explored in a slightly different way. One can ask whether the acquisition of a particular language itself has effects on various cognitive processes and products. For example, can language be responsible for the formation of categories or influence the saliency or availability of concepts?[4] If such effects can be demonstrated, then it is, at the very least, an oversimplification to make strong claims only about the effects of particular prior cognitive developments on language acquisition.

Earlier, three views of the effects of language on *concepts* were mentioned (see p. 57) all of which share the central tenet that language has at least some influence on the possession or development of specific concepts. These were seen as a background against which to examine the competing cognition hypothesis. We can refer to these in general as variations on a 'Whorfian' view.[5] Furthermore, the focus of attention can be widened to include language effects not only on concepts but even on more general cognitive processing mechanisms. What, then, has recent research shown regarding the effects of language on cognition?

Studies of the effects of language on perception

It is obvious that perception depends at some basic level on the anatomical and physiological properties of the receptors. However, what is perceived is the result of interactions between the input and internal representations and interpretations. In this section, the concern is with *linguistically* coded representations and their possible effects on visual perception. Will the fact of speaking completely different languages (such as English, Navajo, Hopi and Dani) have effects on the perceptual categories of the speakers of those languages?

In chapter 1 (pp. 5–6) two experiments were mentioned demonstrating some effects of language on the perception of colour. Brown and Lenneberg (1954) showed that, the more codable colours are, the more easily recognizable they are when subjects are forced to increase their reliance on verbal cues. Lenneberg and Roberts (1956) compared English-, Zuni- and bilingual English–Zuni-speakers. They found that monolingual Zuni-speakers, whose language has only a single verbal label for different kinds of yellow and orange, had difficulty with these colours and often confused them when they had to remember them. By contrast, English-speakers rarely made this type of error, and the error score of bilingual speakers was midway between the monolingual groups. These experiments have often been cited as support for the Whorfian hypothesis. However, this was not the end of the story. As with a great deal of research, problems began to arise when other investigators approached the topic. The usual pattern is that later research leads to refinements of measurements and techniques. But in this case a number of important studies have had a different effect: they have actually led to the opposite conclusion, i.e. an anti-Whorfian position as regards colour perception. The full history to the mid-1970s is recounted by Roger Brown (1976). Here, the main points will first be summarized. Then, just when it appears that an anti-Whorfian position seems justified, more recent studies will be reviewed that cast some shadows where all seemed to be clear.

We can begin by going back to two older experiments. Brown (1976) contrasts the results found by Burnham and Clark (1955) on colour *recognition* and those found by Lenneberg (1961) on colour-*naming*. In the Burnham and Clark study, one colour chip was viewed for five seconds; after a five-second interval, the subject had to identify it from an array of chips. Lenneberg's naming data were collected from 27 women who were asked to name colours as they were shown. The shock was that, when Lenneberg compared these naming results with those from Burnham and Clark's recognition task, he found a negative not a positive correlation between naming (codability) and recognition! Brown cites one of the most glaring examples: the colour chip that was most accurately recognized in the Burnham and Clark experiment was the colour with the least easy-to-code name in English. Now, it should be noted that both of these studies used *unsaturated* colours. Saturation refers to the intensity of a colour. Highly saturated colours are relatively free from dilution with white, e.g. fire-engine red as compared with unsaturated colours like pale pink. Lenneberg argued that, with the unsaturated colours that were used, there was no 'good' instance of each colour. For example, no colour could be coded as 'green' since, instead of one obvious highly saturated green colour, there was a range of unsaturated colours that looked a bit 'greeny'. In fact, the most distinctive points occurred at intersections of colour names, so that 'green-blue' was a more distinctive coding than either 'green' or 'blue'.

Saturation differences may also help to explain another discrepancy. As noted, the Burnham and Clark and the Lenneberg studies, which showed no correlation between codability and recognition, used 'washed-out' unsaturated colours. By contrast, the original Brown and Lenneberg experiment (1954), which did show a correlation between codability and recognition, used highly saturated colours. In order to reconcile these problems, Lantz and Stefflre (1964) used both types of colour arrays: the highly saturated colours that Brown and Lenneberg had originally used, and the low-saturation colours used by Burnham and Clark (1955) and by Lenneberg (1961). In addition, they devised a measure of 'communication accuracy' or 'communicability' which they then contrasted with codability.

Lantz and Stefflre (1964) operationalized *communicability* by having one group of subjects view a series of colours. They had to name (encode linguistically) each of these colours to a second group of subjects, who had to try to pick out the named colours from an array. The number of colours this second group could recognize from the verbal labels represented the communicability score. In the main experiment, both types of colour arrays were used and differing predictions were made in relation to these for the codability and communicability measures. Based on earlier findings, it was predicted that codability scores would be *positively* related to recognition scores for the Brown and Lenneberg highly saturated colours but *negatively* related to recognition scores for the Burnham and Clark low-saturation colours. By contrast, *communicability* would be positively related to recognition for *both* arrays, because the first group of subjects, in trying to communicate particular colours accurately, would try to choose names likely to help the second group of subjects to recognize both high- and low-saturation colours. These predictions were upheld.

This work was extended cross-culturally when Stefflre, Castillo Vales and Morley (1966) examined the effects of communication accuracy on Spanish and Yucatec Mayan speakers in Mexico. Using Lantz and Stefflre's technique, communication accuracy was measured by having 12 encoders from each language group name each of 20 colours 'using the word or words you would use to describe it to a friend so that he or she could pick it out' (p. 113). Twelve decoders had to pick out the colours from the entire array of 100 chips using the descriptions of two decoders (i.e. 40 descriptions). Recognition was examined by having 24 speakers of each language view the 20 colour chips individually for five seconds, and then select that chip from the entire array after a 30-second interval. The results revealed that, within each language, communication accuracy was related to colour memory – i.e. the chips accurately communicated were also those most accurately remembered. However, speakers of the two languages differed in terms of which colours they found most easy to communicate and remember. Furthermore, the typical pattern of the memory errors was to choose a chip in the direction of the one most typical of the term used for encoding. That is, the memory errors were predominantly those of selecting a stimulus more typical of the language description used by encoders rather than being in the direction of the original stimulus. This latter finding shows the importance of the verbal encodings of the stimuli.

Based on these results one might be tempted to conclude that the 'Whorfian' hypothesis is still supported, but that one must use a linguistic measure of communication accuracy rather than codability to predict which colours will be most easily recognized. But a closer look shows that there are major problems with this view. Brown (1976) noted, for example, that the Whorfian hypothesis is concerned with the *linguistic* features of languages. Communication accuracy, however, is also affected by psychological factors such as individual differences in encoding ability; some individuals will be good at encoding and decoding for a given domain and others will be poor. So communicability scores will depend only partly on the verbal labels for colours in a particular language. Recall, too, that the particular terms speakers use to communicate will depend on the characteristics of the colour display from which the decoder must choose. So communicability is not really a language measure in any 'Whorfian' sense at all. This is perhaps most compellingly shown by an experiment of Lantz and Lenneberg (1966). In this experiment, various comparisons were made of communication and memory for colours by hearing and deaf individuals. For our purposes, the result that is of interest is that, while communication accuracy predicted memory performance for both the deaf and the hearing groups, the pattern of errors differed. Lantz and Lenneberg concluded that communication accuracy reflected not only language properties but also the *use* that speakers make of the language. In discussing the Lantz and Lenneberg results, Lucy (1987) goes further. He argues that, since language structure was held constant (i.e. both groups were using the same language), the results could *not* be due to differences in language structure. Furthermore, since recognition accuracy was comparable for the two groups, the results could not be due to differences in cognitive ability or in differential effectiveness of language in aiding cognition. Yet the two groups differed in their errors in ways that were predictable from their communication accuracy. So communication accuracy may affect colour memory, and yet have little to do with the language lexicon or structure *per se*.

But there is a worse problem for the Whorfian hypothesis. Despite cultural differences in verbal labels for colours, there may also exist some *universal* features of colour perception. Some colours may be innately more salient to all human beings. In 1969 Berlin and Kay published a study in which they mapped the perceptual denotations of the basic colour names from each of 20 widely varying languages. To be defined as a basic colour term in a language, several criteria had to be met. The term had to be monolexemic (the meaning is not predictable from the meaning of its parts, thus eliminating terms such as *lemon-coloured*). Its signification could not be included in that of any other colour term (thus eliminating, for example, *crimson* and *scarlet* in English since both are kinds of red). The term must not be restricted to a narrow class of objects (eliminating terms like *blond*, which is predicated only of hair, complexion and furniture). And a basic colour term must be 'psychologically salient' for the informants – defined by Berlin and Kay as, for example, having a tendency to occur at the beginning of lists of colour terms, and stability of reference across informants and occasions of use. Berlin and Kay elicited colour terms from their informants, and by these criteria established the basic colour terms for each language. In the next step in their study, a large colour array was used. This consisted of 320 colour chips of 40 equally spaced hues and eight degrees of brightness, all at maximum saturation, and nine chips of neutral hue (white, black and greys) provided by the Munsell Color Company. These chips were mounted on cardboard and covered with clear acetate. Informants were asked to indicate on the array the best instance of each of their colour terms. This most typical instance was called the *focal area* of the colour term. Informants also indicated the boundary of each colour term on the colour continuum.

When the mappings of the basic colour terms for all the languages were compared, it became evident that the focal colours were very much the same, indicating that at least the basic colours are *universal* for all cultures. Berlin and Kay expanded their study to 98 languages and found that there was even a consistent sequence in the evolution of colour terms. In a language with only two basic terms, these were always black and white. In languages with three terms, red was always the additional term. Next came either green or yellow followed by whichever of these two had not yet appeared. The next colour to be added was blue, then brown, and then an unordered set of four – purple, pink, orange and grey. Given such results, it can be argued that the reason why a relationship is found between colour recognition and codability is that it is these universally salient focal colours which tend to be given easily codable names in all cultures. Instead of linguistic names determining the perception of colours, it may be the other way round: easily perceived colours determine the allocation of colour names in the languages of the world. However, there are serious methodological problems with the Berlin and Kay study, which make interpretation difficult.[6]

Based on studies like that of Berlin and Kay, one might be tempted to conclude that colour perception may have been an especially poor choice of domain on which to test the Whorfian hypothesis. As Kay and McDaniel put it in a later paper (1978), the semantics of colour show substantial linguistic universality since these semantics are based on pan-human neurophysiological processes. Thus strict limits are placed on the applicability of the Whorfian hypothesis. But they do not rule out Whorfian effects altogether. In a later study, Kay and Kempton (1984) made a more direct test of the effects of language on perception by comparing speakers of languages differing in their colour terminology. In this study, speakers of English were compared to speakers of Tarahumara, an Uto-Aztecan language of northern Mexico.

English has separate lexical terms for green and blue. Tarahumara lacks this distinction, using the term *siyoname*, which means green–blue. Kay and Kempton reasoned that, under the Whorfian hypothesis, this linguistic difference will result in differences in the subjective distances between the colours. That is, colours near the green–blue boundary will be subjectively pushed apart by English-speakers since English has words for green and blue. By comparison, Tarahumara-speakers will not show such distortion since they lack this lexical distinction. To test this, colour chips of various shades of greenish blue and bluish green were used. The subject viewed three chips and was asked to indicate which one is the most different from the other two. We can examine one of these comparisons to make the procedure and rationale more clear. Let us take chips A, B and C. For English-speakers, both chips A and B lie on the green side of the green–blue colour boundary. Chip C is on the blue side of this boundary. In fact, in terms of discrimination distance (measured by 'just noticeable differences' or 'jnd's), the distance between chip A and B was 1.27 times greater than the distance between B and C. But, since B and C lie on opposite sides of the green–blue boundary, their distance should be subjectively greater for the English-speakers. This was what was indeed found. The Tarahumara-speakers, on the other hand (who were tested in their native language in their native village), put a bigger distance between

A and B, which agrees with discrimination distance. We have, then, a situation, even in the domain of colour, which appears to support the Whorfian position. But once again things are not so simple.

Kay and Kempton (1984) noted that it cannot be the case that the vision of English-speakers is somehow affected by the language they speak, since the discrimination distances (the very distances the Tarahumara-speakers faithfully reproduced in the subjective-distance task) were established on speakers of English in the first place. They therefore speculated that English-speakers are using some kind of naming strategy in the experimental task. According to their possible scenario, English-speakers might reason (unconsciously) along lines like the following: 'It's hard to decide which one looks the most different. What clues might I use? Well, both A and B are called "green" while C is called "blue". That solves my problem; I'll pick C as the most different.' Tarahumara-speakers cannot use this strategy precisely because their language does not have ready lexical labels for green and blue. Kay and Kempton therefore designed another experiment in which such a naming strategy presumably could not be used. Three chips were placed in a container with a sliding top in which the subject could only see two chips at a time. While the subject viewed A and B, the experimenter said, 'You can see that this chip (points to A) is greener than this chip (points to B).' After sliding the cover so that only B and C could be seen, the experimenter said, 'You can see that this chip (points to C) is bluer than this chip (points to B).' After indicating that the subject could slide the cover back and forth as many times as he liked, the experimenter said, 'I'd like you to tell me which is bigger: the difference in greenness between the two chips on the left or the difference in blueness between the two chips on the right.' Notice that this blocks the naming strategy since the subject has in effect called chip B 'green' when comparing it to chip A and called it 'blue' when comparing it to chip C. Kay and Kempton found that in this second experiment the Whorfian effect disappeared. The subjective similarity judgements accorded with discrimination distance and were not influenced by lexical category boundaries.

Kay and Kempton see this result as still compatible with a 'more cautious Whorfianism'. It is true that some effect of language on categorization in a specific task may have been demonstrated (see the section on the effects of language on categorization, below). But this is quite distant from Whorfian notions that language has effects on habitual thinking processes. In effect, the Kay and Kempton studies merely reinforce the view that the human nervous system severely restricts colour perception and that tests of the Whorfian hypothesis using the domain of colour will reflect these restrictions. A similar finding also using cross-cultural differences had earlier been reported by Eleanor (Rosch) Heider (1972).

Studies of young human infants and of animals lead to the view that perception of the colour spectrum is a basic, given, physiological fact, unaffected by language. When studies have been carried out on the *psychological* salience of basic colours, both in adults and in children, a similar story emerges, although, as will be seen, the data are weaker and there are some contradictions among the various experiments. Bornstein (1985) mentions some of this evidence and presents it in terms of colour preferences, processing and memory; as this is a useful way of organizing the wide range of material, a similar organizational scheme will be used here.

The data on preferences come both from Bornstein's own work and from that of Heider. Bornstein (1985) claims that, when infants are shown exemplar (basic) colours, they look significantly longer at them than they do at boundary colours. In the original experiments (Bornstein, 1975), infants of 4 months of age viewed pairs of eight stimuli, four of which were basic colour-category centres and four of which were colour-category boundaries. At any time, the infant would be viewing two colours and, depending on the group, these might be two basic colours, two boundary colours, or one of each. Their fixation times on the two colours competing for their attention was recorded. It was found that basic colour centres were attended to significantly more than category boundaries.

Heider (1971) carried out a series of experiments on colour preferences of 3-year-old children. 24 children were shown rows of eight chromatic chips, each of which contained one focal colour (of the eight focal colours as defined by Heider). The children were merely asked to show the experimenter a colour – any colour that they wanted from each row. It was observed that the children chose focal colour chips significantly more often than non-focal colour chips. Heider asserted that focal colours attract the attention of 3-year-old children more than do non-focal colours, and this is reflected in their preferences of what to show the experimenter. In a related study in the same report, Heider found that 20 4-year-old children *matched* focal colours more accurately than non-focal colours.

The preferences of both infants and young children, then, appear to support the notion of the existence of basic colour categories, and, in the case of infants, these exist before language experience of particular colour terms. But under close inspection the argument seems less secure. The original data in Bornstein (1975) are, for example, not quite as clear-cut as his 1985 review makes them sound. Close inspection of the data reveals that not all colour centres were attended to longer than boundaries. In fact, the main effect was due to two colour centres – red and blue (a point to which we will return in comparing this study with others); the basic colours yellow and green were actually looked at less than some of the boundary colours. Only as a group were the basic colours attended to significantly more than the boundary colours.

Heider's work, although quoted by Bornstein as supporting his own general conclusion, is in fact at variance with his precise findings. Bornstein's arguments are based on electrophysiological correlates of colour perception. The three retinal colour-receptors excite four classes of chromatic-sensitive cells at the level of the geniculate bodies lateral to the midbrain. Bornstein (1985) reports that these cells show maximal sensitivity (and maximal excitation) in the blue, green, yellow and red regions of the colour spectrum. Bornstein's work uses these four colours as the basic colours. He points out how classic work on colour-scaling supports the notion of these as the basic colours. Indeed, he even notes that in such tasks 'when other, secondary, colour terms are permitted – such as orange or violet – observers use these terms less reliably, and all the wavelengths that they describe can be easily analyzed into the four basic category terms' (pp. 117–18). Colours such as orange and violet are not perceived by adults or infants as primary sensations (Bornstein, Kessen and Weiskopf, 1976).

By contrast, Heider's work on focal colours classifies some colours as focal that are not among the four basic colours of Bornstein. In the colour preference work on young children, the two favoured colours from one type of display were the focal colours yellow and orange; from a differing display, the favoured focal colours were pink and brown. Note that three of these four focal colours would not count as basic colours in Bornstein's terms – and indeed are colours that his theory would predict would not be preferred, not be matched best, etc.[7] Among the infants tested by Bornstein, red and blue were the favoured colours – and that fits in with his notion of basic colours. By contrast, in Heider's work on colour preferences among young children, blue and red were ranked fourth and sixth out of the eight focal colours, both being outranked in preference by orange (ranked second), and with red being outranked by purple (tied with blue) and tied with brown – colours that are not basic in Bornstein's terms. So the work on colour *preferences* is not so clear after all.

What about studies of colour *processing*? Bornstein and Monroe (1980) found that nine adults they studied were faster at naming colours if the stimuli were near the centre of the hue category rather than near the boundary between colour categories. This, on its own, would not be very instructive, since such a finding is compatible with ideal colour categories being defined either physiologically or culturally. However, Bornstein (1981) reported that 4-month-old infants showed the same effects – that is, they became more rapidly habituated to category-central colours blue and red than to category-boundary colours blue-green and yellow-red. This could not be a cultural matter.

Rosch has published a number of experiments (some under the name Heider and some under the name Rosch) examining colour processing by English-speaking adults, adults who speak a variety of different languages including one with a very limited colour vocabulary, and young children. In one set of experiments, Rosch (1975; see also a more general discussion in Rosch, 1977a) used the notion of reference points in relation to which other stimuli in a domain are judged. One way of testing this is through the use of what are called linguistic 'hedges', terms or phrases such as 'x is essentially y', 'x is basically y', 'x is sort of y', etc. The idea is that subjects will more often be willing to say things like '996 is essentially 1000' than to say '1000 is essentially 996'; 1000 is seen as a reference point and such points are placed after linguistic hedges. As applied to colours, the idea is that focal colours will act as reference points for non-focal colours ('crimson is essentially red' rather than 'red is essentially crimson'). Rosch gave colour chips to 960 native speakers of English and had them place these chips in linguistic-hedge frames in a way that 'seemed to be most true or make most sense'. It was found that the subjects significantly more often placed focal colours in the second (reference point) slot than they did colours that were slightly deviant from focal colours. Rosch argues that focal colours are as basic in human perception as Gestalt 'good forms'.

In a series of experiments on subjects who speak languages other than English (Heider, 1972), Rosch found that focal colours were processed more efficiently than non-focal colours. In one experiment, for example, adult speakers of 23 different languages simply wrote, in their own language, what each presented colour would be called. Focal colours were more rapidly responded to, and the names of these focal colours were shorter both in terms of mean number of words used to name the colour and the mean number of letters.

Another experiment in this same series (Heider, 1972) involved 19 Dani, a people of Indonesian New Guinea whose language has only two basic colour terms. These monolingual subjects were shown 16 colour chips as the stimuli – eight of which were focal colours, the remaining eight being non-focal (internominal) colours. These 16 colours had to be learned as associations to 16 response terms – the names of 'sibs', which are descent groupings in Dani society. The task, then, was to learn the 16 stimulus–response pair associations. The results were clear. The Dani subjects learned the paired associates to the focal colours faster than those to the non-focal colours. It would therefore appear that focal colours are processed more efficiently than non-focal colours. Since these results were obtained from subjects whose language does not differentially encode most colours, the effect must be due to the perceptual salience of the focal colours; and this perceptual salience cannot itself be due to differential codability in the language.

Earlier, the notion of eight chromatic focal colours was contrasted with Bornstein's physiological theory which calls instead for four basic colours in human perception. In the series of experiments reported in Heider (1972) a similar contrast was independently hypothesized. The four colours predicted to be basic from physiological evidence were called the 'primary' focal colours, and these were compared to the four non-primary focal colours. Heider reports some 'weak support' for the notion that, within the focal colours, the primary focal colours are processed more efficiently than the non-primary ones. Thus, in the experiment with speakers of 23 languages, the primary focal colours were named significantly more rapidly than the non-primary focal colours. Similarly, in the paired-associates learning experiment with the Dani, the primary focal colours as a group were said to be learned with significantly fewer errors than the non-primary focal colours (though this was only significant using $p < .10$). However, close inspection of the ranking of the terms fails to give unqualified support to a physiological theory. Ignoring the achromatic terms *black* and *white*, the order of response rapidity in the experiment on 23 languages was: yellow, purple, blue, red, pink, brown, green and orange. It can be noted that non-primary purple is high in the list while primary green is low. In terms of codability, the ordering was: yellow, purple, brown, red, pink, blue, orange and green. Here, two non-primary focal colours, purple and brown, are in the most codable half, while primary focal colours blue and green are in the less codable half. Heider herself points out that neither of these orders looks like the order in which Berlin and Kay (1969) claimed that colour terms evolved. We can add that neither are those orders overwhelmingly supportive of a purely physiologically based theory. Similarly, in the experiment on the Dani, the order in which the focal colours were learned, from the fewest to the most errors, was: red, pink, green, orange, purple, blue, yellow and brown. Again it can be noted that two of the primary focal colours, blue and yellow, ranks sixth and seventh out of eight; and two of the non-primary focal colours, pink and orange, were among the most easily learned four.

There are also data on the processing of colours by young children. In a simple matching task, Heider (1971) found that 20 children of mean age $4\frac{1}{2}$ years more accurately matched the eight focal colours than they did non-focal colours. Mervis, Catlin and Rosch (1975) asked children to point to the best example of 11 focal colour terms (the eight chromatic focal colours plus black, white and grey). Groups of $5\frac{1}{2}$- and $8\frac{1}{2}$-year-olds were compared to adults. The resultant foci were exactly the same chips for all three groups (except for purple). However, while the mean focal choices were established by age $5\frac{1}{2}$, the variance had not yet stabilized. In other experiments in this series, it was established that children learn the adult foci for colour categories before they learn the adult boundaries – a point to which we will return in considering the effect of language on colour-perception processes.

In summary, it appears that colour-processing is more efficiently accomplished for focal colours than for non-focal colours. This is true even for individuals who speak languages in which not all of the basic colours are encoded. It is also true for young children and for pre-verbal infants. The explanation of this in physiological terms, however, is not so straightforward, since the findings are often based on focal colours some of which differ from the four basic colours predicted by physiological considerations. Furthermore, some of the findings most supportive of a universalist hypothesis are mainly due to the very focal colours that are not physiologically basic.

The effects of language on *memory* will be dealt with in the next section. However, to round off the discussion of colour perception, it is useful to consider some experiments in which memory for focal and non-focal colours was studied. Bornstein (1981), in experiments on 4-month-old infants, studied recognition memory for simple (physiologically basic) and complex (physiologically non-basic) colours. Groups were habituated to either the simple colours blue and red or the complex colours blue-green and yellow-red. After an interference task, the children were given a retest on the colours they had originally seen. The rationale was that, after habituation and the intervening interference task, a low level of looking at the original stimulus on the retest would be an indication of recognition of the original stimulus to which they had been habituated. By contrast, prolonged looking at a habituated stimulus would be indicative of forgetting (lack of recognition). The results showed that, on the retest, the two groups who had originally been habituated to the complex colours looked significantly longer at those stimuli than did the two groups of infants who had been habituated to the simple stimuli. These results are taken to indicate that memory for the basic colours blue and red is better than for complex (non-basic) colours, and this is true in pre-verbal infants who cannot be benefiting from some effect of language.

Some of Heider's cross-cultural experiments (Heider, 1972; Heider and Olivier, 1972) involved short-term memory for colours. In one, 20 native English-speakers were compared to 21 Dani-speakers, all of whom were monolingual. Subjects were first shown a single colour chip for five seconds. Then, after a 30-second delay, they had to select that colour from a 160-chip array. The test chips were either focal or non-focal colours.

Both the English-speakers and the Dani showed a similar pattern of results: focal colours were remembered significantly more accurately than non-focal colours. This was true in spite of the fact that the Dani language has only two terms for all colours. Furthermore, Heider and Olivier (1972) report that, since there was a good deal of variation in performance among individual subjects in each culture, it would be important to make an analysis of the relationship between naming and memory for each individual. That is, individuals might be more likely to confuse colours to which they had given the same name than those to which they had given different names. Analysis of memory confusions, however, did not support this possibility of within-language linguistic influence. The memory effects, then, appear to be due to universals in the perception of colours and not due to Whorfian-like influences of colour-terminology differences between languages or to labelling influences within single languages.

The story of colour-perception research in relation to the Whorfian hypothesis concerning the effect of language on thought is a somewhat complicated one. For a while, the 'accepted wisdom' was that colour perception was indeed affected by language as viewed through work on linguistic relativity. The experiments by Brown and Lenneberg (1954) and Lenneberg and Roberts (1956) mentioned in chapter 1 and at the beginning of this section, and the colour and communication accuracy experiments by Stefflre, Castillo Vales and Morley (1966), all support the Whorfian view. More recently, and for about 20 years, a universalist position has held sway. This has been based on cross-cultural studies such as those by Berlin and Kay (1969), Kay and Kempton (1984), and the series of studies by Heider (Heider, 1971, 1972; Heider and Olivier, 1972; Mervis, Catlin and Rosch, 1975; Rosch, 1975, 1977a). Even more compelling has been the colour-perception work on pre-verbal infants by Bornstein and his associates, particularly as this has been tied to physiological perception mechanisms (Bornstein, 1975, 1985; Bornstein, Kessen and Weiskopf, 1976). However, we have noted the following problems.

1 The Berlin and Kay work is seriously flawed.
2 Heider's focal colours do not match Bornstein's 'basic' colours. Heider has even found effects of focal colours which in Bornstein's terms should not show such effects (e.g. orange, purple).
3 Bornstein's work has problems in that people, including infants, are not better on all four of the physiologically basic colours, but only on blue and red.
4 Bornstein (1985) himself argues that the perception of basic colours may alter in the course of development through perceptual 'sharpen-

ing' and 'broadening'. That is, although colour categories present near birth may have an identifiable neurological substrate, later development may follow different courses. Bornstein speculates that since colour-naming systems in the languages of the world differ fundamentally from the basic four-colour categorization, language must manipulate basic categorization processes during development; some basic categories observable in infancy may be lost, and other categories may be newly induced or tuned (old categories differentiated). In other words, even if physiological processes can be shown to determine the perception of basic (or focal) colours, language could presumably have an effect by differentially encoding other, non-basic colours and by determining the boundaries of the basic colours. (Recall the Mervis, Catlin and Rosch experiments, 1975, which found that children learn the adult foci for colour categories before they learn the adult boundaries.)

It would therefore seem that even the universalist position on colour perception is not so clear-cut as had been supposed. Nevertheless, in spite of these difficulties, the universalist position seems to be favoured – at least in the specific domain of colour *perception*. With regard to the broader question of the effects of language on cognitive processes, it is therefore important to note two final points.

First, some of the work in the domain of colour that has been most supportive of the Whorfian position, has really been on *memory*, not perception. This is true of the early Brown and Lenneberg and the Lenneberg and Roberts experiments, as well as the Stefflre et al. study mentioned above. The memory experiment in the series of studies by Heider (1972), which, by contrast, did *not* support a Whorfian position, has been criticized on methodological grounds. Lucy and Shweder (1979) claim that Heider's findings – that focal colours are better remembered than non-focal colours – were due to the fact that the focal colours in her display were more perceptually discriminable than the non-focal colours. Using an array in which these differences in discriminability were eliminated, Lucy and Shweder found that memory was no longer affected by focality. They report that, when the influence of focality was removed by taking partial correlations, the correlations between language and memory remained significant; by contrast, when linguistic influences were partialled out, the influence of focality reduced to close to zero. Lucy and Shweder conclude that 'language can serve as a highly effective vehicle for colour memory' and 'it appears to operate independently of "focality"' (p. 599). So the observed effects of language on colour-'processing' may really be only effects on colour *memory*, not colour perception. The influence of language on memory in general will be considered in a later section.

Secondly, while it may be the case that there is little support for the Whorfian notion of the effects of language on *perception* in the domain of colour, such effects may be observable in other domains less closely tied to physiological receptors. That is, colour may have been a particularly poor domain in which to study the effects of language on perception. Whorf's own examples concerned the perception of relationships in space and time. He was concerned primarily with the effects of the grammatical structure of differing languages on the 'world views' of speakers of those languages. The studies of colour perception have all examined the possible effects of colour terms in a language – lexical items, not grammatical structure. And there have been no experiments on the physical 'world views' of the speakers of various languages partly because it is extremely difficult to design such studies. Yet this is what the Whorfian hypothesis is really about.

If language influences our perceptions, perhaps the perceptions it influences are those less dependent on a direct neurological basis. That is, language may affect perceptions in which categorization plays a more important role. In considering social categories, for example, labelling the perpetrator of an act a *freedom fighter* as opposed to a *terrorist* will have consequences for the way the act is perceived. In this sense, how we 'see' the world is a matter of categorization, not of perceptual processes *per se*. Therefore, in considering the possible 'Whorfian' effects of language, it may be more useful to consider the effects of language on categorization.

Studies of the effects of language on categorization

Before considering some domains which appear to show an influence of language on categorization, it may be useful first to ask whether there are domains other than colour in which there are perceptually salient, natural prototypes which, even on a categorization task, would *not* show the kinds of language effects a Whorfian might predict. Gestalt psychologists have long argued for the naturalness of particular forms such as circles, squares and triangles. Rosch (1973) reports that the Dani language does not contain terms for two-dimensional geometric forms. In an experiment analogous to the one on colour perception, 94 Dani subjects had to learn a set of forms as a paired-associate task – a particular Dani sib name being the correct association for the forms. The natural prototypes chosen were a circle, a square and an equilateral triangle. Sets of distortions of each of the forms were also produced by inserting gaps, using curved instead of straight lines, etc. In one set, for example, the good form of a square was 'central' and the distortions were made upon that form. In a different set, a 'distorted' form from this natural set, such as the square with a gap, was taken as central and the distortions were based on that, with the perfect square being one of the peripheral forms. The results (based on the 92 Dani who reached criterion) showed that good forms were learned faster than distorted forms. Furthermore, the sets in which the good forms were central were learned faster than sets in which they were peripheral. This was especially interesting in light of the findings of a pilot experiment that showed that the circles, squares and triangles were not already classified into such form classes by the Dani prior to the experiment.

But, if, in the original sorting pre-test, the Dani did not differentiate circles, squares and triangles, one wonders how they would have performed on that task *after* having learned 'names' for each of the basic forms in the learning experiment. There may be something perceptually basic about 'good forms' that leads to superior performance when such forms are used in the type of learning task employed by Rosch in her 1973 experiment; but language may still have important effects on *categorization*. Rosch (1974) herself cites some suggestive evidence on this point even within the domain of colour. She reports that Greenfield and Childs (1974) had studied pattern concepts in the Zinancantecos of Chiapas, Mexico. They were interested in whether the knowledge of how to weave particular patterns in cloth would have effects on a task in which the subjects had to copy patterns by placing sticks into a frame. The patterns themselves comprised simple groups of red and white threads. To copy the patterns, subjects were given sticks of various widths and colours. It was noted that, while some subjects correctly used only red and white sticks to copy the patterns, others freely substituted pink for white, and orange for red. A separate test showed that all the subjects could discriminate the red, orange, pink and white sticks equally well. However, the subjects who used only red and white sticks to copy the pattern were those who possessed different names for red, pink, orange and white; by contrast, subjects who had only a single term for white and pink, and a single term for red and orange, were the ones who tended to make substitutions.

The effect of language on categorization was nicely shown by Liublinskaya (1957), who had children sort butterflies on the basis of the patterns on their wings. In order to do this, they had to abstract the pattern from the wing colour. Initially, children ignored the pattern and were guided in their choices solely by colouring. Later, however, children in the experimental group were given verbal labels such as *spots*, *stripes* and *nets* for the pattern, while children in a control group were not given any verbal labels. When the patterns were given names, even the youngest children in the experimental group began to turn their attention away from colour and to compare patterns that were different in colour. By contrast, even the oldest children in the control group with no labels could barely distinguish the patterns. They made many mistakes and could not explain their own rare correct solutions.

The studies just reviewed have shown some evidence of the influence of labelling on categorization. But what about the more subtle effects of grammar that Whorf was more interested in? Whorf's hypothesis claims that aspects of the language we speak, and of which we are normally unaware, affect the way we view the world. Is there any evidence that this is so? In 1958, Carroll and Casagrande carried out an interesting experiment using Navajo Indian children in Arizona as subjects. In the Navajo language, verbs of handling such as *to pick up*, *to drop* and *to hold in the hand* have to be modified depending on the *shape* of the object that is part of the action referred to by the verb. For example, when Navajo-speakers ask someone to hand them an object, a long flexible object such as a piece of string will require a different verb form from a long rigid one such as a stick, or flat flexible objects such as paper or cloth. In other words, in the Navajo language, there is an obligatory *linguistic* categorization of objects by shape.

Carroll and Casagrande hypothesized that Navajo children who speak Navajo as their dominant language would be more inclined to perceive shape similarities than Navajo children who predominantly speak English. The children were therefore tested using the 'ambiguous sets' procedure. This consisted of 10 sets of three objects, such as coloured wooden blocks, sticks, and pieces of rope. The objects differed significantly in two respects – for example, shape and colour, shape and size, or size and colour. A pair of objects was put in front of the child. The child was then shown a third object similar to each member of the pair in only one of the two relevant characteristics, and was asked to tell the experimenter which of the pair went best with the third object. Take, for example, a pair consisting of a yellow stick and a piece of blue rope. If the third object is a yellow rope, the basis for classification can be either colour or form. Since different linguistic forms are used in Navajo for a length of rope and a stick, the Navajo verb-form classification may lead a Navajo-speaker to categorize on the basis of form. Thus, the Carroll and Casagrande experiment asked, will Navajo children choose on the basis of colour or by physical forms which are linguistically differentiated? The hypothesis predicted that Navajo-dominant children would select the rope, because in Navajo both the blue and the yellow ropes would be coded by the same form-classifier. However, Navajo children who predominantly spoke English, a language which does not focus the speaker's attention on form, were expected to be equally likely to choose by form or by colour; they would therefore choose the yellow stick more often than the Navajo-dominant group would.

The results showed that the percentage of shape choices by 59 Navajo-dominant children was significantly greater than the percentage of shape choices by the 43 English-dominant children on five out of the seven sets in which shape was contrasted with either size or colour. (On the remaining three sets, size versus colour, there was no pertinent prediction.) Interestingly, four of the five significant differences related to precisely the four sets including shapes coded differently in the Navajo linguistic system. Only where the shape made no difference to the verb (for instance, in the set blue cube, white cube and blue pyramid – Navajo uses the same verb form for both cubes or pyramids) were there no significant differences of choice between the two groups. In other words, the Navajo-dominant group was indeed more likely to categorize on the basis of shapes that are differentially encoded in the Navajo language.[8]

The Carroll and Casagrande study set out specifically to study Whorfian effects of language on thought processes (in this case, categorization). There are other studies that, while made for rather different purposes, nevertheless shed light on the relation between language and thought. One such case is that of the distinction between count noun and mass noun. Like gender, count and mass categories are syntactically defined, but the count/mass categories in English are more closely related to 'real world' categories than are gender categories in languages where gender is importantly marked. Conceptually, count nouns normally refer to individual countable objects (*car*, *table*, etc.) while mass nouns normally refer to non-individuated substances (*water*, *sand*, etc.). This conceptual distinction has been referred to either as the object/substance distinction or, with a different emphasis, as an individuated/non-individuated distinction.

There are several ways in which count and mass nouns are linguistically distinguished from one another. First, singular count nouns must have a determiner, as in 'John likes the car'. (Note the unacceptability of *'John likes car'.) Plural count nouns and all mass nouns may appear without determiners. Thus, one can say either 'John likes cars' or 'John likes the cars'; and either 'John likes water' or 'John likes the water'.

Second, count and mass nouns differ in the quantifiers they can normally take. Only count nouns can be modified by *many, few, several, both, each, every, either, a, another* and numerals (e.g. 'many cars', 'few cars', 'one car', 'another car', etc., but not *'many waters', *'few waters', *'each water', etc.). By contrast, only mass nouns can be modified by *much, little, plenty of*, etc., so that 'much water' is acceptable but 'much car/cars' is not.

Third, only count nouns can be co-referenced with anaphoric *one*. To use an example from Gordon (1988), one can say, 'John has a brown shirt and a blue one too', but not *'John has some red sand and some brown one too.'

This is the 'normal' picture of restrictions on the use of count and mass nouns. However, it becomes immediately apparent that many 'violations' occur in language use – or, rather, that these restrictions are not really correct as formulated. For example, one *can* say 'many waters', but now the meaning is felt to change from that of a mass, unindividuated substance to a different meaning in which the waters are individuated and countable (e.g. 'He has sailed on many waters'; 'She loves mineral water of various types and over the years has tasted many waters'). We nevertheless feel these uses to be 'unusual' or non-prototypical. It is as if we read into these uses that aspect of the object/substance distinction (or individuated/ non-individuated distinction) which is usually associated with count or with mass nouns. If this is so, then interesting questions begin to arise as to the relation between the distributional distinctions on the one hand and the associated conceptual distinctions on the other – both in the acquisition of count/mass terms by children and in the interpretation of such terms in context by adults.

The first thing that needs to be made clear is that regardless of the claimed closeness of the association between count/mass terms and real-world entities, there are numerous exceptions. For example, the word *fruit* while referring to individual, countable objects, is nevertheless a mass term; we can't talk about *'three fruits', we have to say 'three pieces of fruit'. (Note that this is language-specific. The French word *fruit* is treated linguistically as a count noun, and in French it is perfectly correct to say 'trois fruits' – three fruits.) Nor is this an isolated exception. Gathercole (1985, 1986b), Gordon (1985, 1988) and McCawley (1975) provide numerous examples of mismatches between the classification of words as count/mass and the characteristics of their referents in the world. Thus, *silverware*, *cutlery* and *jewellery* denote classes of discrete objects and yet are mass nouns in English. One can also identify pairs of terms, one of which is count and the other mass, that describe similar referents. McCawley (1975) notes such pairs as *noodles* and *spaghetti*, *onions* and *garlic*, and *beans* and *rice*. Thus one says 'I have 12 beans' but not *'I have 12 rices.' Because *rice* is a mass noun one is forced to say 'I have 12 grains of rice', though beans and rice consist of similarly countable entities. And what is one to say about abstract nouns that are categorized as either count or mass? *Example* is a count noun, whereas *advice* is a mass noun; one gives 'an example' but not *'an advice', 'three examples' but not *'three advices', etc.

Note, then, that what we have is a correlation – between the linguistic categories count noun and mass noun and some entities in the world – which is not perfect and is not even applicable to abstract nouns. (More accurately, the correlation, or lack of it, is not between linguistic categories and the real world, but between linguistic categories and conceptual categories – cf. Jackendoff, 1983.) Perhaps as adult speakers we use these partial correlations to interpret what are felt to be non-prototypical uses of count and mass terms – as in the example given earlier of 'many waters'. The question is, how did we achieve this ability during the acquisition of our native language? Furthermore, how did we build up the conceptual categories? After reviewing some recent data on the acquisition of the count/mass distinction by young children, I will claim that this is an area where there may be evidence for a Whorfian-like influence of language on concepts.

Research in this area has been primarily concerned with a slightly different issue: does language acquisition in young children begin on the basis of semantic/referential cues as has been claimed by some child-language researchers (e.g. Macnamara, 1982)? Gordon (1985) reported three experiments to see whether and to what extent young children made use of real-world support (usually – inaccurately – called 'semantic' support) in the subcategorization of nouns into count nouns and mass nouns. The first experiment examined the behaviour of 40 children between the ages of 3 years 5 months and 5 years 5 months. The children were introduced to new (nonsense) words with syntactic cues for either count or mass status. For count nouns, the child was told, 'This is a garn. Have you ever seen a garn before? Here's another garn.' By contrast, the mass-noun cues were 'Here is some garn. Have you ever seen any garn before? This is some green garn and this is blue garn.' These nonsense words in turn described either countable objects or unindividuated substances (what Gordon called the 'semantic' variable). In some conditions the syntactic and 'semantic' cues were in accord, while in others they were in conflict, with mass terms being used for countable objects and count terms for substances. The question of central interest was, which cue would the child make use of in the conflict situation? The so-called 'semantic' or 'meaning first' view predicts that young children will be primarily influenced by the objects described; by contrast, the syntactic or formal view predicts that young children will mainly use the distributional, linguistic cues. The child's subcategorization was assessed by a sentence-completion technique. The experimenter said, 'So, here we have a/some garn, over there we have some more . . . what?' The completion 'more garns' indicates a count-noun subcategorization, while the mass noun would be indicated by completing the phrase with 'more garn'.

Results were tabulated on the basis of 24 children who gave unequivocal replies and who showed no [+ plural] or [− plural] response biases.

Of the 24 children, 22 used predominantly syntactic cues. Only two children approached a 'semantic' pattern of cue use, and neither of these children used the 'semantic' (real-world) cues consistently. Responses were even more consistent in the accord condition. 37 of the 40 children used predominantly syntactic cues. In other words, whether in the conflict or in the accord condition, children primarily used syntactic context as the basis of their categorization. When the cues were incompatible, as in the conflict condition, children overwhelmingly made use of the syntactic cues, not the 'semantic' ones.

In a second experiment, Gordon examined the ability of 39 children aged 3 years to 5 years 11 months to categorize new (nonsense) words either on the basis of 'semantic' (real-world) cues or syntactic cues in isolation. It was found, as predicted, that children were able to use either cue as a basis for category assignment. However, in the syntactic condition, children responded more consistently using syntactic cues than they did with 'semantic' cues in the 'semantic' condition. Indeed, it was only the older children who were able to use the 'semantic' cues as a basis for category assignment. The younger children performed quite randomly in the 'semantic'-cue situation. So the results seem to go against the so-called 'semantic' or 'meaning first' hypothesis about how young children accomplish subcategorization, at least for the count/mass-noun distinction. And the fact that only the *older* children were able even to make use of the 'semantic' cues is an important point to which we will return.

Gordon's third experiment in the series examined children's knowledge of real words. The 'semantic' (real-world) hypothesis predicts that children will initially miscategorize mass nouns such as *furniture, silverware* and *jewellery* as count nouns, since they are used of real-world individuated, countable objects. 40 children between the ages of 1 year 11 months and 5 years 9 months were shown Paddington Bear walking past a number of stores. 'Next he came to a toy store. Do you know what you get in a toy store?' Children were expected to give the count response 'toys'. But how would they perform on non-typical mass nouns? 'Next he came to a furniture store. Do you know what you get in a furniture store?' Here, the reply 'furnitures' would indicate a misclassification of the mass noun *furniture* on the basis of semantic cues. What occurred, however, was that, across a number of conditions and items, children made very few errors. On the crucial mass superordinate terms like *furniture*, where the 'semantic' hypothesis would predict many errors, there were in fact almost none; and the very few that did occur were made by the 4-year-olds. No errors were observed in the 2- and 3-year-olds. The findings with real words, then, like the findings in the first two experiments using nonsense words, all point to the same conclusion: count/mass categories are not represented in terms of an object/substance (or individuated/non-individuated) distinction by young children.

Gathercole (1985) arrived at similar conclusions by approaching the count/mass distinction in a somewhat different way. In one of her experiments, she was interested in children's acquisition of the quantifiers *much* and *many* in relation to count and mass nouns. It will be recalled that mass nouns take the quantifier *much* while count nouns take *many* (e.g. 'how much water', 'too much sand', but 'this many books', 'too many toys'). Young children make many errors on these in their speech, often using *much* where *many* is required. Gathercole (1985) notes such examples as 'Mommy, look how much checkers I got' (age 4 years 8 months) and 'A cargo ship is a ship that doesn't carry very much people' (age 7 years 10 months). To obtain experimental information on the acquisition of these terms, Gathercole designed a task in which the child had to judge the correctness of the speech output of a 'funny-talking' puppet. The child was trained to respond either 'Yes, that's good' or to tell the puppet 'No, you should say . . .'. The terms *much* and *many* occurred with various types of nouns, including prototypical and non-prototypical count and mass nouns, opaque nouns (whose phonological shapes might suggest they are plural when they are singular, or vice versa – e.g. *hose* and *women*), and nonsense words. Based on the various categories, a number of predictions were possible. For example, if young children approach the count/mass distinction on a 'semantic' or real-world basis, they should perform more poorly on non-prototypical count and mass nouns than on prototypical ones. If, instead, young children rely primarily on a distributional analysis, then there should be no difference between these two types.[9] The 'semantic' view would predict no difficulty with the opaque nouns, but the distributional view would predict some difficulty, since the child might be unsure of the singular/plural status of the noun. Nonsense words should be problematic if children base their use of these forms on the properties of real-world referents. On the distributional view, children should have little difficulty with nonsense words.

Gathercole's (1985) results are based on 79 monolingual children, aged 3 years 6 months to 9 years, who successfully completed all the training procedures. The data showed that children performed equally well on prototypical and non-prototypical count and mass nouns (63.9–65.5 per cent correct). They showed poorer performance on opaque nouns (51.4 per cent correct). This pattern of performance is consistent with the distributional view, not with the so-called 'semantic' view of the acquisi-

tion of the count/mass distinction. Children performed poorly on the
nonsense words (46.8 per cent correct), which they shouldn't have done
on the distributional view. However, Gathercole attributes this not to
children's judgements of *much* and *many* in these sentences but to their
lack of familiarity with the nonsense words. They often either questioned
these odd words or corrected them to real words (for example changing
'blicks' to 'bricks'). Gathercole concluded that, 'children begin learning the
mass-count distinction as it applies to *much N* and *many N*, not as a
semantic one, but as a morphosyntactic (distributional) distinction' (p.
411). Furthermore, she also found evidence that at the ages of 8 years and
8 years 6 months there was a switch to a semantic approach. For example,
there was improvement on the opaque nouns and also a sudden decrease in
performance on the nonsense words.

The overall conclusion was, then, that young children use a distributional or syntactic approach to the count/mass distinction; only older
children begin to use 'semantic' or real-world cues to this distinction. This
is the same conclusion reached by Gordon in his experimental studies.
(See also Levy, 1988, for a similar conclusion based on a review of these
count/mass noun findings and findings from gender acquisition by children.)

What relevance do the findings of Gordon and Gathercole on the
acquisition of the count/mass distinction have on the present argument for
the effects of language on conceptual categories? There are at least two
aspects on which we can focus. First, children begin with a distributional
analysis of count/mass terms. The partial correlation with real-world
entities might lead to the formation or, more accurately, the instantiation
of categories such as object and substance.[10] More likely, in this case, such
categories are already part of the child's usable repertoire. However,
having a linguistic distinction partially correlated with particular conceptual categories could make those categories more salient than they would
otherwise be. Second, and obviously related to this, older children and
adults can then make use of those correlations to reinterpret the situation
when count and mass nouns are used in 'untypical' ways – as in the 'many
waters' example. We can treat 'waters' as countable, individuated entities
precisely because of the linguistic cues. If this line of reasoning is correct,
then we have some evidence of a Whorfian-like influence of language on
our interpretation of the world. That is, children learn some types of
linguistic categorization by a distributional analysis. If these are correlated
to some extent with real-world entities, then expectations are built up such
that hearing a new (or nonsense) word of one or another of the subcategor-
izations will lead one to assume that it refers conceptually to what that
word type usually refers to – and this is what happened in experiments

cited, but only in the older children. Furthermore, hearing a familiar word in an 'unnatural' use (as in 'waters') will lead one to reinterpret the referent of that word in the direction of the usual correlation. This argument would be more convincing, however, if another language used something similar to the count/mass distinction in relation to a different set of conceptual categories. We would then expect that speakers of that language would employ those distinctions in a categorization task while English-speakers would use an object/substance distinction on identical material. John Lucy (1987) claims to have shown exactly this.

Lucy (1987) compared the English and Yucatec Mayan languages on indications of grammatical number (e.g. which nouns can take plurals and which cannot) and then designed a number of experimental tasks to see whether the differing linguistic distinctions in the two languages would affect non-linguistic abilities such as categorization. In English, basically only count nouns can take the plural inflection ('two boxes', 'three toys'), whereas mass nouns normally cannot (*'two sands', *'three waters'). This count/mass distinction is itself more intricately based on a number of related distributional facts such as the determiners that can be used with them, which quantifiers are allowed (e.g. *much* or *many*), and other linguistic facts. As has been seen, this count/mass distinction is correlated with the conceptual distinction between objects and substances. By contrast, speakers of Yucatec Mayan, an indigenous Indian language of south-eastern Mexico, use plurals (optionally) primarily for animate entities. Non-animate entities, whether objects or substances, are not pluralized or can only be pluralized by use of a construction that specifies the lack of life (McNeill, 1987, p. 198). To make the contrast clearer, Lucy adopted a set of three categories. The first, [+animate], is pluralized in both English and Yucatec Mayan (though only optionally in the latter). The category [−animate] is divided into two types in order to capture the usual count/mass distinction in English. Thus, the second category, [−animate, +discrete], pluralizes in English while the third category, [−animate, −discrete], does not. By contrast, neither of these two latter categories directly pluralizes in Yucatec Mayan since they are both non-animate. If habitual language patterns affect other non-linguistic activities, then a basic overall prediction becomes possible: English-speakers should notice or pay special attention to numbers of animals and discrete objects whereas speakers of Yucatec Mayan should primarily notice only numbers of animals.

To test this prediction, Lucy designed a variety of related tasks using pictures in which the numbers of animals [+animate], objects [−animate, +discrete], and substances [−animate, −discrete] differed. The animals were dogs, horses, pigs, turkeys and others with which the Yucatecs were familiar. Objects consisted of implements such as machetes, brooms, axes and shovels, and containers such as buckets, barrels, bottles and gourds. Substances included corn dough, meat, rock, puddles, clouds and smoke. One task consisted merely of verbal descriptions of three pictures shown one at a time. 12 Yucatec men were compared to 12 American men on their descriptions of the pictures while those pictures were still in view. (Tasks involving memory will be discussed in the section on the effects of language on memory.) The results showed that the English-speakers indicated number primarily for both animals and objects and much less so for substances. By contrast, the speakers of Yucatec Mayan not only indicated number less often, but, when they did, usually did so only for animals. They indicated number significantly less often for both objects and substances.

So far, this merely shows the differences in the two languages in terms of what they encode. However, another task required the subjects to make non-verbal similarity judgements of an original picture and several alternates in which the numbers either of particular animals, objects or substances differed from the original. The purpose of this task, according to Lucy, 'was to provide evidence that cognitive responses in a task correlate with linguistic patterns even when language is not involved as a mode of response' (Lucy, 1987, p. 415). Each subject was told that the alternate pictures differed from the original in some way. They were then allowed to examine the pictures until all the differences were recognized. Importantly, any differences which were not noticed were pointed out so that each subject was aware of all of the differences. The task was to indicate the picture that was 'most like' the original. The prediction for English-speakers was that, since numbers of both animals and objects are linguistically important, a change in number of either of these would render those alternate pictures different from the original. Thus, the picture that should be chosen as most like the original should be the alternate in which the substance changes. In Yucatec Mayan, however, only animal numbers should be treated as important. Therefore, changes in numbers of either objects or substances should be seen as unimportant, and pictures showing changes in either of these should equally be treated as most like the original. The results strongly supported these predictions. All 12 English-speaking American men chose the alternate with a change in substance as the picture most like the original, with none choosing pictures with changes in the numbers of animals or objects. By contrast, the responses of the Yucatec Mayan speakers were almost equally split between object and substance changes. Six subjects found the alternate with substance changes to be most like the original; five chose the alternate with changes in the number of objects. Only one chose the picture with a change in the number of animals. Even when language is not involved as a mode of response, then, English-speakers treat animals and objects together (count nouns) in contrast to substances (mass nouns). Speakers of Yucatec Mayan treat objects and substances together (non-animate) in contrast to animals – the 'cognitive responses' thus paralleling the categories on which pluralization is based in the two languages.

Lucy noted something else in the Yucatec language that might affect categorization. Yucatec lexical forms often include a range of meanings based on identity of the material of which the items are made. For example, the word for 'wood', *che'*, refers not only to the material itself but also to a variety of things made of wood. Where English encodes things according to their distinctive shapes (tree, stick, board), Yucatec Mayan uses *che'* for all of these (Lucy, 1987, p. 373). Lucy's operating assumption, then, is that due to these language differences Yucatec Mayan speakers will classify by material whereas English-speakers will classify by shape.

To test this, Lucy showed subjects in the two language groups a series of objects one at a time, each with two alternates – a shape alternate and a material alternate. So, for example, when a cardboard box was shown, the shape alternate was a plastic box while the material alternate was a piece of cardboard; and, when the object was a ceramic bowl, the two alternates were a metal bowl and a ceramic plate. There were eight such triads, and subjects were instructed to indicate which of the two alternates was more like the original. Subjects were then classified in terms of their predominant response pattern. Of the 13 English-speaking subjects, 12 classified by shape and only one by material. By contrast, of the 10 Yucatec Mayan speaking subjects, eight classified by material and only two by shape. This difference was highly significant ($p < .0007$). Lucy interprets this as showing that language differences have differential effects on the classification of objects in this task.

Studies of the effects of language on memory

The effects of language, through rehearsal, on auditory short-term memory are well known. (For reviews, see Baddeley, 1976.) In this section, given the focus on 'Whorfian' influences of language on memory, studies concerned with effects of language on long-term, broader memory phenomena will be reviewed.

There are various ways of examining whether language has an effect on memory. One method is to see whether members of a single language community differ in the use they make of language during a memory task and then to examine what effects this has on their memories. This method is illustrated by Bartlett's (1932) classic monograph *Remembering*. In his studies, Bartlett used a number of techniques to study individual differences in remembering various types of material. He found that people did indeed differ in the spontaneous use they made of language and that this in turn affected their memories. In one method, which Bartlett called *the method of description*, a subject viewed five drawings of the faces of men, one at a time, and was later asked to describe these men and to answer questions about them after intervals of thirty minutes, a week, and a fortnight. In another method, the *method of repeated reproduction*, subjects read a story, 'The War of the Ghosts', and were asked to write the story down after 15 minutes and then again after varying intervals – often many hours, days and even years later. A third method, the *method of picture writing* required the subject to view cards on which were drawn signs for particular words. After an interval of 15 minutes, a story was dictated to the subject, whose task was to take down the dictation using the appropriate signs in place of words. Figure 2.5 shows a sample series used by Bartlett.

By using these methods, Bartlett found that subjects could be classified into two groups according to the characteristic methods they used when

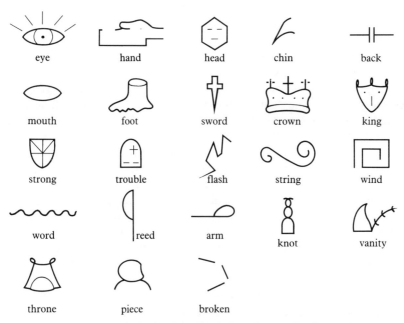

Figure 2.5 *Bartlett's 'picture writing' signs. Source*: Bartlett (1932)

asked to remember things. Bartlett called one group *visualizers*: they relied mainly on visual imagery. A contrasting group, the *vocalizers*, had memories primarily based on language. These two groups were found regardless of whether the material to be remembered was originally pictorial or verbal. Furthermore, a given subject used the same general method of remembering in the different conditions. A person who was able to recall visual features of the men's faces was also likely to be influenced by visual images when recounting the 'War of the Ghosts' story and to replace many of the words with picture signs in the picture-writing task. So an individual who depended largely on visual or verbal cues in one condition did so in the other conditions as well.

More importantly for our purposes, Bartlett found associated effects on the memories themselves. For example, when questioned about the faces, visualizers might suddenly recall an image and would become confident in their replies. By contrast, vocalizers lacked confidence. They recalled verbal judgements or labels about the faces. Bartlett reported that these subjects acted as if they were building up their descriptions as they went along. They were most concerned to make their remarks hang together in a consistent manner. In the picture-writing task, vocalizers placed greater reliance on secondary associations and analogies. The word was often the first thing to be recalled and the sign was then constructed from associations to it. There are obviously many factors that can affect recall in tasks of this type. Within the context of the present discussion, what is worthy of note is that the memories of those individuals who appeared to encode material in a verbal manner were affected by that very method – some evidence that language has an effect on recall.

A second method that can be used to study the effects of language on memory is experimentally to introduce particular labels for items to be recalled in order to study the effects of those labels on memory. In the same year (1932) as Bartlett published his work, another experiment which has become a classic study on the effect of language on memory was published by Carmichael, Hogan and Walter, and it used this technique. Subjects viewed a series of 12 somewhat ambiguous stimulus pictures accompanied by verbal labels spoken by the experimenter. Forty-eight subjects in one group were shown the pictures with one set of verbal labels, 38 subjects in a second group were given a second set of verbal labels, and nine subjects in a third group were given no labels at all. After looking at the complete set of drawings, the subjects had to reproduce them from memory in any order. If a recognizable representation of each figure was not given, the list was shown again. This was repeated until a recognizable reproduction of all 12 figures had been obtained from each subject. Carmichael et al. reported that the number of trials required to

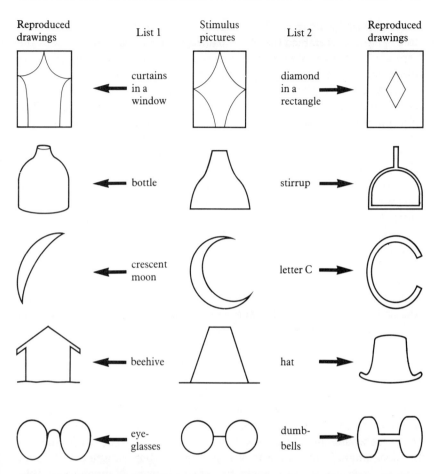

Figure 2.6 *Drawings from memory (left and right) based on stimulus pictures (centre) with alternate verbal labels. Source*: Carmichael et al. (1932)

attain this end in the two experimental groups was between two and eight, with an average of three trials. The small control group working without any verbal labels required an average of four trials. So, to begin with, providing verbal labels helped reduce the number of trials necessary to achieve successful recall of all 12 figures. The middle column of figure 2.6 shows some of the stimulus pictures that were used. To either side are shown the list-1 and list-2 labels that subjects in the two experimental groups were given. The reproductions were then qualitatively rated by two judges on a five-point scale. Those figures assigned quality step 5 were by definition those that showed the greatest amount of change from the original stimulus figures. When these drawings were then examined, close to 75 per cent resembled the object named by the verbal label. That is, the reproduced drawings which were most changed from the originals were differentially 'attracted' by the particular verbal labels they had been given in the two different experimental groups. Examples of these differentially attracted drawings are shown in left- and right-hand columns of figure 2.6. Forcing people to label drawings, then, has an effect on their memory, at least when the labels result in a significant change from the originals. This seems to be clear evidence that linguistic encodings affect recall for pictorial material.

A third method that can be used to study the effects of language on memory is to compare two languages that encode a particular concept differently from one another and to examine whether the speakers of those languages are differentially affected in their memories for the associated concepts. In fact, this is what was done in the early experiments on colour 'perception', whose *positive* results were really to do with colour *memory* (see above, pp. 84–5, 94). And it may be further recalled that Lucy and Shweder (1979) found that, when perceptual influences having to do with the salience of focal colours were controlled, the effects of language on colour *memory* could be demonstrated.

In the series of recent studies by Lucy (1987), effects of language on memory for concepts in domains other than colour have been demonstrated. It will be recalled (see above, p. 105) that Lucy used a similarity-judgement task in which subjects were shown a picture and a series of alternates and had to choose the picture most like the original in front of them. The prediction, which was upheld, was that English-speakers would choose pictures with a substance change (that is, since in English animals and objects get pluralized, but substances do not, English-speakers are less likely to notice changes in numbers of substances). By contrast, Yucatec Mayans were expected to choose pictures with changes in numbers of either objects or substances (since only animals are pluralized and therefore only their numbers are treated as important).

Lucy's memory tasks used the same logic. In a 'shorter-term' memory task, subjects viewed a picture for one minute. After a one-minute delay, they had to pick the original from a set of six pictures into which they had seen the original picture inserted and shuffled. Both English and Yucatec Mayan speakers scored about 30 per cent correct. Where they were wrong, English-speakers mainly chose pictures in which the number of substances was different from in the original. By contrast, the Yucatec Mayan speakers were as likely to err about number of objects as about number of substances.

In the 'longer term' recognition-memory experiments, the task was basically the same, but the interval varied between an hour and an hour and a half. Furthermore, subjects were not warned that they would later have to recognize in an array the pictures that they had been shown. Once again, English-speakers most often mistook for the original those alternative pictures that contained a change in the number of a substance. The results for the Yucatec Mayan speakers were not clear, since they tended to choose at random on this task.

Lucy's basic conclusion is that in these memory experiments, as in the perception experiments, effects of language differences were demonstrated. Subtle differences between the pluralization systems of the two languages had effects on memory.

Studies of the effects of language on thinking and problem-solving

In the past few years the Whorfian arguments as to the relation between language and 'thought processes' have been revived by interesting, and to some people controversial, claims concerning cognitive abilities in Chinese-speakers. This latest episode appears to have begun with a short and highly readable book by Alfred Bloom entitled *The Linguistic Shaping of Thought* (1981). The sad thing is that some researchers and scholars who have criticized Bloom's ideas appear not to have truly absorbed the theoretical parts of Bloom's book, but merely to have turned to the particular experiments themselves. This is important since, as will be seen, some of the criticisms levelled against Bloom seem at a fundamental level to be aimed at Whorfian interpretations he not only did not entertain but explicitly rejected (see the section entitled 'Overreacting to Whorf' in Bloom's book, pp. 2–3).

So what were Bloom's claims and how were they tested? What exactly are the criticisms levelled against those claims? How methodologically sound are the experiments on which those criticisms are based? To begin with, Bloom makes it clear that he rejects the extreme Whorfian notion that the language that one speaks exclusively determines the categories in which one thinks; or that observable differences between two languages necessarily entail corresponding differences in thought. Instead, Bloom makes clear that he believes that the kinds of questions that should be asked are 'When and in what ways do linguistic categories shape thought?' and 'Which linguistic differences entail corresponding cognitive differences?' (Bloom, 1981, p. 3). He then goes on to outline a difference between English and Chinese in the encoding of counterfactual statements.

In English, one indicates the counterfactual in present or future by using a past-tense form of the verb or the phrase *were to* in the first clause, and *would* or *'d* in the second clause. An example is 'If John were to go to the library, he would see Mary.' In the past, one uses a past-perfect form in the first clause, and phrases like *would have* and *might have* in the second, as in 'If John had gone to the library, he would have seen Mary.' These counterfactuals contrast with 'implicationals' which either recount the facts ('John went to the library and saw Mary') or give descriptions carrying no commitment to the truth or falsity of the events ('If John goes to the library, he will see Mary'). By contrast, although Chinese has implicational forms, Bloom claims that 'the Chinese language has no distinct lexical, grammatical, or intonational device to signal entry into the counterfactual realm, to indicate explicitly that the events referred to have definitely not occurred and are being discussed for the purpose only of exploring the might-have-been or the might-be' (Bloom, 1981, p. 16). (This may not be strictly true, since it appears that Chinese-speakers can use a phrase to indicate counterfactuality, the equivalent of 'If X is president . . . but she is not president . . . but if X is president, then . . .'.)

So far we have the claim that Chinese does not encode (or does not easily encode) counterfactuality. This may, of course, have no cognitive consequences. But Bloom claims that there is evidence that the lack of a distinct linguistic device to signal counterfactuals does indeed affect Chinese-speakers, and he quotes evidence from questionnaires, reports of bilingual speakers, Chinese students learning English, and so on, with the aim of showing that Chinese-speakers typically find counterfactual uses in English somewhat difficult and see those uses as a form of thinking characterized as 'un-Chinese'. Bloom is careful to point out that in particular concrete situations Chinese-speakers do make use of counterfactual speech and thought. For example, in a situation where a group of people know that John's coming late has made them late for the movie, saying something like 'If John came earlier, we arrive at the movies on time' is used to express what would be encoded in English as 'If John had come earlier we would have arrived at the movie on time' – the situation itself acting as a concrete equivalent of explicitly pointing out that 'X is not president' in the example given in the preceding paragraph. Bloom is then careful to point out yet again that

> the suggestion that Chinese speakers have not been led by their language to construct schemas specific to counterfactual speech and thought would not imply that Chinese speakers cannot speak or think counterfactually. . . . Such a suggestion would imply, however, that they would typically do so less directly, with a greater investment of cognitive effort and hence less naturally than their English-speaking counterparts. (Bloom, 1981, pp. 21–2)

Bloom then went on to test this in a variety of experiments. A short examination of a typical experiment that Bloom claims confirms his hypothesis will give us the concrete data and interpretations which later researchers have questioned. The basic design was to give counterfactuals using the Chinese form 'A is not the case, but, if A was, then B, then C, then D, etc.' The subjects were then asked in a variety of ways whether the consequents refer to things that have or have not happened. The prediction was that English-speakers would recognize at once that the statement is in the realm of the might-have-been. In outline, 'version 2' of Bloom's statement ran as follows. Bier was an eighteenth-century European philosopher. There was some contact between the West and China at that time, but very few works of Chinese philosophy had been translated. Bier could not read Chinese, but, if he had been able to read Chinese, he would have discovered B; what would have most influenced him would have been C; once influenced by that Chinese perspective, Bier would then have done D; etc. Printed below were questions concerning whether the events had or had not occurred, the correct counterfactual response being that they had not. To these questions, Bloom's American subjects responded 98 per cent of the time with counterfactuals, while the corresponding percentages for several Chinese groups were 6 or 7 per cent. Bloom got results that supported his prediction.

For the later debate, it is crucial to note two things. First, as I understand it, these results obtained precisely because of the extra burden imposed by a *series* of counterfactuals. Bloom nowhere claims that Chinese-speakers cannot think counterfactually – only that such thinking is not supported by their linguistic system and is therefore a somewhat less natural mode which can be overwhelmed by additional complexity (like a series rather than a single counterfactual). Second, and related to this first point, Bloom himself showed that the percentage of counterfactual replies could be manipulated by aspects of the test statement. For example, in 'version 3' of the statement, it was said not that *very few* Chinese works had been translated but that *none* had. Bloom claims that, if the subject misses the structural call for the counterfactual, and gives a straightforward description of the paragraph, 'he soon runs up against an irreconcilable logical conflict that he cannot resolve in a coherent manner without adopting a counterfactual interpretation' (Bloom, 1981, p. 26). In this situation, Bloom found that the percentages of counterfactual interpretations rose dramatically in the various Chinese subject groups – to 46–63 per cent. It is important to keep these two points in mind while examining the claims of his critics.

In a series of experiments challenging Bloom's findings, Au (1983) obtained results that showed that Chinese-speakers do indeed think counterfactually. (For the critical exchange see Au, 1983; Bloom's 1984 reply to Au; and Au's 1984 reply to Bloom.) I hope that I am not doing Au an injustice by reducing the various manipulations in her experiments to what seem to me to be the most important. Au claimed that the Bier story of Bloom was written in very unidiomatic Chinese and she therefore constructed a different story. This story occurred in various versions such that in one version there were three implications (as in Bloom's experiments) and in another only one implication. Furthermore, in English the subject is continually reminded of the counterfactuality by the repetition of the words 'would have', thus reducing 'memory overload'. So, to equate the two languages, Au had versions in English which eliminated the repetitions of 'would have' (cf. 'If I had been you I would have finished my dinner; I would have turned off the TV; and I would have started studying', versus 'If I had been you I would have finished my dinner, turned off the TV, and started studying').

Now, it should be noted that these manipulations have complex implications for Bloom's and for Au's claims that were not made totally clear in the original debate. It is therefore useful to examine them in some detail. For the first variable, if Chinese-speakers did well when there was only one instead of three implications, it could be objected that Au's experiment was not really testing Bloom's claims since it is only when there is overload that the weak Whorfian effect should hold. However, it would support Bloom's predictions if what was found were a significant interaction, with Chinese-speakers doing well only in the one-implication condition but poorly in the three-implication condition. It could be argued that the second variable, equating the linguistic cues, is to some extent irrelevant. If a way had been found to increase the number of cues in Chinese, and if the Chinese-speakers then did well, one could argue that the experimental manipulation had merely undermined what the weak Whorfian position was all about: the Chinese-speakers were not under the processing constraints predicted to lead to observed differences. Au seems to treat memory overload as a separate explanation, whereas Whorfians would view these very language differences as having effects on memory. However, what Au actually manipulated was merely the cues available to English-speakers. If those had made a difference, one could argue that on-line processing variables affect problem-solving in English-speakers. If they had had no effect, one could argue that the Whorfian influences on thought are more pervasive and can not be expected to be influenced by whether particular statements do or do not contain the particular language features that are claimed to affect problem-solving in a more general, long-term way. Either way, the contest between Bloom's and Au's claims does not seem to be affected by the manipulation of this variable.

So the one major result that might help to decide between Bloom and

Au would be a finding that Chinese-speakers either do poorly on both the one- and three-implication conditions, or do well only on the one-implication condition. Unfortunately for Bloom, Au's results showed that the percentage of counterfactual responses for her Chinese subjects was essentially 100 per cent for both conditions. However, these results are not grist for Au's mill either. For, if the number of implications plays no part, and if the number of linguistic cues in English plays no part (the same manipulation on English-speakers led to counterfactual responses of 96 and 97 per cent, respectively), then what leads to the differences between Bloom's and Au's results? One possibility is the difference between their stories, if it is true Au's story is written in a much more idiomatic Chinese – a concept difficult to quantify. Bloom claims that the Chinese versions of his stories were all written by 'native Chinese-speaking professors at the National Taiwan University and judged by them to be in grammatical, acceptable and comprehensible Chinese' (Bloom, 1984, p. 283). Au's claim is that her story is written in a much more idiomatic style than Bloom's. Unfortunately, those of us who are non-speakers of Chinese have very little way of assessing these claims. But there are other differences, some of them methodological (as opposed to theoretical), that could account for the differences in the observed results.

Bloom (1984) claims that Au's story does not really contain a series of counterfactuals in the way that his original testing materials did. Au's story has a number of facts about a native tribe and its beliefs; the only aspect of the story that is counterfactual, according to Bloom, is that the explorer in the story does not know these facts. By contrast, all of the implications in Bloom's original story are counterfactual. Furthermore, one of Au's conditions, in which Bloom's original story was rewritten in more 'idiomatic' Chinese, may simply have eliminated the complexity on which the weak Whorfian effects depend.

Another problem that may account for the differences is a more directly methodological one. Bloom tested various groups of adult monolingual Chinese-speakers, including working people who had had only a basic education. All of Au's Chinese-speaking subjects were in secondary schools, and were bilingual with varying degrees of knowledge of English – all members of her original groups had had 10 or more years of instruction in English as a second language. Au tried in various ways to argue away the possible influence of knowing some English (for example, by later including a group 'who were unlikely to have learnt the English subjunctive' in that they had only four to seven years of instruction in English), but one cannot help feeling that this isn't good enough when testing a Whorfian notion that crucially depends on a language-knowledge variable.

Liu (1985) tested Taiwanese schoolchildren ('ages ranged from 9.5 to 20 with a mean of 14 years') on the Bloom and Au stories – some of the children being young enough not yet to have had instruction in English. She used Au's story both in its original and in a *less* idiomatic version, and Bloom's 'version 3' both in its original form and in a *more* idiomatic version. Liu found that even her younger Taiwanese children gave counterfactual responses. She obtained high percentages of counterfactual responding, and the fact that the percentages of correct responses increased even within the younger groups (grades 4–6), none of whom had yet been exposed to English, was taken by Liu to be supportive of Au and not of Bloom. That is, the developmental trend was not due to number of years of exposure to English. Furthermore, Liu's older children (grades 8–11) had a counterfactual response rate of 82 per cent on Bloom's original story, whereas counterfactual responses by Bloom's adult Chinese sample (shown in Liu as 56 per cent when averaged across groups) were significantly less.

Liu claims that her results lend support to Au and undermine Bloom's claims. What do Liu's results really show? They show that Chinese-speakers, even very young ones, can think counterfactually. Notice, however, that this is not a conclusion with which Bloom would disagree. Indeed, Liu used Bloom's 'version 3' story in her experiments – but this is the very version that Bloom himself used to show that subtle changes in content can lead Chinese-speakers to employ a counterfactual mode of thinking. That is why even Bloom's counterfactual rate was as high as the 56 per cent quoted by Liu. (I can't see any explanation by Liu of why her older groups of children outperformed even Bloom's adults – she reports no effects due to idiom – but, whatever the supposed reasons might be, they are in some sense irrelevant since both researchers show that Chinese-speakers have high counterfactual response rates on Bloom's 'version 3' story.)

In his original book, Bloom also argued that Chinese-speakers would be less likely than English-speakers to give counterfactual responses to the following question: 'If all circles were large and this small triangle were a circle, would it be large?' Testing 173 Taiwanese and 115 American subjects (Bloom, 1981), Bloom found that only 25 per cent of the Chinese-speaking subjects answered 'yes', compared to 83 per cent of the English-speaking subjects – a highly significant difference. Au (1984) basically repeated this test with 33 Chinese-speaking subjects, manipulating the form of the question in Chinese. That manipulation turned out to play no part, with counterfactual replies being found in 72 per cent of the responses to Bloom's original question, and in 73 per cent of the responses to Au's revision. But these percentages are significantly higher than Bloom's original 25 per cent. Again we have major differences between

Bloom's and Au's findings for which no clear explanation is available. Liu (1985) pointed out the problem that Au's Chinese-speaking subjects had had many years of exposure to English. Furthermore, the triangle/circle question was the only one of its type that Bloom and Au had asked. Therefore Liu designed a study using 18 such problems, varying the content along a concrete–abstract dimension, and using what she claimed to be a more idiomatic version of the Chinese question than Bloom had used. The subjects were again the 744 fourth- to eleventh-grade school-children in state schools in Taiwan who had been tested in her earlier experiment.

The percentage of counterfactual responses was found to increase with grade level (age), and, although Liu does not clearly report the percentages for each group for each problem type, it appears from her graph (figure 2 in her report) that even the youngest children were giving about 75 per cent counterfactual responses on most of the problem types, this rising to about 90 per cent in the older groups. In other words, like Au, Liu found that Chinese-speakers engaged in counterfactual thinking to a much greater extent than Bloom had observed (25 per cent) and, at the oldest ages in her student groups, the percentage of children giving counterfactual responses was virtually identical to that for Bloom's American, English-speaking subjects.

With such conflicting results, what can one conclude from this modern debate concerning the effects of language on problem-solving? I personally find it difficult to come to any firm conclusion about which side in this debate is closer to 'the truth'. On the one hand, I find the comments quoted by Bloom from the Chinese-speaking subjects in his experiments persuasive: that they find counterfactual thinking to be to some extent a non-natural mode of thought, and that they have trouble with counter-factual language-forms in English. In the experiment on supposing a particular triangle to be a circle, Bloom reports that most Chinese responded, 'No! How can a circle be a triangle? How can this small circle be large? What do you mean?' (Bloom, 1981, p. 31), and 'I know what you Westerners want me to do, you always want me to assume things, even when they don't make sense. But we Chinese don't do that.' On the other hand, Au's and Liu's studies contradict Bloom's experimental findings. However, the one variable claimed to be responsible for the differences was whether the Chinese versions were written in idiomatic Chinese or not, and this was found to make no difference in Liu's experiments.

Furthermore, the serious lack of comparability among the various groups make any firm interpretative conclusions difficult. Children of varying ages are being compared to adults. Some of the adults are in university while others have a much lower educational level. And in some conditions monolingual Chinese are being compared to bilingual Chinese subjects. I suppose that what I find surprising and disappointing is that none of Bloom's critics has examined groups of monolingual adult Chinese-speakers. Surely there are enough such subjects in the world to make this a not-insurmountable problem.

But there are other and perhaps more crucial reasons for a feeling of disappointment with this counterfactual research as it supposedly addresses the weak Whorfian hypothesis. All of the tests, including the circle/triangle problem, were presented in a paper-and-pencil format by all of these researchers. Though the precise procedures used were often not made clear, it appears that subjects, given written forms in a group testing procedure, were able to go back and reread the story or problem on which they were currently working. If this was so, then the entire edifice on which the varying interpretations of Bloom, Au and Liu were based falls. That is, the tests become nothing more than tests of overall reasoning ability and not of the weak Whorfian hypothesis at all. A comment by Bloom reveals that this may in fact be the case. He reports on the circle/triangle problem that

> when the original question is asked orally, it produces even more dramatic effects. It has been my experience in fact that when subjects are presented with the question orally and informally – in other words, without given time to hesitate, to reconsider or to examine the question from different perspectives – just about every native Chinese speaker who has not been exposed to strong Western influences, and even very many who have, will spontaneously respond 'no', while, by contrast, just about every native English speaker will spontaneously respond 'yes'. (Bloom, 1981, p. 31)

The technology to present materials on a computer display and to measure response times in, say, milliseconds, has been available for years. If the weak Whorfian hypothesis holds in the way Bloom says it does, then the percentages of correct counterfactual responses to counterfactual problems may well be irrelevant. Instead, we might observe significant differences in the ease of processing such problems as reflected in differing response times to counterfactual versus non-counterfactual problems, and these differences may vary according to linguistic background. Until monolingual groups are compared using a better methodology, there will be nothing we can firmly conclude from the Bloom–Au–Liu debate – although many of Bloom's observations remain interestingly suggestive.

Before leaving Bloom's ideas, one last thing is worth noting. If his conception of the weak Whorfian hypothesis turns out to be supported in the way just suggested, most cognitive psychologists are not going to like it. Rather than an all-or-none processing ability that is damaged, faulty, lacking, undeveloped, and so on, the weak form of the Whorfian hypothesis merely claims that language 'influences' processing, making it somewhat more difficult to process information of particular types, especially if working memory is overloaded. This poses a conceptual problem. What exactly does it mean to claim that processing is less efficient? However, in mitigation of this problem, it should be pointed out that those researchers studying processing in mentally retarded individuals have grappled with this problem for many years. (For a modern view on processing efficiency in mental retardation, see Anderson, 1986a, 1986b, forthcoming.)

There appears to have been only a limited amount of work in a Whorfian tradition that has actually focused on cognitive processing. However, some recent research can be interpreted in this context, even though it was not undertaken with a Whorfian view in mind. Ellis and Hennelly (1980), for example, were interested in the effect of length of articulation of digits on measured digit-span performance – an important subtest on many tests of intellectual ability. Baddeley, Thomson and Buchanan (1975) had presented experimental evidence that short-term memory is limited by the amount of time it takes to pronounce the words to be recalled. Ellis and Hennelly reasoned that, if the articulation time for digits is longer in one language than in another, then the average span would be smaller for speakers of the language that takes longer to articulate. Thus, observed differences in digit span would be attributable to this effect rather than to any intellectual differences between the two populations.

It is commonly observed that it takes longer to articulate digits in the Welsh language than in English. So Ellis and Hennelly decided to test their prediction by using 12 Welsh–English bilingual subjects, eight of whom considered themselves to be more proficient in Welsh and four of whom felt more proficient in English. These subjects read aloud single-digit numbers as fast as they could from a sheet containing 20 lines, each containing the digits 0–9 in random order. This list was read eight times alternating language on each trial. The results confirmed that Welsh digits take longer to articulate than English digits. Although only four of the 12 subjects rated themselves more proficient in English, every subject read the digits faster in English. It took on average 385 milliseconds to read a Welsh digit, compared with 321 milliseconds to read an English digit. This essentially means that on average a person can read six digits in English in the time taken to read five in Welsh.

The next step was to investigate whether these articulation-time differences have the predicted effect on memory-span scores. Ellis and Hennelly tested the same 12 subjects on measures of digit span both in English and

Welsh and found a significant superiority in English over that in Welsh. Ellis and Hennelly even speculate that, since any factors that limit short-term storage will make mental arithmetic more difficult, mental arithmetic will be more difficult to carry out in Welsh than in English. They were concerned with equating tests of intellectual ability across languages, but the implications for this review of the effects of language on processing are clear.

Ellis and Hennelly concluded their experimental report by suggesting that there was no reason to doubt that this effect also operates in other languages. And, indeed, in later studies it has been found that they do. Stigler, Lee and Stevenson (1986) compared Chinese (Taiwanese), Japanese and American children on digit span. They tested kindergarten children (mean age 6.1 years), 'first-graders' (mean age 6.8 years), and 'fifth-graders' (mean age 10.9 years). The digit-span scores for the Japanese and American children were roughly the same, but they were very different from those for the Chinese children, who showed superior performance. The set of means for the Chinese, Japanese and American children were, respectively: kindergarten children 5.9, 4.1, 4.6; 'first-graders' 6.4, 4.4, 5.1; and 'fifth-graders' 6.9, 5.5, 5.9.

There may be other, more subtle ways in which different representations of number in the world's languages affect the processing of numbers by speakers of those languages. Languages that are rooted in ancient Chinese (modern Chinese, Japanese and Korean) have numerical naming systems that are congruent with a base-10 numeration system. Thus, 12 is read as 'ten two', 14 as 'ten four', 20 as 'two ten(s)', 43 as 'four ten(s) three', and 80 as 'eight ten(s)'. By contrast, Western languages such as English, French and German lack stability of representation. When 12 is read as *twelve*, it is an arbitrary label with no encoding of the tens and units occurring. Sometimes the spoken and written order of the terms may not agree. Thus *fourteen* in English reverses the digit order of 14. And in German 43 is read as *dreiundvierzig* ('three and forty'). And what does one make of the way French-speakers say 80 – *quatre-vingts* ('four twenties')? Miura, Kim, Chang and Okamoto (1988), from whom these examples were taken, noted that cross-national comparisons of mathematical achievement have consistently shown superiority by Asian students. Though many social and motivational explanations have been offered to explain these differences, Miura et al. suggest that the differences may be due to the differences in encoding just noted. That is, speakers of Asian languages may represent number both more accurately and more flexibly than their Western counterparts.

To test this, Miura et al. examined five groups of monolingual children on a numerical-representation task. Four groups were 'first-grade' children from the People's Republic of China, Japan, the United States and Korea, and their mean ages were, respectively, 6 years 7 months, 6 years 11 months, 6 years 10 months and 7 years 1 month. In addition a kindergarten sample from Korea (mean age 5 years 11 months) was tested. Children were tested individually. They were given blocks that counted as single units and also a 'ten block' – a bar marked into ten segments. The experimenter counted out 10 unit blocks and lined them up to show their equivalence to one ten block. The child was then given a numeral printed on a card and was asked to read the numeral and to show the number using the blocks. As 100 unit blocks and 20 ten blocks were available, the child had more than adequate numbers of blocks available for the tasks. The test items consisted of the numerals 11, 13, 28, 30 and 42 presented in random order.

The representation task for each number consisted of two trials. The child first constructed a spontaneous representation, and, after being reminded of the equivalence of one ten block and 10 unit blocks, the child was asked whether the number could be shown in a different way using the blocks. We thus have both a spontaneous preference for representing the number and an attempt to see whether children could represent that number in alternative ways. Constructions were classified into one-to-one collections – i.e. the child used only unit blocks (e.g. 24 unit blocks to represent 24); canonical base-10 representations, which were defined as using the correct number of ten blocks and unit blocks, and therefore never using more than nine unit blocks; and non-canonical base-10 representations (e.g. a ten block and 14 unit blocks to represent 24). Only correct constructions were categorized. Since the error rate on trial 1 was small, it is possible to report the percentages for each group. The Asian groups predominantly used canonical base-10 representations for their spontaneous trial, with Chinese, Japanese and Korean children doing so in 81, 72 and 83 per cent, respectively, of their constructions. By contrast, the American sample preferred one-to-one collections, using that type for 91 per cent of their representations. The only other group to prefer one-to-one collections was the younger Korean (kindergarten) group, 59 per cent of whose representations were of this type.

But the more startling results came from trial 2, where the child was encouraged to use another means of representation. US first-graders were unable to make correct constructions for 66 per cent of the numbers on trial 2. This compares with only 4 per cent of Chinese children, 7 per cent of Japanese children and 1 per cent of Korean first-graders who failed in this way. Another way to put this is that all the Korean kindergarten children, 98 per cent of Korean first-graders, 76 per cent of the Chinese and 79 per cent of the Japanese were able to show all five numbers in two ways. Only 13 per cent of US children were able to do so. They either said that they could not think of another way to show the number or persisted in rearranging the blocks from the first trial to show the number in a perceptually different way. To summarize across the two trials, 84 per cent of the Chinese children, 67 per cent of the Japanese, 75 per cent of Korean first-graders, and 60 per cent of Korean kindergarten children used a canonical representation to construct all five numbers, while only 8 per cent of US children did so. Half of the US children used no canonical constructions at all!

The strong form of the Whorfian hypothesis is that language affects the processes associated with thinking and problem-solving. But there are other ways of affecting such processes which can be confused with the Whorfian hypothesis. The most obvious of these is through the writing systems used by different cultures. If it can be shown that the ortho-graphic system one uses affects processing, then, the argument goes, this constitutes evidence in favour of a hypothesis resembling Whorf's. Such a position has been advocated by Tzeng and Hung (1981) as part of their more general claim about the influence of notations on information-processing.[11] They note that differences between Chinese and Western orthographies may affect visual information-processing. They are careful to point out that their claim is not that the end products of the thought process will differ, but that only processing will be affected. This is analogous to the way numerical-symbol systems may affect thought processes. Arabic numerals will be easier to multiply in than Roman numerals, and thus the mathematical-symbol system will affect proces-sing. Another example they quote, however, seems to indicate that some 'end products' of thought may also be affected. Thus, it is claimed that calculus made little progress in Britain because originally it used Newton's rather than Leibniz's notation.

The considerable differences between Chinese and Western ortho-graphic systems naturally invite study of the effects of these differences on processing. The Chinese logograph system places a premium on the use of rote memorization and greater emphasis on visual rather than auditory processing. Turnage and McGinnies (1973) asked American and Chinese college students to study a list of 15 words in a serial learning task in which the input modality was varied. It was found that Chinese students learned the character list faster when it was presented visually, whereas American students learned the word list faster when it was presented auditorily. Citing this and other findings, Tzeng and Hung claim that different processing constraints will be built up in our information-processing systems depending on which writing system we have learned. Hoosain (1986) reviews evidence from various studies to show that Chinese subjects are superior to North American and West European subjects on visual motor tests, again presumably because the Chinese orthographic system places greater emphasis on visual-discrimination ability. Scribner and Cole (1981), based on their studies of the Vai in Africa, claim that becoming literate in certain scripts can affect information-processing. Their claims should be approached cautiously, however, since a series of studies did not show the predicted superiority expected of literate subjects on various tasks (see first half of the Scribner and Cole book, 1981, with summary on p. 132), a fact that most researchers quoting their study ignore.

It appears, then, that several specific aspects of culture do have an effect on processing. This is true, for example, of numerical naming systems. The orthographic system used in writing a language, and perhaps even the very act of becoming literate, may also have effects on particular aspects of processing. Whether such results can be accepted in terms of Whorf's original hypothesis is, however, doubtful.

Another area where Whorfian influences on cognition can be seen is in the acquisition of language by children where concepts are in the process of developing. The most important work for showing the effects of language development on particular concepts is Melissa Bowerman's. She claims that in some cases children gradually work out the categories of meaning implicit in the structure of language on the basis of experience of language itself (Bowerman, 1982). Some evidence for this position comes from the development of use of the prefix *un-*, which Bowerman studied longitudinally in her own two children over several years. In English, *un-*, used as a reversitive, can be prefixed to certain verbs but not to others. Thus we can say *uncover, uncoil, undress, unlock, unroll, untangle* and *unwind*; but not **unbreak, *undry, *unhang, *unheat, *unembarrass* and **unmelt*. Whorf used the term 'cryptotypes' to describe the covert semantic categories that determine what items may co-occur with others linguistically. Thus, *un-* in its meaning indicating a reversal of action can only be applied to verbs that share a covering, enclosing and surface-attaching meaning. In some sense, *cover, coil, dress, lock, roll, tangle* and *wind* are said to share this cryptotype. Bowerman studied the children's use of *un-* as a prefix. At first the children used *un-* as an unanalysed unit, usually in semantically appropriate contexts. In a second stage, the children generalized the prefix to novel verbs, but appeared to be unaware of the covert semantic class to whose members *un-* could be attached. Thus, they produced utterances containing such uses as **uncome* and **unhate*. Finally, their errors showed that they recognized a semantic category associated with *un-*, and they began to limit *un-* to verbs fitting that category. In other words, they progressed from the initial use of *un-* with no awareness of internal structure, to a second stage in which they had figured out the semantic force of *un-* and could generate new *un-* verbs with a reversitive sense. Finally, they progressed to a state where they gave evidence of recognizing that verbs that can be prefixed by *un-* share a subtle semantic characteristic.

It is this third stage that is important for the present argument. Bowerman claims that it is the experience of language itself that leads to the construction of the concept that constitutes the cryptotype. For example, the category of actions involving covering, enclosing or surface attachment – a category crucial to correct usage – has little non-linguistic utility, and it is unlikely that children would otherwise form such a category. Bowerman hypothesizes instead that children come to appreciate the semantic correlates of *un-* and thus form what Whorf termed its cryptotype only on the basis of regularities observed in the linguistic forms used originally on a piecemeal basis.

Bowerman (1980) gives further examples of this process in the idiosyncratic uses her children made of *hi* and *gidi*. Bowerman reports that she had sometimes put a finger puppet or an object like the cap of a pen on the end of a finger and, pretending it was a little person, would say 'Hi.' Her child, Christy, instead of interpreting *hi* in its intended meaning as a greeting, apparently constructed the hypothesis that it encoded a concept of 'situations in which something rests on or covers the hand or foot'. Thus Christy used *hi* when she stuck her hand inside her snowsuit hood and held it up; as a washrag drifted across her foot in the tub; as she showed her mother a tiny object balanced on the end of her finger; when a shirt fell off the side of the crib and landed over her foot; and so on (see Bowerman, 1980, p. 291, for the complete list of uses). In a similar way, Eva apparently constructed a concept to cover the use of *gidi* (possibly a rendition of *excuse me*) which involved the actual or anticipated physical displacement of objects. She produced this word as she brushed against a hanging towel, as she set a hairbrush to one side, as she shoved a toy car through a pile of beads, and as she pushed past people or objects in narrow hallways. Bowerman hypothesized that Eva's attention was drawn to physical displacement because she had possibly heard the phrase *excuse me* across a variety of superficially diverse situations, most of which shared this abstract element. Bowerman suggests that the repeated exposure to a particular word or phrase (such as *hi* or *excuse me*) 'started her working on a concept she probably would not have formulated at that time in the absence of this specific kind of linguistic input' (p. 293).

Bowerman's position is an interesting one. It argues that, in some instances, children form concepts on the basis of language. This view is not totally without problems, however. For example, in the case of forming a general concept based on a number of piecemeal uses of a syntactic structure, what purpose would the concept serve? That is, if the child already produced correct syntactic structures on a piecemeal basis, what need would there be of forming a cryptotype to cover instances of productive use? (Such a description, of course, may help to account for productive 'errors'.) More importantly, is it really possible to write a 'semantic' (conceptual) description for every syntactic structure? It is not possible to do this for gender, nor has it been possible to do it for the process/stative-verb distinction. Indeed, it is doubtful that it can be done for any syntactic description or category. (But see Pinker, 1989, for both a criticism of and a new use of this approach.) Even the past tense does not always refer to past time (cf. Maratsos and Chalkley, 1980). Nevertheless, it may still be the case that, for isolated parts of the language system, children do form concepts that they would not form were it not for the linguistic regularities that they observe in the input. Bowerman's careful observations are compelling evidence that this occurs, at least on occasion, for some parts of the language system. There is some evidence, then, that language may play a part in the formation of concepts. Is this incompatible with the cognition hypothesis or can such findings be reconciled?

The Interaction Hypothesis

One of the more recent views on the relation between language and thought can be called the 'interaction hypothesis'. Rice and Kemper (1984) characterize the interaction hypothesis as holding that linguistic expressions can alter the nature of the child's independently developing cognitive processes. It appears that Gopnik, who was cited earlier, in the section on the cognition hypothesis, actually holds this view. The evidence that was given there in support of the cognition hypothesis could be interpreted as supporting the view that language and cognition develop interactively. For example, in one study Gopnik (1984) traced the developmental use of the word *gone* and the concepts it encodes in nine children who were 12, 15 or 18 months old at the start of the study. She found that the children acquired the word *gone* when they were in the midst of developing the concept that it encodes. Conceptual and semantic development seemed to proceed simultaneously. Gopnik speculated that use of the word *gone* may have helped the child to develop the object concept. For example, *gone*, when applied to objects disappearing in all sorts of ways, might lead the child to consider the similarities of these events. Schlesinger (1977a) had earlier put forward a similar theoretical view. As he put it, 'On first dealing with an aspect of his surroundings the child may understand it only vaguely and imperfectly; the manner of

⸺ it then points the way for the child to gain a firmer grasp of ⸺on in question' (p. 166).

Shatz (1987) has been developing a theory which in some ⸺ compatible with the view that language and cognitive develop-⸺ceed in parallel and influence each other. She suggests that seve⸺ ⸺reas of child development consist of what she calls 'bootstrapping operations' – operations that allow children to use the competencies they already possess to attain still more complex competencies. In language acquisition, she argues, there is piecemeal organization and reorganization of an internally represented system. As part of the process, children incorporate bits of heard speech into their own system. They use terms that are not fully understood, but in the process of doing so their attention is drawn to particular regularities, which in turn contributes to cognitive growth.

There is, however, evidence of a different nature that is worrying for the cognition hypothesis even in this weaker interactionist form. Having seen that non-linguistic cognitive processes are not *sufficient* to explain language acquisition, I turn finally to evidence that non-linguistic cognitive processes may not even be *necessary* for language acquisition to occur. That is, the linguistic system may be independent of more generalized cognitive operations and may develop by its own separate routes.

The Two-Routes Hypothesis of Language and Thought

A Chomskian perspective

In the linguistic literature, strong evidence has now been put forward that language acquisition proceeds in a manner that can be interpreted as being independent of the cognitive processes and products as those terms have been used here. Chomsky (1986, 1987, 1988) has given compelling arguments that language acquisition as we know it in the human species could not occur were it not for specifically linguistic innate processes. That is, he claims that language is not learned but occurs as a natural product of growth, much as physical organs in the body grow. What is the evidence for this position, which some psychologists see as controversial?

Chomsky begins with the observation that children need only be exposed to simple sentences in order to acquire competence in the abstract and more complex structures of the language. In one set of examples (1986, p. 8) he focuses on structure dependence of rules. Thus, in the sentence 'I wonder who the men expected to see them' the pronoun *them* can be referentially dependent on the antecedent *the men*; but in the sentence 'The men expected to see them' it cannot. Chomsky asks, 'How does every child know, unerringly, to interpret the clause differently in the two cases?' And why does no one have to direct the learner's attention to these facts? In this case, the correct hypotheses have to do with dependence on grammatical structure, and not on linear word order or on a variety of other hypotheses that the child could logically apply. There are really two aspects to this problem of acquisition. One states the problem and the other is the partial answer to that problem.

Chomsky states the problem as 'Plato's problem': 'How comes it that human beings, whose contacts with the world are brief and personal and limited, are able to know as much as they do know?' (Chomsky, 1988, pp. 3–4). Faced with linguistic structures, the individual is able to make correct judgements on what turn out to be complex matters concerning what the reference of, say, pronouns in the above examples can and cannot be. This is true of structures to which the person may never have been exposed. Language-acquisition data clearly show, moreover, that children do not try out logical hypotheses and then have these disconfirmed either by later data or by explicit instruction of a language-teacher. Chomsky's solution to 'Plato's problem' is that we entertain only particular hypotheses and these are innately determined. That is, certain aspects of our knowledge and understanding are innate, 'part of our biological endowment, genetically determined, on a par with the elements of our common nature that cause us to grow arms and legs rather than wings' (p. 4). The way this works has to do with what Chomsky calls 'parameters'. There are certain universals of language which have 'settings'. According to the input data, these parameters are set one way or another – automatically and without any conscious awareness. Thus, for example, some languages require subject pronouns to be present while others allow them to be omitted. Exposure to a particular language fixes the parameter and determines the child's subsequent responses. That all of this happens automatically and without general learning mechanisms being involved is not a popular conclusion in a culture that has placed such emphasis on an empiricist tradition, yet Chomsky shows that it is hard to suppose otherwise. This brief description of his views may not be too convincing, but the interested reader should consult Chomsky (1986, 1988) for full details of the arguments; Chomsky's logic and empirical examples make for a strong case that language acquisition could hardly occur in any other manner.

What bearing do Chomsky's arguments have on the language–cognition issue? If his views are correct, it would appear that language has its own separate and independent origin and will develop regardless of ordinary impairments in more general cognitive processes. (There may be particular innate language concepts, a point to which we will return.) There is good evidence that this is the case from studies of the blind and of the deaf. But I want to turn now to evidence from a particular case of dissociation between language and general intellectual mechanisms.

The case for language–cognition dissociation

The notion that language acquisition may in some important respects be independent of non-linguistic cognitive processes is not new. The fact that language acquisition is relatively independent of intelligence has often been taken as evidence in support of the idea that language is an independent faculty separate from non-linguistic cognitive abilities. Lenneberg, Nichols and Rosenberger (1964), in their famous early study of 61 Down's syndrome children, found that on language-imitation tests these children performed like younger normal children. It was the passing of particular motor milestones, and not the particular IQ level, that best predicted language development. One could argue that achieving particular motor milestones is a sign of maturational development and language would be one of these. Under this view, language just 'grows' and does not depend on the exercise of any general learning principles.

There is more recent evidence that the relationship between language acquisition and specific cognitive developments is not as close as has often been supposed. For example, Miller and Chapman (1984) report data from a study by Paul, Chapman and Wanska (1980) showing that mean length of utterance (MLU) was a better predictor of complex-sentence acquisition in 3–6-year-olds than was non-verbally measured cognition. In fact, non-verbal cognition *did* account for additional variance, but in the semantic rather than in the syntactic component of the grammar. (See Menyuk, 1975, for other early criticisms of interpretations of a direct relationship between language and specific cognitive developments.)

It has, in fact, often been argued that the early utterances of young children are more adequately characterized by some kind of 'semantic' grammar. (The problem of what it is that psychologists, as opposed to linguists, call 'semantic' will be addressed further on.) This position requires the additional assumption that the child must switch to a different kind of truly syntactic set of principles at a later age, since a semantic grammar is inadequate for characterizing adult language competence. Such a position constitutes a discontinuous theory of language acquisition (Gleitman and Wanner, 1982). This view, however, has been challenged. Levy (1983) has shown through studies of gender acquisition in several languages that very young children rely on phonological properties of the input to decide on grammatical gender of words, rather than taking advantage of natural gender distinctions that the denotation of many of the words involve. (Children can, of course, make use of the semantic distinctions in their use of pronouns when this involves natural gender.) The point is that children often focus on phonological cues instead of using semantics for making grammatical gender distinctions. Levy claims that the early two-word stage grammars cannot, therefore, be exclusively 'semantic'. The child makes non-semantic generalizations; at least some part of language growth would appear to be directed by principles that are independent of meaning in the usual sense.

In a related vein, Corrigan (1979) had reviewed evidence on the cognitive correlates of early language and found many conflicting results. For example, language was found in some studies to be occurring before those substages of sensorimotor intelligence which Piagetians had argued were prerequisite for language. In her perceptive discussion, Corrigan focused criticism on the measures used, on variations in task factors and administration, and on the fact that different criteria were used for assignment of behaviours to particular cognitive stages. In an earlier section of this chapter, studies were cited that made a more careful delineation of the exact cognitive attainments that are thought to be necessary for language to occur. Nevertheless, there have now been studies that undermine that position. The fact that certain associations or correlations are observable in normally developing children, while often compelling, is not definitive.

In this regard, evidence for language acquisition comes from the sometimes rare cases in which the usual picture of development is disturbed. Curtiss and Yamada (1981), Yamada (1981), and Yamada and Curtiss (1981), for example, have presented some case studies of hyper-linguistic children whose language abilities far outstrip the rest of their cognitive development.

One of their cases, Anthony, was studied for six months from the time he was $6\frac{1}{2}$ years of age. They reported a Leiter IQ (Leiter, 1979) of 50 and a mental age of 2 years 9 months when Anthony was 5 years 2 months old. Curtiss and Yamada gave Anthony an array of non-language cognitive tasks. These included batteries of Piagetian measures (conservation, classification, seriation, etc.) and a variety of other measures, including drawing, copying, nesting of objects, hierarchical construction, logical sequencing, auditory-memory span, the Benton Visual Retention Test (Benton, 1965), the Knox Cube Test (Knox, 1974), figure–ground perception tests, tests of embedded figures and many others. Language was assessed through a specially designed battery of tests given in both a receptive and a spontaneous speech form.

Curtiss and Yamada report that on the non-linguistic cognitive tests Anthony scored below all the norms and/or below the 2-year-old level. On only one test did Anthony show normal, age-level performance – a test of auditory (verbal) short-term memory. These performances contrasted sharply with those on tests of his language abilities. His best performance on these tests was on items examining syntactic structure. In his spontaneous speech Anthony was highly advanced in his use of syntactic structures. He used 61 of the 68 different elements and structures that Curtiss and Yamada analysed, including infinitival and sentential complements, relative clauses and other subordinate clauses. He also used a variety of morphological features that were consistent and well-formed. Nevertheless, a number of his grammatical forms were inappropriately used. Curtiss and Yamada gave the following summary of Anthony's performance: 'His ability to use a wide range of syntactic devices . . . to encode his limited and confused thoughts, illustrates the discrepancy between Anthony's grammatical knowledge and his conceptual/cognitive knowledge' (1981, p. 75). They also pointed out that there were certain errors that he never made: 'He did not place verb markers on nouns or vice-versa, and did not use clausal connectors within VP's [verb phrases] or NP's [noun phrases], nor use affixes as prefixes or vice-versa. His errors consisted exclusively of omissions and semantically inappropriate use. Anthony appeared to have extracted purely syntactic and morphological constraints without the semantics which they normally encode' (p. 77).

One nice example of the discrepancy between Anthony's conceptual ability and his linguistic ability comes from his use of pronouns. Curtiss and Yamada reported that Anthony rarely made any errors on pronoun-case categories – only two errors in 347 pronoun uses. In other words, Anthony correctly marked subject and object forms of his pronouns. But he made frequent errors of number and gender, producing such utterances as '*He's* a girl' and '*They* are putting *their* shoes on' (for *she* and *her*). The example of Anthony may give us some clues as to what exactly is prerequisite for syntactic development. At first sight this would appear to be auditory short-term memory, since this was the only cognitive test that Anthony performed at an age-appropriate level. Indeed, in another case that provided strong evidence of good syntactic development in spite of poor conceptual ability – that of a young girl with Turner's syndrome (a chromosomal abnormality in which there is pathological variation in or deletion of the second x-chromosome) – Yamada and Curtiss (1981) again found that the one non-language test on which the subject performed well was a test of auditory short-term memory. However, some doubt is cast on even this 'cognitive prerequisite' for syntactic acquisition by a third case study. Yamada (1981) has reported on the language and cognitive abilities of Marta, a hyperlinguistic, retarded adolescent who also evidenced advanced syntactic ability in spite of limited conceptual abilities. But, unlike the other two cases, Marta also scored poorly on auditory short-term memory tasks.

These cases appear to demonstrate that syntax can be acquired even with severely impaired or limited conceptual and cognitive development. This conclusion is further supported by the condition of children with internal hydrocephaly, who talk excessively, but whose speech, if they are mentally retarded, lacks content. Taylor (1959) described such children as having an impressive vocabulary. Hadenius, Hagberg, Hyttnäs-Bensch and Sjögren (1962) reported on six hydrocephalic children in which mental retardation was observed along with 'a peculiar contrast between a good ability to learn words and to talk, and not knowing what they are talking about' (p. 118). Hadenius et al. described these children as loving to chatter but thinking illogically, and therefore coined the term 'cocktail-party syndrome' for the condition. Similarly, Ingram and Naughton (1962) described nine of 16 cerebral-palsy patients with arrested hydrocephalus who fitted this description. There was a marked disparity between what they could say and what they could do. Ingram and Naughton referred to these children as 'chatterboxes', 'excessively talkative' or 'bletherers'. The term 'chatterbox syndrome' has now come to be used to describe this condition.

Several later studies have provided information on the 'chatterbox syndrome'. Swisher and Pinsker (1971) studied 11 children, ranging in age from 3 years 2 months to 7 years 10 months, who suffered from spina bifida cystica, had a history of hydrocephalus and were considered by clinicians to be hyperverbal. Their language was compared to that of a control group matched for age, congenital physical handicap and a history of exposure to hospitalizations. Results showed a quantitative basis for the impression that these children were hyperverbal. They used significantly more words and vocal response units and initiated more speech than the control group. Utterances were also qualitatively classified as being either appropriate, inappropriate or bizarre. Eight of the 11 hydrocephalic children used some language that was either inappropriate or bizarre, but only two of the control group did so. Indeed, of those eight hydrocephalic children, six produced both inappropriate and bizarre language while none of the control children did so.

Anderson and Spain (1977) reported a study of 145 spina bifida children aged 6 years who had originally been observed when they were 3 years of age. They reported that 40 per cent of the children showed the hyperverbal syndrome although only about half of that number exhibited it to any significant degree. The hyperverbal children were typically female and were poor intellectually, with considerably higher verbal than performance skills. Analysis of the children's spontaneous speech showed that they used quite complex syntax, but often inaccurately. They were described as producing bizarre utterances, as having a tendency to change sentence in midflow, and as making more false starts to sentences and delivering more incomplete sentences than a group of normal children matched for verbal ability on the Wechsler Preschool and Primary Scale of Intelligence (Wechsler, 1967). They also produced many more clichés or adult-type phrases, although they rarely gave the impression of understanding their meaning. Anderson and Spain concluded that these children clearly did not really understand what they were saying.

Finally, Tew (1979) studied 49 children with spina bifida cystica. On the basis of their language in an informal setting, children were classified as showing 'chatterbox syndrome' if they met a number of specified criteria. On this basis, 20 of the 49 children were so classified. These 20 children were then compared to the remaining 29 spina bifida children on a number of measures. One finding is particularly interesting: Tew reported that the children classified as hyperverbal scored from 26 to 32 IQ points *less* than the other spina bifida children on all three measures of IQ – verbal, performance and full-scale. The mean verbal IQ of the 'chatterbox syndrome' group was 65, whereas the mean IQ of the remaining spina bifida children was 92. Full-scale IQ scores in the two groups was 55 for the hyperverbal children and 88 for the non-hyperverbal children. The hyperverbal children, then, exhibited in extreme form fluent speech coupled with poor understanding and limited general cognitive abilities.

It is interesting to explore this dissociation of language and conceptual understanding more closely. For several years I have been exploring in some detail both the language and cognitive abilities of a girl with 'chatterbox syndrome'. D. H. is a spina-bifida child with arrested hydrocephalus (see Cromer, forthcoming, for details of this case). Her speech is fluent, appropriate and not bizarre, is filled with complex syntactic forms, shows the correct use of semantic constraints, an extensive vocabulary, and incorporates the use of normal pragmatic devices. She gives every evidence of understanding the conversation. Table 2.2 presents a small part of her verbal output in an attempt to convey the fluency of her speech. There are two issues that must be dealt with before any claims can be made about this case. First, is D. H.'s intellectual ability so limited? And, second, is her language really so good?

Her intellectual ability has been explored at some length. On a large variety of standardized tests, she performs at the severely retarded level. Suspecting that the typical tests required some ability on which she was failing, we tried an inspection time task that does not require reflection (Anderson, 1988). She again responded at the severely retarded level.

Table 2.2 Two samples from transcripts of D. H. in conversation with R. C.

D. H.	R. C.
	Ah, I see. So there's a whole story there. She might fall in. If she fell in the water what would happen then?
Well, she . . . if she . . . if she was a good swimmer she could probably swim to safety.	
	Uh-hmm.
But . . . and also she's got a life-jacket on.	
	Right.
So that would save her.	
	Right.
Like I fell in. . . . I'm a guide you see and we went to. . . . We go to this river to do canoeing and I fell in the river once.	
	Ah.
That wasn't funny; that was frightening. I said I'd never go . . . I said I'd never go canoeing again, and I still go canoeing now. And that's three years later that was. But my Dad's got a canoe and we go canoeing. I threw my Dad in once. Me and my brother threw him in together.	
	Uh-hmm.
That was funny that was.	
	Would you like to see another picture?
Yes.	

★   ★   ★

D. H.	R. C.
	So how long have you been here then?
Two and half years.	
	Uh-huh.
And Dad's getting fed up with moving around. He thinks it's time that I settle down – to school, which is fair enough. To him, it . . . he feels it's going to ruin my whole life if I don't settle down sometime.	
	Uh-huh.

Table 2.2 *continued*

D. H.	R. C.
So I'm gonna have to, at some point, settle down, somewhere,	
	Uh-huh.
somehow. Mum didn't mind me moving about, but Dad objected to it because he knew it was bothering me and it was bothering my school work.	
	Um-hmm.
And now I'm [getting on] like a house on fire he doesn't want to destroy it. He said I'm not going to destroy this for her, she can just keep going.	
	Uh-huh.
I love to move around with my Dad because of his work.	
	Um-hmm.
But he's feels if he keeps on doing that to me, I'm never gonna get anywhere.	
	Um-hmm.
Which is fair enough. I've got friends here.	

Source: Cromer, forthcoming.

Finally, she functions in everyday life at the retarded level. She has been unable to learn to read and write in her late teenage years and cannot handle money. As for whether her language is really so good, everyone talking to her or seeing a video of her agrees about her excellent use of syntax, semantics and pragmatic discourse devices. Curiously, on standardized language measures she performs below age level although much higher than on non-language tasks. This has been reported for other 'chatterbox syndrome' individuals as well. But it may be that our current language tests have a metalinguistic component which is not a problem for normal children but tends to prevent 'chatterbox syndrome' subjects from displaying competence. Moreover, such a metalinguistic component is not necessarily involved in grammaticality judgements of various complex linguistic forms. Making such a judgement merely requires *use* of the linguistic competence to indicate whether the utterance can be parsed or not. Indeed, D. H. performs almost without error on grammaticality judgements.

So the question remains of how she can have acquired excellent linguistic competence in spite of limited conceptual knowledge. One can speculate that she in fact has a particular kind of conceptual competence that is not measured by tests examining what are usually referred to as 'concepts'. This competence would relate to what have been referred to as 'language concepts', including such things as 'agent of an action', 'object of an action', and so on. Such language concepts do not have to be learned and may well be innate (Chomsky, 1988). D. H. possesses these language concepts and the semantic underpinnings of language, as well as phonology and syntax. It has been increasingly popular to speculate about whether there are modular components of human knowledge. 'Language' has often figured prominently in these speculations, but the different advocates of this position often disagree about what a module includes. Does modularity apply only to the core syntax? Or does it apply to the language system in a broader sense, as in Tim Shallice's notion (Shallice, 1988) of 'isolable subsystems' seen from a neurological point of view, in which modularity is to a great extent defined by what aspects of language are impaired by specific neurological damage? Or is modularity broader even than the syntax itself, as Fodor (1983) seems to suggest in discussing modularity? A case such as that of D. H. may help to illuminate these issues. What can be said is that D. H. appears to possess the basic phonology, the crucial pragmatics, semantic mappings and syntax. If these interpretations of our observations of D. H. are correct, then language acquisition proceeds on a different course, basically independent of general cognitive development.

Conclusions

The first two sections of this chapter reviewed evidence for the 'cognition hypothesis' – the idea that concepts and developing cognitive abilities have effects on language acquisition; and for the contrary, Whorfian position – the view that language can have effects on the development of concepts. An interactionist position has also been reviewed. But 'correlations' based on the development of normal, unimpaired individuals are never decisive. What cases such as that of D. H. seem to show is that general cognitive mechanisms are neither necessary nor sufficient for the growth of language.

Notes

1 There has been some controversy over whether the present perfect *to refer to relevance*, a late acquisition in the American children, is used earlier by

children in language communities where perfect-tense forms are more frequent in adult speech. Fletcher (1981), for example, using data from British children collected by Wells (1979), reports that all 60 British children studied used a form of the perfect by age 3 years 6 months and that 50 per cent of them had done so by age 2 years 6 months. Fletcher's more detailed analysis, however, showed that the forms included under the adult category of 'perfect tense' in fact encoded recent past events, or were used by children as a stative present to refer to possessions and attributes. Fletcher's functional analysis of the use of various forms of the perfect by British children is surely a welcome advance, but I can see nothing in his data that undermines the cognitive interpretation that I put forward in 1968 concerning the children's failure to refer to relevance.

Gathercole (1986a) has shown an earlier acquisition of the present perfect by Scottish children, who are exposed to the form with far greater frequency than American children. However, she was considering the perfect as used to encode a variety of meanings. Examination of the categories of meaning in her data reveals that the category that requires the present perfect to encode relevance ('perfect of a persistent situation', in which the verb form is used in reference to an event or state that began at some past moment and has continued up to the present) is also acquired late by the Scottish children – the only two children (out of the sample of 12) who used the form at all doing so at ages 4 years 4 months and 4 years 11 months. Gathercole makes clear in her conclusion that her study was not concerned with the issue that is of importance to the cognition hypothesis. As she put it, 'This study did not address the question of when the child begins to appreciate that the present perfect, in contrast to the simple past, entails relevance to the time of utterance' (p. 558). Her data do not dispute the cognition hypothesis as regards acquisition of the perfect tense. Where that form is used to encode cognitively simpler meanings, as in some uses in Scottish English, one would reasonably expect to find children using it – as Gathercole's data indicate. By contrast, the position supporting the cognition hypothesis claimed that 'the reason why [American] children were not producing the perfect tense at an early age was that they were not making reference to what the perfect tense usually expresses' (Cromer, 1974a, reprinted here as chapter 1; see p. 36). (The logic of trying to account for what the child appears to be attempting to express regardless of the *forms* used to encode that expression is discussed below.) Gathercole's data, rather than undermining that claim, in fact reinforce it, since the Scottish children, in spite of greater exposure to and even use of the perfect tense, do not use it to refer to relevance until the same age as the American children – age 4 years 4 months being the earliest in her data.

Weist (1986) cites evidence of earlier use of perfective forms by children acquiring Mandarin Chinese and Finnish. However, without knowing how the forms were used in context by the child, nothing can be concluded as regards the cognition hypothesis. It is simply not the case that one can take the meanings often associated with particular linguistic forms and attribute them to children. Johnston (1985) makes this particularly clear in her discussion of the relation between the acquisition of spatial concepts and their encoding as locatives in children's utterances: 'Parallels between developing spatial concepts and locative acquisition are thus clearest when we consider plausible child meanings rather than the full range of meanings assigned to these words by the adult grammar. Failure to recognize this distinction has yielded mixed results . . .' (p. 970). Gopnik and Meltzoff (1985) have made the same important point in their study of the relation between language and cognition at the one-word stage: 'We must take into account the *way* in which the child uses the word, not just *that* he or she uses it, when we are testing for the relationship between early linguistic and cognitive development' (p. 510; see also Gopnik and Meltzoff, 1986a, p. 1042, and 1986b, p. 199, for similar caveats). As regards the perfect tense in English, Gathercole (1986a) has demonstrated that it encodes a variety of meanings, and even these vary from one dialect of English to another. It is therefore imperative to study the situational context for clues as to what aspects of meaning the child may have been attempting to encode – ideally, independently of the particular linguistic forms used.)

2   The new work of Baillargéon and Spelke (e.g. Baillargéon, 1986, 1987a, 1987b; Baillargéon, Spelke and Wasserman, 1985; Spelke, 1987, 1988) opens up the whole question of the very nature of the development of the object concept. This will no doubt reopen the debate on the relationship between sensorimotor development and language.

3   These spatial notions are Piagetian terms, used to describe the development of the child's representation of space. According to Johnston's brief summary, the earliest spatial notions are bound to object functions such as containment and support. Next, the child has spatial notions based on relations between objects such as proximity, separation, order and surrounding. Finally, projective relations among objects are represented, such that, when a child is asked to place lamp-posts along an imaginary street, he or she will not only place the items next to each other, in a 'meandering row' (Johnston, 1985, p. 969), as during the previous stage, but will also create the projective axis, thereby representing a spatial perspective.

4   It should be carefully noted that I am not entertaining the 'strict' Whorfian position that one would not be able to think particular thoughts unless one had learned a particular language. Rather, what is being considered here is a Whorfian-like notion that the language one is acquiring can *influence* the concepts that one eventually has. See Fodor (1975) for a thorough discussion of this point in relation to an inner language of thought. For example, Fodor notes, 'it is necessary to distinguish the concepts that *can* be entertained . . . from the ones that actually get employed. This latter class is obviously sensitive to the particular experiences of the code-user, and there is no principled reason why the experiences involved in learning a natural language should not have a specially deep effect in determining how the resources of the inner language are exploited' (pp. 85–6).

5   Strictly speaking, some of the experiments that are reported in the following sections are not 'Whorfian' in that they do not identify and examine the 'world

view' that the particular linguistic forms may embody. See McNeill (1987, pp. 196–7) for a good discussion of this. Here, however, the object is not to examine the Whorfian hypothesis *per se*. Rather, the interest is in a more general question: does the acquisition of a particular language *influence* various cognitive processes and their products (categories, concepts, etc.)?

6 The Berlin and Kay study is often cited as evidence both of the universality of human colour perception (at least for focal colours) and of an evolutionary sequence of the number and ordering of focal-colour terms within languages. It should be noted, however, that this study is in fact seriously methodologically flawed to the point where one might even claim that its conclusions are simply unwarranted. For example, most psychologists who cite this work appear unaware that the informants for 19 of the 20 languages originally studied were bilingual speakers residing in the San Francisco area (usually, it seems, only one speaker per language). Hickerson (1971), in an important examination of the Berlin and Kay work, notes Erwin's carefully controlled 1961 study of colour terms used by Navajo monolinguals and Navajo–English bilinguals; this concluded that the colour categories used by the bilinguals differed systematically from those used by monolinguals. Similarly, Lenneberg and Roberts (1956) had found significant differences in the colour-mapping of monolingual and bilingual Zunis. In a more extensive study, Caskey-Sirmons and Hickerson (1977) examined the colour categorizations of 50 informants, who were either monolingual speakers of Korean, Japanese, Hindi, Cantonese or Mandarin Chinese (five groups of five) or bilingual speakers of English and one of these other languages (five groups of five). This study showed that in every case there were regular patterns of difference between the monolinguals and the bilinguals; the colour categorizations of the bilinguals, whatever their first language, had come to resemble to some degree that of monolingual speakers of their second language. This result is especially damaging for the conclusions of Berlin and Kay, since those were based almost entirely on bilinguals.

The study was then extended to 98 languages. Again, however, many researchers who cite these data seem unaware as to what this extension actually entailed. It was based on a library search for anthropological descriptions of colour terms in these languages, a good number of which dated back to the late nineteenth and early twentieth century; it did not consist of experimentally examining native informants as to the location of their colour terms on the colour charts. Furthermore, Hickerson (1971) has given details as to the extremely limited range of languages and language groups represented by the 98 languages in a way that raises doubts as to the claimed universality of the findings.

Perhaps most important of all is the problem of 'data reduction' and the associated classification of the basic colour terms. Hickerson (1971) gives several examples of problems in this aspect of the analysis by Berlin and Kay. One, which particularly well illustrates the problem is the analysis made of the colour terms of the Murray Islanders based on the 1901 publication by W. H. R. Rivers of the Cambridge anthropological expedition to the Torres

Straits. It will be recalled that Berlin and Kay restricted their definition of basic colour terms in a language by a number of criteria. One of these was that 'colour terms that are also the name of an object characteristically having that colour are suspect'. Rivers had elicited a large number of colour terms; Berlin and Kay pointed out that many of these were formed by reduplication from the names of various natural objects. Thus, *mammam* (red) is related to *mam* (blood); *bambam* (yellow, orange) to *bam* (turmeric); *siusiu* (yellow) to *siu* (yellow ochre); *soskepusoskep* (green) to *soskep* (bile, gall-bladder); *bulubulu* (blue) to the English term *blue*; and *pipi* (grey) to *pi* (ashes). Two other terms are also given: *kakekakek* (white), though also obviously a reduplication, is shown as having an unknown derivation; and *golegole* (black) is related to *gole* (cuttlefish), which is then listed as a 'suspicious' derivation. Through the (inconsistent) application of their criteria, Berlin and Kay analyse this language as having only two basic colour terms – white and black! (Interestingly, the term *orange* is allowed as a basic colour term in English.)

Reduplication itself was used to eliminate colour terms from some languages on the criterion of morphological complexity; basic terms had to be morphologically simple according to the Berlin and Kay analysis. However, Michaels (1977) has challenged the very use of this criterion as in any way meaningful. He points out that it is difficult to see in what way morphologically complex words are necessarily non-basic in a definable semantic sense. As he put it, 'Is *blackboard* less basic than *slate*, *headache* less basic than *migraine*, *handkerchief* less basic than anything? In English, the BCT's [basic colour terms] are non-compounds. However, English utilizes compounds for basic terminology in other semantic domains' (p. 336).

One can see the absurdity of the Berlin and Kay criteria for eliminating colour terms from various non-Western languages by considering particular cases. Wescott (1970), for example, applied the Berlin and Kay criteria to Bini colour terms. (Bini is the native language of about 300,000 people in Nigeria.) By so doing, they reduced 42 colour words in Bini to zero basic colour terms!

Some data reduction takes the form not of the elimination of colour terms, but of incorporation of their meanings into what appear to be preconceived categories. Hickerson (1971) examined Berlin and Kay's classification procedure for Tiv, an African language. Tiv is shown as having three basic colour terms: *pupu* is said to refer to very light blues, light greys and white. Berlin and Kay have chosen to gloss this as *white*. The term *ii* refers to green, some blues, some greys, dark colours and black. This is glossed as *black*. Finally, *nyian* is used by the Tiv for 'all warm colours through red to yellow, brown', and this is arbitrarily glossed as *red*. From reductions of this kind, Berlin and Kay claim the existence of a universal evolutionary sequence, such that, if languages have only three basic colour terms, they are always black, white and red. Such problems of data reduction are serious, for they undermine the very claims made by the authors.

The Berlin and Kay findings are often cited as showing identical focal-colour categories across the speakers of diverse languages. My own inspection of their data graphs for the 20 languages (Berlin and Kay, 1969, pp. 114–33) leaves me with the impression that their claim is overstated in any case. Each page contains a set of the 329 squares corresponding to the 329 chips used. The focal colours and the boundaries of those colours are shown on the graphs, one language per page. These graphs, however, do not seem to show identical focal categories for these speakers but merely general areas of colour similarities. That is, the informants from the various languages had not chosen absolutely identical colour chips as their focal colours; and the colour boundaries varied rather widely across the languages.

7   It is also interesting to note that Heider herself (1971) points out that her findings do not match Berlin and Kay's evolutionary order. She states that this may be due to the unreliability of the literature on which Berlin and Kay based their evolutionary account.

8   Carroll and Casagrande also tested 47 white, middle-class, English-speaking children from Boston. Surprisingly, this group behaved like the Navajo-dominant group: they tended to categorize objects by form. By way of explanation, Carroll and Casagrande claim that middle-class children in America have a great deal of practice with form-board type toys, i.e. wooden or plastic shapes that have to be fitted into their corresponding holes. Inspection of the results for each set, however, reveals a major difference between the two cultural groups. The Boston children chose by shape across all the categorization sets – the percentage of children doing so never falling below 70.2 on any set where shape was involved. By contrast, the Navajo-dominant children chose by shape mainly on those items that are linguistically differentially encoded in the Navajo language. The Navajo-dominant children did *not* differ from the English-dominant Navajo children on two of the three sets which the Navajo language does not differentially encode. Carroll and Casagrande concluded that the tendency of a child to match objects on the basis of shape rather than size or colour is enhanced by two types of experience. One of these is the acquisition of a language like Navajo in which the grammatical structure requires the speaker to make shape discriminations. The other is the general learning experience in which the child partakes – in the case of the Boston children, practice with toys involving the fitting of shapes into their corresponding forms.

9   For consistency in the present chapter, I am contrasting what most current researchers call the 'semantic' view with a linguistic distributional view. Gathercole herself, however, is more precise, and in her 1985 paper compares three views. She is more accurate in using the term 'semantic' to refer to the meanings of the terms themselves. She then contrasts this with the 'ontological' view, which claims that the count/mass distinction resides not in the words themselves, but in the objects to which they refer in the world. However, within the framework of her experiment, the semantic and ontological views make the same predictions. These are contrasted with what Gathercole calls the 'contextual' view, which attributes the count/mass distinction to a distinction in the use of terms – a view closely related (but not identical) to what is usually called the distributional view. In a later paper, Gathercole (1986b) defines the contextual view in a way that allows either the linguistic or

non-linguistic context to define the count/mass distinction. She further adds a 'deep structure' view. For our present purposes this is not important. Her experimental predictions are applicable to the simple distinction captured in contrasting the 'real-world' view – mistakenly referred to by most child-language researchers and psycholinguists as the 'semantic' view – with a linguistic distributional view.

10 If one takes a Fodorian view, such concepts are not 'acquired' but are part of the human language of thought. They may, however, remain unexploited by the individual in the absence of particular experiences. See above, note 4.

11 Unfortunately, Tzeng and Hung (1981) tend towards overinterpretation of the data they review when they say 'In other words, the linguistic-deterministic view does have much empirical support' (p. 252). In my view, the orthographic system is not strictly part of the linguistic system.

3

Developmental Strategies for Language

Introductory Comment

After 15 years, this essay remains relevant for the study of language use by adults and children. A brief discussion of some recent interesting new ideas and experimental methodologies is added here because they provide a new perspective to the discussion of strategies.

The main thrust of the original essay was to examine the roots of the strategy notion, and to portray the roles it had played in the investigation of language use and language acquisition. Throughout the essay it is emphasized that investigating children's and adults' use of perceptual and general cognitive strategies does not, and cannot in principle, contribute to an understanding and explanation of *linguistic* competence and its acquisition. It is argued that strategies reflect what children do when they *lack* certain linguistic structures required for solving a particular task, and also reflect the short-cuts which adults use in order to avoid a full syntactic analysis.

In recent years interesting suggestions have been put forward which, in effect, extend this chapter's conclusions. Researchers in developmental psycholinguistics have paid increasing attention to the subject of *strategies* as they have re-examined the relationship between linguistic competence and performance. Trying to establish ways of testing linguistic knowledge proper has become more than merely

This chapter (copyright © 1976 by Academic Press Ltd) was first published in Vernon Hamilton and Magdalen D. Vernon (eds), *The Development of Cognitive Processes* (London and New York: Academic Press, 1976), pp. 305–58, and is reprinted here by kind permission of Academic Press.

Richard Cromer had intended to write a short update to this chapter. In the event he was unable to do so himself. The Introductory Comment was therefore written by Sigrid Lipka on the basis of several conversations with Richard Cromer.

an experimental problem. Stephen Crain, in particular, has emphasized that non-linguistic factors, some of which had previously been studied under the heading of strategies, might conceal knowledge of linguistic structure that an individual actually possesses. Crain presents convincing data to illustrate this point (see Crain, 1987, for a summary). Young children, for example, demonstrate linguistic knowledge of relative clauses, co-ordination and subordination, and temporal terms at a much earlier age than previously assumed (i.e. at about age 3). The catch is that this is only found if the test situation is optimal with regard to planning the sequence of actions required in giving a test response, if pragmatic presuppositions are fulfilled, and if no unnecessary demands on working memory are made. In other words, the non-optimal performance demands limit the linguistic competence which can be revealed.

Both Crain's recent work, and the essay reprinted here – even though they seem to reach different conclusions about early linguistic competence – are concerned with maintaining a clear distinction between knowledge of linguistic structure and the outcome on performance measures. What is needed is a framework within which to decide which factors contribute to performance on a linguistic task. If there is confusion of these matters, there is a danger of incorrectly attributing linguistic knowledge to a child (or adult) when the task can actually be solved by use of strategies alone. On the other hand, one might incorrectly attribute too little linguistic competence if the way the task is constructed makes it impossible for linguistic competence to be displayed.

Introduction

In the 1950s, Bruner, Goodnow and Austin (1956) posed the question, 'How do people achieve the information necessary for isolating and learning a concept?' In the course of analysing the data from a series of experiments on concept attainment, these authors arrived at the conceptualization of 'strategies' to account for the behaviour of individuals in various laboratory experiments. A strategy describes regularities observed in decision-making. In a concept-attainment task, subjects were first shown a positive instance of a concept on a card. They were then allowed to choose cards for testing, one at a time, and were told whether or not they were positive instances of the concept. Particular strategies were inferred from the patterns of decisions made on successive cards. These strategies included simultaneous scanning (testing hypotheses to see which were still tenable and which had been eliminated), successive scanning (limiting new choices to those instances that provided a direct test of a particular hypothesis), conservative focusing (finding a positive instance of the concept to serve as a focus, and then making a sequence of choices in which one attribute at a time was altered), and focus gambling (in which more than one attribute value was changed at a time). The authors were careful to point out that such strategies did not necessarily represent conscious plans by people for achieving and utilizing information. They were merely inferred by the experimenters from the pattern of decisions actually observed.

During the years since the publication of the work on strategies, there has been a renewed interest in the acquisition and development of language. This has partly resulted from the theoretical attack on traditional theories of learning as being incapable of explaining language acquisition (Chomsky, 1959), and from a number of empirical studies which indicate that the child is engaged in a very active process in acquiring language rather than passively responding to differential frequencies of language input and reinforcement (see for example Bellugi-Klima, 1969; Brown, 1973; McNeill, 1970a; and Miller and McNeill, 1969). It is this change of emphasis to the child as an active organism which has sparked an interest in the methods by which he goes about acquiring his native language, and has led to the increasingly frequent use of the term 'strategy' to describe observed developmental language behaviour. In this chapter, a number of different strategies which have been proposed to account for language behaviour will be explored. To begin with, a number of strategies apparently used by very young children will be reviewed. Some of these strategies may help the child to 'get into' the linguistic system, although such a notion is also open to dispute. At some point, it appears that certain perceptual strategies become relatively more important than the earlier action-based strategies. Experiments on these perceptual strategies, particularly those concerned with word order, will be discussed in some detail. As part of that discussion, the problem of individual differences will be raised, and some strategies used by some children will be reviewed. The emphasis will then be changed to one in which broader cognitive strategies associated with language are considered. The penultimate section will raise the issue of whether there are any specifically linguistic grammatical strategies which are used in the acquisition of language. Finally, the entire notion of 'strategy' as applied to language acquisition will be examined, and we can ask whether we have learned anything about that mysterious process, language acquisition, from such an approach.

Some Early Strategies

It has often been assumed that children at a very early age acquire the word order of the grammar of active declarative sentences. It is said that the extension of this word order to other grammatical forms leads to misinterpretations of such forms as the passive, in which the first noun is mistakenly believed to be the actor. For example, children about 4 years of age will often interpret sentences like 'The black cat was chased by the white cat' as if it meant 'The black cat chased the white cat.' As part of a study of this phenomenon, Strohner and Nelson (1974) discovered that the usual assumption that very young children understand the word order of *active* sentences may be false. They presented various sentences to children of age 2–5 years. The child's task was to carry out the action of the sentence with various puppets and toys which were provided. As will be seen in a later section, several investigators have examined the differences between what are called reversible and non-reversible passives. The example just mentioned with the cats, in which either noun could logically serve as the actor, is a reversible passive, but sentences like 'The marble was rolled by the boy' cannot be reversed and still make sense. Strohner and Nelson, however, extended their testing to active sentences as well. Thus, they included not only the various types of passive, but also reversible active sentences and what they called improbable active sentences. An example of the latter would be 'The fence jumps the horse', for which the 'probable' form would be 'The horse jumps the fence.' A reversible active sentence, of course, would be one in which either noun could serve as the actor, as in 'The boy hit the girl.' The results on the 4- and 5-year-olds show strong evidence for a word-order strategy, but the results from the younger children present quite a different picture. The 2-year-olds were not tested on passive sentences, but the 3-year-olds were 100 per cent wrong on improbable passive sentences, which is not surprising since such a result is predicted by both a word-order strategy and by a strategy based on the probability of the event. However, the 2- and 3-year-olds, while 100 per cent correct on probable active sentences, were nearly always wrong on improbable active sentences (83 per cent wrong by 2-years-olds, 90 per cent wrong by 3-year-olds). Strohner and Nelson interpret this as evidence of a 'probable event strategy' used by the younger children, which leads them to interpret sentences describing improbable events as if they referred to probable events. Furthermore, they point out that, although by the age of 5 a child knows even more about event probabilities, such information only occasionally leads the older child to make errors in interpreting improbable sentences. It is also of note that the younger children, when they are not able to extract information about the actor and the object of sentences from syntactic structure, nevertheless do not behave randomly. Instead, they are likely to apply extra-syntactic strategies such as the probable-event strategy in order to interpret sentences.

It is even possible to affect the 'probability' of some sentences by the surrounding linguistic context. In one interesting experiment, Hazel Dewart (1975) studied the comprehension of passive sentences by 20 children aged 3 years 5 months to 4 years 10 months. Some sentences were given without any context. For example, children had to act out with hand puppets sentences like 'The duck is bitten by the monkey.' But some sentences were embedded in an 'appropriate context' ('Poor duck. The duck is bitten by the monkey' and 'Bad monkey. The duck is bitten by the monkey'), while others were given an 'inappropriate context' ('Bad duck. The duck is bitten by the monkey' and 'Poor monkey. The duck is bitten by the monkey'). When the children were divided into those who knew passives and those who did not (as judged from the no-context condition), significant differences emerged. Of the group of 13 children who failed no-context passives, the inappropriate-context condition led to 90 per cent errors (against 63 per cent errors on the appropriate-context condition). In other words, sentence comprehension in $3\frac{1}{2}$–$4\frac{1}{2}$-year-olds can be affected by a short linguistic context which bears on the appropriateness or likelihood of the action. But again this appropriateness affects mainly those children who do not otherwise know how to interpret the structure, and has very little affect on children with adequate syntactic knowledge. This matches the results of Strohner and Nelson on event probability.

Research is beginning to explore the use of other extra-linguistic strategies by young children to interpret certain kinds of sentence. Margaret Donaldson and her associates have been looking at the development of the understanding of certain relational terms such as *more* and *less* (Donaldson and Balfour, 1968; Donaldson and Wales, 1970). She has proposed (Donaldson and McGarrigle, 1974) that lexical and syntactic rules, in some situations, do not provide enough guidance for assigning truth values for such terms. Instead, the child applies a number of what are called 'local rules', which, while not linguistic in any narrow sense, interact with the lexical and syntactic rules when the child is interpreting the sentence. As Donaldson and McGarrigle put it, these local rules determine which features of the referent will be selected as criteria for the assignment of meaning when the child's linguistic rules leave the matter vague. In their experiment, children were presented with differing numbers of cars on two shelves, five cars on one shelf, and four on the other. They were asked, 'Are there more cars on this shelf or more cars on this shelf?', with the experimenter indicating the two shelves in turn. Then, a set of garages was placed over the cars. The set of garages placed on the shelf with five cars had six garages, so that one garage remained empty. The other garage set consisted of four garages, so that every car on the other shelf had a garage over it. The children were then asked the same question again. Of the 40 children aged 3 years to 5 years 2 months, 21 were consistently correct both with the cars alone and with the garages, as adults presumably would be. Another five children consistently chose the less numerous subset as being 'more', with or without the garages in place. But 14 children changed their choice when garages were introduced or removed. Of these, 13 correctly chose the greater number of cars as being 'more' in the absence of garages, but chose the smaller subset as being 'more' when the garages were in place. They would point at the shelf with four cars and say such things as 'There's more on that shelf because there's enough to go in there.' Donaldson and McGarrigle suggest that, instead of assuming that the 'meaning' of an utterance changes frequently for the young child, we should consider the possibility that the child is guided by local rules which determine that an utterance be interpreted first one way and then another. There are 'more' cars in the garage structure which is full although shorter, yet 'more' cars in the longer row when the garages are not there. Only as children grow older will purely linguistic constraints on the interpretation of such utterances become stronger, and the local rules correspondingly come to have a reduced part to play in interpretation. It is not yet clear what these various local rules may be that influence the interpretations of sentences by young children. Perhaps the probable-event strategy mentioned earlier is one type of local rule. Other rules, such as the judgement of differing amounts, would presumably be based on broad developmental cognitive strategies which would be observed in non-linguistic behaviour as well.

Some local rules may be highly specific. Eve Clark (1973b) has proposed two rules for the interpretation of prepositions and has suggested that such rules may interact with the child's linguistic hypotheses about the meanings of words. In one experiment, 70 children between the ages of 1 year 6 months and 5 years were given toy animals and asked to place them *in*, *on* or *under* six reference points. Two of the six items, a box on its side and a tunnel, allowed either *in* or *on*. Two more, a dump truck and a crib, allowed *in* or *under*, and the last two, a table and a bridge, allowed *on* or *under*. The child had to place 24 items, i.e. eight for each of the three prepositions. Each preposition occurred twice with each of the four reference points it was allowed by. The results appeared to show that even the youngest children knew the meaning of *in*. *On* appeared to be of intermediate difficulty, and *under* was the developmentally latest acquisition. However, Clark proposed that two strategies for placing the materials could account for the results. One rule says that if the reference point is a container then X is *in* it. The second rule says that, if the reference point has a horizontal surface, then X is *on* it. These non-linguistic rules are strategies used by young children in a comprehension test in the virtual absence of comprehension. If one looks carefully at what possibilities are allowed by each of the six reference points, it becomes clear that the use of these two rules would lead to results in which the child would appear to know the meaning of *in*, to have no knowledge of *under*, and to perform intermediately on *on*. It is also apparent, however, that such an analysis tells us nothing about how the child acquires language. It merely tells us how he answers questions about the meaning of sentences when he does not yet possess the linguistic structure (semantic or syntactic) necessary for correct interpretation. But Clark proposes that such non-linguistic strategies may play a role in the acquisition of language. Clark cites the suggestion by Slobin (1973) that the main determinant of linguistic acquisition is cognitive complexity. One problem with such a proposal, however, is the difficulty of quantifying or measuring cognitive complexity. Clark proposes that non-linguistic strategies may provide the basis for the child's linguistic hypotheses about such phenomena as the meaning of words, and as such could be used as a kind of cognitive measure. For example, if a strategy coincides with semantic knowledge, there is nothing for the child to learn. But, when a strategy does not coincide, the child has much to learn in order to acquire the meaning. In terms of Clark's experiment, *in* is cognitively simpler than *on* or *under* because it requires minimal adjustment of the child's hypothesis about its meaning. Clark also mentions the possibility of additional non-linguistic strategies which might explain the order of acquisition of other linguistic behaviours. A strategy such as 'Always pick the greater amount' would lead to children treating the word *less* as if it means *more*, as Donaldson and Balfour (1968) and Donaldson and Wales (1970) have found. A strategy of retaining the description of a series of events in time in the order in which they occurred might lead to the linguistic hypothesis that the order of mention reflects actual order. This has been observed by several investigators (Clark, 1971, 1973a; Cromer, 1968, 1974a; Ferreiro, 1971).

Wilcox and Palermo (1975) have challenged Clark's explanation of the acquisition of *in*, *on*, and *under*. Rather than specific rules about *in* and *on* as Clark proposed, they considered that the results she obtained might be due to the objects she used in her experiment, and that a more general explanation was possible. With three age groups whose mean ages were 1 year 9 months, 2 years 3 months and 2 years 9 months, Wilcox and Palermo tested comprehension of the same terms, but using different materials. Furthermore, they used sentences which were what they called congruent or incongruent with the materials. For example, with a toy truck and a toy road, they might give a congruent sentence ('Put the road under the truck') or an incongruent one ('Put the road in the truck'). It can be seen that these terms are used in the way 'probable' and 'improbable' events were used in the Strohner and Nelson study, and 'appropriate' and 'inappropriate' context used in Dewart's experiment. The results using this material were very different from Clark's. Many children now treated *in* as if it meant *under* or *on*, and they treated *on* as if it meant *under*. Wilcox and Palermo suggest two reasons for these results. One is the tendency to put objects in their most congruent contextual relationship. This was most pronounced in the older children and may be due to their knowledge of what relations objects should be in. Notice that these older groups are ages 2 years 3 months and 2 years 9 months and are thus equivalent to Strohner and Nelson's youngest groups. Here is more evidence, then, of children aged approximately 2 and 3 years using a probable-event strategy. However, the youngest group in Wilcox and Palermo's experiment actually did better on the incongruent (improbable) tasks. It was the older children who were affected by congruency (probability). This too represents a development. Children below 2 years old use a different strategy. Wilcox and Palermo suggest that the youngest children are following a tendency to make the simplest motor response. Their errors are motor errors, and this leads them to make such responses as putting the road *in* rather than *under* the truck.

Huttenlocher and her associates have also studied the motor responses of children and the effect they may have on performance with some types of verbal material. In one test of children's comprehension of relational statements of the type, 'The red block is on top of the green block' (Huttenlocher and Strauss, 1968), children performed differently depending on which block they had to place. The task was to place a block which they held in their hands in relation to a block fixed to the middle rung of a ladder in such a way as to match the experimenter's verbal description. The results revealed that it was much easier for children to place the block they were holding if it was the grammatical subject of the descriptive sentence than if it was the grammatical object. For example, it was easier to perform the action required by 'The red block is on top of the green block' if they were holding the red block (corresponding to the grammatical subject) than if they were holding the green block (corresponding to the grammatical object). Huttenlocher and Strauss suggested that this was so because comprehension is aided by a correspondence between the form of a linguistic description and the extralinguistic state of affairs. Furthermore, in this case, the block being held is the 'actor' (the block to be moved), and the grammatical subject of a sentence often plays the role of the actor. However, as this was confounded by temporal order of the mention of the two blocks, a second experiment was undertaken (Huttenlocher, Eisenberg and Strauss, 1968). In the second experiment, both active and passive sentences were used. Children had to carry out the action of placing a truck which they held in their hands (the mobile truck) in relation to a fixed truck so that their truck was pulling, pushing, being pulled by or being pushed by the fixed truck. The results showed that for active statements it was easier to place the mobile truck when it was the grammatical subject, as the earlier experiment had shown. But for passive sentences it was easier to place the mobile truck when it was the grammatical object (i.e. the logical subject or real actor). In other words, the ease of placing the truck matched the action of the sentence – the logical rather than the surface grammatical feature. Children, then, seem to co-ordinate the logical subject and the actor.

The children in the Huttenlocher experiments were 9 and 10 years of age. The kind of motor preference mentioned earlier was said to be a strategy used by very young children, at ages prior to their recognition of the importance of word order. Hazel Dewart (1972) obtained results similar to Huttenlocher's but with somewhat younger children – 5 and 6 years old. In later experiments (Dewart, 1975), using 4-, 5-, and 6-year-old children, a strategy based on treating the mobile toy as actor was observed. In this experiment, the child had to carry out the actions described under conditions in which sometimes the *actor* was mobile (the toy to be the actor was placed in the child's hand before the sentence was given), and sometimes the *object* was mobile (the child held the toy to be acted upon). First the child performed six passive sentences holding neither toy (no-context condition). This was done to gauge his ability on passive sentences generally. Then a pre-test was given consisting of active sentences. The test itself consisted of 12 passive sentences, six with the actor mobile and six with the object mobile. The results were in agreement with the Huttenlocher studies. There were significantly fewer errors in the actor-mobile condition, and there were significantly more errors on the object-mobile condition than even on the no-context condition. Furthermore, the context did not affect the known active sentences at these ages. Since the active sentences were not affected, one may assume that the results are not just due to an assumption by children that they are supposed to move the toy in their hand. Some children consistently used a strategy of treating the mobile toy as the actor for any passive sentence. If one compares children who knew the passive with those who did not (in the no-context condition), it becomes apparent that children use a strategy when they do not know how to interpret passive sentences. Of children who were correct on the no-context passives, none was misled into using the strategy that the mobile toy was the actor. But many children who did not yet know the passive form used that kind of action strategy. Many of these, indeed, had used strategies in answering the unknown passives. For example, 13 children used a strategy in which they consistently treated the first noun as the actor for all passive sentences in the no-context condition (a strategy which will be discussed in the next section). Of these, seven abandoned that word-order strategy on the 12 passive test sentences and used the contextual cue of treating the mobile toy as the actor. It appears, then, that a child uses an extra-linguistic strategy when he does not know how to make use of grammatical structure in the adult manner. At the much younger age of about 1 year 9 months, when children did not know the meaning of *in*, *on* and *under*, and before they knew or made use of event probabilities, they used a strategy of making the simplest motor response (Wilcox and Palermo, 1975). Similarly, some children of 4 and 5 years of age, who might normally be making use of a word-order strategy on structures they do not yet know, used a motor-related strategy of consistently treating the easily mobile toy (the one in their hand) as the actor.

It was noted that the effect in the Huttenlocher studies was not due to position in the sentence as such, but to the role of the item. Thus, if a child was holding a toy, he performed with fewer errors if that toy served in an 'actor' role. The actor is the surface grammatical subject in active sentences, but is the surface grammatical object in passive sentences. It has been suggested, therefore, that perhaps performance is related to the role that is played by particular grammatical units, rather than to the grammatical units themselves. This would call for analysis along the lines of a case grammar (Fillmore, 1968) or one of the more semantic grammars (for instance, Chafe, 1970). In a series of experiments, Suci and Hamacher (1972) found some evidence that sentence-processing by undergraduate subjects was more affected by the action role of the noun in the sentence (that is, whether the noun was agent or patient) than by the position or grammatical category. In an experiment on 10- and 12-year-old children, Suci and Hamacher investigated whether the effect on processing was indeed that of action role or whether it was based on case grammar units. Suci and Hamacher claim that for Chafe (1970) there are two dimensions to the agent category: the action role of the noun–verb relation and the animateness of the noun. Fillmore's case units (1968) divide the domain somewhat differently. The agentive and instrumental cases are really both agents, but the agentive is an animate agent ('The man opened the door') while the instrumental is an inanimate agent ('The key opened the door'). Similarly, one might say that the dative and objective cases differ in that the dative is an animate patient and the objective is an inanimate patient. Questions about the subject–adjective or object–adjective relations were asked, and the response latencies timed. Adult subjects had been found to be affected by both action role and animacy. Thus, case grammar distinctions seemed to be observed. On the 10- and 12-year-olds, however, it was found that case units by themselves (agentive, instrumental, dative and objective) did not produce significant differences in processing. But there were effects due to action role. Suci and Hamacher concluded that action role is a psychologically valid concept for children but that the case units were not. It appears, then, that the Suci and Hamacher results show that animacy is important for adults but not for 10- and 12-year-old children. However, there are drawbacks both in the technique that they used and in the fact that the sentences for the children and for the adults were not the same. It is very difficult to interpret their complex results at some points. Other investigators have observed that animacy is a very important variable in the interpretation of sentences by young children. One such study was that carried out by Hazel Dewart (1975) in which younger subjects than those used by Suci and Hamacher were tested for their comprehension of sentences in which the animacy of various nouns was varied in conjunction with various sentence positions.

In Dewart's experiment, 20 children aged 3 years 3 months to 5 years (median age 4 years 3 months) were given a total of 24 sentences in which one noun was a nonsense word. The child's task was to choose from a pile of toys which one he thought the nonsense word referred to. The toys included six dolls and animals which would be named by animate nouns, and six objects which would be named by inanimate nouns. The sentences were of four types: active-voice sentences with either the actor or object being a nonsense word, and passive-voice sentences with either the actor or object being a nonsense word. The verbs in these sentences were chosen to include (1) those which required an animate actor (e.g. *fight*, *kiss*) and (2) those which could take either an animate or inanimate actor (e.g. *wake*, *scare*). These two types of verbs (based on requirements of the actor) were cross-classified into three types in terms of the object which they necessitated: animate, inanimate or either. A concrete example will make this clearer. The verbs *fight*, *read* and *send*, all require animate actors (type 1). But in addition *fight* requires an animate object, *read* requires an inanimate object, and *send* can take either an animate or inanimate object. Similarly, *wake*, *break* and *hold* can take either animate or inanimate actors (type 2), but *wake*, requires an animate object, *break* requires an inanimate object, and *hold* can take either. In the 24 sentences of the test, four verbs from each of these six categories were used, one in each of the four sentence types. Although the results of this experiment are complex, the main findings can be easily summarized. Nonsense words functioning as actors were more likely to be replaced by animate nouns if they were in pre-verb position as in active sentences than when they followed the noun as in passives. Similarly, those functioning as objects were more often replaced by animate responses in passives, again where they were first noun, than in actives, where the object comes second. In other words, children aged 3 and 4 years behaved as if they were using a strategy that the first noun is animate and the second noun is inanimate. However, this tendency was less strong on passive-voice sentences. Dewart hypothesizes that perhaps children at this age are progressing from that strategy towards the adult pattern of response.

It has now been seen that young children make use of a variety of strategies in order to perform on tests of their comprehension of linguistic knowledge. One early strategy has been described as a probable-event strategy (Strohner and Nelson, 1974), the use of which, by very young children, even appears to lead to incorrect interpretations of active sentences. Others have spoken of 'appropriate' and 'inappropriate' contexts (Dewart, 1975), or 'congruent' and 'incongruent' relationships (Wilcox and Palermo, 1975), in order to describe a similar phenomenon. A second type of conceptualization has used the term 'local rules' (Donaldson and McGarrigle, 1974) to describe the way a child may approach sentence and word interpretation in various cognitive tasks. Some of these local rules may be very specific, such as placing things *in* a container but *on* a surface (Clark, 1973b). Even earlier than all these strategies may be one based on the child's carrying out the simplest motor response (Wilcox and Palermo, 1975). Related to this type of strategy may be those based on various features of the action role of the actor. Treating the mobile toy as the actor was observed not only in young children (Dewart, 1972, 1975), but in older children as well (Huttenlocher and Strauss, 1968; Huttenlocher, Eisenberg and Strauss, 1968). In experiments where error scores rather than reaction times were used as the measure, it appeared that older children used this strategy only when they did not know the syntactic structure (Dewart, 1975). In other words, the older children fell back on the use of a strategy found in much younger children when comprehension based on grammatical principles failed. Finally, it was noted that, while in adults the action role included the use of animacy for agents and inanimacy for patients (Suci and Hamacher, 1972), younger children, about age 4, used animacy in relation to sentence position, with the first noun being animate and the second noun being inanimate, to some extent independently of grammatical role (Dewart, 1975). This last observation, the importance of sentence position at particular ages, has been noted by many investigators of child language. Sentence position is claimed to be the basis for several strategies used by both children and adults. These strategies are seen as being part of a perceptual processing apparatus which acts on the surface features of language. They are 'perceptual' in that they deal with such phenomena as word order, segmentation of the incoming speech sequence, and interruptions of that sequence. It will be suggested that some of these strategies which have been called perceptual may really be part of broader cognitive mechanisms.

Perceptual Processing Strategies

A theoretical background

In the Strohner and Nelson experiment (1974) mentioned in the previous section, young children aged 2 and 3 years old were found to act in accordance with a probable-event strategy, even to the extent of performing incorrectly on simple active-voice sentences about improbable events. However, children of ages 4 and 5 were also tested, and here the findings were quite different. The 4- and 5-year-olds were no longer greatly influenced by the event probabilities. The 4-year-olds often made use of a strategy that the sentence word order corresponded to actor–action–object. They did well on active sentences, but poorly on passive ones. Even some of the 3-year-olds had begun using this type of word-order strategy, at least on reversible sentences, i.e. sentences in which either event was equally possible. By the age of 5 years, the child was found to rely mainly on syntactic information, both ignoring event probabilities and no longer using the actor–action–object word-order strategy. It is clear, then, that, although the youngest children may comprehend the language they hear in terms of what they know about events in the world, there comes a point in development where the structures of language become comprehensible in their own right even if they do not match reality. This is, after all, what we mean when we say that a linguistic structure is acquired – that it will be employable without context, and even in spite of conflicting context. This is the point where 'The fence jumped over the horse' is acted upon correctly even though it may appear amusingly silly to the child. It is the basis for the glee with which young, but not too young, children greet

> Hey diddle, diddle
> The cat and the fiddle,
> The cow jumped over the moon,
> The little dog laughed to see such fun
> And the dish ran away with the spoon.

In order to understand language acquisition and how it occurs, it would appear to be necessary to do more than merely state how language is related to reality. Syntactic structure, however it is acquired, becomes something which is separate from and beyond that reality. This resembles an issue in linguistics which is the subject of much controversy.

For some time certain linguists have been proposing a type of grammatical analysis that differs from Chomsky's particular formulation of transformational grammar. Chomsky's position is usually referred to as 'standard theory' (Chomsky, 1965) or, in a later modified version, 'extended standard theory' (Chomsky, 1972; Jackendoff, 1972). The proposals which disagreed with the standard theory have often been referred to under the broad term 'generative semantics' (see for example Lakoff, 1971; McCawley, 1971a, 1971b, 1973; and a collection of reprinted articles edited by Seuren, 1974). It is not appropriate here to give a detailed analysis of the differences between the two types of theory. For our purposes we need only centre attention on what Katz and Bever (1974) have called the issue of absolute notions of grammaticality versus graded ones. The older standard theory of Chomsky paid little attention to the semantic or meaning component of the grammar. This was its weakest point. Furthermore, the generative semanticists claimed that a Chomskian analysis was inadequate to deal with many sentences, and that this inadequacy was traceable to the lack of consideration given to meaning in the generation of sentence structures. Both the extended standard theory and the theory of generative semantics were reactions to the inadequacies of the earlier view. However, those adhering to the extended standard theory still emphasize the autonomy of the syntactic component. Although they have given more attention to the semantic component and its interaction with the syntax, this semantic component is conceived of as a set of interpretation rules which act on or are applied to the syntax. The followers of that theory have come to be called 'interpretative semanticists'. By contrast, the generative semanticists claim that the meaning component plays an essential part in the generation of the structures themselves, and cannot be separated from them. They claim that the two components (semantics and syntax) are inextricably entwined and that sentences are generated from a syntactic–semantic base. Indeed, another way of characterizing the two broad schools of thought is to call the theory of the latter 'semantic syntax' and to label the Chomskian position as 'autonomous syntax' (Seuren, 1974). Both theories are concerned with specifically linguistic entities. The word *semantics* is not identical to *thoughts, cognitions* or *meanings*. Semantics is concerned with the representation of meaning in language. Many psychologists have shown some confusion about this, and have drawn on the generative semanticists as support for a relatively anti-linguistic view. Bloom (1973) has called attention to this problem of misinterpretation. As she puts it, the semantic versus the syntactic basis for a grammar is an important issue for psychologists only to the extent that the formal correlates of such a difference make different predictions, if any, about cognitive and behavioural aspects of language use. Bloom claims that the more important distinction for those studying child language is not within linguistic categories (grammatical and semantic), but between linguistic categories on the one hand, and cognitive categories on the other.

However, Katz and Bever (1974) point out that aspects of Lakoff's theory of grammatical competence include a number of non-grammatical facts about the world. For Chomsky, a theory of competence relates to the principled knowledge which explains the intuitions that speakers have about sentence structure. For Lakoff, by contrast, well-formed sentences depend in part on knowledge of the world and on the beliefs of the speaker. For example, Lakoff's theory would claim that sentences like 'My frying pan enjoys tormenting me' depend for grammaticality not on a structural notion of '+human', but on whether the speaker considers the subject of the sentence to be sentient. If so, then and only then would the sentence just quoted be grammatical. In other words, the notion of the well-formed sentence is not absolute, but is relative, depending on the belief of the speaker. This may sound sensible as a theory of 'acceptability', but as a theory of 'grammaticality' this view seems very odd. Surely we can use grammatical sentences to talk about nonsense or about improbable or unlikely occurrences whether we believe them or not. Even 5-year-olds, as well as adults, have been empirically observed to know what to do with the toys when given the sentence 'The fence jumped over the horse', and such a sentence is still grammatical even though it violates what we expect about events in the real world. Moreover, as Katz and Bever point out, deviant sentences can be used to make true statements. Furthermore, they claim that Lakoff's view would entail the belief that there is no distinction between a speaker's knowledge of grammatical and semantic properties of language and the speaker's beliefs about the things to which the language refers in the world. In other words, such a theory would claim that there is no distinction between 'language' and 'cognition'. Such a view would, it seems to me, be somewhat of a hindrance when one tries to study the language acquisition of children, and even more so when studying such conditions as developmental aphasia in children and various types of adult aphasia.

Katz and Bever suggest that we need to know precisely what the specifically grammatical relations are, and that many of the problems raised by the favourite examples quoted by generative semanticists should more properly be regarded as being due to considerations which are outside the grammar entirely. An early example of this kind of problem was that raised by the unintelligibility of multiple centre-embedded sentences such as 'The rat that the cat that the dog that the cow tossed worried killed ate the malt.' Miller (1962b) and Miller and Chomsky

(1963) dealt with problems of this type by turning to non-grammatical considerations. They argued that centre-embedded sentences may be 'grammatical' but perceptually complex. For example, memory limitations put such structurally complex sentences involving recursive features beyond the analytic power of any finite device. Furthermore, severe memory limitations may put any sentence of sufficient complexity beyond comprehensibility even when it lacks properties such as self-embedding. Short-term memory limitations have in fact been implicated in the language deficiencies observed in some mentally retarded children (Graham, 1968, 1974) and in other language-deviant groups (Menyuk, 1964, 1969).

In generative semantics, all sorts of performance factors count as a legitimate part of the grammar. Lakoff's theory, for example, insists that anything whatsoever which influences the distribution of observed linguistic forms is to be accounted for in the grammar. However, a Chomskian type of grammar rejects a conception of grammaticality which is based simplistically on the principles of distributional linguistics. Instead it is based on the notion of explication (Chomsky, 1972; Katz and Bever, 1974). It is meant to explain syntactic behaviour, and, although it is based in large part on distributional phenomena, many of the principles which help account for the distribution of linguistic forms are not included in the notion of grammaticality itself. As we will see further on, this is certainly not to say that such principles are unimportant; they are essential to the understanding of child language acquisition. Indeed, the rest of this section will be concerned with a number of perceptual processing strategies used by adults and by young children acquiring language. But it will be necessary to ask later whether these principles *explain* language acquisition, and to examine what they tell us about developing grammatical processes.

Some perceptual strategies

Having said that some aspects of language organization are explicable on the basis of perceptual mechanisms as distinct from grammatical mechanisms, Bever (1970; Katz and Bever, 1974) has comprehensively examined what some of those perceptual processes might be. In this subsection, some of the strategies he has outlined will be reviewed, and mention will be made of work of a few others which might conceivably be viewed in this framework.

Some of the processing strategies relate to the segmenting of the incoming speech sequence. It has been found that the lexical sequences that are placed together as units correspond to underlying structure. In a series of well-known experiments (Fodor and Bever, 1965; Bever, Fodor and Garrett, 1966; Garrett, Bever and Fodor, 1966) the subject hears a click while listening to a sentence. Subjectively, the click appears to migrate to the clause boundary. For example, in the sentence 'Because it rained yesterday, the picnic was cancelled', a click, which in reality occurred either during the word *yesterday* or during the word *the*, appears to occur *between* the two words. This migration will vary according to the structure of the sentence even when the heard sequence is identical. For example, if the sequence '. . . eagerness to win the horse is quite immature' is preceded by 'Your . . .' the click seems to occur just after the word *horse*; but if that same sequence is preceded by 'In its . . .' the click is subjectively heard just after the word *win*. From this Bever concludes (1970) that adults have a strategy of perceptually organizing adjacent phrases in the surface structure which correspond to sentence units at the level of internal structure. That is, as Bever puts it, 'As we hear a sentence we organize it perceptually in terms of internal structure sentence units with subjects, verbs, objects, and modifiers.'

Sometimes perceptual strategies inhibit the understanding of the sense of certain structures and mislead the hearer into an unintended interpretation. Katz and Bever (1974) give the example 'The friend of my brother's fiancée left town.' It is very difficult to interpret this sentence as meaning that it was the fiancée who left town. This is because of the perceptual attractiveness of N + N (noun plus noun) sequences. However, any aspect of the sentence which would perceptually separate *brother's* from *fiancée*, or which emphasizes the word *fiancée* as head noun, would have the effect of making acceptable the interpretation of *fiancée* as subject. Thus, 'The fiancée of my brother's friend was discovered to be a cat burglar so the friend of my brother's fiancée left town' (Katz and Bever, 1974) serves to render the meaning of the sentence as something which could be written as 'the friend-of-my-brother's fiancée left town', where *friend-of-my-brother's* becomes a phrase modifying *fiancée*. In other words, as simply given, the sentence first quoted is ambiguous. Most people would interpret it as meaning that *friend* left town, and would find it difficult to see the possible meaning that *fiancée* left town; this is due to what Katz and Bever call a perceptually suppressed sense which is caused by the perceptual attraction of the two adjacent nouns.

Amongst the processing strategies which Bever reviews is one which predicts that sequences which interrupt one another are especially complex. In addition, the complexity of a sequence varies in proportion to the complexity of the intervening sequence. It may be, however, that some of the principles that Bever has isolated in this set of related strategies should not be designated as narrowly perceptual. Perhaps they are really broad cognitive strategies that affect not only the perception of language but other human behaviours as well. One theory has been proposed which relates the difficulty of interrupted sequences to the relative difficulty of various motor strategies for handling material objects (Goodson and Greenfield, 1975). It is a theory which has developmental implications as well, and it will be discussed in some detail in the next section of this chapter.

One special kind of interrupted sequence was mentioned earlier: self-embedded or centre-embedded sentences. It was suggested that memory limitations may play an important role in the unacceptability of longer sequences of this type. However, it has also been found that some self-embedded sentences are easier than others with the same number of self-embeddings (Fodor and Garrett, 1967; Fodor, Garrett and Bever, 1968). For example, in one of these experiments, it was found that the presence or absence of relative pronouns affected performance on embedded sentences of the same length. Therefore the differences in difficulty cannot be attributed to memory limitations. Bever (1970) has since also proposed that the difficulties of other types of centre-embedded sentences may lie in a perceptual principle and two related word-order strategies rather than on memory limitations. Suppose one has the following sentence: 'The dog the cat was scratching was yelping.' In this sentence, the basic relations can be more clearly shown as

N_1	N_2	V_1	V_2
The dog	the cat	was scratching	was yelping

The main sentence is 'The dog . . . was yelping', into which has been embedded the clause 'the cat was scratching'. Bever proposes two perceptual strategies that yield correct interpretation of this construction. One is that, with a V_1–V_2 combination in which both verbs are finite, V_2 is taken to correspond to the main verb of the sentence with V_1 being the subordinate verb. Second, with N_1–N_2–(VP) sequences in the surface structure, N_1 is the internal object of the internal sentence-structure unit of which N_2 is the subject. In the example above, N_1, the dog, is the object of an internal sentence, 'The cat was scratching the dog', of which N_2, the cat, is the subject. Notice that N_1 thus serves a 'double function' as Bever calls it. It is a subject of one sentence (the main sentence), yet an object of the embedded sentence. Bever proposes a general principle that a stimulus may not be perceived as simultaneously having two positions on the same classificatory dimension, i.e. a stimulus can't be perceived in two incompatible ways at the same time. According to Bever, it is this that leads to the difficulties with self-embedded sentences of this type.

This is very similar to a problem posed by some sentences with relative clauses which has been studied by Amy Sheldon (1974). In such sentences, the co-referential nominal may have the same function in both clauses, or there may be a change of function or role. Take, for example, two sentences with subject relatives:

The dog that jumps over the pig bumps into the lion
The lion that the horse bumps into jumps over the giraffe

In the first of these, the dog is co-referential nominal. Furthermore, it serves the same function in both clauses. It is the subject who both jumps over the lion and bumps into the pig. In the second sentence, however, the co-referential nominal (the lion) serves different functions in the two clauses. The lion is the object of the first clause (the horse bumps into the lion), but is the subject of the second clause (the lion jumps over the giraffe). The first sentence, where no role change of the co-referential nominal occurs, is referred to by Sheldon as exhibiting 'parallel function'. Where changes of role occur, as in the second sentence, the term 'non-parallel function' is used. The two examples just given are of subject relatives. Sheldon also included object relatives, some of which exhibit parallel function and some of which have non-parallel function of the co-referential nominals:

The dog stands on the horse that the giraffe jumps over
The pig bumps into the horse that jumps over the giraffe

With all four sentences, there is the further difference that the two subject relatives have the main clause interrupted, while the two object-relative sentences do not. If interrupted sequences are more difficult than uninterrupted ones, the subject relatives should be harder. There are also differences based on whether the relativized noun phrase is a subject or object. For example, in the two object relatives just cited, the horse which is relativized in the first sentence is the object, while the horse which is relativized in the second is the subject. Thus, if difficulty is due to word order, then relative clauses in which the subject noun phrase is relativized should be easier to process than relative clauses in which the object noun phrase is relativized, because the underlying word order is preserved in the surface structure of the former, but it is not preserved in the latter.

Sheldon tested 33 children between the ages of 3 years 8 months and 5 years 5 months, by having them act out the sentences with toy animals. Each child received 12 sentences – three examples of each of the four types of relatives. The results indicated that interruption played no part in difficulty, nor did word order. There were no significant differences between subject relatives and object relatives; and there were no significant differences between sentences in which the subject was relativized and those in which the object was relativized. However, performance on parallel-function relative sentences was significantly better than on non-parallel-function sentences. Analysis of errors showed that in some sense word order plays a part in that some children used a strategy of identifying the antecedent to the relative pronoun on the basis of treating the relative clause that followed a main clause as if it were an extraposed subject modifier. For example, in 'The dog stands on the horse that the giraffe jumps over' many children understood the giraffe to be jumping over the dog, as if the entire relative clause modified the subject (the dog). Sheldon concludes that children use two strategies on relative-clause sentences. In trying to find the antecedent to the relative pronoun in object relatives, children rely on an extra-position strategy; in attempting to assign a function to the relativized noun phrase, they use a strategy of assigning parallel function.

Sheldon's discussion is concerned only with linguistic interpretations. Bever's analysis of self-embedded sentences attempts to identify the difficulty in terms of the broader perceptual principle of the same stimulus serving a double function. Perhaps the principle is broader still, and encompasses various cognitive phenomena which go beyond perception. Furthermore, Bever does not relate this particular principle to developmental phenomena. Something very similar to Bever's 'double function' can be said to be lacking in what Piaget calls pre-operational-stage children. When operational thinking is attained, the use of double functions becomes possible. In the well-known conservation experiment, the water which is higher is, at the same time, now co-ordinated with being narrower. On seriation tasks, the interposed sticks are now conceptually known to be at one and the same time larger than some and smaller than others. Goodson and Greenfield (1975) have referred to this same type of double-function thinking as 'role change'. For them, role change is a cognitive process in which a single element plays different roles in relation to different parts of a complex structure. The developing ability for employing this process accounts for the developmental changes in sentence interpretation. We will return to the Goodson and Greenfield study in the section on cognitive strategies for language. It is apparent from the Sheldon study that role retention and role change have a part to play in the interpretation of some sentences.

The retention of the same role within a sentence has also been found to be an important principle in the young child's understanding of the referents of certain pronouns. Maratsos (1973a) studied sentences of the following type:

> John hit Harry and then Sarah hit him
> John hit Harry and then he hit Sarah

In these sentences, we are concerned with the problem of the referents of the pronouns *him* and *he*. In the first sentence, the usual interpretation is that *him* refers to Harry. In the second sentence, *he* refers to John. Notice that with these interpretations the grammatical relations are the same in both clauses. In the first sentence, *Harry* is the object of the first clause. *Him* is the object of the second clause, and, if it is interpreted as referring to Harry, then the grammatical categories for Harry have been maintained. Similarly, in the second sentence, *John* is the subject of the first clause. *He* is the subject of the second clause, and, if it refers to John, then John is functioning as the subject in both. However, in conditions of contrastive stress, adult English-speakers know that a change has been signalled. If one reads 'John hit Harry and then Sarah hit *him*', with special stress on *him*, then *him* is taken as referring to John. Similarly, special stress on *he* in the second sentence leads to the interpretation that it refers to Harry instead of John. In other words, stressed pronouns signify a change in roles. In the first sentence, *John*, the *subject* of the first clause, becomes *him*, the *object* in the second clause. In the second example, *Harry*, the *object* of the first clause, becomes *he*, the *subject* of the second. Maratsos tested 106 3-, 4- and 5-year-olds for their comprehension of sentences of this type. All children performed similarly on the unstressed sentences, retaining the same role from the first clause to the second. However, performance on sentences in which the pronouns received contrastive stress improved with age and language ability (as measured by an imitation task). The youngest group interpreted the stressed pronouns just like the unstressed ones. Maratsos interpreted this as being due to a general heuristic strategy used by young children to interpret pronouns in order to change the grammatical and semantic roles as little as possible. Correct performances on the stressed pronouns requires one to violate this strategy. As mentioned earlier, the nature of the learning that allows one to begin to violate certain strategies remains unclear; it is by no means apparent that the mechanism is a simple one of learning exceptions to rules based on such principles as frequency of occurrence.

Semantic considerations can also affect perceptual strategies. Katz and Bever (1974) claim that one perceptual rule is that relative pronouns usually modify an immediately preceding noun phrase. Sequences which violate this principle may be grammatical, but nevertheless unacceptable due to perceptual complexity. Thus, in the sentence 'The man likes the girl who lives in Chicago', the interpretation that *who* refers to *the man*, rather than to *the girl*, is unacceptable. However, that such an interpretation is nevertheless allowed by the *grammar* can be seen in a sentence of identical structure, 'The man likes your idea who lives in Chicago.' In this case, *who* refers to *the man*, since semantically, *ideas* can't live in Chicago. In other words, perceptual, not grammatical, features determine the unacceptability of the first sentence.

Similarly, behavioural variables, not grammatical structure, can affect the acceptability of certain sequences with co-referential pronouns. Bever gives the example 'He and he like juice', which is unacceptable. Note, however, that the grammatically identical 'He and she like juice' is acceptable. Bever further notes that even 'He and he like juice' is acceptable if it is accompanied by appropriate gestures.

It appears that what Bever is arguing is that the usual interpretation of pronoun reference in several different conditions is based on perceptual strategies, mainly relating to word order. However, these perceptual strategies can be overridden by semantic and behavioural factors. In other words, the principles determining interpretation in these cases are not entirely 'grammatical'. Rather, perceptual phenomena play a major role in interpretation, and these perceptual features are in turn subject to modification by semantic and behavioural variables.

As can be seen, most of the perceptual strategies that Bever has proposed are based on considerations of surface-structure word order, and these perceptions can be overridden at times by semantic or behavioural considerations. These basic perceptual strategies are not unlike some kinds of strategy which other experimenters have observed in young children. Carol Chomsky (1969), for example, examined the acquisition of some linguistic structures which violate a more general principle observed in sentences of similar structure. Take the following sentences:

John told Bill to leave
John wanted Bill to leave

These sentences are of the form $NP_1 + V + NP_2 + Infinitive V$. In both of these, NP_2 (*Bill*) is the subject of the infinitive verb; it is Bill who will be leaving. Some verbs, like *told* in the first example, mandatorily take an object (*Bill*); 'John told to leave' is not a sentence. But with other verbs, like *wanted* in the second example, the object is optional. One can say either 'John wanted Bill to leave' or 'John wanted to leave.' In the first of these, Bill is the subject of the infinitive verb, but, in the second, the first NP (*John*) now becomes the subject of the infinitive. Where the second NP is optional, the description can be written:

$NP_1 + V + (NP_2) +$ Infinitive V. In other words, when the second NP occurs, it is the subject of the infinitive; when it is omitted, the first NP becomes the subject. Carol Chomsky described this as the 'minimum-distance principle', for it is the NP closest to the infinitive verb which is taken as the subject. This works for most verbs in English. However, a few verbs violate this principle. One of these is *promise*. In the sentence, 'John promised Bill to leave', it is John, not Bill, who will be leaving. Even more complicated is the verb *ask*. When used as a request, as in 'John asked Bill to sing', the minimum-distance principle is applied, and it is Bill who will be singing. But, when *ask* is used as a question, as in 'John asked Bill what to sing', then the minimum-distance principle is violated and it is John who proposes to provide the entertainment.

Chomsky tested children between the ages of 5 and 10 years on sentences of these types by using procedures and materials with which children could cope. For example, to test sentences with *promise*, children were given small Donald Duck and Bozo the Clown figures. Then, after various practice and warm-up sentences, they were given such test sentences as 'Donald promised Bozo to hop up and down. Make him hop.' Chomsky found that correct interpretation of sentences with *promise* and *ask*, which are exceptions to the minimum-distance principle, is a rather late acquisition. Children at the lower end of the age range usually failed, and they did so by consistently applying a strategy based on the perception of word-order relations – the minimum-distance principle. It is not known when children begin to apply this strategy, but, at least at ages when it is applied, it leads to incorrect interpretations until new learning intervenes. Here, then, is a strategy which children, but not adults, apply to perceived surface-structure relations. They do so at about ages 5 and 6 (and possibly younger). It gives them a means of performing on comprehension tests set by psycholinguists, but it does not yield a correct interpretation of underlying sentence structure as judged by adult grammatical analysis. Precisely how the exceptions to this strategy are learned is not yet at all clear and some of the complexities associated with the attainment of adult-like performance with the verb *ask* will be mentioned in the final section of this chapter.

Most of Bever's perceptual strategies mentioned earlier were intended by him to account for adult performance on various linguistic structures. However, one strategy in which he was particularly interested is used primarily by 4-year-olds. It is that of treating noun–verb–noun sequences as referring to actor–action–object (Bever, 1971). The basic strategy has been conceived more simply as one in which the first noun is taken as the actor. A good deal of experimental research has been directed at discovering the use and developmental changes of this perceptual, word-order strategy.

The strategy that the first noun is actor

It has already been noted that Strohner and Nelson (1974) observed that children aged 2 and 3 years old were likely to make use of a probable-event strategy, but that by age 3 some children had begun to change to a strategy based on word order. On reversible passive sentences there were many errors, which is consistent with the strategy of interpreting the first noun in the sentence as the actor. Wetstone and Friedlander (1973) similarly were interested in the degree to which word order carries communicative information for young children. They studied 20 children aged from 2 years to 3 years 1 month, presenting them both with questions to be answered and with commands to be carried out in three conditions. One condition consisted of normal word order, as in 'Show the clown to Mommy.' A second condition had a misplaced word order: for example, 'Show clown the Mommy.' This was formed by reducing the normal form to 'telegraphic' speech (as often used by children of this age for sentences of this type) and reinserting the non-referent words out of their normal order. The third condition was a scrambled word order, as in 'Mommy clown to the show.' Although children were of about the same age, they were divided into a developmental order which consisted of non-fluent children, who were described as being either at the stage of holophrastic word use and had a mean utterance length (MUL) of 1.75 morphemes, or at the stage of telegraphic word use (MUL = 2.79 morphemes). The developmentally most advanced children were described as fluent children, and they had an MUL of 3.73 morphemes. The children's responses were scored as being either relevant or non-relevant, the latter being a failure to respond, acting outside the context of the question or command, or showing marked puzzlement, a demand for explanation, and the like. The results showed that for both groups of non-fluent children there were no differences between normal, misplaced and scrambled word orders. By contrast, the fluent children performed significantly worse on the scrambled word order – significantly worse than on the other two conditions and than the other two groups. Wetstone and Friedlander conclude that for non-fluent young children word order carries little or no communicative value. But fluent children seem to utilize syntactic as well as semantic information, since they did significantly worse when the word order was scrambled. The least developmentally advanced children make do with context and with content words of specific reference. Developmentally more advanced children have entered the syntactic system. Studies of this kind show the unsatisfactory nature of theories incorporating only communicative intent and meaning.

In relatively early experimental work on the developmental course of sentence interpretation by young children, Bever, Mehler and Valian

(1968) noted a number of stages based on different interpretation strategies. They claim that in Stage 1 (age 2–3) the child understands simple declarative sentences even when improbable. Performance on passive sentences was found to be near random even when correct interpretation was aided by semantic constraints. Only physically impossible sentences were responded to incorrectly. It is only in Stage 2A (boys: age 3–4; girls: age 3 to 3 years 8 months) that results similar to those later reported by Strohner and Nelson were found. In this stage, semantic probability determined the interpretation on improbable active and passive constructions. That is, there was poorer performance on improbable active and passive sentences than during the preceding year. Performance on other passive sentences continued to improve until Stage 2B (boys: age 4 to 4 years 4 months; girls: age 3 years 8 months to 4). In this stage, sentences without semantic constraints (i.e. reversible passives) were responded to such that any noun–verb–noun sequence was interpreted as actor–action–object. Thus, the children evidenced poorer performance on reversible passives now than at the immediately preceding stage. Finally, in Stage 3 (boys: 4 years 4 months and upwards; girls: age 4 and upwards) performance on all types of sentences improved steadily. In later writing, Bever (1971) has treated the strategy of the noun–verb–noun sequence as a perceptual processing strategy that continues to affect adult interpretation of sentences. He claims that as a processing strategy it allows the listener to short-cut the use of full linguistic rules. Support for this comes from a number of experimental investigations which indicate that, when there are no semantic constraints, the passive is harder to understand than the active (see Bever, 1970, 1971, for a review of these experiments).

The strategy affects the interpretation of sentences other than passives. For example, Mehler and Carey (1968) have observed that adults find progressive sentences such as 'They are bombarding cities' easier to verify than participial constructions like 'They are performing monkeys.' This could be interpreted as being due to the perceptual expectation of actor–action–object order. Bever reports (1970) that cleft sentences of the type 'It's the cow that kisses the horse', where the actor is first, are easier for children of about 4 years of age than cleft sentences such as 'It's the horse that the cow kisses', where the object occurs first.

Hazel Dewart (1975), whose work on the effect on sentence comprehension of such variables as animacy, linguistic context, and mobility of the object to be moved has already been mentioned, has also carried out a number of experiments on structures possibly affected by the strategy of treating the first noun as the actor. In one of these experiments, sentences containing both direct and indirect objects (double-object constructions) were presented to 50 children between the ages of 3 years 1 month and 7 years 7 months. The children were given two carts which each contained an animal. Then they had to carry out instructions which used the double-object construction. Some of these were of the type 'Send the cat to the dog', which has the direct object (DO) first, the preposition *to*, and then the indirect object (IO). This structure can be designated V–DO–*to*–IO. Others, such as 'Send the dog the cat' have the indirect object before the direct object, and in adult English do not contain a preposition. These are of the form V–IO–DO. In order to study the kinds of strategies children used, however, Dewart also presented a number of other constructions which are deviant from the adult point of view, but which are nevertheless comprehensible by adults. These included sentences such as 'Send to the dog the cat' (V–*to*–IO–DO), 'To the dog send the cat' (*to*–IO–V–DO), 'To the dog the cat send' (*to*–IO–DO–V), 'The cat to the dog send' (DO–*to*–IO–V) and 'The cat send to the dog' (DO–V–*to*–IO). Notice that, given the task, it is the DO which is to be moved. In a sense, then, the DO is the actor. The prediction from the strategy that the first noun is the actor would be that sentences with DO as the first noun should be easier than those with IO as the first noun. Dewart's results confirm this. Similar findings have been reported by Cook (1974), Cromer (1975b), Waryas and Ruder (1973) and Waryas and Stremel (1974). However, Dewart was more interested in whether children used consistent strategies for their answers. Possible cues to interpretation included not only order of mention, but also the proximity of one or the other of the nouns to the verb, and the presence or absence of prepositional marking. By making an error-by-error analysis, Dewart found that, of 39 children who made at least one error, 16 used consistent strategies for their answers. Eight used the strategy of treating the first noun as the actor (DO). Six consistently chose as the DO the noun not marked by *to*. One child used the strategy that the DO (actor) was the noun nearest the verb, and one child always chose the second noun as the DO (the opposite of the particular hypothesized word-order strategy). In other words, at least one child used each of the possible types of strategy, but the most popular was that based on order of mention (nine of the 16 children who used any consistent strategy at all), and almost all of these (eight out of nine) treated the first noun as actor (DO). Thus, although Bever's notion receives support, it must be qualified by the fact that these eight children are the only children who consistently used the hypothesized strategy. And as Dewart points out, their mean age was 4 years 6 months, and not 4 years as reported in the Bever studies.

Another structure where the strategy that the first noun is the actor could be employed is called the instrumental structure. In sentences of the form 'Hit the X with the Y', Dewart (1975) asked, what cues do children use to determine what is hitting and what is being hit? Sentences were used with equally likely interpretation, such as 'Hit the dog with the cat', and 15 children between the ages of 3 years 2 months and 4 years 6 months had to carry out the action described. Again, Dewart used various combinations of word order which result in deviant but interpretable sentences to adults. These included the orders 'Hit with the cat the dog', 'With the cat hit the dog', 'With the cat the dog hit', 'The dog with the cat hit', and 'The dog hit with the cat.' This allowed the experimenter to observe whether children's answers were following a consistent strategy. The results indicated that instrumental sentences were very difficult for the children. They actually made more errors on normal-word-order instrumentals than on the various forms of deviant word order. But, again, interest centres on the error analysis and on what, if any, strategies the children consistently employed. Three types of strategy are possible: one based on the order of the two nouns; one based on the noun marked by the word *with*; and one utilizing the position of the noun in relation to the verb. Of the 15 children, five were found to employ consistent strategies (on the strict criterion of using that strategy for every sentence) for identifying the instrumental noun, i.e. the one to be manipulated in the task. Four of these always chose the first noun as the instrument. The remaining child always used the noun marked by *with*. Thus, although one child used a different strategy, the most popular strategy was that of treating the first noun as the actor (that is to say, as the instrument in this structure).

Another experiment by Dewart included the cleft sentences mentioned earlier. There are various types of cleft structures, including 'It's the wolf that bites the duck', 'It's the wolf that the duck bites' and 'It's the wolf that is bitten by the duck.' Dewart had 80 children between the ages of 3 years 4 months and 7 years 7 months carry out these kinds of instruction, but in addition she was interested in the generality of the strategies used. Therefore, in addition to the cleft sentences the children were given a battery of linguistic tests which included passive sentences, double-object constructions and instrumental constructions. As before, the sentences were given with normal word order and also with various non-English orders. In all, there were 27 sentences on which the child had to perform. Of the 80 children, eight performed correctly on all 27. An analysis by strategy was carried out. A child was credited with using a strategy if he used that method of answering significantly more often than chance. This meant that if a child answered 20 or more items of the 27 in accordance with the strategy, he was counted as using that strategy (0.05 2-tail binomial test). When this criterion was applied, it was found that 24 children had used the strategy that the first noun is the actor across the various sentence types. In fact, eight of these 24 children used the first noun as actor on all 27 items. The children had been divided into eight age groups of 10 children each. Below are listed the median ages of the eight groups along with the total number of children in each who used the 'first noun as actor' strategy:

3 years 8 months	3	5 years 7 months	1
4 years 1 month	7	6 years 4 months	0
4 years 4 months	6	6 years 10 months	1
4 years 8 months	6	7 years 6 months	0

It can be seen that the strategy is mainly used by the 4-year-olds. This confirms Bever's original finding and the later results of Strohner and Nelson, that very young children do not yet use the word-order strategy. It is mainly used at about 4 years of age. It can also be seen in Dewart's results that use of the word-order strategy drastically declines after 4 years 8 months. Note too that Dewart's results show that the more accurate description of the strategy is indeed that the first noun is the actor, rather than that, as formulated earlier, noun–verb–noun sequences are to be interpreted as actor–action–object. This is clear from the deviant word-order sentences where children treated the first noun as actor in spite of varying noun and verb combinations.

Finally, Dewart makes the important point that the actor in these sentences, in the sense of being the thing moved, serves a number of different functions. In terms of the surface structure, in double-object sentences the moved piece or actor is the direct object of the verb. In instrumental sentences, the moved piece is the head noun of the prepositional phrase. In passive sentences, it is the grammatical object of a passive-voice verb and is marked by *by*. In cleft sentences with the object first and an active verb, it is the grammatical subject of a complement clause. In cleft sentences with passive verbs, the moved piece is the grammatical object of a complement clause and is marked with *by*. If instead one looks at the sentences in terms of an underlying case grammar, such as Fillmore's (1968), then in double-object sentences the moved piece or actor is the dative; in instrumental sentences it is the instrument; and in passive and cleft sentences it is the agentive case. It is apparent, then, that children use the same strategy, that the first noun is the actor, to identify a number of disparate grammatical functions.

A number of questions can be asked about the development and use of this strategy. For example, does it continue to be used in some form by older children or adults? Although Dewart's data seemed to indicate a sudden decrease in the use of this strategy after the age of 5 years, it may be that children were acquiring enough information about the structures tested to make use of the strategy unnecessary. She found that both passive sentences and cleft sentences with passive verbs appeared to be acquired by the age of 5½ years, and instrumental sentences were acquired soon after (by about age 5 years 8 months). On the other hand, performance on cleft sentences with active verbs was mixed to the end of her age range (the median age of her oldest group was 7 years 6 months), and the prepositionless form of the double-object construction ('Send the dog the cat') was not acquired by the end of the age range. It could be that knowing the 'easier' structures led to a score on strategy use well under that required for significance overall; that is, perhaps some of the older children were making use of the strategy only for the more difficult structures. Or it could be the case that, even though they had not yet fully acquired these more difficult structures, they knew enough about them to attempt various answers not based on constant application of the strategy.

Davis and Blasdell (1975) studied the comprehension of centre-embedded relative clauses in both normal-hearing and hard-of-hearing children at ages somewhat older than we have been considering. The hard-of-hearing group consisted of 23 children aged 6–9, with hearing losses of between 35 and 70 dB in the 500, 1,000 and 2,000 Hz range. These children were congenitally hard of hearing. They were of normal intelligence and attended an American public school at least half the day. The normal group was made up of 15 children aged 6–9. When presented with sentences such as 'The man who chased the sheep cut the grass', they had to point at pictures of the action. Apparently Davis and Blasdell counted as 'correct' only the picture of the man cutting the grass. Normal-hearing children did this 78 per cent of the time and the hearing-impaired did so 51 per cent of the time. Pointing to the picture of the man chasing the sheep was said to be evidence of the strategy treating N_1–V–N_2 as actor–action–object. This response was made 14 per cent of the time by the normal-hearing group, and 23 per cent of the time by the hearing-impaired group. Thus, some older children were said to be using the strategy more typically found in younger children. The hard-of-hearing did one additional thing. Several of them seemed to shift the strategy to the end of the sentence. They seemed to process only the last few words ('. . . the sheep cut the grass'), and, in order to use *sheep* as the actor, would 'mis-hear' the verb as *ate*, and point to a picture of the sheep eating the grass.

Adults would appear to use strategies either to short-cut full linguistic processing (observable in such measures as response-time differences, perceptual suppression of other possible meanings, etc.) or when they do not otherwise know how to perform on a test of their comprehension. It has been emphasized throughout this discussion on strategies that children use them not to acquire language, but to interpret structures they do not yet understand. The area in which this might arise for adult speakers is when they are attempting to learn a foreign language. Susan Ervin-Tripp (1973) reports that English-speakers who know the passive nevertheless use the 'first noun as actor' strategy in their first foreign-language utterances.

Another question that can be asked about this strategy is whether it is really a perceptual strategy or a purely linguistic abstraction. By the latter is meant merely that the child abstracts a rule from the more common active-voice sentences that he hears and generalizes this rule to other types of sentences such as the passive. If, however, the strategy is an induction from experience, why should it be preferred to other possible generalizations which would be equally justified by experience? Bever (1970) claims that a nativistic component selects certain possible generalizations but rejects others. Furthermore, he argues that it is not at all clear that all perceptual strategies are based on experience. Whatever the exact status of this strategy's origin, Bever believes that all children pass through a phase of using it.

However, the results of Dewart's study leave a good deal of room for doubt. Many children at all the age ranges did not give any evidence of using the strategy. Of course, it may be that they had not yet entered or were already past the stage of using it. As she suggests, only longitudinal studies can answer this question. In addition, however, her studies showed that many children made no use of any strategy, while others used different, less frequent strategies for comprehending the various types of structure. A study by Margaret Harris (1976) on the cues used to interpret agent-deleted passives such as 'The boy got hit' (also called truncated passives) revealed that, although children in the two youngest groups studied (up to 4 years 5 months; and from 4 years 6 months to 5 years 11 months) could not yet perform passives correctly, they were aided by such cues as non-reversibility and by the lack of an agent in the truncated form. She found that very few children used a consistently inappropriate strategy. In fact, the pattern of cue use for her groups was so mixed that she suggested that the processes involved in comprehending the passive voice are not identical for all children. A more general question can be raised, then, about the use of any strategy for comprehending sentences: are there consistent differences among children in the strategies they use in their approach to comprehending and acquiring language?

Strategies Accounting for Individual Differences

Katherine Nelson (1973) was interested in the language-acquisition processes of very young children. Specifically, she wanted to know how the child proceeds from the one-word stage to the stage where short sentences begin to be used. To this end, she made a study of 18 middle-class children in Connecticut, who were between 10 and 15 months old at the beginning of her study. Nelson visited the home once each month for half an hour over a period of about one year, depending on the starting age of the individual child. In addition to this data base, the mothers kept records of the child's first words as they were acquired. The first 50 words of each child were analysed. Mother–child interaction was also recorded and analysed at two points during the study. Some psychological testing was carried out, and the children were seen during a follow-up session when they were approximately 30 months old.

One of the interesting things that emerged from this study was that children differed greatly in their early use of words. For example, one child would have many general nominals or names for objects. In contrast to this, another child would be observed to have a large number of what can be called personal and social words. Nelson found that she could divide the children into two groups on the basis of these differences in language use. One group, which she called the referential group, was object-oriented. The other, the expressive group, was self-oriented. This expressive group used many more two-word utterances than the referential group. Nelson describes their language as being a very personal, social language for expressing feelings and needs.

Nelson used this division of the children and analysed the data to see if various features of acquisition were associated with one or the other 'strategy' of using language. She found that there was no difference in the ages at which the first 10 words were acquired. However, the referential group showed a faster rate of acquisition of words per month and attained a higher vocabulary at age 2 years. But the age at which they acquired their first 10 *phrases* was later. In other words, for the referential group it is the lexicon and not syntactic acquisition which is advanced. The phrases of the referential group were usually two-word telegraph-like utterances (for instance, 'more car'), whereas the expressive group's phrases were more complete grammatically (for instance, 'Don't do it').

In addition to affecting the size of vocabulary at age 2 years and the content and form of the language acquired, these different acquisition strategies affected the pattern of development as well. Nelson proposed that semantic-structure acquisition differs from child to child. Fundamental to all children, however, are some basic distinctions such as that between object and non-object. The object side of the semantic tree is itself divided into animate (which is again subdivided into people and animals) and inanimate (which is subdivided into personal items such as toys, food and clothing, and impersonal items such as vehicles and furniture). The non-object side of the tree is divided into categories which are person-related (action, expressive) and object-related (action, various object properties). All of these subcategories on both sides of the tree continue to subdivide. According to Nelson, the manner in which semantic development proceeds differs for the two basic groups. The referential-group children show greater development on the object side of the tree, whereas the expressive children develop the non-object side. The manner in which the semantic tree is filled in also differs, with the expressive group children establishing greater diversity in their categories.

In the latter part of her monograph, Nelson elaborates two other dimensions which affect language acquisition. One of these is the relative degree of match between the child's concepts and the environmental linguistic usage. The other relates to mother–child interaction and is characterized as acceptance or rejection on the mother's part of the child's attempts at verbalization. In conjunction with the referential/expressive dimension, eight language-learning patterns are shown to be possible. The contribution of the child's linguistic strategies, however, is seen mainly in the referential/expressive distinction.

Other investigators have also drawn attention to differing 'strategies'. Dore (1974) approached language acquisition from the rather different point of view of studying what are called primitive speech acts, which consist of single words or single prosodic patterns which function to convey an intention. Some of the primitive speech acts he has observed include labelling, repeating, answering, requesting an action, requesting an answer, calling, greeting, protesting and practising. Although his empirical data were based on the video-taping of only two children, a girl from the age of 1 year 3 months to 1 year 5 months and a boy from 1 year 3 months to 1 year 7 months, he observed a distinction which is very similar to that found by Nelson. The girl evidenced what he called the 'code-oriented style', which was made up basically of labelling, repeating and practising words. It consisted mainly of primitive speech acts which were not addressed to other people. This would match Nelson's referential strategy. The other child, the boy, used what Dore called the 'message-oriented style', a style which used language mainly to manipulate other people. Of the boy's primitive speech acts, 63 per cent involved other people, compared to only 26 per cent of the girl's speech acts. This message-oriented style would be what Nelson called the expressive strategy.

In another study, Susan Starr (1975) visited 16 children longitudinally from the age of 1 year to 2½ years. Each visit lasted for about an hour and a half, with about an hour and a quarter of recording for each session. When the child was observed to have 10 or more two-word combinations in a single session, he was said to be in the sentence stage. Analysis was then made of the single words in the session exactly two visits prior to this stage, in order to have a developmentally similar data point for all the children at the single-word stage. Similarly, the data from the session two visits after the one which marked the beginning of the sentence stage were analysed for the two-word-stage data. Starr found that there was a functional continuity between single words and two-word sentences. She found that children use language either to describe objects or to talk about themselves. Again, these are the same two strategies as Nelson found. Starr noted that whichever strategy the child was observed to use at the one-word stage was the same as that he used at the two-word stage, showing a continuity of strategy use across developmental milestones.

Nelson has also speculated on whether some other observed differences in language use might be described as different individual strategies of acquisition. One of these concerns the comprehension/production distinction. Children who use a comprehension strategy appear to attend selectively to the talk around them, enlarging the number of utterances which are understood. Nelson says that this strategy is especially noticeable in children who talk 'all of a sudden' after months or years of little or no verbal response. The reverse is true of children who use a production strategy, in which they constantly test their conceptions of words and sentences against their acceptance by the environment. Yet another possible strategy is the use of questioning by some children. Nelson found a positive correlation between the use of questioning at age 2 years and the other language indices, especially vocabulary acquisition. It was not, however, related to the referential/expressive-strategy distinction. Nelson points out that, since there is merely a correlation, it could be that questioning is an activity which is engaged in by more advanced speakers, rather than a strategy for acquiring a larger lexicon.

In most of the earlier studies of children's language, more attention has been paid to generalities across children in their methods of acquisition. It may be that a closer analysis will reveal that children use several different paths in the particulars of acquiring the structure of their native language. Some evidence for this has been presented in this section; and we saw in the previous section that slightly older children may use rather different processing strategies on similar linguistic structures, while some children may use no strategies at all. There may nevertheless be some broad similarities in the language-acquisition process which may be due to similar cognitive stages through which the normal developing child must pass. If cognitive abilities underlie the language-acquisition process, it may be possible to trace a number of strategies used by children of similar cognitive levels to deal with linguistic structures.

Broader Cognitive Strategies

After much initial interest in the structural descriptions of child language, a number of psychologists began to turn to underlying conceptual processes and their development to help explain language acquisition (see for instance Bloom, 1970; Cromer, 1968; Macnamara, 1972; Slobin, 1973; and reviews of the field by Cromer, 1974a, 1976a). The initial impetus for this change in direction came primarily from the Piagetian school of psychology. Piaget's view of language is rather complex. Language obviously plays a major part in the person's internal representation of the world. For example, when language begins in the child, it serves as the major contributor to the interiorization of action into thought. Nevertheless, language is seen as only one part of what is called the symbolic function. Other parts include deferred imitation, mental imagery, symbolic games and drawing. The symbolic function allows thought to be detached from action, and language is particularly important for this formative process (Piaget and Inhelder, 1969b). Piaget's main emphasis, however, is that language builds on and affects a number of cognitive abilities which have already arisen in the sensorimotor period of intellectual growth. In fact language acquisition is said to be able to begin only at the conclusion of the sensorimotor period because it is dependent on some of the intellectual accomplishments of that period.

   Hermine Sinclair (1971) has put the Piagetian case most succinctly. She has noted a number of sensorimotor schemes which she considers can account for corresponding linguistic abilities observed in language acquisition. For example, it is the developing ability to put things in spatial and temporal order which would also allow for the linguistic equivalent of being able to concatenate linguistic elements. The child's developing ability to classify actions (such as using entire categories of objects for the same action or applying a whole category of action schemes to one object) also makes possible the linguistic classification ability of placing verbal elements into major categories like noun phrases and verb phrases. The ability to relate objects and actions to one another provides the basis for the functional grammatical relations, such as 'subject of' and 'object of'. The achievement of the ability to embed action schemes into one another allows for the kind of linguistic recursive property in which phrase-markers can be inserted into other phrase-markers, as found in some of the types of sentence mentioned earlier, such as centre-embedded structures and relative clauses.

A similar theoretical approach has been proposed by Greenfield, Nelson and Saltzman (1972). They argue that the existence of action structures formally similar to grammatical structures may provide a cognitive base for language-learning itself. In order to study action structures, they presented five cups of increasing size to 64 children between 11 and 36 months of age. The experimenter demonstrated an advanced strategy for seriating the cups. The children were then, in the first trial, allowed free play with the cups. In a second trial, they were handed the smallest cup first; in a third trial, they were handed the middle-sized cup first; and, in a fourth trial, they were given the largest cup first. With each child, whenever he had accomplished a seriated arrangement, he was handed a cup midway in size between the third and fourth cups and told to put it 'where it belongs'. Responses were scored in terms of 'final structure', defined as the largest cup structure attained before dismantling. Three distinct strategies were identified for handling the cups, and they were associated with different age levels. The strategy which was dominant at 11 months of age was 'pairing', where a single cup was placed in or on a second cup. A second strategy, which reached its peak at about 20 months of age, when it became the dominant strategy for most children at that age, was the 'pot method'. Here a stationary cup functions as a pot which holds the mobile cups. In this strategy, the child successively holds a number of cups which move into or onto a single stationary cup. The most advanced strategy, and the one which was used most by the oldest children, is called the 'sub-assembly method'. In this strategy, a previously constructed structure consisting of two or more cups was moved as a unit into or onto another cup or cup structure. In this method, the stationary cup which was acted upon in the first move becomes the acting cup in the second move. Some cups, then, serve a double function or double role. They change from being acted upon to being the actor. It was also observed that children using a particular strategy did so fairly consistently, using that strategy about 80 per cent of the time. Greenfield et al. relate these strategies to particular grammatical constructions. The pairing strategy, for example, is said to be parallel to the subject–verb–object grammatical ordering. That is, the first cup (actor) enters (action) the second cup (acted upon). The second strategy, the pot method, is said to involve multiple actor–action–acted-upon sequences which would be similar to conjoined linguistic structures. The first cup (actor) enters (action) the cup acting as the 'pot' to hold the other cups (acted upon), and another cup (actor) enters (action) the cup acting as the 'pot' (acted upon). Finally, the sub-assembly method is thought to be parallel to the linguistic structures in which the first object in the sentence becomes the subject of the following clause. The first cup (actor) enters (action) the second cup (acted-upon object), which then (now becoming subject) enters (action) a third cup (acted upon object). This would be parallel to the kind of relations found in relative-clause sentences like 'The dog chased the cat that caught the mouse.'

Greenfield et al. argue that the same human capacities may be responsible for both the action structures and the linguistic structures. That is, both the cup strategies and the language strategies are said to be behavioural manifestations of underlying internal forms of organization. These forms of organization may have other concrete applications as well. There are, of course, problems with such a view. First, although the cup strategies are said to be analogous to certain linguistic features, and although the linguistic features are shown in terms of increasing complexity (and are observed to be acquired in an order which matches the increasing complexity), there is no direct evidence of a link between the two classes of phenomena. Children using the most advanced cup strategy were under 3 years of age in the experiment, but we have seen that much older children have difficulties with relative clauses in which role change occurs. Second, although one may well suppose that the ability to handle certain types of relationship linguistically must depend on an underlying cognitive ability to handle those relationships on a non-linguistic level, such an observation does not explain the language-acquisition process itself. But it would tell us that certain cognitive abilities which result in certain strategies for dealing with the non-linguistic world might well be used in attempting to handle linguistic input. We would also expect that the inability to deal with certain structural principles on the non-linguistic level would be paralleled by the inability to use similar principles on a linguistic plane.

In a later study, Goodson and Greenfield (1975) examined three structural principles which are common to linguistic behaviour and manipulative play. They labelled these principles hierarchical complexity, interruption and role change. Hierarchical complexity occurs when a sub-assembly is constructed and used as part of a larger construction. It occurs in both manipulative tasks and in linguistic constructions, and was the most advanced strategy in the experiment of Greenfield et al. just discussed. Interruption can be observed in manipulation tasks when one activity is stopped in order to complete an intervening activity before the first activity is resumed and completed. In grammar, the interruption of one sequence by another would be seen in centre-embedded sentences such as 'The boy who was sick stayed home', where *who was sick* constitutes the interruption. In both motor activities and grammar, interruption is said to make the sequence more complex. Role change is observable when a single element plays different roles in relation to different parts of a complex structure. The experiments of Amy Sheldon (1974) mentioned earlier, and the similar speculations by Bever (1970) concerning 'double functions' in centre-embedded sentences are examples of the difficulties caused by role change. It will be recalled that role change, or what Sheldon called 'non-parallel function', made the largest contribution to the difficulty experienced by the 4- and 5-year-olds that she studied. In the study of Greenfield et al. role change occurred in the sub-assembly construction, which was also an example of hierarchical complexity. Thus the two principles, role change and hierarchical complexity, were confounded in that earlier study. Goodson and Greenfield, then, designed their experiment in order to study these various principles separately.

The materials used were various blocks, boards, nuts and bolts, from which various objects could be constructed. Two objects were chosen for study, a bench and a propeller. The bench may be constructed by means of two strategies. In one, the subject can place the board on one support, screw it in, and then move to the other side to attach the second support. In the second strategy, however, one can interrupt the sequence. One can place the board on the two supports, and then move to one side to place the screw, returning to the other side to place the second screw. The first method could be called a simple sub-assembly, while the second would be a sub-assembly with interruption. The propeller can also be constructed by two different strategies. In one, the various pieces are merely piled onto a single piece, the nut or bolt. That is, the nut or bolt always serves as the recipient of the action and defines the locus of the action. This strategy is called 'piling' and is similar to the 'pot method' of the earlier experiment. A second strategy, however, is much more complex. One can place the two blades of the propeller together and then the nut and bolt through them. This does not involve interruption, but it does require that the pieces which served as actor in the first action become the acted upon pieces in the second action. This strategy was termed sub-assembly with role change. Noting Sheldon's data that role change was more difficult than interruption, Goodson and Greenfield predicted the following order of difficulty of the four strategies: piling (propeller), simple sub-assembly (bench), sub-assembly with interruption (bench) and sub-assembly with role change (propeller).

36 children who ranged in age from 2 to 7 years were tested. Pilot testing had revealed that all 8-year-olds tested were capable of employing all four strategies. First, a completed bench was shown and the child was asked to build another just like it. In this way, the child's spontaneous strategy could be observed. But Goodson and Greenfield were interested in what a child was *capable* of doing. So, as the next step in the experiment, the experimenter took the model apart and asked the child to copy a new method of constructing it. The experimenter then modelled the strategy that the child had not used. If the child had used the advanced strategy spontaneously, he should easily be able to copy the less advanced method. If he had spontaneously used the simpler strategy, then this step would show which children were capable of the more advanced assembly technique, and which were not. In the third step in the experiment, the experimenter took out a completed propeller and asked the child to make one. Finally, as in the procedure with the bench, the experimenter demonstrated the method opposite to that spontaneously used by the child and asked him to make the propeller in that manner. The results corresponded exactly with the predicted order of difficulty. Furthermore, the strategies were scalable; a child could perform up to his most advanced strategy and not beyond it. Only three of the 36 children revealed a gap in the strategy order. The increasingly complex strategy use also correlated with age $(r = 0.75)$. Goodson and Greenfield interpreted their results as suggesting two developmental steps in strategy use: the acquisition of complex hierarchical structures, and the acquisition of the ability to deal with role change. An inspection of their table of the individual strategy use of the 36 children revealed that interruption itself did not affect competence very much, and this is in line with Sheldon's findings on relative clauses.

Once again, as in the earlier study, one can ask whether there is any direct link to strategies used in comprehending or producing linguistic structures. Goodson and Greenfield argue that one need not find a specific parallel between manipulation and language, due to the differences in the media. Rather, these strategies are really general principles which appear many times in development. But this claim is somehow unsatisfying. A child may need to have the cognitive underpinnings which make him capable of carrying out certain types of operation before they are observed in either action or language. This is essentially what Sinclair's argument, using the Piagetian framework, insists on. It was claimed that, in order that language should begin, certain accomplishments of the sensorimotor period had to be achieved. But we are again faced with the problem concerning how these are specifically encoded in a linguistic system. It is one thing to speculate that certain cognitive abilities are *necessary* in order for certain aspects of language acquisition to occur, but it is another to claim that they are *sufficient*. Since these cognitive strategies appear a good deal earlier in manipulative play, what exactly is it about language that 'prevents' a child from applying the same strategies to that medium? Dulay and Burt (1974) ask a similar question in a slightly different context. They were looking just at linguistic structure, rather than at the commonalities of structures found in action and in language. But they argue that, even if one is solely concerned with linguistic structure itself, a linguistic description only tells one *what* is eventually learned and not *how* it is learned. It may of course be that certain cognitive strategies will be used by the child gradually to reconstruct his more primitive linguistic system until it more closely matches the adult system, but these will have to be more closely specified. The strategies will have to be shown to be directly related to the language-acquisition process, and not merely related by analogy.

A number of other important questions also arise. How are these various cognitive mechanisms or strategies thought to be organized in the brain? For example, what is one to say about children who have difficulty acquiring linguistic structures (developmentally aphasic children), but who are otherwise intellectually normal? What about adults suffering from some form of traumatic aphasia, who lose certain grammatical abilities? Would one claim that they also lose precisely the same cognitive structures in their action patterns? In both of these cases one might be tempted to speculate about specific language mechanisms beyond the cognitive ones, although alternatively one could suppose that the impairments are purely in the auditory modality. But, in addition, what about unimpaired adults attempting to learn a foreign language? Since they have presumably passed through all the developmental stages and possess all of the necessary cognitive equipment, what prevents them from easily acquiring in the second language hierarchically complex forms, embedded structures, structures with interrupted sequences, and structures which incorporate role change? It is possible to accept that specific cognitive underpinnings are necessary for language acquisition to occur and yet still assume some specifically linguistic mechanisms in addition to these.

Specifically Linguistic Strategies

One area of linguistics in which evidence of strategies is available is the study of phonology, and some of the strategies which have been observed appear to be specifically linguistic. Even in studies of the perception of language there is strong evidence that speech is analysed differently from non-speech sounds (Liberman, 1970; Liberman, Cooper, Shankweiler and Studdert-Kennedy, 1967; Studdert-Kennedy, 1974). This appears to be the case in infants 2 and 3 months old (see for instance Eimas, 1974a). Even infants as young as 4 weeks of age are able to discriminate linguistic and non-linguistic stimuli (see reviews by Eimas, 1974b; Morse, 1974).

In the production of speech, it is becoming generally accepted that the young infant does not acquire his sounds by imitating them. Rather he appears to produce them in accordance with a systematic set of phonological rules. This was the position put forward originally by Jakobson in 1941, though not translated into English until 1968. Basically, his theory proposes that the infant makes a series of discriminations of the features of the language that he hears. These features are represented by phonological contrasts such as vocalic/non-vocalic, voiced/voiceless, nasal/oral, grave/acute, etc. It appears that the child first dichotomizes sounds on the basis of one feature, and begins to classify all sounds on that basis of that feature. Later, new contrastive features are added to his system, and in this way he progressively adds to his differentiations until all the sounds in the language to which he has been exposed have been identified on the basis of the distinguishing features. These features are rules which act across particular sounds. For example, when the child acquires the contrast voiced/voiceless, he creates not one but a number of distinctions based on the voicing feature. There include /g/ versus /k/, /b/ versus /p/, /d/ versus /t/, and /v/ versus /f/. Moreover, Jakobson claims that these contrasts appear in the child's productive speech in a constant order, and this order is said to correspond to the number of languages in the world which contain the particular feature. In other words, the strategies the child uses to discriminate sounds follow a constant order which appears to be some kind of species-specific and language-specific system, and is observable in the universal distributional characteristics of human language sounds. Details of theories of this type can be found in Chomsky and Halle (1968), Jakobson (1968), Jakobson and Halle (1956), and Jakobson, Fant and Halle (1952).

Neil Smith (1973) in a longitudinal study of phonological acquisition mentions several strategies that the child employs in his early productive speech. One of these is constant harmony, in which a child changes the sound of the adult form so that the consonants of the syllables are identical. An example of this would be the child's producing [keɪki] *or* [teɪti] for *Katy*. Another common strategy is systemic simplification in which classes of sounds are reduced to one of their common elements. A third strategy is cluster reduction. Here, certain sound combinations are reduced to simpler sounds. An example would be the child's rendition of *flower* as 'fower'. Barbara Dodd has found the same types of strategies to be used by deaf children (Dodd, 1976b) and by severely subnormal non-Down's-syndrome children (Dodd, 1976a).

The Jakobson type of theory of the acquisition of distinctive features emphasizes the generalities across children in acquisition order. Some deviations from this order are found, however, in individual children. Ferguson and Farwell (1975) claim that some of the differences are attributable to the different strategies adopted by children in acquiring the adult phonological system. Amongst the individual strategies that they mention are the use of 'favourite sounds' (that is to say, the preference for certain sounds, sound classes or features), extensive use of reduplication, special markers for certain classes of words, preference for either lexical expansion or phonological differentiation at the expense of the other, and persistent avoidance of particular 'problem sounds'.

If there are certain phonological strategies some of which can be thought to be specific to the language system, one may ask whether there are any strategies which children use in acquiring grammar which may be specifically linguistic. Dan Slobin (1973) calls attention to the cognitive prerequisites for grammar, but he also notes that formal linguistic complexity plays an important role in language acquisition. He points out that cognitive development and linguistic development do not proceed in unison. The child must find the linguistic means to express his intentions and understandings. According to Slobin, it is possible to postulate a number of what he calls 'operating principles' which the child seems to apply to language input. These operating principles are inferred from child language-acquisition data which have been gathered cross-culturally, and are meant to represent universal strategies used by children. However, most of these strategies would seem to be explicable as linguistic manifestations of broader cognitive strategies. For example, the principle 'avoid interruption or rearrangement of linguistic units' has already been discussed by Goodson and Greenfield (1975) as being observable in manipulation strategies used by young children. Similarly, it is not difficult to imagine the broader cognitive strategies of which these language-acquisition principles are a part:

pay attention to the ends of words;
pay attention to the order of words and morphemes;
avoid exceptions;
the phonological forms of words can be systematically modified.

Even two principles which at first appear to be slightly more linguistically specific –

underlying semantic relations should be marked overtly and clearly;
the use of grammatical markers should make semantic sense;

– can be seen as part of a number of general, non-linguistic principles for coping with information.

Whatever the exact status of these strategies, whether linguistic or more broadly cognitive, their adequacy for accounting for observed language behaviour has been questioned. Dulay and Burt (1974) ask what is predicted when two apparently conflicting principles are applicable to a certain structure. For example, in utterances like 'no Daddy go' and 'wear mitten no' the child has avoided the interruption of the main sequence, but he has not paid attention to the proper placement of the negative morpheme. Of course, this could be dealt with by ordering the principles. But Dulay and Burt have other criticisms as well. They point out that some common observations appear to confute certain operating principles. The principle 'pay attention to the ends of words' is violated by English-speaking children who regularly omit functors at the ends of words even after having acquired several prepositions. Also, such a principle would not apply to prefixing languages such as Navajo. As Dulay and Burt put it, there is no evidence that Navajo children acquire their morphological structure later than children acquiring suffixing languages such as Turkish.

It is difficult to see what might count as a specifically linguistic strategy, unless it was one which is not applied to other material or which exhibits certain features which are unlike other cognitive strategies. An example of the latter might be the observation that such a strategy is not used beyond some sort of critical period for language acquisition (Lenneberg, 1967). I made a series of studies (Cromer, 1970a, 1972a, 1972b, 1974b, summarized in Cromer, 1975a) in which I hypothesized that such a strategy was being used in the acquisition of new linguistic material. The structure used in these experiments was one studied by Carol Chomsky (1969). It is usually rendered by linguists as the contrast pair 'John is eager to please' versus 'John is easy to please.' In the first, John is the actor of the sentence, but in the second, he is acted upon; someone else finds it easy to please John. Correct interpretation of the second type of sentence is acquired at a rather late age by children. The reason for this appears to be that they must learn to violate their expectation that the surface subject is the actor. The experiments were designed with materials the children could handle and which studied comprehension of a number of examples of the structure. The child had wolf and duck hand puppets and had to act out the meaning of such sentences as 'The wolf is happy to bite' and 'The duck is glad to bite', in which the surface subject is indeed the actor, as well as sentences such as 'The wolf is fun to bite', and 'The duck is tasty to bite', in which it is the surface object which is the actor. In all, there were eight sentences which served as a clear test of this structure, four of each of the two types, with appropriate controls for which animal was named first and which animal acted as the biter. The results indicated that young children persist in the interpretation that the surface subject should be the actor even at an age when they can correctly perform passive sentences of the type 'The wolf was bitten.' These children can be labelled as being at a 'primitive-rule stage' since they apply a rule that the named animal is the actor in this particular structure. At about 6 years old, however, children enter what can be called the 'intermediate stage'. At this stage they no longer always treat the surface subject as the actor, but they do not yet perform correctly. They get some sentences right and others wrong. Furthermore, they are not simply acquiring the semantic markings or syntactical understanding of the particular words like *happy*, *glad*, *fun* and *tasty* which indicate which deep structure to recover when they are used in this structure. Rather, they are inconsistent from day to day in their answers, and this intermediate period lasts for about three years. Finally, at about 9–10 years old, they fairly rapidly become capable of performing correctly in the adult manner on all the exemplars of this sentence type. How this learning occurs is a mystery, but an attempt was made to examine it by having the children learn new material (nonsense words) which could be used in the structure. For example, it is the case that words like *happy* and *glad*, which serve as the cue to the fact that the surface-structure subject is the actor in the sentence, are allowable in sentence frames such as 'I'm always —— to read to you.' The words like *fun* which indicate that the surface subject is *not* the actor are excluded from this frame. One cannot say 'I'm always *fun* to read to you.' Similarly, there are frames which allow the latter types of words, but exclude the former. For example, one can say 'Reading to you is *fun*', but it is ungrammatical to say 'Reading to you is *glad*.' It was suggested that perhaps children learned the structural properties of words such as *glad* and *fun* by hearing them in these and similar transformational frames which serve to differentiate them. In various experiments, normal children at the different stages of acquisition of this structure, subnormal children and normal adults were given nonsense words in related differentiating frames, and then asked to perform with the wolf and duck when these same words were used in the test structure. Although the learning hypothesis was not supported, a number of strategies were observed, and these differed in the different groups. In normal children, those using the primitive rule on normal sentences continued to do so on all the sentences with the nonsense words.

Of intermediate children, about 50 per cent used a consistent strategy for interpreting all new material. Half of these applied the primitive strategy of treating the surface subject as the actor, but half applied a strategy of treating the surface subject as acted upon. Amongst children capable of adult performance, about a quarter applied a consistent strategy, but now it was always the strategy of treating the surface subject as acted upon. This strategy might be loosely characterized as 'bending over backwards' to expect a change in the basic grammatical relations. It was hypothesized to be related to a linguistic universal to do with marked and unmarked forms. What is intriguing is that this strategy was never used by adults. More than 40 per cent of the adults used a strategy to interpret all the sentences with the nonsense forms, but they always used the strategy used by the youngest children – treating the surface subject as the actor. Educationally subnormal children behaved just like the normal adults, and it was suggested that this might be because they were 14, 15 and 16 years of age, and thus beyond a critical period when the 'surface subject equals acted upon' strategy was likely to be used.

Cook (1973) studied the acquisition of this structure by adults who were learning to speak English. He found that in the normal sentences with real words (*happy*, *glad*, *easy*, *fun*, etc.) adults were progressing through the same stages as children. This was inferred both from the average amount of time they had been living in England and from the average amount of time that they had been learning English in their home country. Those who performed on all sentences in accordance with the primitive strategy of treating the surface subject as actor had been in England an average of two months, and had been learning English in their home country for an average of two years two months. Adults who were intermediate on this structure had been in England seven months, and learning English for three years five months. Those who were capable of performing in the adult English fashion had been in England an average of one year, and had been learning English an average of four years eight months. However, on learning new instances (the nonsense words used first in the frames meant to differentiate them), they performed differently from the children. The primitive-rule users on real sentences did not use that strategy on the new words. And the strategy of treating the surface subject as acted upon was not observed in any adults, just as it was lacking in the native English-speaking adults in Cromer's experiment. Cook's experiment has two implications. First, these foreign adults can be presumed to have the ability to use adult cognitive operations, but they are observed to go through the same stages as children in learning this structure. Second, the strategies they apply to new instances of the structure are not the same as those applied by children.

It was hypothesized that the strategy used by children who were advanced on this structure was related to an observed linguistic universal concerning marked and unmarked grammatical forms. Since it did not appear in adults, it was further hypothesized that it is the kind of strategy which is somehow tied to a critical period in which language is more easily acquired and by different methods. It was thus concluded that the strategy observed in the advanced children may be a purely linguistic one. But one would like a more direct experimental test of a supposed linguistic strategy. I have carried out such a test (Cromer, 1975b) on a strategy suggested by McNeill, Yukawa and McNeill (1971): that of expecting overt inflectional marking to indicate the indirect rather than the direct object. Using English-speaking children in a language game in which they had to break codes, one of which was in accordance with the universal expectation and one of which was against it, no differences were observed in the error scores in the two groups. Various possibilities can be suggested for this negative result, but another important question arises instead. How does a strategy allow learning to occur in any case? In a language in which only indirect objects are marked, it would allow for quick and easy acquisition of the form. But most inflectional languages provide special word-endings for both the direct and indirect objects (accusative and dative cases). A strategy of treating all marked forms as the indirect object would lead to a high proportion of incorrect comprehensions. Similarly, in the wolf-and-duck experiments, the strategy of treating the surface subject as the one to be acted upon led to a 50 per cent error rate. Perhaps the whole notion of 'strategy' as applied to language acquisition needs to be examined.

The Notion of 'Strategy' as Applied to Language Acquisition

In an earlier section which dealt with the use of various perceptual processing strategies by children, a complication was observed. Children were seen to differ in their use of some commonly observed strategies, many not using them at all. Yet all the children acquire the adult forms. How does the acquisition occur? This is not necessarily a difficult problem. In the Bruner, Goodnow and Austin experiments on concept formation, individuals used widely varying strategies to learn the same concepts and these strategies were classified into four basic types. Similarly, we saw that there are many strategies that account for individual differences in the language-acquisition process. There are further complications with these language-acquisition strategies, however. Not only do not all individuals use them, but even those who do do not apply them to all linguistic input. For example, whereas 6-year-old children apply the rule that the surface structure is the actor in sentences like 'The wolf is fun to bite', they do not apply that strategy to passive sentences such as 'The wolf is bitten.' What makes children apply a particular strategy to one structure but not to another? Perhaps they have a broad strategy (such as first noun is the actor) which they apply to many structures and slowly learn the particular structures which are exceptions to it. This kind of explanation would be compatible with the results obtained by Dewart (1975) across a number of different sentence types. But, again, this is really a description which in essence says that, as the learning of various linguistic structures occurs, particular comprehension strategies which often lead to an incorrect interpretation are no longer applied to them.

Even more complex are cases where the linguistic structure itself seems to determine whether a strategy is to be used or not. Earlier, the minimum-distance principle hypothesized by Carol Chomsky (1969) was mentioned. The strategy consisted of treating the noun nearest to the complement verb as the subject of that verb. Verbs like *promise* violate that rule, and children must learn that the first of the two nouns is the actor. Thus, in 'John promises Bill to sing', it is not until a rather advanced age (8 or 9) that children begin to realize that it is John and not Bill who will be singing. However, in experiments on interpreting *ask*, further difficulties were observed. First, it is more complicated for children because it has two meanings. When used as a question, as in 'John asked Bill what to sing', the minimum-distance principle is violated as with *promise*; it is John who will be singing. But, when used as a request, the minimum-distance principle is observed. Thus, in 'John asked Bill to leave the room', in British English, Bill must leave the room. In American English, the sentence is ambiguous, and the context can influence the interpretation. Compare, for example, 'The teacher asked the boy to leave the room' and 'The boy asked the teacher to leave the room.' To Americans, the boy will be leaving in both cases. To British English-speakers, the second sentence does not sound quite grammatical. But in both dialects *ask* as a request is treated differently from *ask* as a question. For both dialects *ask* as a request observes the minimum-distance principle – consistently for the British, inconsistently for Americans.

When Chomsky tested a number of children on their interpretation of *ask*, she was surprised to find that many children treated the sentences as if they meant *tell*. She therefore changed her study to an investigation of when the child could correctly interpret *ask* as a question instead of using *tell*. Two children were seated at a table with various toys and objects. The task was for one child to ask and tell the other child certain things. Chomsky found that there were three structures in which *ask* could be used, which varied in difficulty. She called these Cases 1, 2 and 3. Examples are

Case 1   Ask Laura what colour this is
Case 2   Ask Laura the colour of this book
Case 3   Ask Laura what colour to make the square

In Case 1, the child merely has to change 'what colour this is' to 'What colour is that?' in order to form the question. Case 2 is slightly more difficult. The child must now supply a question word and a verb in order to form the appropriate question. Thus, 'the colour of the book' must be changed to 'What's the colour of the book?' In Case 3, the most difficult case, the child must not only supply the auxiliary verb, but must specify the correct subject. In the example, 'what colour to make the square' must be changed to 'What colour *should I* make the square?' To do this, the child must refer outside the complement clause to retrieve the subject and must essentially choose between NP_1 and NP_2 (i.e. it is not appropriate to say 'What colour should you make the square?').

Chomsky found that the children could be divided into five developmental stages on the basis of their answers. Treating *ask* as if it means *tell* is scored as a failure. Treating it correctly to mean asking a question was scored as success. Given these definitions, the five stages were

Stage A   Failure on Cases 1, 2, and 3
Stage B   Success on Case 1; failure on Cases 2 and 3
Stage C   Success on Cases 1 and 2; failure on Case 3
Stage D   Success on all cases, but wrong subject assignment for Case 3
Stage E   Success on all cases and correct subject assignment for Case 3

The interesting stages for this discussion are Stages B and C. At these stages, children can be said to know the meaning of *ask* and can perform correctly in the situation – as long as the simplest linguistic structure is used. At all other times they seem to apply the strategy 'treat *ask* as if it means *tell*'. The moment a slightly more advanced linguistic structure is used, they fall back to the use of that strategy. Here is an example of one Stage C child taken from Carol Chomsky's report:

> *Experimenter*. Ask Joanne what colour this book is. (Case 1)
> *Laura*. What colour's that book?
> *Experimenter*. Ask Joanne her last name. (Case 2)
> *Laura*. What's your last name?
> *Experimenter*. Tell Joanne what colour this tray is.

Laura. Tan.
Experimenter. Ask Joanne what's in the box. (Case 1)
Laura. What's in the box?
Experimenter. Ask Joanne what to feed the doll. (Case 3)
Laura. The hot dog.
Experimenter. Now I want you to *ask* Joanne something. Ask her what to feed the doll. (Case 3)
Laura. The piece of bread.
Experimenter. Ask Joanne what *you* should feed the doll. (Case 1)
Laura. What should I feed the doll?

Of the 39 children between the ages of 5 and 10 who took part in the experiment, nine evidenced this kind of behaviour and were classified as being at Stage C. A close inspection of the example dialogue shows that the child understands the meaning of the word *ask*. Furthermore, she can form the appropriate questions structurally. What she does, however, is to use a strategy, as it were, of supplying a *tell* interpretation for any linguistic *structure* which is beyond her competence. In order to apply the correct interpretation, she must already know the structure of the sentence. In other words, once again one can observe a strategy which is applied when the child doesn't know what to do. It does not tell us how the child acquires the structural knowledge which determines whether a strategy is used for interpretation or not. And this is really the central problem of strategies as applied to language acquisition.

At the beginning of this chapter, the work of Bruner, Goodnow and Austin was cited as providing the basis of definition for the concept of 'strategies'. But the strategies they explored were very different from those now being proposed for language acquisition. Concept-formation strategies provide a means for testing hypotheses which are easily disconfirmed. By contrast, young children use strategies sometimes for years to produce utterances they do not hear others producing around them, and which in the linguistic community are being constantly disconfirmed. A more essential difference, however, is that the 'strategies' of Bruner et al. are *methods for acquiring new information*. The strategies proposed to account for language acquisition do nothing of the sort. As has been repeatedly emphasized throughout this chapter, the various strategies which have been proposed are merely ways of answering a psycholinguist's questions on a comprehension test, or a way of interpreting sentences in the world when their structure is not yet understood. Nelson (1973) recognized this distinction and wrote of the differences between strategies for *acquiring* language and strategies for *processing* language. She characterizes the former as being strategies for adding new elements to the original repertoire, whereas the latter match elements to the existing repertoire. We do not seem to have discovered many acquisition strategies as yet.

The emphasis on 'strategy' has had, overall, a beneficial effect. It has made us aware of some of the ways by which the child may possibly 'get into' the linguistic system. It has shown us the importance of perceptual mechanisms for interpreting utterances, and how as adult speakers with full linguistic competence we nevertheless rely on a number of short-cuts to understanding. We are even misled at times by some perceptual strategies, as we saw, for example, when some interpretations of a structure are perceptually suppressed. The emphasis on 'strategy' has also made investigators much more aware of the individual differences exhibited by children learning language. Psychologists have also begun once again to realize the crucial importance of underlying cognitive operations which are necessary for any language behaviour to occur. Some operations may be specifically linguistic, but little is yet known about them. The concept of language-acquisition strategies has told us much – except how the child acquires language.

4

Reconceptualizing Language Acquisition and Cognitive Development

At this point in the development of language-intervention programmes, it is important to take stock of the directions taken by those working on the acquisition of language in normal, unimpaired children. The focus of this chapter is on the acquisition of the structure of language. Any intervention programme that is intended truly to deal with 'language' cannot confine itself merely to 'communication'. Understanding the development of grammar for language-training programmes was emphasized by Waryas and Stremel-Campbell (1978).

Although there has been a good deal of interesting work on the communicative and pragmatic aspects of language, our knowledge of the structure of language has barely increased, and those acquisition processes are still shrouded in mystery. There has been little progress in this area partly because many psychologists are confined by a number of conceptual prejudices that prevent the emergence of an adequate understanding not only of language acquisition but of cognitive development in general. This chapter suggests that the recent directions taken by language-acquisition research, although valuable for the advancement of knowledge of important aspects of communication (and therefore of great interest to those designing language-intervention programmes), have nevertheless failed to fulfil their promise to explain adequately the acquisition of the linguistic

This chapter (copyright © 1981 University Park Press Inc.) was first published in Richard L. Schiefelbusch and Diane D. Bricker (eds), *Early Language: Acquisition and Intervention* (Baltimore: University Park Press, 1981), pp. 51–137, and is reprinted here by kind permission of University Park Press.

structure of language. It is further suggested that at least two major reconceptualizations of development may be in order. The first part of this chapter reviews recent research directions in language acquisition with the aim of indicating the reasons why such research has not solved the problem of the acquisition of language structure. In the remainder of the chapter, two reconceptualizations are suggested.

The first reconceptualization stresses the importance, for language acquisition, of internal factors in the child. Two frameworks are mentioned within this first reconceptualization – one stressing possibly innate factors and the other emphasizing the child's treatment of the language system as a conceptual puzzle space to be dealt with in its own right. Although these two frameworks are different, they are not incompatible. They share the feature of being critical of purely environmental/ associationistic approaches to the acquisition of the structure of language. This section is introduced by a brief outline of how the mechanisms of growth and development can be reconceptualized to give a modified account of Piagetian mechanisms of development so that innate mechanisms can be considered more seriously. The fact that these concepts are stated in a Piagetian framework does not imply that they are limited to that theoretical position. In fact, it is preferable to see the suggestions that are offered as part of a broad 'epigenetic' framework for development, but the ideas are stated in terms of Piagetian mechanisms because these are currently popular. The other framework – treating language as a structural system that is acquired – draws on work by Karmiloff-Smith that analyses in some detail how the child deals with particular structural subsystems of language.

The second reconceptualization deals with the content of cognitive stages. This reconceptualization asserts the need to look in more detail at the cognitive processes that comprise any putative stages. Some examples are given from research on language-disordered individuals to support the claim that, to have effective intervention programmes, there is no substitute for finding the true deficit. In a review of language-intervention programmes, Siegel and Spradlin (1978) reasoned that differential diagnosis and the discovery of specific underlying causes of language impairment would be important if it could be shown that these had significant consequences for the type of treatment and/or instructional programmes undertaken. They concluded somewhat pessimistically, however, that, given the present state of knowledge, the instructional task seemed to be identical regardless of whether the individual child was labelled autistic, brain-damaged, retarded or congenitally aphasic. Although their conclusions are not unwarranted given present knowledge, the examples that are given of underlying deficits being uncovered by research will perhaps give a more optimistic outlook for the future. The emphasis on the need to look at specific cognitive deficits in the various types of language-disordered individuals is related to the second reconceptualization. It is argued that mere correlations between broadly conceived Piagetian stages and various indices of language development are of little value for language-intervention programmes.

The concluding section presents recent advances in language acquisition that take into account what the child brings to the language-acquisition process, and suggests some links to language-intervention procedures.

Research Directions that Have Not Fulfilled Expectations to Advance Knowledge of the Acquisition of the Structure of Language

This section discusses three topics and originally also discussed a fourth, research on language-acquisition strategies, which in this book is already fully discussed in chapter 3. Not all of these are strictly 'research directions'; at least one of them is really only a theoretical orientation for research. It should be noted that the research mentioned below is not being criticized. Much of it is excellent in quality and has led to real advances in our broad understanding of communication. In every case, however, there has been a failure to shed any light on the processes involved in the acquisition of the structure of language. This is true despite the claims often made that only by understanding the broader aspects of language acquisition will the acquisition of linguistic structure be made clear. Such claims have so far proved empirically empty.

Research on parent–child interaction

One of the more interesting recent developments has been the close analysis of parent–child interaction. Because the child's exposure to the linguistic system in the first few years consists primarily of the speech of the parent, it certainly seems that the features of that system will be important in determining the child's language growth. Several questions are posed in this section: what is special about this language input? Why is it used by parents? What effects does it have?

One of the criticisms of the early studies of the growth of structure in child language was that it left meaning and communicative intent un-explored. Researchers began to make a more detailed analysis of the relationship between the mother and the child, and they especially focused on the pre-linguistic communication (Bates, 1976; Bruner, 1974–5, 1975).

Much time is devoted in the mother–child relationship to the development, in Bruner's words, of joint activity and joint attention. Language is seen as an instrument for regulating this activity, for example by ensuring joint reference. It was also noted that much of the mother's activity was shaped by the child. This is in contrast to the more purely empiricist view that the child's actions are primarily shaped by external experience. The issues raised by studies of the communicative interactions are important for those dealing with language-intervention programmes. Nevertheless, when the question of how the acquisition of the structure of language is to be explained, the answer is unclear. Developing cognitive processes, meaning, communicative intent and the like are examined in the next section. Here, the speech of parents to infants is examined to see what effects it does and does not have.

The special characteristics of baby talk   In the early 1960s it was assumed that the input the child was exposed to was, like speech of adults to one another, filled with pauses, hesitations and false starts. It was thought to constitute a degenerate signal from which to extract the syntactic regularities of the linguistic system. The ability of the child to master the system in only a few years was seen as even more remarkable given the characteristics of this input. People began to question, however, whether the speech to children was really as ill-informed as had been believed. After a good deal of observational study, much of it cross-cultural in nature, it is now established that adults speak to infants and young children in ways that are markedly different from the ways they talk to other adults. Brown (1977) noted that there are over 100 features that can be detailed for 'baby talk', or 'motherese', as some researchers call it. Baby talk is a special register in which adults speak to infants and young children (Ferguson, 1977). An excellent collection of original research articles on this topic can be found in Snow and Ferguson (1977). Sachs (1977) found that adults use a higher fundamental pitch when speaking to young children. In addition, special intonational patterns are used as well as special rhythmic patterning. Certain sounds are more commonly used – for example, initial stop consonants, especially the voiced forms. Garnica (1977) also noted the use of higher pitch and such features as the assignment of more than one primary stress to short and simple sentences, the prolongation of certain content words, and the use of rising sentence-final pitch terminals in sentences in which the adult grammatical form would call for a falling pitch. Cross (1975, 1977) called attention to such discourse features as the self-imitations and self-repetitions by the mother. In addition, there are several structural features that have been observed. Wills (1977) noted the use of third-person forms for both the 'sender' and 'receiver' of the message (e.g. 'Where are Mommy's eyes?' 'Did Adam eat it?'), replacement of a singular 'sender' and 'receiver' with a plural form (e.g. 'Let's get you some mittens, huh?', 'We'll put some music on, wait, wait, wait'), and the deletion of independent pronouns from the surface structure of declarative sentences (e.g. 'Got that duck on ya now', 'Shouldn't talk with your mouth full'). Other structural features of baby talk include low mean-utterance length, less use of long utterances (Cross, 1977) and low semantic complexity (Cross, 1977; Snow, 1977). These are only a few examples of the kinds of features noted in the special baby-talk register.

Why is baby talk used?   Before discussing why baby talk is used by parents, it is interesting to note some other uses of baby talk, or at least of registers resembling it. Brown (1977) pointed out that baby talk is found not only in speech addressed to infants but also in speech to animals, to foreigners and between lovers. It is usually thought that the use of a simplified register is to ensure communication. This can hardly be the case with the use of the register with domestic animals and between lovers. There are several other possible uses for the register. For example, as used in speaking to animals, or by the 4-year-old to the 2-year-old, or by nurses to patients, the use of the register may be to assert power or status (Gopnik, personal communication). Brown (1977) suggests that these are different registers, and that baby talk is more specific in that it is created by a specific conjunction of two main components. One of these deals with the dimension of communication clarification; the other is an expressive–affective dimension. The registers used with animals or with lovers do not contain both of these components.

Why parents use baby talk as a special register to infants or young children is an interesting question. Brown (1977) pointed out that in response to this query parents often answer that they are teaching the child to speak, but Brown questions this assumption. He gives evidence (e.g. from Cross, 1977; Garnica, 1977) that the real aim is not to teach but to communicate. The parent uses the various features of the register not with a tutorial purpose but to control attention, improve intelligibility, and to specify that those particular utterances are directed to the child. These are significant aids to learning. Many of the functions of baby talk are important in the design of intervention programmes for the language-handicapped, although some of the principles, such as the need for clarity and control of attention, are obvious and have always been employed. A close study of spontaneous 'motherese', however, will be useful in revealing a number of techniques that serve less obvious functions that can be used in such programmes.

What effect does baby talk have? In addition to discussing the specific effects baby talk may have on the language-learning of the child, it is useful to ask what effects the mother–child interaction studies have had on our notions of language acquisition in general. It is possible to put the question in a stronger form. The parent–child interaction studies are referred to here under the heading of research directions that have not fulfilled expectations to advance knowledge of the acquisition of the structure of language. In what way have they not done so? Underlying most of the research is an assumption that the child is acquiring what the environment has to offer. Chomsky (1967) argued that children acquire their language system on the basis of a restricted amount of evidence – evidence that is moreover of a degraded sort, consisting largely of utterances that break grammatical rules in that they are made up of false starts, disconnected phrases, and other deviations. The mother–child interaction studies have shown that the speech the child is receiving is a far less degraded sample than Chomsky and others had hitherto believed. This has been taken by some as evidence that there is no innate component to the language-acquisition process, or that, at the very least, innate mechanisms should be de-emphasized (Brown, 1977; Garnica, 1977). Such conclusions, however, are unwarranted. To show that the input signal to many children is far clearer than had been assumed in no way explains how the grammatical structures that the child uses are developed. Even those mother–child interaction researchers who conclude that the child is an active participant and indeed the participant who shapes the interaction (e.g. Bruner, 1974–5, 1975; Gleason, 1977; Seitz and Stewart, 1975) – as opposed to the older behaviourist view of a passive child almost totally influenced by environmental input – do not extend those notions to the linguistic structure of language itself. It is asserted in this section that what is known about children's use of grammatical structures is not incompatible with a strong internal component. A close analysis of the structural acquisitions of the child reveals that there is not a close fit between the nature of the structures that the mother uses and those that the child is producing. One important experimental study makes this especially clear and is therefore reviewed here in some detail.

Newport, Gleitman and Gleitman (1977) analysed the motherese directed by 15 mothers to their young daughters. The children were in three groups: ages 12–15 months, 18–21 months and 24–27 months. They were visited twice for two-and-a-half hour sessions, held six months apart. Both the mother's and the child's utterances were coded on a variety of features. The mother's speech was coded in terms of well-formedness, sentence length, structural complexity (as determined by the number of sentence nodes per utterance and derivational length), sentence type, intelligibility and expansions. Child measures included mean length of utterance (MLU), the frequency and length of noun phrases and verb phrases, and the use of various inflections (marking of plurals, modals and tenses). Newport et al. found that there is a pattern (which they called 'motherese') that incorporates many devices that aid in clarity. For example, the utterances to the young children were significantly shorter than those to other adults (mean MLU of 4.24 to children compared to 11.94 to other adults). The utterances also were highly intelligible (only 4 per cent of utterances to children were unanalysable because of mumbles and slurs, compared to 9 per cent in speech to other adults) and well formed (only one utterance of 1,500 spoken to the children was disfluent; in speech to other adults there was a 5 per cent disfluency rate). Most utterances to both children and adults were *bona fide* grammatical sentences (60 per cent of those to children, and 58 per cent to other adults) – the rest were primarily well-formed isolated phrases. These results showed that the mothers' speech is indeed shorter and clearer than had been supposed. However, Newport et al. also pointed out that the sentences of motherese were not structurally simpler in terms of other important aspects. The canonical structure of English sentences is the active declarative sentence of the form subject–verb–object. Although 87 per cent of sentences to other adults were of this type, in motherese only 30 per cent were. There was also a wider range of sentence types to children than to adults. To children, 18 per cent of the utterances were imperatives and 44 per cent were questions. Newport et al. also found that derivational complexity is significantly higher in speech to children than in speech to other adults. This measure is suspect, however, and indeed open to an interpretation that so-called derivationally complex sentences are in fact psycholinguistically easier than less derivationally complex ones. In any event, it is the case that motherese in general is a simpler form of the adult language because it is shorter and has fewer sentence nodes. This is reflected in the rare use of sentences involving embedding and conjunctions. Even this latter finding, however, is seen in terms of a move towards brevity and not in terms of syntactic simplicity. This interpretation is supported by the fact that there was no correlation between the number of sentence nodes used by the mother and the child's age or any of the measures of the child's syntactic sophistication.

Newport et al. concluded that motherese is not a special register for teaching language structure. They claimed that one can envisage three basic principles for teaching a language to a beginner: (1) use the canonical sentences of the new language first; (2) introduce one new construction at a time; (3) move from simple to complex sentences over time. Newport et al. pointed out that none of these holds for motherese.

For example, canonical declaratives actually increase over time, and the range of sentence types used by the mother narrows as the child grows older. The increases in MLU and a number of sentence nodes are not statistically significant. As Newport et al. concluded, 'there is no compelling evidence in our data that mothers tune their syntactic complexity to the growing competence of their children through this crucial age of syntax acquisition, the period from one to two and a half years' (1977, pp. 123–4). This is not to say that motherese has no effects on the acquisition of certain aspects of language (this is discussed in detail on pp. 199–201, where the positive effects found by Newport et al. are examined). At this point it is worth noting, however, that Newport et al. are making two major claims. First, motherese is not a register designed for teaching the syntax of language. Others (e.g. Brown, 1977) have reached a similar conclusion. As Newport et al. stated, motherese arises in order to communicate with a cognitively and linguistically naïve child in the here-and-now. It is a style designed to get the child to do something now, not to teach him structure. Second, Newport et al. accept that the child, in addition to being affected by the communication setting, possesses language-specific mental structures – that is, hypotheses for evaluating incoming linguistic data. The usual assumption of studies of adult speech styles directed to children is that the carefully structured input determines the child's acquisition. In contrast, Newport et al. concluded that 'nativist assumptions are left intact by a close look at motherese – they neither gain nor lose plausibility' (1977, p. 123). It is possible to go further than what Newport et al. suggest by looking at what the child is producing in conjunction with the motherese he or she is receiving as input.

The data from the first serious language-acquisition studies of the 1960s revealed one important feature: the child actively organized the structure of his or her productions in ways that did not match the structure of what he heard others saying. The productions were not 'telegraphic' – merely shortened forms of the adult input – as had at first been postulated. Consequently, it was claimed that imitation was not the method the child used to acquire the structures of his or her language. There are numerous examples demonstrating that children produce utterances that are structurally ordered in ways quite different from the input (e.g. Bellugi-Klima, 1969; Brown and Bellugi, 1964; reviewed in Cromer, 1970b, 1980). When young children produce negative utterances by prefixing *no* or *not* to affirmative sentences, as in 'No wipe finger' and 'Not fit', they are not simply associatively picking up adult language forms or imitating the adults around them, no matter how short and clear the sentences are that are directed at them. Bellugi's analysis (Bellugi-Klima, 1969) of the development of self-reference by the child, which attempts to specify the rules by which the child first uses his or her own name and then *I* or *me* dependent initially on sentence-position rules and later on rules of grammatical structure, shows that the changes over time are not related to the use of these terms in the mother's speech. A clear example of the lack of correspondence between the adult input and the child's utterances comes from Bellugi's careful analysis of the child's use of auxiliaries. For example, at first the child always produced the full, uncontracted form of *will*, thus producing utterances that sounded very precise: 'We will put it here', 'It will go away.' In contrast, the mother almost invariably used the contracted form, *'ll*, leading to inputs to the child of numerous forms like 'He'll', 'You'll', 'It'll', 'That'll' (as in 'It'll hurt you', 'That'll be enough'). The mother only used the complete form of 'will' in interrogatives, as in 'Will it be fun?' 'Will you finish it?' As Bellugi pointed out, the child must have organized the forms *will* and *'ll* into a single system leading to the production of forms by the child that differ from the adult input in significant ways.

Although these are only a few examples, close analysis of child-language data shows that this is the rule, not the exception. Children construct their own productive rule systems. They constantly produce utterances and sentence forms that do not match the adult model. Of all the recent studies on mother–child interaction, not one mentions this basic and important fact – clear findings from the 1960s that to date no strictly empiricist theory has adequately explained. This neglect of basic observations is primarily attributable to the conceptual prejudice of most psychologists to consider only concepts that show direct association with environmental input. The mother–child interaction studies have not explained or accounted for the acquisition of linguistic structure. This is clearly pointed out in the Newport et al. study, in which the attempt was made to relate specific features of input to specific features of child production.

The studies reviewed in this section are often referred to as studies of mother–child *interaction*. Indeed, some researchers have emphasized the interactiveness of the process and are thus thought to be in advance of those conceptions that saw the child as passively receiving environmental input. But the 'interactiveness' is ignored when the question of the *structure* of language arises. Some psychologists even allow the child to have innate capacities and/or innate schemata to deal with behavioural exchanges between the self and others. By fiat, however, the child is not allowed to have innate capacities for the organization of language. Part of the reason for this is the continued misinterpretation of the nativist issue in terms of an either/or situation. It is mistakenly assumed that, if a theory allows for an innate component, environmental influences have only a moderate or little or no part to play in development. Such a belief is misconceived, and a truly interactive theory is advanced as part of the first of the reconceptualizations presented in this chapter. It is helpful, however, to continue examining the Newport et al. study to clarify these issues and to show that the structure of the input does play an important part in the acquisition process.

Newport et al. studied the relations between the maternal speech styles and language acquisition by carrying out a series of correlations between differences in those styles and the child's language growth rate when both the child's age and the initial level of linguistic achievement had been partialled out. They found that certain aspects of the mother's speech did have an effect on some aspects of the child's learning. That is, while many properties of motherese had no effect on the child's language growth, some aspects did exert an influence. They claimed that this was true only for what they called language-specific structures – that is, the surface morphology and syntactic elements that vary between languages. Even these, however, only had an effect through what they called the filter of the child's selective attention to portions of the speech stream. Newport et al. claimed that the child has a means for restricting and organizing the flow of incoming linguistic data. He or she filters out some kinds of input and selectively listens for others. (This notion of filtering is referred to on pp. 251–5, where some suggested links to language-intervention programmes are considered.) According to Newport et al., then, learning does respond to narrowly specified features of the environment, even though 'it is contingent on what the children are disposed to notice in that environment, on their stategies of listening and the hypotheses they are prepared to entertain' (1977, p. 131). Newport et al. then considered what aspects of the child's language were affected by the input. The number of auxiliaries used by the child correlated positively both with the mother's use of yes/no questions and the number of her expansions. The number of nominal inflections (e.g. formation of plurals on nouns) was positively correlated with the mother's use of deixis (use of *this* and *that* as in 'That's a dog'). The growth of a number of language features, however, was not sensitive to individual differences in motherese styles. Thus, the number of verbs per utterance or the number of noun phrases per utterance were dependent on cognitive and linguistic maturity – not on specific aspects of environmental input.

Newport et al. claimed that what is and what is not affected by maternal speech style are very different aspects of language. The universal aspects of language structure and content are basically unaffected by differences in motherese. This supports the view of a semi-autonomous unfolding of language capabilities in the child. In contrast, those features that are specific to the surface features of different languages are the ones on which motherese exerts an influence (although even these are subject to a filtering system noted above). These findings are similar to differences recently observed in the written language samples by aphasic children and congenitally profoundly deaf children (Cromer, 1978a, 1978b). The aphasic children evidenced problems with basics of linguistic structure. In contrast, the deaf children used structural relationships that the aphasic children seemed incapable of using, but made many 'surface' grammatical errors such as inconsistent use of plural inflections, and possessives (see below, pp. 247–9).

The studies of parent–child language and interactions have made an important contribution to our knowledge of the growth of communication processes. They have not, however, provided a solution to the problem of how children acquire the structures of their language. The Newport et al. study, in contrast, does succeed in showing how a reconceptualized viewpoint, incorporating in a truly interactive manner what the child brings to bear on the process, can contribute not only to a better understanding of how language acquisition occurs but how language-intervention programmes can use those principles. Most studies of baby talk fail to explain the acquisition of structure because of a primarily environmentalist viewpoint and the implicit empiricist assumptions made about the mind of the child when acquisition of linguistic structure is considered.

Semantically based theories

Many recent reviews and discussions of language acquisition criticize child-language research in the 1960s for concentrating on syntax and neglecting the field of semantics. This was certainly true, and a great deal of research effort has been invested in righting this imbalance (e.g. Bowerman, 1976; Clark, 1973c; Donaldson and Balfour, 1968; Klatzky, Clark and Macken, 1973; Maratsos, 1973b; Nelson, 1973; Nelson and Bonvillian, 1973; Wales and Campbell, 1970). Although most researchers were clear about what aspects of the child's developing language system they were studying, psychologists with more general interests frequently misunderstood and confused such notions as semantics, thought and syntax. A good example of this is the use made by psychologists of 'case grammar' theory from linguistics.

Case grammar (Fillmore, 1968) incorporated features of meaning into the syntax. That is, it was suggested that 'case' categories should appear in the base component of the grammar. According to Fillmore, grammatical concepts such as 'subject' and 'object' are constituents only of the surface structure of some but possibly not all languages. What was important in the new view was the underlying case assignment that relied on the covert meaning of sentence relations. For example, in English, the subject of a sentence may express a variety of case functions. In 'John opened the door' *John* is an agent, but in 'The key opened the door' *key* is an instrument, not an agent. In other sentences the subject serves other functions. In 'John received a gift' *John* is a recipient, in 'John received a blow on the head' *John* is a patient; and in 'Chicago is windy' *Chicago* functions as a location. Case-grammatical conceptions, then, express some aspects of meaning not found in the linguistic constituents 'subject' and 'object'. In contrast, these latter terms express a different level of generalization. As in the examples above, the 'subject' of a sentence can serve various case functions. But 'grammatical subject' is a linguistically relevant constituent in that speakers use these constituents in a number of transformations or changes independently of their particular case functions. Psychologists proposed that case grammar might better capture the essence of young children's utterances. Bowerman (1973) demonstrated that very young children's grammars were more adequately described using case-grammar terminology during the initial phases of language acquisition. But she also noted that at some point in development it was necessary to invoke grammatical notions such as 'subject' and 'object' to account for the more purely syntactic relations that were observed.

Although case grammar is itself a linguistic theory – and one which virtually no linguist still accepts as an adequate description of language – many psychologists have taken case notions as if they were identical to non-linguistic concepts, equating them with more general 'meanings' or 'intentions' of the speaker. To clarify this problem, and also to relate it to language intervention, the interpretations of some research findings should be examined. There have been a number of attempts to teach non-human primates to use 'language' or at least to 'communicate'. The distinction between these terms is crucial for the argument of this section. In one successful venture of great interest and importance, Premack (1969; Premack and Premack, 1972) used plastic shapes backed with metal that a chimpanzee, Sarah, could manipulate and place on a magnetic board. Each plastic abstract shape was associated with a particular stimulus. Although Premack used reinforcement techniques gradually to shape the chimpanzee's behaviour, he did not claim that this was the way in which language functions were acquired by human beings. He was interested in investigating whether language functions similar to those found in humans could be established in another species. Premack had a good deal of success. Sarah acquired the basic communication units that he taught including what he termed the names for objects, verbs that described various actions, modifiers, questions and negations. Some of these consisted of the judgement and communication of complex concepts. Not only did Sarah learn symbols for *yes, no, same* and *different,* but she combined these in understanding and answering questions. For example, given the symbols for

(X) $(same\ as)$ (X) $(?)$

she would answer with the symbol for *yes.* She would similarly answer *yes* to

(X) (not) $(same\ as)$ (Y) $(?)$

Given the symbolic strings

(X) (not) $(same\ as)$ (X) $(?)$
(X) $(same\ as)$ (Y) $(?)$

she would answer *no* to both. Premack taught Sarah communication structures built from simple structures to more complex ones. For example, Sarah was first taught simple messages with symbols corresponding to 'Sarah insert banana pail' and 'Sarah insert apple dish'. After Sarah could understand both messages separately, as gauged by her being able to carry out the appropriate actions, Premack then combined them. Thus, he progressively introduced the more condensed instructions 'Sarah insert banana pail insert apple dish' and 'Sarah insert banana pail apple dish', in which the second uses of *Sarah* and *insert* were eliminated. Again, Sarah was able to perform appropriately on these more complex tasks. These are amazing feats, and research of this type makes more probable the exciting prospect of being able to communicate with other species in a direct fashion. In the context of the problem of the acquisition of the structure of human language, however, and in terms of intervention programmes with language-handicapped individuals, it is important to make the conceptual distinctions mentioned above.

On the basis of Premack's results (and those of other researchers, e.g. Gardner and Gardner, 1969, 1975; Rumbaugh, 1977; Rumbaugh and Gill, 1976), some psychologists have concluded that chimpanzees have been able to learn 'language'. The actual results of these studies have now been the subject of strong criticism (e.g. Sebeok and Umiker-Sebeok, 1980; Seidenberg and Petitto, 1979; Terrace, 1979). Even if the claims that have been made for communicative abilities in non-human primates were true, however, there is little evidence that the production of these primates would be correctly characterized by claiming that these constitute subject–

verb–object strings. Cromer (1978a, reprinted below as chapter 5) argued caution must be used in making such interpretations. The terms *subject*, *verb*, and *object* are terms for linguistic constituents, and, although they often express the meanings 'actor', 'action' and 'acted upon', they need not do so, as the examples from case grammar indicated. The former linguistic terms are not identical to the latter specific conceptual meanings. Perhaps the systems acquired by chimpanzees are communication systems encoding the linkages of meanings rather than of linguistic elements. If this is true, then chimpanzee messages may be more accurately described in terms such as *actor, action, acted upon* rather than in terms such as *subject, verb, object*, which imply a different level of linguistic generalization that human children have been observed to eventually build upon (Bowerman, 1973).

This distinction between meaning and the linguistic structures in which meaning is encoded is important to language-intervention programmes. It is possible, for example, that in some types of aphasia certain conceptual meanings may be preserved while the more purely linguistic structures in which these meanings are usually encoded break down. On a suggestion by Dr Hermelin, Hughes (1972, 1974–5) carried out a study to see if children with developmental or early acquired aphasia could acquire the type of communication system that Premack used. The four children she studied were of average or above average intelligence as measured by non-verbal tests. They were unable to comprehend and to produce normal language, and this was true either from birth or from an early age despite the fact that no known brain trauma had occurred. The children were trained individually in 30-minute sessions twice a week for about nine weeks, using materials similar to those used by Premack – plastic symbols backed with metal that could be placed on a magnetic board. Hughes reported that the aphasic children rapidly acquired all of the functions she taught. These included the names for objects and persons, names for attributes of these objects, actions such as *give* and *point to*, negatives and questions. Despite an inability to comprehend or use normal linguistic forms – and this was not merely because of auditory modality defects (see below, chapter 5) – these aphasic children acquired a fairly sophisticated communication system without much difficulty.

Glass, Gazzaniga and Premack (1973) reported similar findings with adult aphasics. Seven patients with global aphasia resulting from cerebral vascular accidents were trained in the use of cut-out paper symbols varying in colour, size and shape. These symbols were arranged on a table in a set left–right direction. Glass et al. found that with an average of one month's training all seven patients acquired same/different and interrogative constructions. In addition, two of the patients learned simple sentences consisting of what were described as 'subject–verb–direct object' strings, to a level of accuracy of about 80 per cent. There was evidence that the other five patients also would have progressed to the same level had training continued, but for administrative reasons (e.g. patients being discharged from the hospital) this was not possible. Glass et al. concluded that global aphasics may not suffer a cognitive impairment as severe as their linguistic impairment; globally aphasic patients are capable of sophisticated and abstract symbolic thought despite severe language deficits.

The demonstration by Hughes and by Glass et al. that developmentally aphasic children and globally aphasic adults can acquire abstract plastic-symbol systems despite known language disability is evidence that these systems, although encoding some of the functions that language encodes, are nevertheless not really the same as *linguistic* systems. Conceptual distinctions like these, which psychologists have blurred, are important if one tries to improve the language abilities of language-handicapped individuals, and not just their communication abilities.

A similar confusion of meanings and language is found when psychologists have considered another movement within linguistic theory – generative semantics (see for example Lakoff, 1971; McCawley, 1971a, 1971b, 1973; and a collection of reprinted articles edited by Seuren, 1974). An earlier version of Chomsky's particular formulation of transformational grammar (Chomsky, 1965) was criticized for its neglect of the semantic component of the grammar. This earlier version is sometimes referred to as 'standard theory'. As a reaction to these criticisms, which showed inadequacies in the theory for dealing with various sentences, two types of theories were developed. One of these was a modified version of the earlier Chomskian theory, and is referred to as 'extended standard theory' (Chomsky, 1972; Jackendoff, 1972). It still emphasized the autonomy of the syntactic component of the grammar. Although more attention was given to the semantic component and its interaction with the syntax, this semantic component was nevertheless conceived of as a set of interpretation rules that acted on or were applied to the syntax. The followers of that theory, therefore, also came to be called 'interpretive semanticists'. The followers of the other theory were called 'generative semanticists'. They believed that the meaning component itself is important in the generation of sentence structures and cannot be separated from them. Indeed, it was claimed that syntactic phenomena could not be explained without reference to semantic factors. In other words, the claim by the generative semanticists was that the semantic and syntactic components of grammar are inextricably entwined. To capture these essential differences, this broad school of thought was also called 'semantic syntax' in contrast to the 'autonomous syntax' of Chomskian theory (Seuren, 1974).

Although linguistic theory has progressed from these positions – the Chomskian tradition now embraces 'trace' theory (Chomsky, 1975), and the theory of 'generative semantics' is said to have collapsed about 1975 (Newmeyer, 1980) – it should be noted that these two main positions, the extended theory or interpretative semantics and the generative semantics theory, were both reactions to the inadequacies of the earlier Chomskian viewpoint. More importantly, both theories were concerned with specifically linguistic entities. The issue between them was the exact placement of the semantic component in the grammar. The term *semantics* is a linguistic term that refers not to meaning, but to meaning-in-language. It is in no way identical to *thoughts*, *concepts* or *meanings*. Many psychologists have been confused about this, and have even drawn on the arguments used by linguists of the generative-semantics school as support for a relatively anti-linguistic view. This confusion still exists although Bloom (1973) called attention to this misinterpretation. Bloom argued that the semantic versus the syntactive basis for grammar is not an important issue for psychologists unless the differences in formal theory lead to different predictions about cognitive and behavioural aspects of language use. She also claimed that the important distinction for those studying child language was not within linguistic categories (syntactic and semantic) but between linguistic categories on the one hand and cognitive categories on the other.

Psychologists tend to view semantic theories as if they were identical to 'cognitive' theories. (The reasons why such theories have not explained the acquisition of the structure of language are discussed in the next section.) Obviously, there is a close relationship between *meaning* (in the broad sense), *semantics* and *syntax*. Schlesinger (1977b) tried to formulate a theoretical position that would relate a speaker's intentions to his or her production of utterances, but there is still little direct evidence concerning how such systems actually work. One of the most interesting works on this problem is that by Carey (1978). It is especially valuable because it is one of the only experimental papers in which the distinctions between the conceptual system, the semantic system and the syntactic system are made clear. She was concerned with the acquisition of the meaning of particular lexical items. By the age of 6, the average child has acquired the meaning of some 14,000 words. As Carey put it, assuming that such learning begins in earnest at age 18 months, the child learns an average of nine new words per day, or one per waking hour. After the age of 2, conscious drill on words – for example, by parents pointing at and naming referents – is not typical; therefore, the child learns most of those 14,000 words by hearing other people use them in normal contexts. In order to study this acquisition and the means used to accomplish it, Carey experimentally introduced a 'new' word, *chromium* (an actual colour name), for olive-coloured objects, in natural situations in a nursery school atmosphere. The 14 3- and 4-year-olds originally applied either the label *green* or *brown* to the olive colour when they were asked to name the colour of various objects at the beginning of the study. The ways the children changed their concepts over the months of study were the focus of the investigation. Carey developed a theory in which children engage in 'fast mapping', which allows them to hold onto fragile new entries in their lexicon while the meanings are built up. She also criticized a simple 'missing features' hypothesis in which a child merely fills in those lexical features that are not yet part of the representation. The details of her arguments are relevant for those interested in the growth of lexical knowledge. What is pertinent for this review is that Carey clarified some of the distinctions that most psychologists currently gloss over. Most important is the differentiation of the conceptual domain from the lexical domain. The conceptual domain is the mental representation by which one describes or understands the world or one's own actions. The lexical domain is the structured set of words that encodes aspects of the conceptual domain. As Carey put it, in terms of colours, there are many things that we know about colours that are not captured in the structure of the colour lexicon. Indeed, each domain has its own identity and structure. According to Carey, in the child there can be development within each domain separately before any mapping of one domain onto the other occurs. To illustrate this point she noted that pre-verbal infants, and even animals, have knowledge of the conceptual/perceptual domain of colour. This point can also be illustrated by Rosch's study of the Dani of Indonesian New Guinea, whose language has only two colour words, *mili* and *mola*. According to Rosch (1977b), the Dani evidence knowledge of the same focal colours as other groups despite the lack of individual lexical entries for them. In contrast, regarding the lexical domain Carey noted that individuals who are blind can learn a great deal of the structure of the lexical domain of colour without ever mapping it onto perceived colours. She also cited Bartlett (1978), who demonstrated that children can list the names of colour hues in response to questions such as 'Do you know any colours? What colour is this?' before they know how to map those colour terms correctly onto the conceptual/perceptual domain.

It is possible, then, to have concepts without any corresponding lexical or semantic encoding (as in the examples of young children, animals and of groups with a limited vocabulary of colour); and it is possible to possess certain aspects of lexical and semantic knowledge without the corresponding perceptual experiences or conceptual knowledge. Semantics is not the same as meaning. Carey studied both aspects by observing how children restructured their lexicon to find the right place for the word *chromium*, and how they restructured their conceptual domain by learning that olive was not included in green or brown but had its own name. Her experiments make it clear why it is important to make the distinction between semantics and conceptual meanings even though they interact during development.

Cognitively based theories

Despite recent work on semantics by the psychologists mentioned above, the interest of more broad-based, mainstream psychologists has been not so much in the development of semantic theory as in theories relating conceptual knowledge and language. These theories have taken two major forms: theories concerning the development of specific aspects of conceptual knowledge and their consequent effect on language acquisition; and theories concerning the development of the structures of thought (usually Piagetian) and their effect on the language-acquisition process. The two approaches are somewhat similar and are not always distinct in practice. For example, theories that propose that specific concepts must develop before the child encodes them in language, even by imitation, may themselves be based on the assumption that such concepts can only develop when the child is capable of certain cognitive operations. There are many studies and reviews of cognitive theories of language acquisition (e.g. Beilin, 1975; Cromer, 1974a, 1976a, 1979; Macnamara, 1972; Moore, 1973); therefore, they will not be examined in detail here. A few examples can illustrate what a cognitive theory of language acquisition would claim.

In a study of the development of reference to time in language (Cromer, 1968), it was observed that certain aspects of language acquisition were dependent on prior development of particular concepts. The two children were Adam and Sarah of Roger Brown's study (Brown, 1973). In looking at their development of reference to various aspects of time, two contrasting methods were used. In one, the child's intention was judged from situational cues and from context. For example, the child would be credited with referring to some aspect of time, even if this was encoded inadequately or incorrectly from the adult grammatical point of view. What the child seemed to be attempting to express was contrasted with the data from the second method – examining the linguistic form and context of the utterance. It was found that children did not attempt to produce certain linguistic forms until after the point in their development when they were making use of the *concepts* that those forms encoded. This was true for a variety of temporal features. One of these was reference to hypothetical situations. True hypotheticalness of predicating a future event on the basis of another event also in the future, as in 'If it rains [future] I will take an umbrella [later future]', developed from earlier uses of pretending. Another was 'relevance', or the ability of the speaker to note the importance of a referred-to-event to the time indicated by his or her utterance. This is usually encoded in English by use of the perfect tense: 'The lamp has fallen' usually indicates that the lamp is still in a fallen position at the time of the utterance or is in a state effected by its fall, whereas 'The lamp fell' merely indicates that the lamp fell at some time in the past but does not imply anything about the current state of the lamp. Another type of time reference was 'timelessness', in which the speaker refers to an event that normally occurs in some timed context but in such a way as to lift it out of any particular situation and so to imbue it with a timeless quality. This is not the same as descriptions, which are usually references to things in the present. Rather, the timeless quality as expressed by one of the children in the utterance 'Playing a banjo is good exercise for your thumb' is what is intended here.

When these and other time reference categories were explored, it was found that children began to use the concepts shortly before using the linguistic forms in which they were usually encoded by adults. Furthermore, it was demonstrated that many of the forms had been used by adults in the child's presence, sometimes for years, before the child began to use them productively. This was true not only for linguistic forms, but for specific lexical items as well. For example, it was only after age 4 that the children began to use words like *always*, *sometimes* and *never* productively – and they began to use these only when they began to express 'timelessness' by other formal means.

There is a great deal of evidence that can be cited in support of the view that conceptual understandings precede the acquisition of linguistic forms used to encode them. Slobin (1966) postulated that the late emergence of the hypothetical form in children who speak Russian, a language in which the hypothetical is exceedingly simple grammatically, is attributable to conceptual difficulty. Brown (1973) cited examples of children making reference to the concept of possession (e.g. 'Mommy nose', 'Daddy nose') before they acquired the *'s* inflection by which it is commonly encoded. (Bloom, 1970, gave similar evidence from three other children.) Brown (1973) also noted that the first verb inflections that children acquired during Stage I of language acquisition encoded the concepts they seemed to be trying to encode when they used only the generic unmarked form of the verb. That is, given the situation and context, adults interpreted the child's verbal meaning in one of four ways: (1) as an imperative, as in 'Get book'; (2) as a reference to immediate past, as in 'Book drop'; (3) as a form of intention or predication, as in 'Mommy read' (pronounced *reed*) in a context where she was about to do so; and (4) as an expression of present temporary duration, as in 'Fish swim', where an adult would use the progressive form 'The fish is swimming.' During Stage I, the children modified the verb in three ways. One of these was to begin marking the past with *-ed* or with an irregular allomorph (e.g. 'It dropped', 'It fell'). A second way the verb was modified was to use it with a semi-auxiliary such as 'wanna' and 'gonna' in utterances such as 'I wanna go' and 'It's gonna fall.' The third modification was that the child used a primitive progressive form – producing the *-ing* but omitting the copula verb (e.g. 'Fish swimming'). What is interesting is that these first three modifications of the verb form encode three of the four meanings that the child was credited by adults with trying to express before he acquired the ability to do so in the adult way. For the fourth meaning, the imperative, Brown noted that, although there is no special imperative form in English, it is just at this age that the children started to use the word *please*.

These are a few examples illustrating the kinds of observations that support the position that specific aspects of conceptual knowledge have an effect on language acquisition. The examples of time reference also illustrate the second type of theory concerning the effect of cognitive variables on language. Some of the more complex types of temporal reference, such as true hypotheticalness, relevance and timelessness, were observed to emerge more or less together in the child and at similar points in development in the different children. It was hypothesized (Cromer, 1968, 1974a, reprinted in this book as chapter 1) that this emergence at about the age of 4 could be accounted for by a more broadly based stage-related development of the ability to decentre. The lessening of 'egocentrism' allows one to move from one's own viewpoint as a speaker and to place oneself at other perspectives and at other points on the time continuum. This enables the speaker to use true hypotheticals (predicating a later future on an earlier future), relevance (relating events of other times to the time indicated by the utterance) and timelessness (the ability to stand outside of the actual order of events in time). This is an example, then, of using a Piagetian notion of cognitive development to explain the emergence of several concepts concerned with understanding time. More direct uses of Piagetian stages to account for aspects of language development have included theories about both what sensorimotor intelligence allows, and, later, what operational thinking makes possible (e.g. Edwards, 1973; Morehead and Morehead, 1974; Piaget and Inhelder, 1969a; Sinclair, 1970, 1971; Sinclair-de-Zwart, 1969, 1973).

These two cognitively based theories can be termed the 'conceptual underpinnings of language theory' and the 'cognitive-operations theory of language acquisition and use'. Although they both have some very interesting things to say about language acquisition, they both have dangers. The first theory is flawed, and the second is usually (but not necessarily) interpreted in a way that does not explain language acquisition. It is useful to examine the theories separately.

Conceptual underpinnings of language theory   One problem with the theory that language depends on the formation of prior concepts is that, despite the demonstrated conceptual influence in some areas, not all of what is encoded in language is necessarily dependent on prior conceptual knowledge. The examples above from Carey (1978) illustrated that some aspects of the lexicon in children were developed independently of conceptual knowledge. Thus, children knew when colour terms were required in discourse, but not how to relate these to the perceptual/conceptual domain of colour. A similar finding was reported in a different context by Blank and Allen (1976). They noticed that children used *why* before they comprehended its meaning. Furthermore, it was noted that at first children only used *why* for verbal stimuli and never to ask about non-verbal events. According to Blank and Allen, the early use of *why* by the child is not with the adult sense of the word, but represents the child's search to determine the meaning of *why*.

Curtiss, Fromkin and Yamada (1978) presented some evidence that there is no link between syntactic and morphological ability and what they call general cognition. They studied six mentally retarded individuals, aged 6–9. A seventh subject was Genie, age 20, who was isolated from language input throughout her childhood. They were compared to a control group of 74 normal children, aged 2–6. The subjects in the experimental group were seen once a week for 20–45 minutes, for a period of 10 months. The control group was seen two or three times a week for two months. The language recorded was the spontaneous conversation between the child and the experimenter. Tests for various aspects of comprehension of language were also administered. These included studies of word order, uses of *before* and *after*, complex modifications, negation, disjunction, tense and aspect, verb pluralization, and *wh*-questions. The children were also given tests of non-language mental abilities. These included a variety of tests of memory, perception, construction tasks, copying, drawing, tests of Piagetian skills (classification, conservation, etc.) and conceptual sequencing. Their spontaneous play was also noted for evidence of symbolic activities. In the matrices of correlations among the various measures, it was noted that expressive *semantics* correlated with a number of non-language tasks, including conservation ability, conceptual sequencing, drawing ability and spatial operations. Expressive *syntax*, the measure of structural complexity of language use, however, correlated only with auditory short-term memory. This means that memory constrains the length and complexity of utterances in child language, but conceptual and even broader Piagetian cognitive abilities are not related to structural measures of language. Curtiss et al. contrasted two extreme cases in their sample. Genie scored lower on expressive syntax than on all the other measures. It was her semantic ability that was most comparable to her cognitive level. Indeed, her level of performance on Piagetian tasks fell within the 6–12-year-old range, indicating that she was in the stage of concrete operations, but her expressive language ability was barely above the 2-year level. Thus, even operational cognitive structures and the concepts they allow are not sufficient to account for grammatical development. It might be said, then, that such operations are therefore necessary but not sufficient for language acquisition and development. But the analysis of another child in the sample raises doubts even on this point. This child's profile revealed that expressive syntax was high, as was his auditory short-term memory, but his scores on non-language tasks were very low, as was the measure of his expressive semantic ability. As Curtiss et al. put it, this child was able to acquire a highly complex grammar while possessing only limited conceptual abilities in other spheres. He had complex syntactic and morphological structures, but his language often lacked appropriate semantic reference and many of his utterances were semantically anomalous. He demonstrated the structural use of *wh–* words, but had trouble distinguishing one *wh–* form from another. He produced all the English tense and aspect verb forms and the auxiliaries, but did not use them appropriately. His syntax was highly complex and his morphology was normal, but his utterances were often semantically irregular. Lenneberg (1967; see also Lenneberg, Nichols and Rosenberger, 1964) similarly found that intelligence was not highly related to language development. It seems then, that conceptual knowledge and language are separate systems and can develop independently.

A second problem with the theory that language depends on the formation of prior concepts is that, even in some conceptual areas where this seems to be true, nothing is explained about the ability to encode those concepts in language. As noted above, developmentally aphasic children, and indeed adults suffering from traumatic aphasia, have concepts that they cannot encode into linguistic structures. This is seen most clearly in those studies that showed that they could learn the symbolic concepts of the communication system that Premack designed even when their language abilities were impaired. The so-called 'weak form of the cognition hypothesis' (Cromer, 1974a, reprinted here as chapter 1) was put forward precisely because of the inability of non-linguistic, purely cognitive theories to explain the acquisition of the structure of language:

> Our cognitive abilities at different stages of development make certain meanings *available* for expression. But, in addition, we must also possess certain specifically linguistic capabilities in order to come to express these meanings in language, and these linguistic capabilities may indeed be lacking in other species or in certain pathological conditions. (Above, p. 54)

This basic criticism of purely conceptual or cognitive approaches to language acquisition was illustrated by Slobin (1978) in what he calls the 'waiting-room metaphor'. In this metaphor there is a box, or 'waiting room', for each linguistic form. The entrance to this room is an underlying notion or concept. The entry key is thus cognitive development that results in discerning the existence of a given notion. The problems to be solved in the waiting room are both semantic and morphologico-syntactic. That is, the semantic problem is the necessity to figure out just what aspects of the particular conceptual notion are encoded in the language. The morphologico-syntactic problem involves determining what linguistic means are used for that encoding. The solution will take various amounts of time and effort depending on linguistic features, and the exit from the waiting room is accomplished by the appropriate linguistic form.

The basic problem with some conceptual theories of language acquisition, then, was the notion that, once the child had the concepts, there was nothing more to explain. All the child had to do was to see how these concepts that he or she was now capable of forming were encoded in everyday language. The trap was the old purely associationistic view of language acquisition – this time an association between the concept and its encoding by adults. Clear input signals such as baby talk or motherese were seen as solving the remaining obstacle to the theory by removing the problem of the child having to form associations between his intentions and signals replete with hesitations, false starts, and the like. As pointed out earlier, the productive utterances by normal children in their natural environment are at variance with such a theory. One of the frameworks for the first reconceptualization proposed in the next section suggests the important part linguistic factors play in the acquisition of the structure of language.

Cognitive operations theory of language acquisition and use Theoretical approaches that concentrate on cognitive operations are less concerned with the specific concepts made possible by such operations, and concentrate instead on the operations themselves and the direct effects they might have on the language-acquisition process. For example, sensorimotor schemata are said to account for corresponding linguistic abilities observed in language acquisition (Piaget and Inhelder, 1969a). That is, a number of sensorimotor schemata are said to account for specific linguistic abilities. The child's ability to order things both spatially and temporally has its linguistic equivalent in the concatenation of linguistic elements. The child's ability to classify actions – using whole categories of objects for the same action, and applying an entire category of action schemata to one object – is observed in the linguistic realm as the ability to categorize linguistic elements into major categories like noun phrase and verb phrase. The ability to relate objects and actions to one another provides the basis for the functional grammatical relations 'subject of' and 'object of'. The ability to embed action schemata into one another is the same operation as that which allows phrase-markers to be inserted into other phrase-markers in language behaviour.

Experimental techniques have been devised to demonstrate action structures in behaviour and problem-solving that are formally parallel to the grammatical structures of language (Goodson and Greenfield, 1975; Greenfield, 1978; Greenfield, Nelson and Salzmann, 1972). At the same time, there has been an unfortunate trend in recent research to do mere correlational studies between measures of cognitive capacity and language ability. Theories of cognitive operations as the foundation of language development are often claimed to be supported by demonstrated positive correlations between measures of behaviour in these two domains. The usual assumption is that, if one has a particular cognitive ability, it is manifested both in non-linguistic actions and in linguistic structure. But the criticisms of the previous sections hold here as well. Curtiss et al., by analysing individual cases, gave examples that counter this view. They found children who had operational ability but who lacked the grammatical structures these are supposedly paralleled by; and they found children who had complex grammatical structures who lacked the cognitive abilities that are supposed to make the use of such structures possible. In addition, cognitive-operations theories suffer from the other problem mentioned in the previous section. Just as having concepts does not explain how these concepts come to be encoded in language, so, too, having the ability to perform particular cognitive operations fails to explain how those operations come to be used in linguistic structures.

There is, however, another way to view cognitive operations. One of the problems in Piaget's approach to language has been to treat it as only one factor of the symbolic function as a whole. Language was not really viewed as different in kind from other symbolic factors such as deferred imitation, mental imagery, symbolic games and drawing. Of course, language was seen as especially important, and the advantages it confers and the developments it allows have been discussed in some detail (Piaget and Inhelder, 1969b). Nevertheless, it was still considered part of the overall symbolic function, although a very important part. It is possible, however, to take a slightly different view. If language itself is seen as constituting a complex body of knowledge that must be discovered on its own terms (Slobin, 1978) in addition to being a part of the symbolic function, then it is possible to apply Piagetian notions concerning the child's acquisition of any system to the acquisition of the language system itself. The other framework for the first reconceptualization proposed in this chapter draws on the work of Karmiloff-Smith (1977a, 1977b, 1978, 1979a, 1979b). Her experimentally based work demonstrates the advantages of viewing the child as an active organism with internally generated procedures and operations addressing himself to the linguistic system as a problem space to be solved.

There has been another effect of cognitive-operations theories and the general upsurge of interest in Piagetian stages as applied to language acquisition. Many researchers have shown an increasing tendency merely to accept the broad Piagetian periods as they have been theoretically presented and to treat these as explanatory of all correlated behaviours. For example, children are given tests designed to measure their stage-related abilities, and on the basis of these measurements they are classified as being pre-operational or concrete operational, or occasionally substages of these. These stage-grouped children are also compared on their language abilities. On the basis of such correlational studies, claims are then made that the achievement of this or that broad developmental stage is a necessary prerequisite for the acquisition of particular features of language. Quite apart from the logical flaws in such arguments, this is not a very useful procedure for advancing the kind of knowledge needed for language-intervention programmes with the linguistically handicapped. The second reconceptualization presented in this chapter is concerned with the necessity to look in more detail at exactly what cognitive processes make up the stages of growth and development.

The Basic Assumption Blocking Real Progress

In the previous section, three directions in recent research were reviewed.

The claim was made that in some sense they have failed to provide insight into the nature of the acquisition of the structure of language. To what is this failure attributable? Research on language-acquisition strategies also needs to be brought into the discussion here (it was omitted from the previous section only because it has already been discussed in chapter 3). The shortcomings of this research direction are slightly different from those of the others. Most such research has actually revealed what children do in interpreting certain structures when they do not yet have the linguistic competence to comprehend these structures in the adult manner. It does not, however, really show how children acquired that competence. In fact, it would be more accurate to say that most of the research on children's strategies has been on strategies for *processing* language, and that very little is known about strategies children use for *acquiring* language. Nelson (1973), who originally pointed out this distinction, characterized acquisition strategies as methods for adding new elements to the original repertoire. There has been some work done on such strategies, and it is referred to as part of the argument for the first reconceptualization. It should be noted that strategies for acquisition, in so far as they go beyond the more traditional theories of acquiring any new information, presuppose an important contribution from the child, and one that may be specifically linguistic (the first framework) or at least composed of general cognitive principles for solving problems by members of the human species (the second framework).

The other three research areas, in contrast, fail to provide an understanding of the acquisition of the structure of language for a different reason. Work in those areas has often been characterized by the assumption of an empiricist theory of mind, which gives no place for specifically linguistic internal procedures. With the exception of the Newport et al. study, the parent–child interaction research has proceeded as if the child merely matched his or her productions to the input signal – which was shown to be clearer than had been supposed. Few attempts have been made to analyse the linguistic patterns used by both participants in the fine-grained manner necessary to demonstrate an empiricist claim, and the fact that child-language productions do not match that input has been virtually ignored. Research on semantic theory is not reviewed in this chapter, but the misinterpretation that many psychologists make of semantic theories in linguistics by confusing them with psychological theories of concepts was noted. Such errors are further promulgated by the misappropriation of the term *semantics* from linguistic theory for a variety of theoretical notions in psychology.

One prominent example of this terminological misuse is found in so-called semantic memory theories, most of which are concerned solely with concepts and not at all with semantics. True semantic theories were not evaluated. The criticisms in the subsection on semantically based theories pertained to the confusion of terms. It was in the discussion of cognitively based theories that inadequacies were discussed. The review of conceptual and cognitive theories pointed out how these theories do not account for the acquisition of linguistic structure. The reason is the same as that claimed for the failure of the parent–child studies: the naïve assumption that, once certain cognitive properties (either concepts or operations) have developed, they will be encoded in linguistic structure. There is an implied associationistic assumption. Children associate the ideas they wish to encode with the linguistic structures they hear in the environment around them. The inadequacies of such theories for language acquisition have been pointed out since the 1960s (e.g. Bellugi, 1967, 1971; Bever, Fodor and Weksel, 1965a, 1965b; Brown, Cazden and Bellugi-Klima, 1969; Ervin-Tripp, 1966; McNeill, 1966, 1970a, 1970b; Miller and McNeill, 1969; Sachs, 1971; and Slobin, 1971a, 1971b, 1973). Empirical research on the utterances children actually produce while acquiring language supports these anti-associationist claims. Yet the real challenge of these findings has been for the most part systematically ignored.

The kind of theoretical reconceptualization that is needed to encourage research in the acquisition of the structure of language to proceed along useful lines is not limited merely to language. The same reconceptualization is needed if the development of broad areas of cognition is to be understood. Since the publication of Neisser's *Cognitive Psychology* (1967), it has been popular for an increasing number of psychologists to assume 'a constantly *active* organism that searches, filters, selectively acts on, reorganizes, and creates information' (Reynolds and Flagg, 1977). In spite of these protestations, a great deal of research on the development of cognitive processes, like much of the work on language acquisition, in reality assumes a much more externally oriented approach than is either professed theoretically or is warranted by the evidence. A good example of this is the explosion of research into the development of conservation ability by 6-year-old children. Piaget's demonstration that young, pre-operational children believe that the amount of liquid changes with the shape of the container was intended to illustrate the inability of the child at that stage of thinking to perform particular operations. Thus, a child who answers that there is more juice in the tall, narrow container than in a container identical to the one from which it has just been poured, is considered a non-conserving child. The child's answers, but more importantly, the child's methods of reasoning, are taken as evidence of pre-operational thinking; he or she is unable to compensate the two dimensions. Note that what is important for the Piagetian view is not the child's answer. Indeed, there are tasks for which pre-operational children almost always give correct answers (for the 'wrong' reasons), although most adults give incorrect answers. In problems concerning area, for example, changing the layout but not the overall length of the perimeter so as to transform a square into a rectangular shape leads children to claim that the area (the space that 'cows can graze over') is less, as it actually is, while adults 'conserve' and incorrectly claim that the amount of grass to graze over must be the same; what is lost in one dimension is made up by the other. Adults use compensation, and are led to the wrong answer. In other words, tasks, like the typical conservation problems, were intended to show evidence of the limits of children's thinking when their thought structures could be characterized in particular ways. Whether Piaget is right or wrong over the particular descriptions of those structures (or even whether children's thinking can in fact be characterized by stage-like thought structures) is an empirical question that can be settled by observational and experimental research. What is at issue here is the approach that was taken to these problems by researchers mainly in America and Great Britain.

Although Piaget was 'translated', his intentions and theoretical orientations were not. Psychologists in English-speaking countries have been concerned much more with a purely externally oriented approach to development. What followed were scores of studies purporting to show that pre-operational children could be taught conservation by various techniques. (The number of articles that share this orientation in child-development journals is too numerous to list. The interested reader can refer to collections of reprinted research articles that come under headings such as 'training research', as is found, for example, in Siegel and Hooper, 1968.) This was, of course, not Piaget's point. More important, such training-oriented research misses the real significance for development that Piaget had observed. Piaget's equilibration process, which is made up of assimilation and accommodation (this is discussed in the next section), considers what the child brings to any problem-solving task. In contrast, the question as to how the structures of thought are acquired is often ignored in training research, which is primarily concerned with external influences.

The claim being made here is that research that is founded on the theoretical assumption that what is crucially important for development is found almost exclusively in external influences will be unable to explain development adequately. This is true for the acquisition of the structure of language, and it is true for cognitive development in general. The usual rationale for such research is that, if it can be demonstrated that children can be taught particular concepts, such as conservation, then it follows that all children must be acquiring these and similar concepts from environmental input. Not only is such a claim illogical; it is not empirically supported. In order to show this clearly, it is useful to quote the results from an early training experiment. Smedslund (1961) demonstrated that he could train a number of non-conserving children to acquire the concept of the conservation of substance and weight. Smedslund reasoned that, if children were truly acquiring the concept of conservation on the basis of learning theory, it ought to be extinguishable, and this should be true whether the concept was acquired in the laboratory or in natural life. In contrast, Piaget's equilibration theory predicts that a genuine principle of conservation would be practically impossible to extinguish because it is thought to reflect an inner logical necessity. Smedslund pre-tested 5–7-year-old children on the conservation of weight. He was thereby enabled to see which children were natural conservers. The non-conservers were those who showed no trace of conservation. These non-conservers were then given training sessions. 11 children were successfully trained to become conservers. They then undertook a series of extinction trials that were also administered to 13 children who had been found to be natural conservers. The extinction trials were carried out by cheating the child. That is, when the plasticine was deformed into other shapes, pieces were inconspicuously taken away so that the two objects would not balance. The results were very interesting. Of the children who were taught to conserve, none showed any resistance to the extinction trials. Smedslund reported that they showed little surprise and rapidly switched back to non-conservation answers supported by explanations referring to the perceptual appearance of the objects. By contrast, almost half of the natural conservers maintained conservation in the face of apparent non-conservation, and this was evidenced in statements such as 'I think you have taken away some of the clay!' and 'We must have lost some clay on the floor.' Smedslund concluded that children who had acquired a notion of conservation in the training sessions had learned only a relatively arbitrary empirical law. As he put it, they were not very shocked or surprised when the law was falsified, and they rapidly modifed their answers and explanations. This contrasted with the resistance shown by many of the natural conservers.

This experiment has often been quoted as showing that trained conservers differ from those acquiring conservation naturally. Since that time, many experimenters have attempted more comprehensive training techniques or have disputed some of the specific details of Smedslund's procedures. But to do so – and even to demonstrate the existence of a tutorial programme on conservation that is resistant to extinction – is to miss a much more crucial point. That some concepts can be taught, and truly acquired, in no way explains how a concept is nevertheless acquired by children who have not undergone such training procedures. The usual empiricist assumption (and it should be noted that it is merely a theoretical assumption) is that, if children can be trained in a particular concept, then other, untrained children are similarly acquiring that concept but by less direct means of environmental input. There is something in Smedslund's study, however, that has never been discussed. If it is assumed that children become conservers because of incidental environmental learning, and this process can be accelerated by direct tuition and environmental demonstrations of the concept, then another prediction is necessary. In Smedslund's study, the so-called extinction trials constituted direct tuition and environmentally supported demonstrations that conservation of weight in fact does not hold true in the world. By any reasonable learning theory, then, we would have to suppose that these children were made into non-conservers, and it must be assumed that they remain so because the normal environment offers only very indirect, incidental learning to the contrary. Although no proper follow-up has been made, it is doubtful that we would find these 11 Swedish children to be non-conservers as adults – or even that they had been delayed in their acquisition of operational thinking. There have been experiments that indicate that some aspects of development can be accelerated by tuition, but such techniques in no way *explain* that development, especially in those who have not had the benefit of that tuition, or, as in the case just cited, in those who have been directly trained in incorrect concepts.

The First Reconceptualization: Internal Factors

The current emphasis on purely empiricist theories is as inadequate as are purely rationalist theories. What is needed is a reconceptualization of development that stresses the interaction of inner determinants and environmental factors.

The first framework: an epigenetic–interactionist viewpoint

What is here called an epigenetic–interactionist viewpoint is really nothing more than the assertion that there is inherent in the human species a number of unfolding developmental phenomena, some of which may be specifically linguistic, that interact with environmental variables. Such a position does not claim that children are born in possession of particular structures, but that structures are built up from an interaction of innate potential with environmental factors. There is a sense in which Piaget's genetic epistemology can be viewed in these terms although Piaget would disagree with the nativist component of such a view. In the Piagetian system, the structures of thought are said to develop through a process of assimilation and accommodation. Assimilation is the process of incorporating elements in the environment into the structure of the organism. These external elements are said to be assimilated to the system. In the process of assimilation, however, the organism is also undergoing modification. This modification is termed accommodation. Accommodation, then, is the modification of assimilatory schemata or structures by the elements that are assimilated.

Seiler (1979) attempted to employ Piaget's equilibratory system to notions of differentiation as a model of cognitive development. In doing so, he emphasized the relationship between assimilatory and accommodatory processes and innate and environmental variables. Seiler equated what he calls 'pure' assimilation with predetermined aspects of behaviour. 'Pure' accommodation, in contrast, is environmentally determined. But, of course, there is no such thing as 'pure' assimilation and accommodation. As Seiler put it, the linkage of the two concepts dissolves the contradiction. Environmental objects do not enforce the accommodation that children 'endure'. Rather, the children themselves accommodate their structures while acting. Assimilation and accommodation are both actions of the developing child. As Seiler stated, 'Development is not suffered, but done.' But, at the same time, development depends on the structures that determine the actions. The activity of the organism is constructive. Development is therefore seen as the active formation of new structures through modification and integration of existing ones.

The view that developmental growth depends on internal processes in interaction with the environment is certainly not new. The problem for understanding the acquisition of the structure of language is that most research assumes a rather strong empiricist/environmentalist orientation, as was indicated in preceding sections. Very little research proceeds from the assumption of the possibility of specific innate factors. This is partly because the term *innate* is usually misinterpreted as being in total contrast to environmental influences on development. It is therefore necessary to take a closer look at what 'innateness' could possibly mean in terms of language acquisition, and in what ways research could provide useful ideas concerning how to implement intervention and remedial programmes.

Interpretations of innateness The usual reaction by psychologists and educators to the suggestion of innate components for any behaviour is to reject the notion out of hand. That there should be any innate component to the acquisition of language seems especially absurd in view of the necessity to acquire the specific structures of the language to which one is exposed. Such rejection usually represents the mistaken view, however, that innate and environmental factors are opposite poles. There is, in addition, the assumption that positing innate aspects of behaviour is a way of cloaking one's ignorance of environmental factors that at present are unknown. Because any discussion of innateness often becomes obscured by these and other misunderstandings, it is necessary to present the epigenetic–interactionist viewpoint in some detail. One way to do this is to give an example of theory and findings in the field of perception.

Until only recently, it was usual to encounter almost totally empiricist theories of perception in textbooks of psychology. For example, depth perception was said to depend on the development of a number of cues. One of these is interposition or superposition of objects in which one learns that, if one object seems superimposed on another, the interrupted object seems to be further away. Another set of cues include learned features of perspective such as linear perspective (where parallel lines seem to converge in the distance), decreasing size with distance, height in the horizontal plane, and gradients of texture. Still other cues include the acquired knowledge with experience of the muscular feelings accompanying accommodation and convergence of the eyes. It was seen as somewhat of a breakthrough when the experiment by Gibson and Walk (1960) demonstrated that young infants seemed to have the knowledge of depth perception by as young as 6 months of age. They tested 36 infants between 6 and 14 months of age on a 'visual cliff' that consisted of a large sheet of heavy glass, one side of which was several feet over a patterned floor (the deep side) or flush against it (the shallow side). The mother called to the child from both sides in turn. Almost all of the infants crawled off the shallow side, but refused to do so for the deep side. Even this demonstration was criticized because the infants were already 6 months old, and a great deal of perceptual learning had already taken place. It has also been demonstrated, however, that chickens, goats, lambs and kittens would venture out over the shallow side but not the deep side of the visual cliff as soon as they were able to walk – which in some cases was less than 24 hours after birth. Other aspects of perception, which had formerly been believed to be learned, have now been shown to be either innate or at least present at very early ages. For example, Bower (1966) showed that infants as young as 2 months of age possess size constancy. Having trained a baby to respond to a 30 cm cube, he then presented it both with a cube three times the size but farther away so that the retinal size was identical, and with the original 30 cm cube at varying distances. It was found that the baby primarily responded to the original stimulus in spite of distance and retinal size changes, and not to objects of the same retinal size.

The experiments on depth perception and size constancy have to do with functional properties of vision. Of course, psychologists have always accepted that certain physiological structures are prerequisite for vision. No one would argue that humans can, by mere experience, learn to 'see' ultraviolet rays, although such stimuli can, of course, be experienced by conversion through mechanical means to stimuli that can be perceived. Experiments on properties of receptor cells in the visual cortex, however, have not only provided evidence of inborn detectors of a very specific nature, but have led to some discoveries that illustrate the interaction between innate and environmental factors in development. Hubel and Wiesel (1959) found that cells in the visual cortex of cats showed the greatest amount of activity to stimuli that were lines of a certain width located in a particular plane in the visual field. It seems that there are inborn receptors for horizontal and vertical lines. Some of the innate detectors are species-specific. For example, frogs have visual cells that respond to certain types of movement – a kind of 'bug detector' as it has been called.

The finding that cats have inborn receptors for horizontal and vertical stimuli has led to further research on how such cells develop functionally, and it is here that a good example of environmental interaction has been observed. Blakemore and Cooper (1970) raised kittens in either a vertical or horizontal striped environment. After more than five months of this visual experience, it was observed that the adult neurons were all responding within 45 degrees of the expected orientation. Hirsch and Spinelli (1971) similarly found that kittens raised seeing only vertical or horizontal lines – one set to each eye in special goggles – developed monocular receptive fields that had the orientation of the experience of the eye to which they were connected. Blakemore (1974) concluded on the basis of these and other similar results that binocularity is innate, but that it can be modified by experience. Furthermore, early visual experience can modify the orientation of cell receptivity selectively. Blakemore noted that the human visual system is also subject to the same types of inborn/environmental interaction. He cited evidence that humans who grow up with severe astigmatism of a type that weakens the contrast of patterns of one orientation are left with *meridional amblyopia* (reduced acuity for the orientation that was originally out of focus). This cannot be rectified by eyeglass correction of the eye's optics. It has also been found that humans have higher resolution acuity for vertical and horizontal patterns than for diagonal ones. Blakemore speculated that this may be because of the predominance of rectilinear orientations in Western urban environments. It seems then, that inborn biological structures that are genetically determined are very much affected by environmental experience. Such environmental effects are within limits, however. Cells responding to linear orientation can be made to react to specific orientations in accordance with environmental experience, but those same cells do not respond to other aspects of visual input.

Regarding the possibility of certain innate mechanisms for language acquisition, it is best to be quite clear. The proposal being advocated here is not an acceptance of the nativist position for language acquisition, although that may seem to be the case from this section. Rather, the claim being made is (1) that it is dogmatic and unscientific to dismiss such claims; (2) that, even where nativist claims are not explicitly rejected, much research proceeds without a true appreciation of internally generated factors; (3) that purely environmental (empiricist) theories have so far proved to be inadequate to account for the acquisition of the structure of language; and (4) that it is possible to conceive of theories of development that place a greater emphasis on epigenetic–interactionist principles and that take species-specific structures and functions into account. Furthermore, this view is especially important for intervention programmes dealing with language disorders in that, in the most obvious case, the impairment of specific biological structures determines not only the basic cause of the problem but gives clues as to techniques of remediation. No one pretends that someone who is congenitally deaf is not deaf. Similarly, it is important to determine whether other structural and functional properties that underlie language as we know it are impaired in certain groups. One major objection to studying innate factors – that finding something to be innate is to take a very pessimistic view for remediation – can be reversed; indeed, the opposite can be concluded. For purposes of effective intervention, it is obvious that, if it is known at the biological structural level what the impairments are, there is a far better chance of undertaking appropriate remediation procedures. This is equally true if the deficits are of functional or organizational properties rather than physiological ones. The notion of physiological deficits is fairly easy to comprehend. In discussing the possibility of a nativist position for language acquisition, however, the importance of innate functional and organizational properties of language must be considered. One way this has been done has been by appeal to language universals.

Universals that may be innate It is somewhat dangerous to use the phrase that one way to study possibly innate organizational properties of language is to look at linguistic universals. The whole appeal to universals has often been misunderstood. It should be made quite clear at the outset that no competent psycholinguist has made the claim that because certain aspects of language are found universally they must be innate. To do so is illogical because it is equally possible that certain things that are found universally arise through similarities of environment. A circular mandala need not be an innate symbol as Jung (1959) and others have claimed. All peoples share the important experience of a circular-appearing sun and moon. The argument by Chomsky (1965, 1968) for innateness was based on very different considerations. These included the arbitrariness of certain types of rules and constraints on the structure of language, the regularity of onset of language acquisition, the ease and rapidity of that acquisition, the fixed sequence of typical primitive language forms representing broadly similar approaches to language across children (in spite of more specific individual differences in that acquisition), and the observation that the unfolding of the sequence of acquisitions is not greatly affected by practice and reinforcement variables nor even by large variations of intelligence, except in cases of severe retardation.

In other words, language was claimed to reflect a number of innate properties. Because these properties are innate, they are found universally. Thus, the search for linguistic universals was not to offer evidence of innateness; that is illogical, as was pointed out above. Rather, the search has been to discover what specific aspects of language reflect the inborn, species-specific human linguistic ability. What are some of these universals?

There are two approaches to this problem. One is to claim that specific linguistic rules or rule types are somehow inborn. The second is to claim that certain procedures or operating principles are brought to bear by human individuals on language input. Catlin (1978) pointed out that claims of the first type constitute a pre-formationist rather than an epigenetic view of innate factors. According to Catlin, Chomsky's position seems to be of this pre-formationist type. This contrasts with Lenneberg's position (1967), which is compatible with epigenetic theories. Chomsky claimed that the child has a set of specifically linguistic inborn structural properties and constraints that are applied to linguistic input. According to his view, there is a genetically determined universal grammar that permits a range of possible realizations. Individual experience acts only to specify the particular grammar and performance system within the range of possible grammars allowed by universal grammar.

When psychologists looked for clues in the linguistic literature as to what constituted particular linguistic universals, they found little that could help them in designing specific experimental tests of these claims. Most of the linguistic universals that are posited are not couched in absolute terms. For example, Slobin (1978) pointed out that in a long review of word-order types in languages of the world Greenberg (1966) did not make the absolutist claims that psychologists have attributed to him.

Rather, his study focuses on statistical tabulations of dominant order types in conjunction with co-occurring linguistic features. In other words, universal linguistic features and constraints only operate within certain structural environments. It has nevertheless been possible to isolate a few instances that seemed to lend themselves to observational and experimental attempts to study whether children acquiring language behave in ways that would be predicted on this basis. McNeill, Yukawa and McNeill (1971), for example, provided some data from Japanese children indicating that children expected the language input to match observed universals. The universal in question concerned direct and indirect objects. Many languages provide case-markings for these forms. In some languages, only one of the forms is marked. It had been noticed that, if a language marks only one form, it is always the oblique or secondary form that is marked – in this example the indirect object. In Japanese, both forms are marked. McNeill et al. reasoned, however, that, if Japanese children who had not yet fully acquired the system were presented with slightly deviant sentences with only one form marked, they would expect it to be the indirect object in accordance with the universal. This can be made clearer with an anglicized example. In Japanese, the post-particle *ni* marks the indirect object, and *o* marks the direct object; this contrasts with English, in which word order plays an important part instead. Thus, a sentence something like 'Turtle-*ni* fish-*o* give' would be identical to 'Fish-*o* turtle-*ni* give' – that is, 'Give the fish [direct object] to the turtle [indirect object].' In contrast, in English word order would affect the interpretation, as in sentences like 'Show the baby the cat' and 'Show the cat the baby.' McNeill et al. presented sentences to Japanese children in which only one of the two forms was marked. Although they are deviant sentences, they are interpretable by adults because one of the two forms still retains its marking. What was observed with the children, however, was that some of them performed in accordance with the expectation based on linguistic universals. They actually performed better when only the indirect object was marked than when both direct and indirect objects were marked appropriately, as is done by adult Japanese. They did the poorest when only the direct object was marked, treating it as the indirect object. The results suggested that children made use of innate tendencies that matched this linguistic universal. Attempts to see whether speakers of other languages share these universal expectations, however, have failed. Cromer (1975b) presented 6–8-year-olds with a language game in which they had to learn which animal to push or to give to another on the basis of post-particle markings. Children in one group received sentences with the direct object marked; children in the other group heard sentences with marked indirect objects. After each trial they were shown which animal should have pushed the other, and trials continued until they had learned the 'secret language'. The experiment was designed so that both groups received word orders such that the correct answer to the very first trial violated English word order for acting on the sentences in the game. The expectation was that, if children are acting in accordance with the linguistic universal, the children in the marked-indirect-object group should learn the secret language in fewer trials and with fewer errors than children in the direct-object group. This did not occur: there were no observed differences between the two groups, and this was true even when the children were subdivided according to their knowledge of the adult English word-order rules for structures of this type. This one ex-perimental test of children's expectations matching a particular structural universal in language has given negative results. There are, of course, possible drawbacks in this study concerning the nature of the particular linguistic universal chosen for investigation, the age of the children (perhaps being beyond an age when they might make use of expectations based on universal grammar), interactions with the particular grammar of English that does not make use of this type of case-marking, etc. Other studies should be designed to investigate the claim that children make use of innate properties of universal grammar in the acquisition of the language to which they are exposed. Unfortunately, the most common reaction to Chomsky's pre-formationist claims has been to deny them dogmatically without adequate empirical investigation.

Another approach to the study of possibly innate factors is based more directly on Lenneberg's epigenetic view of what might be innate than on Chomsky's pre-formationist view. One such approach looks at the kinds of procedures that children bring to bear on language production. These procedures or operating principles may constitute true language-*acquisition* strategies as opposed to the language-*processing* strategies reviewed above. Some studies in this area have yielded encouraging results.

Slobin (1978), whose 'waiting-room' analogy was mentioned above, believes that language acquisition cannot be explained without under-standing the connection between cognitive development and specific linguistic encoding. He argued that pre-linguistic cognitive and social development obviously prepares the child for the acquisition of his or her native language, but those developments do not give the key to the particular categories and structures of the language. Linguistic expression is not in a one-to-one correspondence with thought. The child has to learn which possible notions receive formal marking in his or her language and how to form these notions in producing an utterance. To illustrate this point, Slobin gave the example of the English sentence 'Daddy gave me the ball.' This sentence has four essential categories – actor, action, recipient, object. One of these, *gave*, is marked for past. There is an additional notion of definite/indefinite contrast encoded in the word *the*. To express this same thought, the German sentence would be 'Der Vater gab mir den Ball.' Slobin pointed out that the notions that the German speaker must encode, in addition to the four essential semantic categories, are

Der definite, singular, masculine, subject
gab past, third person, singular
den definite, singular, masculine, object

These notions change yet again and/or appear in different combinations in the examples Slobin gave of the same sentence in Hebrew, Turkish, Kaluli, Tagalog, etc. Furthermore, as he pointed out, still other languages require the speaker to encode, for example, the shape of the object and considerations such as whether the action took place recently. In other words, as Slobin showed, there is a large gap between a communicative intention and the semantic structure that contains the notions that must be mapped onto the grammatical utterance in a particular language. Each language, then, presents the child with a different problem in terms of discovering the notions that have to be encoded and the means of encoding them. Slobin posed the question directly by asking what kinds of linguistic structures might facilitate language acquisition. This is seen in terms of operating principles like those given in Slobin (1973). They include, for example, the principle that underlying semantic relations should be marked overtly and clearly; and the principle that postponed markers (suffixes and postpositions) are more salient than preposed markers (prefixes and prepositions). Although Slobin presents these principles in terms of the structures of the language the child is acquiring, his view is compatible with a view that focuses on the procedures the child brings to bear on the acquisition of such structures. The ease or difficulty with which particular features of language are acquired presupposes internal (and possibly innate) factors favouring some types of structures over others in terms of ease or speed of acquisition.

  Slobin (1978) reported the results from his Berkeley Cross-Linguistic Acquisition Project, in which the acquisition by children of four languages was investigated – English, Italian, Serbo-Croat and Turkish. These languages contrast in certain basic ways. For example, Turkish and Serbo-Croat are inflectional languages in that, unlike English, the greater portion of syntactic contrasts involves modification of word-stem forms. These two languages themselves contrast in that Turkish is a pure inflectional system with maximal freedom of word order. It is an agglutinating language in which words are typically composed of sequences of morphs (word parts) with each morph representing one morpheme or meaning unit. Turkish is often cited as an example of an agglutinating language that approximates very closely to the 'ideal' type (Lyons, 1968). Serbo-Croat is a fusional language whose words are not readily segmentable into morphs. It relies on a mixture of both word order and inflections. In contrast to these two inflectional languages, English is considered an analytic or 'isolating' language. Fixed word order is one of the main ways grammatical relations are encoded. Of the languages studied, English has the most fixed word order; Italian has more flexibility, as has Serbo-Croat; and Turkish has the maximum freedom of word order.

For each of the four languages 48 children were studied. These samples were composed of six children at each of eight age levels that were set at four-month intervals between the ages of 2 years and 4 years 4 months. Each child was studied intensively for a total of 15–20 hours in a 10-day period. A battery of linguistic and non-linguistic tasks was administered. Language production, both free and elicited, was studied, as was language comprehension. Specific investigations were made of the agent–patient relation, causatives (which are reported in more detail in Ammon and Slobin, 1979), locatives, and the understanding of before/after. The basic finding was that the languages patterned differently according to the task. For example, for causatives, the two inflectional languages were superior; for before/after, Turkish was the easiest for the children; for locatives, Turkish and Italian were in the lead. The conclusion was that the child's acquisition of the means of encoding particular relations was influenced by the types of linguistic structure involved. In addition, there was something about Turkish that made these structures especially easy to discover. Turkish uses a stock of regular particles for expressing single elements of meaning. These particles demonstrate word harmony and exist without irregular forms. In the findings, there was no support for the use of word-order strategies or for the notion that certain word orders are more natural than others. In languages in which word order plays an important role (English, Italian), sensitivity to word order was not found initially; it was not observed until the children were between 2 years 8 months and 3. It is interesting to note in this regard Slobin's claim that word-order languages impose a greater burden on short-term memory and this may account for the later emergence of word-order strategies in sentence comprehension.

For Serbo-Croat, the child must learn an interaction of both inflections and word order. When an inflectional contrast is not available to distinguish certain grammatical relations, then a particular word order is used. Slobin claimed that the inflectional system of Serbo-Croat, being fusional rather than agglutinating, lacks the clarity of the Turkish system. In Serbo-Croat, there are interactions of case with number, gender and animacy, and there are many irregular forms. Some of the case forms are homonyms. There are no unique markers for number, case or gender. As Slobin put it, it is a challenge to theories of language acquisition that such confused systems are learned at all in the first few years of life.

There are other aspects of the acquisition of these four languages that Slobin noted. When it comes to aspects of language that are typically acquired late – for example, instances where surface forms are very different from their underlying representations – languages like Turkish that seem to have an advantage in early acquisition are at a disadvantage. Relative clauses in Turkish may be difficult because, unlike in Indo-European languages, such clauses do not look like surface sentences. In languages in which relative clauses do have such a resemblance, normal sentence-processing strategies with minimal adaptations can be used to interpret them. Slobin concluded that languages may not differ considerably in the overall ease of their acquisition. Advantages in morphology are compensated for by disadvantages in syntax and vice versa.

Slobin's work shows the importance of considering the particular linguistic features of the language to be acquired. As he put it, the child behaves as if he expects to find a certain consistency in the linguistic system. The child interprets new and deviant forms on the basis of rules or strategies that he has already established from earlier input. Beyond this internal aspect, however, Slobin speculated that perhaps children only attempt to interpret sentence structures that fit their notions of language. Although Slobin did not commit himself on the point, some of these acquisition strategies or operating principles could conceivably reflect innate organizational principles that may be specifically evolved for dealing with language structure. In whichever manner this is viewed, his overall approach is significant because he takes serious consideration of the internal aspects that the child brings to bear on the very specific system of language structure.

Linguistic specificity of possibly innate processes　If the child brings to bear on language acquisition certain processes that may possibly be innate, the question arises as to whether such processes are specifically linguistic or whether they merely represent broader cognitive procedures that may be applicable to the acquisition of other structures of knowledge. The processes studied by Karmiloff-Smith, which are discussed below as part of the second framework for viewing internal factors, seem to be the same processes as the child uses in approaching any problem space. The contrasting view, that some processes may be specifically linguistic, has met with a good deal of scepticism.

It is true of course that language as a human communication system depended evolutionarily on the anatomical and physical features of the human species. The issue of what is meant by 'specifically linguistic' is therefore very complex. Obviously, an impairment of any of those other systems on which language depends will result in an impairment of language. These can include defects of anatomical structures that impair the speech mechanism – but these are considered as speech problems and not as language impairments as such. Other physical structures, however, may be crucial for true language-functioning. These may include such systems as auditory processing, auditory storage, abilities to deal with interruption, abilities to process hierarchically ordered materials, and long-term memory, among others. If one can isolate impairments in one or another of these systems in various language-disordered groups, there will be important implications for intervention programmes.

There is also the question of whether there are some specifically linguistic principles that are innate. Chomsky concluded that there are. It is difficult to specify whether the types of operating principle that Slobin proposed (1973) are purely linguistic or whether they represent somewhat broader cognitive approaches to the language system. Although little is known about the psychological reality of possibly innate linguistic processes, there is no logical *a priori* reason for dismissing the possibility of their existence. Certainly the observation of widespread constraints on certain linguistic structures across wide divergences in language (see for example Keenan and Comrie, 1977) points to the existence of some mysterious and unexplained natural phenomena; empiricist theorists have been unable, when not unwilling, to account for their existence.

Uniqueness of the human species   Of all the arguments against the possibility of innate linguistic principles, the charge (e.g. Linden, 1975) that those who propose such principles are attempting to hold onto a vestige of human uniqueness in an anthropocentric sense must surely rank as one of the most illogical. To argue for species-specificity of a particular behaviour in no way implies holding such a viewpoint. It would be as absurd to claim that the discovery of innate releasing mechanisms in greylag geese or in sticklebacks implies an attempt to defend their uniqueness in the quasi-religious sense of which proponents of species-specific language behaviour in humans are accused. Indeed, to believe that human beings somehow do *not* share with other animal species various types of innate mechanisms is more akin to arguing for a human soul. That the issue has been raised is because of the interest in teaching 'language' to closely related species. These studies are interesting and important; indeed, the techniques on which they provide information may give valuable clues to *methods* for intervention with persons who have impaired language abilities.

There are two points about these studies that should be clarified. First, so far it has not been possible to demonstrate the acquisition in other species of a linguistic system as distinct from a system of meanings and/or communication. Second, and more importantly, even if it is eventually demonstrated that other species can be taught linguistic structures, this would in no way address the problem concerning how children acquire language in the ways that they do nor would it account for the universal existence of particular linguistic structures, principles and constraints in human languages. The argument that any positive results of teaching language to other species would falsify the claims of an innate component of language in human beings is illogical. It is possible to train a pigeon to react aggressively to a red patch. Such training does not invalidate the fact that robins do so as the result of innate releasing mechanisms (Lack, 1943; a good review of literature on innate releasing mechanisms can be found in Eibl-Eibesfeldt, 1970). Limber (1977) made the same point: 'Some may interpret the achievements of . . . trained apes as disproving Chomsky's hypothesis. Presumably, such individuals would also consider the successful training of a dog to move about on hind legs as evidence against the hypothesis that humans are genetically predisposed to walk' (p. 292n).

In summary, the overall claim that is being made here is not that certain aspects of language acquisition are necessarily innate. But problems do arise concerning why only certain types of linguistic procedures and constraints, and not others that are logically possible, are found universally in particular language environments; why children acquiring language evidence a regularity of onset, ease and rapidity of acquisition, and sequences of acquisitions not greatly affected by practice, reinforcement and wide variations in intelligence; and why children acquiring different languages seem to make use of particular operating principles and not others during that acquisition. In addition, one must also consider the continued failure to explain the acquisition of the structure of language by purely empiricist theories despite years of intensive research into this issue. If the continual misunderstandings and misinterpretations of what constitutes an epigenetic–interactionist viewpoint can be cleared away, it may be possible to consider in an unbiased fashion the biological underpinnings that exist for language acquisition. The continued dogmatic rejection of such a viewpoint is unwarranted in the face of empirical evidence, and is in fact detrimental to the development of effective intervention programmes.

The second framework: language as a specific structural system to be acquired

There is another approach to language acquisition that focuses on the child's contribution. It is that of viewing language as a structural system to be acquired, and one that children will approach in ways not unlike the manner in which they approach other conceptual tasks. This is the view proposed by Karmiloff-Smith (1977a, 1977b, 1978, 1979a, 1979b). She believed the reasons usually offered to explain why children begin to use new linguistic devices were inadequate. The new linguistic forms used by children are not just due to communicative pressure. As has been pointed out by many researchers, the child is understood most of the time anyway even when he is using forms quite different from the adult model. Furthermore, the child is not progressively accommodating to the linguistic input that he or she hears – a point made clear by all of the careful observational studies of child language acquisition in the 1960s. Karmiloff-Smith offered evidence that the reason why the child uses new forms is quite different; it is because of a metalinguistic push to deal with the structured language system. When children first begin to use particular forms, they do so primarily for themselves, not for communication purposes. According to Karmiloff-Smith, there is an attempt by the children to get a grip on the linguistic system. The children are trying to come to terms with their own budding organizational activities, language, and all of their environment.

In one of her experiments, Karmiloff-Smith (1978) studied the acquisition and use of gender distinctions by French-speaking children. She first noted that there is no foolproof way to predict gender on conceptual grounds. Furthermore, although prediction of the correct gender is often possible from word-endings, there are many exceptions. The only foolproof strategy is to use grammatical gender – that is, to use as definitive the gender of the article, and then to make adjectives, past participles and pronouns agree with that gender. Karmiloff-Smith wanted to know what acquisition strategies children used for gender. To do this, she carried out a set of experiments on 339 monolingual French children, aged 3 years 2 months to 12 years 5 months. To test knowledge of gender agreement, she used 30 nonsense words that were assigned to pairs of identical but differently coloured pictures. The nonsense words had either typically masculine, typically feminine or neutral word-endings. For example, the nonsense word *bicron* had a masculine ending; *bravaise* had a feminine ending; a word like *fediste* is audibly typical of neither gender. Note that the colour-word pronunciation depends on the gender of the noun with which it is used. The masculine and feminine forms for 'white' in French are *blanc* and *blanche*.

The child was asked questions about the different nonsense words. He was confronted with five types of problems. In one, the article and the noun were consistent, as in 'un bicron' and 'une bravaise'. In another type, the article and noun endings were inconsistent. In a third problem, no article gender was provided, as in 'deux bicrons' and 'deux bravaises'. In a fourth type of problem, the sex of the pictured person was inconsistent with the noun ending and no gender marked article was provided. The child had to give spontaneous responses containing the definite article (*le/la*), the nonsense noun, and an adjective of colour (e.g. *blanc/blanche*). In a fifth task, the child was asked to create names for pictures of imaginary people of both sexes. The questions used forms in which gender was not audibly marked, as in 'Ça', 'quel/quelle *x*?' and 'Ça c'est quoi?' Karmiloff-Smith reported that the results from these tasks showed that the youngest children used a very powerful implicit system of phonological rules based on the consistency of phonological changes of the word-endings. They did not use syntactic cues (gender of the article) nor semantic cues (the sex of the person in the drawing) to determine gender agreement. She also noted that young children even made errors on frequently used words such as *la maison*, whose masculine ending but feminine article are inconsistent with regard to phonological rules. The young children responded, 'la maison vert' using the masculine form of the French word for 'green', to make it agree phonologically with the masculine noun ending, even though the article shows it to be feminine. Older children, however, took syntactic and semantic cues into consideration and changed the suffixes so that they agreed with the definite article or with the sex. They spontaneously changed 'une bicron' into 'la bicronne'. In some cases they simply avoided pronouncing the suffix by using only the definite article and the agreeing adjective, as in 'la grise' (the grey one) instead of 'la bicron grise' (where *bicron* would have needed to be changed into *bicronne*).

In this experiment, the use by the youngest French-speaking children of a predominantly phonological strategy, and thus one which is specifically linguistic, has been demonstrated for the system of gender. Karmiloff-Smith's paper discusses the intricacies of this system and how it interacts with other aspects of the language system – for example, how older children go on to use the phonological rules for more extended syntactic cohesion, as in the use of gender endings to govern anaphora and lexical concord. In this short review of her findings on phonological rules for gender, one does some injustice to the complexity of her arguments, and the interested reader should refer directly to her writings. In the context of the issues raised in this chapter, her work is cited with the more specific aim of giving an example of how one can take account more directly of the kinds of strategies the child brings to bear on language acquisition and how some of these may be specifically linguistic. Karmiloff-Smith noted that the phonological strategy used by French-speaking children on the gender system is input-dependent. In German, the noun-endings are not good clues to formal gender and German-speaking children may use quite different strategies in acquiring that system. Furthermore, other aspects of French may depend to a greater extent on semantic, syntactic or pragmatic procedures.

These results can be interpreted by others in a variety of ways. One possibility is to view the phonological strategy as reflecting some kind of innate language-specific procedure used in conjunction with environmental language input of particular types. In that sense, this work could have as well been reviewed in the previous section on the epigenetic–interactionist viewpoint. It should be noted that Slobin's work, although reviewed in that section, could have been summarized here as research that takes account of language as a specific structural system. The placement in this review of the results of Slobin's and Karmiloff-Smith's studies is merely intended to illustrate one or another of the viewpoints being presented and is not meant in any way to imply that these researchers see their work in the light of those viewpoints. Both of these researchers would, however, agree as to the importance of considering the internal factors that the child brings to bear on language acquisition, regardless of how such processes are seen to arise; both would find an empiricist theory of purely external input inadequate; and both would view the linguistic system as an organized structural entity to be understood and acquired.

Karmiloff-Smith (1977b, 1978) also showed the kinds of strategies children use in an attempt to separate linguistic functions that overlap. She found that the child tries to keep separate two meanings normally represented by a single reference element so that he can consolidate the two meanings independently. The child actually creates forms that are ungrammatical from the adult point of view in order to accomplish this separation. For example, in French *une voiture* means both 'a car' and 'one car'. When the child wants to specify 'one', he will often produce 'une de voiture', a form which is slightly ungrammatical in adult French except in some dialects where it is used for emphatic contrast – which was not the case with these children. Children similarly distinguish the determiner and descriptive functions of adjectives. Thus, when describing a red crayon, they will correctly say 'Je prends le crayon rouge.' But in a task requiring the determiner function, they produce 'Je prends le rouge de crayon', which again is slightly ungrammatical in adult French.

Another example of keeping distinct meanings encoded by separate forms can be seen in the child's use of *même* ('same'). Karmiloff-Smith pointed out that *same* has two meanings: *same kind*, as in 'Jane is wearing the same dress as Mary', and *same one*, as in 'Jane is wearing the same dress as yesterday.' In comprehension tasks, Karmiloff-Smith (1977b) found that children interpreted 'the same *x*' as 'another *x* with the same attributes' and not 'one and the same *x*'. The child was given various objects. Some were identical, some were of the same class but differed in colour, and others were of the same class but differed in several ways. Also included were objects that were the only members of their class available in the experiment. Forty-seven children between the ages of 2 years 10 months and 7 years 11 months were tested by the Genevan method of changing items, asking the child questions, etc. Not only did the youngest children treat 'the same *x*' as 'another *x* with the same attributes' (= another one) but they understood the word *another* for the contrast case (= another kind); they would refuse to carry out a task on 'another *x*' unless the objects differed in some way. It is interesting to note that older children (age 6–7 years) created a slightly ungrammatical form to express 'the same kind'. They avoided using the economic and correct 'J'ai la même' ('I have the same') and produced such utterances as 'J'ai *une de même de* vaches chez moi' ('I've got *one of the same of* cows') or 'la *même de* vache', which were ungrammatical in the context in which they were used (Karmiloff-Smith, 1978).

In addition to creating ungrammatical forms, children also make use of what Karmiloff-Smith calls the 'overmarking' of forms. That is, they add redundant markers for clarity – and again they seem to do this for themselves and not to aid communication (Karmiloff-Smith, 1977a, 1979b). Thus, children will not place the burden of anaphoric reference on articles and pronouns in contrasts where ambiguity of reference might occur. Instead of saying 'The girl pushed a dog and then the boy pushed *it*', they will make utterances like 'The girl pushed a dog and then *also* the boy *re*-pushed *again the same* dog.' Karmiloff-Smith (1979b) also showed that such overmarking is not necessarily limited to approaches to language. In an ingenious memory task in which children had to recall a very long series of T-maze-type choices, the same types of overmarking were observed. The interest in the task was not in the child's learning of the choice points. Rather, the memory aids the child used were studied. The path was drawn on a long roll of brown wrapping paper. As the next choice came into view by unrolling the wrapping paper, the earlier choices disappeared as the other end of the paper was being rerolled. When it was demonstrated to the child how difficult it would be to remember all the choice points, he was given pencils and paper and told he could make what notes he wanted in order to trace the path correctly later. At first the child would overmark in his notes, and even during the course of the experiment would simplify his system by dropping redundant features in later notes. For example, for a particular choice point, he might first draw a forked path with an arrow indicating the correct side to take and a cross blocking the incorrect path. Later, he might drop the blocking cross, and merely show the arrow along the correct choice of the two paths. Eventually, he might no longer draw the entire fork in the path, but merely that part going up in the correct direction.

Karmiloff-Smith argued that some of the strategies or principles that children bring to bear on language acquisition, then, are not necessarily specific to language. They are procedures for attempting to cope with any system or task. What is emphasized is the child's contribution to the acquisition process. No stand is necessarily taken as to how these internal processes arise. It is possible to interpret her results as showing some procedures that may be purely linguistic. Others are strategies that the child might apply to any problem space. But, in an important extension of such an approach, Karmiloff-Smith emphasized that language is to be viewed as a structural system and not merely as a collection of auditory stimuli, or as merely one of several aspects of a general symbolic function. Her own theories are more complex than is evident here. For example, the relation between language and cognitive processes is seen in terms of a constructive interaction, and Karmiloff-Smith (1978) presented evidence that some advances in language acquisition also provoke other cognitive changes.

It has been asserted that a reconceptualization concerning development is necessary in which internal factors within the child are taken into more serious consideration. Although this was emphasized as regards the acquisition of the structure of language in the theoretical positions of the 1960s and was supported by the observational studies of children acquiring language, much subsequent research has drifted back to an approach that can be described as being based on assumptions of an empiricist theory of mind as regards language. Although the child is likely to be seen as a more active participant in general cognitive development, that same active structuring is ignored when studying the acquisition of the specific structural system of language. Two frameworks have been proposed within which to emphasize the importance of internal factors on that acquisition – one advocating an epigenetic–interactionist view and the other advocating that language be understood as a specific structural system to be acquired. The second reconceptualization is different and concerns the content of cognitive stages.

The Second Reconceptualization: Specific Deficits

Recently, a number of controversies have developed over the specific aspects of some of Piaget's developmental periods. One of these controversies pertains to the ability to make a transitive inference of the type that if $A > B$, and $B > C$, then $A > C$. According to Piaget, such an inference should not be possible until the child has reached the stage of concrete operational thinking, which occurs at about the age of 6 or 7 (Piaget and Inhelder, 1956; Piaget, Inhelder and Szeminska, 1960). Bryant and Trabasso (1971), however, challenged this view and claimed that children could indeed form transitive inferences if it could be ensured that they could recall the premise information at the time of making the transitive inference. In their experiment, they used five sticks in order to eliminate a labelling strategy – that is, learning to label particular sticks 'large' or 'small'. Children were overtrained on the specific comparisons. Each adjacent pair had to be learned to a stringent criterion. When this was done, 4-year-old children were found to be able to make the correct judgements of relative size on the non-adjacent sticks that had not been specifically contrasted. In other words, it was claimed that they could now make correct transitive inferences. If this is true, then it would challenge the assumption in Piaget's theory that a certain type of logical structure is not attained until operational thinking is possible, as seen in a variety of other tasks. Smedslund (1963, 1965), however, had previously rejected a memory interpretation of the Bryant and Trabasso type when he reported that some of the children he tested sometimes were unable to make the transitive judgement even when they were able to recall the specific comparisons immediately before the test on the transitive relation. More recently, Halford and Galloway (1977) specifically tested for memory of the shown comparisons after the transitive inference. Of 163 children, aged 4½–9 years, 107 did not make the transitive inference. Of these, however, only 20 were unable to remember the comparisons; 87 remembered both comparisons but still failed to make the transitive inference. It has also been argued that success in the Bryant and Trabasso task may be attributable to other factors, and that the children had not really made inferences of the Piagetian type. Riley and Trabasso (1974) came to this conclusion. They claimed that, if by operational transitivity is meant the co-ordination of the members of the premises by way of a middle term at the time of testing, then the young children they have tested do not use operational transitivity. They present a process model of how the transitive judgements are made by these children, but also assert that their results and those of Bryant and Trabasso (1971) are irrelevant as far as

Piaget's theory is concerned. Whether this is so or not, the point can be made that at the very least, transitivity judgements cannot be correctly made until the child has developed a sufficient memory span to recall the initial comparisons. A certain memory span is at least necessary for certain aspects of operational thinking to occur, and whether it is sufficient, as Bryant and Trabasso had originally claimed, is another issue.

However they are interpreted, the Bryant and Trabasso results suggest that it may be wiser to consider more specific aspects of cognitive functioning rather than merely to rely on broad Piagetian stages. Those broad developmental periods such as the sensorimotor and concrete operational stages were a very valuable and useful way of describing the child and of making sense of the way the child approached very disparate aspects of the world. There has been a tendency, however, for research on the relationship between language acquisition and cognitive functioning to focus only on such broad stages, often using correlational techniques. These studies are not very useful for language-intervention programmes. Instead of concentrating on the macro level of broad developmental stages (if they do indeed exist), a more useful approach would be to concentrate on the micro-level processes that contribute to making such intellectual accomplishments possible.

Memory

One of the specific processes that might be impaired in some language-disordered groups is short-term memory. That short-term auditory memory plays a role in verbal comprehension has been demonstrated in a variety of experiments. For example, Conrad (1972) presented evidence supportive of the notion that verbal stimuli pass into an auditory short-term store in order for various operations to be performed to extract meaning. Rapin and Wilson (1978) noted that lesions involving the supramarginal and angular gyri of the left parietal lobe have been found to interfere with short-term verbal acoustic memory, thus producing amnestic aphasia (Geschwind, 1967; Warrington, Logue and Pratt, 1971). There has been speculation that short-term memory impairment may be responsible for the language disorders of some children. Menyuk (1964, 1969) studied a group of children, aged 3 years to 5 years 11 months, who were described as using infantile language. Menyuk found that their language was in fact deviant and not merely infantile or delayed. In conjunction with some imitation tasks that she gave, she concluded that the differences were possibly attributable to a short-term memory impairment. Leonard (1979) challenged this view. He claimed that the manner in which she made her statistical comparisons of spontaneous speech with a younger normal group was unusual, and that the comparison even at a descriptive level showed that only two structures out of 33 that were examined were used by one group but not the other. Leonard argued that the language structures used by language-disordered children are not different from those used by normal children but are merely *like* those used by younger normal children. In his own study of nine language-impaired children, aged 4 years 10 months to 5 years 10 months, who were compared to nine normal children of the same ages (Leonard, 1972), he found that the two groups differed not in absolute terms (one group using a structure that was never evidenced in the other group), but in terms of the frequency of use of particular structures.

The observation that one or another language-disordered group does not differ absolutely in the use of structures found in younger normal children does not invalidate the claim that they are not necessarily behaving like normal children. To look at the language structures that are or are not used only in themselves is to take a rather narrow view of what can be learned from such studies. Structures that are rarely or never used by language-disordered groups but are used by normal children or adults may give clues as to the nature of underlying deficits. Furthermore, as noted above, Menyuk's conclusion concerning a memory deficit was based not only on the examination of spontaneous language. She also gave the language-disordered group a sentence-imitation task that was administered to younger, normal children as well. This sentence-repetition task revealed significant differences between the groups. The normal children made use of sentence structure and were able to repeat some sequences that would have exceeded their memory span as measured by traditional methods. In the imitation task, repetitions were constrained by syntactic structure and not by sentence length as such. The correlation between sentence length and inability to repeat sentences was only 0.04 – that is, at chance level. The imitations by the language-disordered group showed rather different results. For these children, the correlation between sentence length and inability to imitate was 0.53. In addition, the kinds of errors that were observed differed from those made by the normal children. The normal children made errors and omissions that consisted primarily of modifications of transformational structure. In contrast, the omissions that were made by the language-disordered children were almost invariably from the first part of the sentence. The last thing heard was more frequently recalled, which seems to indicate a short-term memory deficit. Short-term memory even for utterances as short as 3–5 morphemes in length seemed to be impaired. Menyuk speculated that, if these children were able to keep in memory no more than 2–3 morphemes, they would be unable to carry out a deepening linguistic analysis on the language input. This would result in utterances that would be impoverished and limited. Such utterances would not be qualitatively different from those used by younger, normal children, who also have a limited short-term memory span. Such a hypothesis would not be at variance with Leonard's findings. However, Menyuk also suggested, however, that such a short-term memory limitation would result in qualitatively different utterances because they would be based in some cases on different hypotheses and rules concerning language. Menyuk (1978) summarized work on language-disordered children as showing that the intentions of sentences (to command, declare, negate and question) are preserved, as are the main relations (actor, action and object). She also noted that these children preserve the syntactic rule of word order to express those relations. They do not, however, preserve certain transformational modifications. Lee (1966) provided evidence that a language-disordered child that she studied did not produce some types of utterance even at the two-word level that is found in normal children. Bloom (1967; see also Leonard, 1979) raised some doubts concerning Lee's findings particularly because the language samples of the two groups were obtained in a different manner. In any case, because the differences observed were at the two-word level, short-term memory was not implicated, and the deficit was attributed to other factors.

Graham (1968, 1974; Graham and Gulliford, 1968) presented a memory-limitation hypothesis to account for language observed in educationally subnormal children. Repetition and comprehension scores on various sentence types increased regularly with short-term memory as measured by the repetition of random words and digits. By relating the notion of short-term memory to the amount of computation required by sentences of various structural types, Graham concluded that the children in his study were unable to process sentences that made demands on short-term memory and that were beyond their capacity.

Processing-deficits in autistic children

In discussing Menyuk's work, it was noted that normal children made use of sentence structure in the repetition task that she administered, but that her language-disordered group was more greatly affected by sentence length than by sentence structure and a memory impairment was therefore hypothesized. Similarly, most subnormal children have extremely short memory spans. This is not true of autistic children who are also subnormal (O'Connor and Frith, 1973). But non-autistic subnormal children have been observed to increase the amount of information they can process by making use of sentence structure, whereas autistic children do not do so to the same degree. Hermelin and O'Connor (1967) compared 12 subnormal autistic children with 12 severely subnormal non-autistic children matched on the basis of their immediate memory span for digits and on scores from the Peabody Picture Vocabulary Test. The task was to repeat words that were arranged either randomly or in sentences. The results showed that, although the severely subnormal non-autistic children. performed significantly better with sentences than with random sequences, no significant difference was found for the autistic children.

Frith (see Aurnhammer-Frith, 1969) compared 16 autistic children with 16 normal children on a similar task. The autistic group included only those children who had some speech. Their chronological age was 11 years 6 months. They were compared with a normal group (mean chronological age 4 years 3 months) that was matched on digit span. The two groups were of comparable mental age as measured on the Peabody Picture Vocabulary Test. The results showed that, although both groups benefited from grammatical structure and performed better for sentences than for words arranged randomly, the normal children benefited significantly more than the autistic group did. It was as if the autistic group was impaired in the ability to deal with sentence structure as compared with the normal children. This result is especially interesting when one recalls that the two groups were prematched for digit-span performance. Fyffe and Prior (1978) replicated this finding.

There have been other studies that have shown that autistic children may be suffering from specific language or communication deficits. Ricks (1972, 1975) found differences in the early cries of autistic children, subnormal non-autistic children and normal children. The autistic children were 3–5 years old, as were the matched non-autistic, subnormal children. The normal children were 8–12 months old. Different types of cry were obtained from the children in standardized situations designed to elicit messages of frustration, request, greeting and pleased surprise. These cries were tape-recorded and test tapes were made by splicing the four cries of four children onto a single tape, resulting in 16 cries on each tape. These tapes were played to six parents of normal children and six parents of autistic children. Parents of normal children heard tapes of the four cries of their own child, the four cries of two other normal English babies, and the four cries of one baby being raised by non-English-speaking parents. The cries were spliced onto the tapes in random order. Parents of an autistic child heard the cries of their own child, two other autistic children, and one non-autistic retarded child of the same age. The parents' task was to identify and label the meaning of all 16 cries and to identify their own child. In addition, parents of normal children were also asked to identify the non-English child; parents of autistic children had to identify the non-autistic subnormal child. Finally, all of the parents were presented with the request sounds of six babies and had to pick out their own child from among these. The results showed that parents of normal children could easily identify all 16 messages including those of the non-English baby, although they could not identify which child was the non-English one. To their surprise, they were unable to pick out the cries of their own baby. It seems that the cries of normal children have a marked similarity and these signals seem to be independent of language background. The results from the autistic group were quite different. The parents of autistic children could only identify the idiosyncratic messages of their own child and the cries of the non-autistic retarded child. They could not identify the messages of the other two autistic children. Furthermore, they could easily identify their own child. Retarded children who are not autistic seem to have normal cries that can be identified by adults. But autistic children have their own idiosyncratic and distinctive cries that can only be identified by adults familiar with them; they do not share the vocabulary of intonated signals used by normal and even subnormal children.

Because of their language impairment, autistic children have often been confused with or compared to developmentally aphasic children. However, Bartak, Rutter and Cox (1975; see also Bartak and Rutter, 1975) provided evidence that the two groups can be reliably differentiated. They present entirely different kinds of language impairment. For example, autistic children show significantly greater *I–you* pronoun reversal and echolalia, and make significantly more stereotyped utterances and inappropriate remarks than do aphasic children.

Deficits in developmentally aphasic children

Short-term storage deficit A number of recent reviews of possible deficits in childhood aphasia are available in Wyke (1978), Benton, (1978), Cromer (1978a, reprinted here as chapter 5), Menyuk (1978), and Rapin and Wilson (1978). One such deficit is that of an impairment of short-term storage of the type mentioned above. Eisenson (1968) speculated that the aphasic child's storage system for speech signals may be defective. Stark, Poppen and May (1967) studied eight aphasic children, of mean age 8 years 3 months, on a task that involved pressing keys with pictures on them in the same order as the order in which the items were auditorially presented by the experimenter. Five of the eight aphasics performed very poorly on this task. Furthermore, most of their errors occurred on the item in the first position. Verbal stress put on this item led to an improvement of their scores. Although Stark et al. concluded that the results were evidence for a sequencing disability, they can also be interpreted as showing an impaired auditory memory.

Rosenthal and Eisenson (1970) presented short speech sounds either singly or in pairs to aphasic and normal children. The child's task was to put the paired sounds in temporal order. The time taken to do this was compared with the time taken for the same task with non-speech sounds. Both normal and aphasic children could identify the sounds presented singly. The aphasic children, however, did poorly when they had to report the order of two sounds that were presented in close temporal proximity. Rosenthal and Eisenson took this as evidence that the aphasic children they studied were suffering from an auditory storage deficit. The auditory trace that could be identified when presented on its own could not be retained long enough to allow a perceptual analysis of temporal order.

Rate of auditory processing deficit   Tallal and Piercy (1973a, 1973b, 1974, 1975, 1978) conducted a series of studies on the processing of temporal order by aphasic children. They found that, when the rate of presentation of auditory signals is too great, the child is unable to analyse their order. A deficit that affects the rate of auditory processing may even cause difficulty in discriminating particular speech sounds. Tallal and Piercy (1974) indeed found that aphasic children had difficulty in discriminating between stop consonants that have rapidly changing spectra provided by the second and third formant transitions – in the range of about 50 milliseconds. They had no trouble, however, in discriminating vowels that have steady-state frequencies that remain constant over the entire length of the stimulus – approximately 250 milliseconds. In a later experiment, Tallal and Piercy (1975) showed that aphasic children similarly could not discriminate specially synthesized vowel–vowel syllables in which the discriminable information occurred in the first 43 milliseconds, but they could distinguish consonant–vowel syllables in which the transitional period of each stimulus was increased from 43 to 95 milliseconds. In other words, it was not some specific feature of the stimuli (steady state versus transitional features) that caused difficulty for the aphasic children. They had no trouble distinguishing syllables when the discriminable components were of long (95-millisecond) durations regardless of whether they were transitional in nature, but they could not discriminate syllables of either type when the discriminable components were brief (43 milliseconds). Tallal and Piercy concluded that the language deficit in aphasic children is due to an inability to process rapidly occurring acoustic information.

Sequencing deficit   The idea that some adult aphasics may be suffering from a kind of temporal disorientation or temporal order deficit has been discussed for some time (e.g. Critchley, 1953; Hughlings-Jackson, 1888). Hirsh (1959) emphasized the importance of a central temporal-sequencing ability for making sense of auditory input and language. Monsees (1961) speculated that the basic disability in aphasic children was a central disorder involving the perception of temporal sequences. In adult aphasics, Efron (1963) observed that the ability to say which of two sounds came first was seriously impaired unless the sounds were separated by a gap of over 500 milliseconds. Because normal-speech sound segments occur at the rate of one every 80 milliseconds, such a deficit could prevent the processing of normal speech because the order of phonemes could not be sorted out. That such sequencing may be important at the phoneme level is supported by a study by Sheehan, Aseltine and Edwards (1973). They found that the comprehension of adult aphasics could be aided by the insertion of silent intervals between phonemes. These same patients were not aided by the insertion of silent intervals between words.

Lowe and Campbell (1965) studied eight children classified as 'aphasoid', who were between 7 and 14 years old. They were compared to a matched group of normal speaking children. Two types of tasks were studied. In succession tasks, the time required by the child in order for him or her to hear two auditory signals as separate signals was measured. In temporal-ordering tasks, what is measured is the slightly longer time needed for the child to say which of the two signals occurred first. On succession tasks, the two groups did not statistically differ from each other. But on the temporal-ordering task, there were large differences. The aphasoid children required an average of 357 milliseconds to separate the two signals. This compared to only 36 milliseconds required by the normal children. Lowe and Campbell concluded that a temporal-order deficit may be the major factor causing language difficulties in these children.

Other researchers also observed a sequencing deficit in aphasic children. Some of these have claimed that the deficit is not limited to the auditory modality. Withrow (1964) studied immediate memory for visual stimuli that were presented sequentially to aphasic, deaf and normally hearing children. The deaf and the aphasic children performed significantly worse than the normal children. Poppen et al. (1969) had six aphasic children (aged 5 years 8 months to 9 years 3 months) press three frosted panels in the same order as they saw them lighted. Although they performed better on this visual task than on auditory sequencing tasks, they still performed poorly, achieving only a 75 per cent success rate. These authors also gave the children five different types of sequencing tasks. The Kendall coefficient of concordance for these tasks was 0.71. They concluded that there is a general sequencing ability and that aphasic children are deficient in that ability.

Although there has been much interest in the possibility of a sequencing deficit in aphasic children, there are some problems with such a theory. Efron (1963), whose results on aphasic adults have been cited above, found a curious anomaly in his study. The subjects who showed the poorest performance on his temporal-ordering task were patients with expressive aphasia, and those patients with receptive difficulties had little trouble with auditory sequencing. This is the opposite of what would be expected. That is, Efron found that the expressive aphasics, who needed so large an interval between auditory stimuli in order to sequence them correctly, nevertheless understood normal speech, even though this comes at the rate of one phoneme per 80 milliseconds. Efron later noted (in Millikan and Darley, 1967) that he found no significant correlation between the severity of the aphasia and the degree of difficulty aphasic patients have with sequencing. Some of his patients who were profoundly aphasic scored near normal on sequencing tasks. An even stranger finding is that a number of patients whom he described as 'hopeless' on auditory sequencing tasks could understand speech reasonably well.

Rosenthal (1972), whose findings implicating an auditory-storage deficit were mentioned above, similarly had problems concerning how his results could explain the language behaviour of the children. All of the older children who were subjects in his experiments possessed usable language in spite of the fact that most of them evidenced impaired auditory-processing abilities.

There are other problems for a sequencing-deficit theory of aphasia in children. If the sequencing disability is purely or primarily in the auditory modality – for example, caused by a more basic problem in rate of auditory processing and thus at the level of the phoneme – one would expect aphasic children to exhibit jumbled words, not disordered syntax. Furthermore, if the deficit was specifically auditory, these children would be expected to acquire language easily by lip-reading, or to acquire written language through the visual modality. This, however, does not seem to be the case.

Leonard (1979) pointed out that the nature of the speech used by language-impaired children suggests that auditory-processing and sequencing deficits are a corollary to and not a cause of the language difficulties. He noted that, if such theories were truly causal, the children should evidence word-order reversals in their syntax. But, instead, the syntactic problems they have take the same form as those of younger normal children – that is, the deletion of elements that are obligatory in adult syntax. It should also be noted that sequencing difficulties have often been found in deaf children, but no one would claim that such deficits are the 'cause' of their deafness. Furthermore, O'Connor and Hermelin (1973a, 1973b) showed that the lack of auditory input does not prevent deaf children from being able to appreciate temporal order, but it makes them unlikely to use that mode of ordering. For tasks in which various strategies can be used, deaf children were found to prefer spatial left-to-right orderings rather than temporal first-to-last ones. But this was shown to be an elective strategy. In experiments in which they were instructed to retain only temporally ordered information they were able to do so. In children with developmental aphasia, a temporal-order disability has sometimes been observed, but it remains to be shown whether this is an elective strategy. In any case, the notion that a temporal-ordering or sequencing disability causes the language impairment in these children needs to be further scrutinized.

Hierarchical-planning deficit   In some cases it may be possible to analyse the types of sentence structure being produced by language-disordered children in an attempt to uncover a more basic deficit. Such an approach has been taken with a very special group of aphasic children (Cromer, 1978a [chapter 5 below], 1978b). There is a rare aphasic syndrome that has been referred to in the literature as 'acquired aphasia with convulsive disorder in children' (Landau and Kleffner, 1957; McKinney and McGreal, 1974; Van Harskamp, Van Dongen and Loonen, 1978; Worster-Drought, 1971). Children who are described by this syndrome, either from birth or from a very early age, have neither comprehended nor produced language. As Landau and Kleffner (1957) described it, 'For most of these children the deficit seems to be congenital, since they have failed to acquire the ability to use speech or language normally. Some of them, however, have acquired the ability to use language in an apparently normal fashion and have subsequently lost it' (p. 523). Most of these children have an associated convulsive disorder and EEG abnormalities (McKinney and McGreal, 1974). The aetiology of the syndrome is unknown. The special group of 10 aphasics with a median age of 13 years 6 months that Cromer studied seem to fit this basic pattern. Deafness, mental deficiency, motor disability and severe personality disorder could be excluded as the cause of their language difficulty. The non-verbal IQs of the children as assessed by the Collins–Drever Test were in the normal range with a median of 99.5. Most of these children could produce and comprehend single words that seemed to be semantically correct in the sense of being appropriate to the situation. The children were bright and interested and gave the appearance of being frustrated by their lack of communicative ability. Although they had been taught to read and write, they were still handicapped in these abilities.

In order to study the grammatical constructions they used, a standardized situation was devised. The children were presented with a nonverbal story enacted by hand puppets. After viewing the puppet show, they wrote a description of what they saw. The story was designed to elicit a range of grammatical devices. For example, two characters of one of the types of animal were used in order to stimulate the use of plurals in later descriptions (e.g. 'two ducks') and to force a differentiation of the characters by the use of adjectives and other descriptive devices (e.g. 'the duck with the little eyes'/the duck with the big eyes') when these characters differed in their motivation in the story. Themes in the story were repeated in order to try to elicit various adverbial expressions such as *at first* and *again*. Materials such as low wide containers and tall narrow ones were used in order to encourage the use of more complex descriptions.

Of the 10 children, the two youngest merely drew pictures. Two produced written samples that were so severely disordered that a grammatical analysis has not yet been attempted. The remaining six samples were compared with the writings of six deaf children with a median age of about 10 years 6 months, who viewed the same show and similarly wrote free descriptions of what they had seen. Both groups of children wrote about the same number of words per sentence. Despite this overall similarity, significant differences were observed when the sentences were broken down into phrase-structure categories such as noun phrases, verb phrases, adverbial phrases. The deaf had a significantly greater mean number of categories per sentence (4.51) than the aphasic children (3.73). The number of different verb types used was also significantly greater in the deaf than in the aphasic children's writings. But the two groups were most different when the types of sentences they wrote were examined in a different way. The sentences of the deaf were more complex in that they attempted to combine units using devices such as embedding some constituents within others, and in general using processes that involved the interruption of simple sequences. The aphasics, in contrast, used very few such structures. Of all of the sentences written by deaf children, 35.9 per cent included one or more embedded or conjoined structures. In contrast, only 12 per cent of the sentences of the aphasic children evidenced such embedding and conjoining. When the aphasic children did use what could be classified as embedded structures, the second verb was always omitted. Furthermore, the aphasic writings differed significantly from those of the deaf in that the aphasic children never produced sentences that involved more than one embedding or conjoining. Of the sentences written by the deaf, 10.9 per cent did so.

It should be noted that a child was credited with attempting a structure even if he or she made grammatical errors. The sentences of the deaf were not correct by adult standards. Their grasp of various grammatical devices was inconsistent and limited; they made many errors on all sorts of surface features such as the inflections and suffixes indicating possession, plurality, tense-markers, and the like. The aphasic children seemed to make fewer errors, but this was because they attempted less. They confined themselves to fairly simple forms. This was not thought to be attributable to differences in educational methods used with the two groups because other groups of aphasic and language-disordered children in the same residential school as the aphasic group in this study, and thus learning by the same instructional methods, did not evidence this lack of embedding and interrupted structures when they undertook the same task.

Whether the structures used by the aphasic children are qualitatively different from the structures used by younger normal children is a difficult question. The two severely disordered samples that were not analysed are certainly unlike the writings of younger children. But the writings of the six aphasic children that were analysed could be viewed in such terms. The question that arises, however, is not whether the outputs of two groups look similar but whether anything can be inferred about an underlying deficit from the structures that are lacking. The writings of this particular aphasic group seem to reflect an inability to plan or programme sentences that incorporate hierarchical structuring in the sense that the production of some parts is postponed during the performance of other parts. The writing of somewhat younger deaf children did not show such a deficit. The utterances of normal speaking children as young as age 3 contain features that have been described as requiring this type of hierarchical-planning ability.

Evidence that these aphasic children may have a hierarchical-planning deficit comes from another source. It has often been observed that developmentally aphasic children have an almost uniformly poor sense of rhythm (Griffiths, 1972). They often cannot march in time or clap to the rhythm in music. Kracke (1975) found that aphasic children performed significantly poorer on tasks of identifying rhythmic sequences than did either normal or profoundly deaf children. This was true even when the rhythms were presented to the child in the tactile instead of the auditory modality by applying the rhythms to the child's fingertips with a vibrating disc. It is often assumed that rhythms are merely a sequential concatenation of beats. Martin (1972) challenged this assumption. He claimed that the view of rhythm as consisting merely of periodic, repetitive behaviour is misconceived. Such a series of sequential elements would have no structured internal organization. The alternative, for which Martin presented a strong case, sees rhythm as being composed of hierarchically structured units in which the change of any one element alters the interrelationships of all the elements to one another. Altering one rhythmic element does not merely affect its relationship to the immediate preceding and succeeding units; the whole rhythmic structure is affected.

Just as a hierarchical-planning or structuring ability is said to underlie the appreciation of rhythm, so such an ability is said to be necessary to describe normal language. Lashley (1951) asserted that associative chain explanations are unable to account for a variety of behaviours including rhythmic activity, motor movements, piano-playing, typing, speech and language. He claimed that theories that attempted to account for grammatical form in terms of the associative linkages of words in a sentence would overlook the essential structure of sentences. Such theories would also be unable to account for the processes by which sentences are produced or understood. Most modern linguistic theories since Chomsky (1965), regardless of their competing claims as to specific details, assign an important place to processes of embedding and interruption that would be difficult to account for in terms of simple temporal sequences. The alternative is that processes that are not themselves sequential underlie the sequential output of surface strings. The suggestion by Cromer (1978a [chapter 5 below], 1978b) is that the causal or at least associated condition found in the special group of developmentally aphasic children with convulsive disorder is some form of hierarchical-planning disability. Such a deficit prevents them from dealing adequately with rhythm and makes the structure of normal language difficult.

In order to test this disability more directly, a task was devised in which a child had to copy a two-dimensional drawing of a 'tree structure' and to build a replica with constructional straws of a three-dimensional mobile that was hierarchically ordered (Cromer, 1978c). This task is described in detail in chapter 2 of this book. The results obtained supported the view that some aphasic children may suffer from a hierarchical-ordering deficit. This is shown by their inability to deal with rhythm, their poor performance on drawing and construction tasks when asked to do them in an interrupted manner, and their relative lack of use of linguistic structures using embedding and interruption, which would necessitate hierarchical planning. Semenza et al. (1978) found that adult aphasic patients also evidenced what they call a constructional-planning defect. In copying various designs they used primarily an analytic strategy, whereas normal and non-aphasic brain-damaged subjects used a mixture of analytic and global strategies. This lack of global constructions by the aphasic patients was linked by these authors to modern linguistic theory in which global planning of utterances is necessary because language structure cannot be accounted for by a mere chain-like, sequential process.

Summary

In this section, a number of hypotheses about impaired processes have been mentioned as well as the experimental procedures designed to study them. Studies of deficits in memory, linguistic processing, auditory processing, phonological processing, sequencing and hierarchical planning have been reviewed. This list of possible deficits is not exhaustive. Others have proposed, for example, that language impairment can be due to limitations of production-span capacity and to attentional deficits.

The so-called reconceptualization urged in this section is not really a reconceptualization at all. Those doing research on language disorders have always been aware of the need to be specific about the kinds of deficits that may exist in one or another group of language-disordered individuals. Some work on normal language development, however, has focused exclusively on broad Piagetian stages in an attempt to explicate the relationship between cognitive development and language acquisition. It has been argued in this section that such a broad-based approach is not valuable, especially for those concerned with language disorders. Furthermore, the grouping of children in a broad category such as developmental aphasia for purposes of intervention programmes is equally poor. It has been difficult in the past to tie intervention programmes to specific disorders. Although this is still true, the next section offers some suggestions on how to begin that difficult task.

Implications for Intervention

Two reconceptualizations are suggested in this chapter. What are the implications for language intervention programmes that these reconceptualizations suggest? In a review of semantic and syntactic development, Bowerman (1978) suggested the basic necessity of viewing the child as an active participant in the language-acquisition process. It is argued in the first part of this chapter that recent research has not always done this. The underlying but not stated assumption that has emerged shows a reversion to studies that are at base extensions of purely empiricist theories, at least where the structure of language is concerned. One way to take account of the linguistic processes that children bring to bear on language acquisition is to see if some of the operating principles suggested by Slobin can be incorporated into the procedures used by intervention programmes. A good example of the direct but unconscious exploitation of such procedures by mothers was found in the study by Newport et al. (1977). Although they found that what they described as universal aspects of language structure were not sensitive to individual differences in styles of 'motherese', certain specific individual properties of language were indeed responsive to environmental input. The number of auxiliaries that the child used was correlated with the mother's use of expansions and her use of yes/no questions. The latter is especially interesting in that yes/no questions require the auxiliary to be moved to sentence-initial position (e.g. *'Can* you do it?', *'Will* it be fun?'). This position may be more salient for young children, and easier to process. It may be, then, that aspects of the input play an important part when they fit in with the child's processing strategies. The kinds of operating principles suggested by Slobin, and the methods noted by Karmiloff-Smith that children bring to bear on language acquisition, serve to indicate the kinds of principles that can play a role in specific language development. Newport et al. also noted a number of features of 'motherese' that were positively correlated with the child's vocabulary development. These include deixis (using words that point out and identify a referent, as with *this, that, here, there*) and exact imitations with expansions. Deixis was also correlated with the child's use of nominal inflections (mainly plurals). Partial imitations with expansions by the mother were positively correlated with every measure of the child's linguistic sophistication. It is also interesting to note that the mother's self-repetition was negatively correlated to many of the measures of the child's sophistication in language. Nelson (1973) similarly found a negative correlation between the rate of language acquisition and the mother's efforts to control and direct the child. These findings should give pause to any language-intervention programmes that do not take sufficient account of what the child brings to the situation.

Newport et al. concluded that maternal speech does exert an influence on the child's language acquisition, but only on structures specific to the individual language. These are such aspects as surface morphology and the syntactic elements that vary between languages. More importantly, they noted that even these are only influenced through the filter of the child's selective attention to portions of the speech stream. In their study they found these to be basically utterance-initial positions and items whose referents were clear. They concluded, in other words, that learning does respond to narrowly specified features of the environment, but it is still contingent on what children are disposed to notice in that environment, on their strategies of listening, and on the hypotheses they are prepared to entertain. Particular aspects of the mother's style interact with the child's processing biases for language and this can lead to differential rates of acquisition. This matches the epigenetic–interactionist viewpoint presented in this chapter.

The second reconceptualization emphasized the need to examine specific deficits in language-disordered children. One immediate problem that must be faced in intervention programmes is whether to undertake procedures designed to aid in communication or whether to concentrate on language. It was pointed out above that the two are not identical. It may be that, if irreversible deficits of a kind crucial for language are discovered, intervention procedures may be better directed to the establishment of more broadly based communication systems. The importance of language, however, both for communication with the majority of the people in the community and for internal processes of thought and development suggests that such a step should be taken only with some reluctance and after careful consideration of all the issues involved. In any case, language-intervention programmes are the concern of this chapter, not communication programmes. In this regard, the discovery of the existence of specific impairments requires that attempts be made to structure the input material or instructional methods to make use of unimpaired processes. An example of the discovery of specific impairments and their implication for remedial programmes comes from work on dyslexia.

Studies of adult aphasic patients with acquired reading difficulties have given a good deal of insight into the various processes that can be used in that skill. Marshall and Newcombe (1973, 1977) classified patients according to the method they used for reading on the basis of the errors they made in a task requiring them to read single words without context. Two basic methods were described. One was the use of a phonemic route in which the word is converted into a sound before it is interpreted. The other is a direct semantic route in which the meaning of a word is recovered directly from its visual appearance. Shallice and Warrington (1975) reported in detail a patient who showed impairment of the phonemic route and whose grapheme-semantic route (i.e. visual route) was relatively unimpaired. Patterson and Marcel (1977) tested this notion with two patients exhibiting a similar impairment. They found that, although the patients could *repeat* non-words, they could not *read* them. Furthermore, they gave these patients a lexical decision task in which the requirement was to make a judgement as to whether the presented stimulus was a real word. Normal subjects are usually slower in making such judgements when the presented stimuli are non-words that sound like real words when pronounced (e.g. *caik*). Their two patients, in contrast, did not show such an effect. It seems that they too suffer from a grapheme–phoneme impairment.

Snowling (1980) studied a group of dyslexic children who were substantially behind their peers in reading ability but whose low reading scores could not be attributed to low intelligence. 18 such children with a mean chronological age of 12 years 1 month and mean IQ of 106 were matched for reading age with 36 normal readers, whose mean age was 9 years 5 months and whose mean IQ was 105. The task was to make a same/different judgement for pronounceable nonsense words presented either auditorily or visually. The four conditions consisted of auditory or visual presentation of the first word coupled with either auditory or visual presentation of the word to be judged as the same or different from the first. The results showed that both groups did well on the auditory–auditory task, thus showing that the dyslexic children had no problems with auditory discrimination. There was a significant difference in performance, however, on the visual–auditory task (the condition most like real reading), with the dyslexic group scoring poorly. Snowling concluded that dyslexic readers perform in a qualitatively different manner from other readers, for it should be recalled that they were matched to the normals in terms of reading age. As Snowling put it, they are not just the low end of a normal distribution of readers; they have difficulties in visual–sound decoding. These children develop strategies to read whole words and this leads to a considerable sight vocabulary. But they have difficulty in decoding unfamiliar words. The dyslexic children in her sample, then, evidence a specific impairment in grapheme–phoneme translation.

Jorm (1979) reviewed evidence also leading to the conclusion that developmental dyslexics have difficulty with a phonological route to meaning, although he attempts to explain this in terms of a short-term memory deficit. Whatever the true reason for their grapheme–phoneme impairment, Jorm offered some suggestions for remediation programmes. He argued that, because dyslexics can access words visually but have difficulties in using the phonological route, methods of instruction should capitalize on their intact system. He suggested that the look–say method may be more effective for this group of children than phonic methods that try to teach grapheme–phoneme correspondences. The value of a phonic method is that it allows one to access the meaning of unfamiliar and novel words. But the designers of remediation programmes are left with a dilemma. Does one teach to the strength, as Jorm seems to suggest, or does one teach to the weakness in the hopes of improving a poorly functioning system but one which has advantages for the individual?

Other issues arise as well. Teaching to the weakness results in the experience of failure. There may be important motivational reasons for avoiding such failure. Cooper and Griffiths (1978) made a similar point in regard to educational programmes for aphasic children. They noted that the language failure of such children is not due to a linguistically deprived environment. Therefore, language enrichment and stimulation should not be the sole means of treatment. They point out that children who are subjected to stimulation and demands beyond their abilities may react with disorganized, disturbed or withdrawn behaviour.

Cooper and Griffiths (1978) suggested that, from an educational point of view, children should be identified in terms of their disabilities and impairments. Once these have been ascertained, children whose handicaps are amenable to the same teaching approach should be grouped together. They gave an example of five types of aphasic children that they found valuable to differentiate in terms of educational considerations.

It is clear that a child is not a passive entity to be subjected to one intervention programme or another based on broad learning principles and the assumption that all children, and even all animals, learn in one and the same way. For language-intervention programmes, the general features, predispositions, procedures and operating principles that human beings bring to bear on the language-acquisition process need to be considered. Some of these procedures may be specifically linguistic. The individual child must also be examined for specific disabilities and impairments affecting language acquisition. The conjunction of the two reconceptualizations outlined in this chapter may help to encourage a reconceptualization of intervention.

5

The Basis of Childhood Dysphasia: A Linguistic Approach

Introduction

There are basically two approaches to the study of any psychological behaviour. One consists in centring attention on the specific behaviour itself. This approach leads to description, classification, and also to studies of a correlational nature which attempt to interrelate various phenomena which may be associated with the behaviour in question. Another approach, however, is to 'dig deeper' and to try to uncover the underlying processes (or deficiencies) which lead to or produce the observed behaviour. Obviously there must be an interaction between these two approaches. It is the behavioural phenomenon that must, eventually, be understood or explained. But, in order to know how to bring about changes in that behaviour, or to produce a remedial effect, one must come to an understanding of the basic processes that are affecting or causing that behaviour. Moreover, quite different deficiencies may underlie the same or similar observable phenomena – especially when those phenomena are abnormal behaviour patterns.

There are dangers, however, in approaches that attempt to deal exclusively with the underlying processes. One of these stems from the fact that the way in which underlying processes are conceived often reflects one's assumptions about the structure of the behaviour itself. This becomes a danger because a particular conception becomes outmoded or else reflects a contemporary misunderstanding of the structure of that behaviour. A second problem is that one may lose sight of the behaviour that is to be explained, and as a result hypotheses and theories put forward are unable to account for that behaviour. A good example of this was in the 1950s when the emphasis was put on stimuli, responses, frequencies, associational mechanisms and reinforcement principles as applied to language acquisition by the young child, with little awareness that the actual language behaviour of young children differed considerably from the patterns that would be predicted on the basis of those processes. The study of disordered language is particularly vulnerable to these two problems. In the first place, one's understanding (or misunderstanding) of the nature of linguistic structure may greatly influence the search for the types of processes likely to be impaired and which therefore prevent language comprehension or production. Secondly, the hypothesized process impairments must be able to account for the kinds of disordered language actually observed. In the course of the first part of this chapter, the author will put forward the possibility that some of the recent work on the processing difficulties underlying childhood dysphasia may have been influenced by the shortcomings outlined above.

In an early paper, Lashley (1951) discussed the problem of serial order in behaviour. He pointed out the difficulties inherent in associative chain explanations of certain sequences of actions, for example rhythmic activity, typing, speech and, most important for our purposes, grammatical structure. Lashley claimed that such sequences cannot be explained in terms of the successions of stimuli. Rather, underlying these overtly expressed sequences are a number of integrative processes which can only be inferred from the final results of their activity. This constitutes what Lashley called 'the essential problem of serial order': namely, the existence of generalized schemata which determine the sequence of specific actions. In line with this view Lashley, when looking specifically at language, claimed that any theory that describes grammatical form as due merely to the associative linkage of the words in the sentence overlooks its essential structure. This is also one of the main points made by recent linguistic theory (see Chomsky's 1959 criticism of Skinner's model of language acquistion). Miller and Chomsky (1963) have argued strongly against the theory which explains acquisition of linguistic structure in terms of sequential links. They demonstrated that any theory of language acquisition based on the sequence of words (Skinner, 1957) or even on the possible sequences of grammatical categories (Jenkins and Palermo, 1964) would be mathematically impossible for the child to learn. For example, in the relatively long sentence, 'The people who called and wanted to rent your house when you go away next year are from California', the listener detects a dependency between the second word (*people*) and the seventeenth word (*are*) – a string of 15 sequential dependencies. The reader can easily demonstrate this to himself by substituting the word *person* for *people* or, alternatively, substituting *is* for *are*, for this will produce a sentence which is unlikely to be uttered (or written) or which would jar the listener or reader if it were. Based on certain assumptions concerning the average number of categories in a given sentence, Miller and Chomsky estimated (conservatively) that the listener, in order to have detected this dependency, would have had to learn 10^9 different possible transitions between sequential grammatical categories in – as they put it – a childhood lasting only 10^8 seconds. It can similarly be demonstrated that attempts merely to modify sequential theories by notions such as context generalization or by adding rules which allow one to insert or embed certain strings of linguistic elements within other strings are also inadequate. In any case, the idea of the ability to embed some structures within others implies the existence of that same underlying planning or integrative capacity which Lashley claimed to be necessary in order to explain externally observed sequences.

Despite this significantly different conception of language structure, the predominant emphasis in research on disordered language has been based on a sequential view of language units. In other words, the earlier assumption that language is a sequential ordering of elements has led to a great deal of research into temporal-ordering difficulties in individuals with linguistic impairments. In view of the more recent assumption of the hierarchical nature of linguistic structure, it may be that the importance attributed to the processing of temporal order is misconceived. The results of a linguistic analysis of the written productions of some dsyphasic children, discussed later in this chapter, tentatively support the view that the difficulty with language in these children stems from an inability to deal with hierarchically ordered relationships of the type inherent in the structure of language. But before discussing that research it is useful to review some of the hypotheses advanced to account for language difficulties in dysphasic children.

Some Theories of Childhood Dysphasia

Dysphasia is generally defined as the disturbance or the loss of ability to comprehend, elaborate or express language concepts. In adults this may take a variety of forms which have been classified in various manners, for example on the primary type of dysfunction (i.e. whether receptive or expressive), or else in terms of the nature of the language disturbance (i.e. whether the patient is agrammatical, anomic, etc.). Dysphasia in childhood, although it can sometimes be classified in similar ways, may in fact be very different in nature. In adult dysphasia, a previously functioning linguistic system has been impaired, whereas in developmental or even in early acquired dysphasia the child has been prevented from the initial acquisition of a complete language system. The underlying dysfunction in dysphasic children may furthermore be quite different from the impaired processes studied in the various types of adult dysphasia, although studies on adults may provide some interesting clues as to the nature of the dysfunction in children. There is also the additional problem that the basic defect may differ from one child to another, and this has led some researchers either to despair or to redefine childhood dysphasia to fit the purposes of their study. However, using certain criteria of exclusion, it is possible to obtain small numbers of subjects showing the same underlying difficulties, thus providing a homogeneous group. Griffiths (1972) provided a working definition of the condition when she described 'developmental aphasia' as being a failure of the normal growth of language function when deafness, mental deficiency, motor disability or severe personality disorder can be excluded. Several researchers have noted an inattention and an inconsistency of response to sound (Benton, 1964; Eisenson, 1968; Lea, 1970; Petrie, 1975; Schuell in Millikan and Darley, 1967), although it is unclear whether this is a contributory cause or an effect of the language disability. The main theories put forward to account for the lack of language in dysphasic children are as follows:

1 a specific defect of auditory perception;
2 an impairment of the auditory storage system;
3 impairment of rhythmic ability;
4 a defect in sequencing and temporal-ordering abilities; and
5 a specific linguistic-system impairment.

These theories are briefly reviewed before presenting research findings which have shown that the linguistic structure of dysphasic (and deaf) children does not lend support to the theories so far proposed. Instead, the underlying difficulty in dysphasic children may lie in an impairment of a hierarchical-structuring ability.

Auditory imperception

Word deafness or congenital auditory imperception implies that in spite of intact peripheral hearing mechanisms auditory speech cannot be processed by the central nervous system (see Worster-Drought and Allen, 1929). It is not easy to assess the auditory abilities of aphasic children. In addition to the inconsistency of response to sound, it is often noted that these children show no orienting reflex to sounds, even non-speech stimuli. Mark and Hardy (1958) studied 36 language-handicapped children with auditory imperception (median age $6\frac{1}{2}$ years) who had orienting-reflex disturbances. These children failed to respond to newly introduced sounds and to sounds which elicit orienting responses in normal children. Psychogalvanic skin-response audiometry established that the failure to respond to sound stimuli was not attributable to a peripheral hearing disorder. What, then, is the cause of their orienting-reflex disturbance? Mark and Hardy collected evidence to show that a significant number of these children did possess, in infancy, an orienting reflex to sound. The evidence was derived from the study of the age at which the first symptom occurred – i.e. the earliest age at which the informants (usually the parents) 'had the slightest cloud of suspicion that anything at all was wrong with the child' – and the character of the alerting symptom (whether speech or response to sound). In addition, anecdotal evidence of early responses to sound was collected. Especially in cases when the first symptoms occurred late, there were also detailed reports of startle responses, orienting reflexes and readiness-to-listen behaviour patterns. In some cases there was even evidence of early sound imitation and speech, and in a very few cases expletive or interjectional speech in children who were later on considered totally non-speaking. Mark and Hardy attempted to account for the lack of orienting reflexes to sound at later ages by hypothesizing that some cerebral damage or faulty development interfered in the establishment of the links between sounds and meaning. They argued that the child disregards sound later because the impressions from this sense modality remain unreinforced.

There are some problems with this interpretation. An inspection of the table in the Mark and Hardy paper reveals that in 23 of the 36 children the alerting symptom was a hearing symptom. But 11 of these were under 1 year of age, and six of these were less than 6 months old. It is somewhat difficult to see in what way a linkage between sound and meaning could be impaired at these very young ages to the extent of producing an apparent 'hearing' disturbance. More crucially, some experiments have shown that dysphasic children are not impaired in their ability to attach meaning to particular sounds (see for example Barna, 1975, to be discussed in a later section). Rather than a link between sound and meaning, other research-ers have argued that the basic impairment lies in the perception of speech sounds.

It may be that one major defect in dysphasic children is not the perception of sounds *per se*, but the perception of sounds in context. It is known, for example, that the perception of vowels is greatly dependent on context (Fry et al., 1962). Eisenson (1968) has suggested that dysphasic children may suffer from an inability to generalize sounds into phonetic contexts. That is, they can discriminate phonemes when presented in isolation, but not when they are incorporated into phonetic contexts. He conjectured that this results from a narrow and premature rigidity of the speech categories of the dysphasic children. In an experimental study, McReynolds (1966) found that dysphasic children between the ages of 4 and 8 years performed as well as normal children when discriminating isolated speech sounds, but did significantly worse when the same speech sounds were embedded in a phonetic context. McReynolds offered a number of possible explanations for this finding. But she seems to favour the above-mentioned interpretation of Mark and Hardy – that is, a lack of reinforcement for auditory perceptual responses which has led to an inhibition in the response to auditory signals, especially in language-like tasks, in which the dysphasic child may have experienced constant failure. Thus the inhibitions for language-like signals are stronger and more habitual than they are for auditory signals which do not resemble language. Again, there are several problems with this interpretation. For example, why have these children been unrewarded for language be-haviour in the past? If such poor reinforcement contingencies for language have led to the lack of auditory response, especially for language-like signals, then this lack of auditory response cannot be responsible for the poor language abilities in the first place. But, more importantly, there is no proof that language development in normal children is based on especially good reinforcement contingencies.

McReynolds offers several other alternative explanations for her results. For example, she thinks that dysphasic children suffer from an inability to deal with more than one perceptual skill at a time. In the sounds-in-context task, the child must not only discriminate the sounds, but retain and sequence them, and the simultaneous use of these skills may be beyond the child's capabilities. On the other hand, it is possible that the impairment may be merely in the ability to sequence the sounds. Theories of these types will be discussed in later sections.

Rosenthal (1972) has suggested several possibilities to explain the performance of dysphasic children on auditory processing tasks (Rosen-thal and Eisenson, 1970; Rosenthal, 1971). One of his theories postulates a basic auditory perceptual dysfunction. Rosenthal (1971) conducted an experiment designed to study the relationship between intensity of an auditory signal and its duration. He claimed that in normal subjects, at near threshold levels, the auditory system seems to summate or integrate the moment-to-moment energy into continuous signals. Consequently, if the duration of a signal is decreased, greater signal intensity would be required for detection. Since other experiments, however, appear to have demonstrated that dysphasic children are put at a severe disadvantage when temporal constraints are placed on auditory processing, Rosenthal hypothesized that signal intensities would have to be increased abnormally for this group in order to maintain normal detectability. The results were, in fact, somewhat equivocal. Only half of the dysphasic subjects showed a significant abnormal relationship between signal duration and detection thresholds. Nevertheless, as a group, the dysphasic subjects did require substantially greater increases in signal intensity than did the normal subjects. But there were other problems. These differences were only found at the shortest signal durations. Moreover, while the data at a 1000 Hz frequency supported Rosenthal's hypothesis, no reliable differences were found between dysphasic and normal subjects at a higher, 4000 Hz, frequency signal. He attempted to explain this in terms of a complex theory based on a notion of 'critical bands'. Basically, this theory holds that the ear does not respond to sounds outside particular frequency ranges (the critical band). The critical band for certain frequencies is thought to widen at short signal durations. Rosenthal suggests that in dysphasic children this widening of the critical band does not occur to the same extent as in normal children. Rosenthal raises the question of whether such critical bands are to be viewed as a fixed physical property, for example of the cochlear or other mechanism, or whether they are a function of some kind of internal filtering which is subject to cognitive control. In either case the possible cause of the child's lack of language ability may stem from a type of auditory imperception, but one which would not necessarily be limited to speech-like sounds.

Impairment of the auditory storage system

One explanation by McReynolds (1966) for the inability of dysphasic children to deal with sounds in context was mentioned earlier. It was claimed that, in order to carry out such a task, the child had to make simultaneous use of more than one perceptual skill – for example, not only to discriminate sounds but to retain and sequence them. This view is compatible with theories which seek to explain the basic difficulty of dysphasic children as a limitation of auditory storage ability. While a number of experimental investigations have studied various aspects of auditory imperception, very little specific work has been done on this second type of theory. Eisenson (1968) speculated that the dysphasic child's storage system for speech signals may be defective. That is, immediate recall of signals measured by matching procedures may be adequate, but the storage of such signals may be defective.

There are some experiments concerned with sequencing disabilities in dysphasic children, the results of which, on the basis of the procedures used, could be interpreted as showing a memory-storage problem. Stark, Poppen and May (1967) studied eight dysphasic children (mean age 8 years 3 months) and eight normal controls (mean age 5 years 3 months) on a task which involved depressing three keys with pictures on them, in the same order as the items were auditorily presented by the experimenter. Three of the dysphasics did well on the task but five did not. Of the errors made by these five children, 76 per cent occurred on the item in first position, whilst in the normal children and the other three dysphasics only 40 per cent of errors were on the first position. Furthermore, verbal stress put on the first item improved the scores of the five dysphasics, but did not help the normal children. Stark et al. concluded that the results showed that dysphasics have impaired auditory memory for sequences. The difficulty was mainly related to the forgetting of the first item in the sequence, but, when the first item was stressed, recall of the entire sequence was enhanced. Although Stark et al. saw the inability primarily in terms of sequencing difficulty, it could be argued that what this experiment really shows is an impaired memory function in five of the eight dysphasic children.

Poppen et al. (1969), in a later set of experiments, studied visual sequencing by a similar technique. In one experiment, nine dysphasic children (mean age 9 years 3 months) and nine normal children (mean age 8 years 8 months), viewed pictures on three frosted panels. The task was to press the keys in the order they had flashed. The results will be discussed in more detail in the section on sequencing, but here it is relevant to note that when a delay (ranging from two to 17 seconds) was introduced between presentation and response the number of errors increased significantly; however, the delay had a greater effect on the dysphasic than on the normal children. Reading from the graph presented in their paper, it appears that the errors of the dysphasic group were about 25 per cent with a two-second delay, but increased to 40 per cent with a 17-second delay. By contrast, the errors by the normal children increased from about 8 per cent (with a two-second interval) to about 12 per cent (at a 17-second interval). Although Poppen et al. were mainly concerned with a sequencing explanation, they suggested that memory and attention may be basic to that ability.

Rosenthal (1972) was also concerned, in some of his experiments, with sequencing disabilities, specifically in the auditory modality; but his results are also compatible with a theory of an auditory storage impairment. In a study of temporal-order effects Rosenthal and Eisenson (1970) presented short speech sounds, either singly or in pairs, to dysphasic and normal children. When the sounds occurred in pairs, the subject's task was to order them temporally, and the time taken to do this was compared with their performance on non-speech sounds which were similarly contrasting. The results showed that the dysphasic as well as the normal children could learn and later identify with a high degree of accuracy the stimuli which were presented singly. When those stimuli were paired in close temporal proximity, however, and the children had to report the order of their occurrence, performance by the dysphasic children broke down. Rosenthal and Eisenson take this as evidence that the nature of the auditory processing defect in dysphasic children is primarily one of short-term auditory storage. That is, the auditory trace, which can be identified singly, is not retained long enough to allow a perceptual analysis of temporal order; thus their interpretation of the difficulty of temporal ordering is that it results from an auditory storage deficit. Not all theories of sequencing disability agree with this, and many would emphasize that the temporal-order dysfunction itself is the primary disability. It should be pointed out that these different theories will lead to different predictions. A theory of auditory memory impairment would appear to predict greater difficulty with increasing numbers of auditory items, whereas temporal-ordering disabilities, which will be discussed in a later section, should affect even the shortest auditory strings.

Impairment of rhythmic ability

Clinical observations often suggest that certain types of adult dysphasic patients (e.g. those diagnosed as suffering from conduction aphasia), have difficulty reproducing non-verbal rhythmic sequences (Tzortzis and Albert, 1974). One of the most common observations by those who work closely with dysphasic children is that these children lack the ability to appreciate or deal with rhythm. Griffiths (1972) reported that dysphasic children show 'an almost uniformly poor sense of rhythm' in such lessons and activities as music and movement, dancing and singing. She studied 24 dysphasic children, six of whom were considered to be receptive dysphasics, while the remaining 18 were classified as expressive dysphasics. These children ranged in age from 6 years 9 months to 9 years 10 months (mean 7 years 11 months), and their IQs from 70 to 128 (mean 98) on the Performance or Full Scale of the Wechsler Intelligence Scale for Children. They were compared with 40 normal children on a number of tasks involving the sequencing of digits, the comprehension and repetition of sentences, and the repetition of non-verbal rhythms. This last task required the child to repeat a rhythm on a tambourine, immediately after the experimenter. There were four rhythm tests, each consisting of 10 items arranged in increasing order of complexity. The results showed that, while the dysphasic children were less successful on all of the tasks than the normal children, the task which most sharply differentiated the groups was the rhythm-repetition task. The errors made by normal children on the rhythms tended to be very minor. But Griffiths reports that, when the dysphasic children attempted to copy the rhythms, their productions often showed no apparent relationship to the rhythmic pattern presented, and gave the impression that some of their 'successes' were a matter of chance.

When certain disabilities are observed in a group, one must always question whether those disabilities are the cause or merely the effect of the basic condition by which the group is defined. In an early paper, Rosenstein (1957) assumed that the absence of hearing should have a significant effect on the ability to perceive rhythmic patterns, even if these rhythms are presented in a non-auditory modality. He used 30 pairs of rhythmic patterns presented tactually and compared matched groups of normal, blind, deaf and dysphasic children. The task was to render a judgement of 'same' or 'different' to the second of two vibratory rhythms delivered to the right index fingertip. Contrary to prediction, the blind group performed best, with the deaf, dysphasics and normals performing about equally and more poorly than the blind. Rosenstein felt, however, that there was some support for his hypothesis, since with practice the two normally hearing groups (the blind and the normals) improved their performance slightly, while the two groups who suffered from an auditory impairment (the deaf and the dysphasics) did not. Rosenstein concluded that auditory experience perhaps plays some role in the *improvement* of rhythmic discrimination, but he admits that his results do not show that auditory experience contributed to superior *initial* rhythmic discrimination.

Kracke (1975) starts with a different assumption, based on observations of deaf and of dysphasic children. She claims that these children display many behavioural similarities including 'normal play activities, good inter-personal relationships, efficient non-verbal communication between the children, not much verbal interaction, [and] little reaction to sound including their own names'. There is, however, one very noticeable difference. Deaf children are observed to enjoy rhythmic activities such as clapping, dancing and using percussion instruments. Dysphasic children, by contrast, cannot clap or beat rhythms which they hear and often are out of step with each other's movements. Kracke tested this observed difference experimentally; the aim of the study was also to ascertain whether the rhythmic disability is specific to the auditory modality or whether it transcends it. After a series of warm-up tasks to get the children to render same and different judgements to various pairs of stimuli, Kracke presented rhythmic patterns consisting of three stimuli, repeated three times to make up a rhythmic sequence. This was compared to a subsequent rhythmic sequence for a 'same' or 'different' judgement. 12 comparisons were made on auditory rhythms, and 12 on rhythms which were applied to the child's fingertips by a vibrating disc. 12 children were tested in each of the three groups (i.e. receptive-dysphasic, profoundly deaf, and normal children) matched for sex, age (8 years 4 months to 15 years 3 months) and non-verbal intelligence. The auditory rhythms were presented at levels of high intensity for the deaf children, and only children who could hear the experimental tones were included in the experiment. The results showed that, regardless of modality, the hearing and the profoundly deaf performed similarly, with the average number of correct responses of the two groups on the two tasks between 10.3 and 11.6 out of 12 rhythmic sequences. By contrast, the dysphasic children performed significantly worse, the group average of correct responses being only 6.6 for rhythms presented auditorially, and 5.8 for the vibrotactile rhythms. Thus, it seems clear that the deaf do not suffer a deficit in rhythmic ability, but dysphasic children do. Kracke claims that some underlying process apparently fails in dysphasic children, a process which enables unimpaired subjects 'to learn to recognise lawful relationships in temporal gestalts'. If this process is impaired, it may well have an important effect on sentence perception. These results, with a slight change of emphasis on the interpretation of what this disability may be, will be discussed in the final part of this chapter when several findings are brought together. Furthermore, it should be noted that Kracke's results suggest that the rhythmic disability is not limited to the auditory modality, but is of a nature that transcends other sense modalities.

The findings briefly reviewed here indicate that even profoundly deaf children do not suffer impairment of rhythmic ability. Rosenstein's results also support this conclusion, although in fact he started with the opposite assumption. What remains puzzling is the fact that, in his experiment, the dysphasic children were not especially impaired on rhythms when compared to the deaf and normal groups, despite the common observation concerning their poor performance on such tasks.

Sequencing and temporal-order deficits

There is another area of study where there is some question as to whether the hypothesized deficit is limited to the auditory modality or whether it is more general in nature – sequencing and temporal-order deficits. Problems of temporal disorientation and temporal ordering in certain types of brain damaged patients have been discussed for some time (e.g. Hughlings-Jackson, 1888; Critchley, 1953). Hirsh (1959) emphasized the importance of a central temporal-sequencing ability for making sense of auditory input and language. Monsees (1961) speculated that the basic disability in dysphasic children was a central disorder involving the perception of temporal sequence. The most commonly cited early experimental work on the impairment of such abilities in dysphasic patients, however, was that by Efron (1963). He found that in adult dysphasics the ability to say which of two sounds occurred first was seriously impaired unless the two stimuli were separated by a gap of as much as 575 milliseconds. This was contrasted with the fact that in normal speech sound segments occur approximately every 80 milliseconds. It was suggested, therefore, that dysphasic patients are unable to process normal speech because they cannot sort out the temporal order of the phonemes. That such sequencing may be important at the phoneme level is also supported by a study made by Sheehan, Aseltine and Edwards (1973). They found that the comprehension of some adult dysphasics was aided by the insertion of silent intervals between phonemes, but not by the insertion of silence between words. Efron (1963), however, commented on the difficulties that exist in this simplistic interpretation of the findings. For example, the dysphasic adults who showed the poorest performances on his temporal-ordering task were patients with expressive dysphasia, while those with receptive difficulties had little trouble with auditory sequencing. That is, the expressive dysphasics, who needed so large an intervening gap between auditory stimuli in order to sequence them correctly, nevertheless understood normal speech, even though this comes at the rate of one phoneme per 80 milliseconds. Efron admits that these findings are puzzling, and as he later put it in Millikan and Darley (1967) there is no significant correlation between the severity of the dysphasia and the degree of difficulty these patients have with sequencing. Some patients who understand speech reasonably well are very poor on a sequencing task. Others, who are profoundly dysphasic, score near normal results on sequencing. Further studies have turned up similar conflicting findings. Malone (1967) examined the relationship between the ability of dysphasics to resolve the temporal order of pure tones differing in frequency, and to identify sentences played at rapid speeds. No relationship was found between these two tasks ($r = 0.08$). Indeed, subjects were able to identify speech even when its mean rate of presentation exceeded their rate for ordering two tones by a ratio of more than two to one. Rees (1973), relying on evidence of this type, criticizes theories of dysphasia based on auditory processing difficulties. She cites Day's (1970) hypothesis that there are at least two different levels of temporal-order perception – a non-linguistic and a higher, more potent, linguistic level. Theories based on auditory processing of discrete phonemes or speech sound segments will not be able to explain the perception of connected speech. Experiments like those of Bever, Lackner and Kirk (1969), in which it was shown that the processing of sentences is carried out on the basis of major clause constituents, are taken as evidence that there is no basis for the assumption that the comprehension of heard speech depends on a more fundamental ability to analyse utterances into an ordered set of phoneme strings.

Perhaps these linguistic experiments provide a clue to the partial solution of Efron's puzzle. The adult expressive dysphasics who can comprehend speech yet need a large separation of two signals to make a correct judgement of temporal order may, in some sense, be relying on formerly learned language patterns in order to process sentences. They are, after all, people who prior to their illness possessed a normal language system, and having once known a linguistic system they can make use of different processing mechanisms, such as Day's (1970) higher-order linguistic processing, to understand speech even when its rate exceeds that necessary to order temporally non-linguistic stimuli. By contrast, a temporal-order disability in children could prevent them from acquiring a full linguistic system in the first place, and could conceivably be the cause of their dysphasia.

Lowe and Campbell (1965) studied auditory temporal processes in a group of children classified as 'aphasoid'. Eight such children, aged 7 to 14 years, were compared with a group of matched normal speaking children. Two types of temporal task were studied: 'succession' tasks to measure the amount of time required by a subject in order for him to hear two auditory events as separate events, and 'temporal-ordering' tasks to measure the slightly greater amount of time which is needed for the subject to be able to state which of the two auditory events occurred first. In succession tasks, the aphasoid children needed, on average, 35.8 milliseconds, compared to the normal average of 18.5. This difference, however, did not reach statistical significance. On the temporal-ordering task, the aphasoid children required 357 milliseconds as compared to only 36.1 for normal children. This very large difference was highly significant. Furthermore, since the average of 357 milliseconds required by the aphasoid children is far above the rate of normal speech (80 milliseconds per phoneme), Lowe and Campbell concluded that temporal-order malfunction may be the major factor in the language difficulties in these children.

Tallal and Piercy (1973a, 1973b, 1974, 1975) have conducted a series of studies on temporal-order processing by dysphasic children. They have found that, when the rate of presentation of two stimuli is too great, the child is not able to ascertain their order of occurrence. But Tallal and Piercy do not conclude that the impairment is one of sequencing inability as such. Rather, they believe that the basic inability is an impairment in the rate of auditory processing, to which a sequencing difficulty is secondary. That is, for developmental dysphasics, the time available for auditory processing is critical for adequate performance. Their perform-ance improves when the rate of presentation of stimuli is reduced, as was done in these experiments either by increasing the durations of the stimuli or by increasing the interval between them (cf. Sheehan et al., 1973). Tallal and Piercy also note, however, that the dysphasic children were impaired on all auditory serial memory tasks even when the durations and the inter-stimulus intervals were maximal. It is therefore necessary to postulate additional deficits, such as a specific defect of auditory memory, or the need by these children for disproportionately more time to process more elements (Tallal and Piercy, 1973b).

In spite of the need for additional explanations, Tallal and Piercy nevertheless emphasize the importance of the lowered speed of processing in the auditory modality shown by these children. It may, indeed, have the effect of causing difficulty in discriminating speech sounds. In a recent experiment (1974), Tallal and Piercy found that dysphasic children have difficulty in discriminating between stop consonants which have rapidly changing spectrums provided by the second and third formant transitions, which in fact are of relatively short duration (50 milliseconds). By contrast, they show no difficulty in discriminating vowels which have steady-state frequencies of the first three formants which remain constant over the entire length of the stimulus (approximately 250 milliseconds). That is, Tallal and Piercy found that dysphasic children performed as well as matched non-dysphasic normal children on the vowels, but their performance was significantly worse on the stop consonants. Indeed, only five of the 12 dysphasic children were even able to make the initial discrimination between two stop consonants. It could be, of course, that dysphasic children suffer from an inability to process transitional stimuli, regardless of their duration, and that this is why they performed adequate-ly on the vowels but not on the consonants. To test this, Tallal and Piercy (1975) used a new set of stimuli including specially synthesized vowel–vowel syllables in which the discriminable acoustic information occurred only within the first 43 milliseconds of the stimuli. These differ from the consonant–vowel syllables, which also contain the discriminable informa-tion in the first 43 milliseconds, in that the information in the former is of a steady-state character, while that in the latter is of a transitional nature. In conjunction with this they tested consonant–vowel stimuli but modified these so that the initial transitional period of each stimulus was increased from 43 to 95 milliseconds, although they were still of a transitional nature. The results showed that the dysphasic children were impaired when the discriminable components of the two stimuli were brief (43 milliseconds) but unimpaired when these components were longer (95 milliseconds), regardless of whether or not they were transitional in nature. Thus, the impairment in dysphasic children's discrimination of consonants is due to the brief duration of the discriminable components. Tallal and Piercy (1975) conclude that the language defect in dysphasic children is not specifically linguistic but is secondary to an impairment in the ability to process rapidly occurring auditory information. Their argument seems to be that this impaired processing ability underlies the sequencing difficulties which they have observed in the auditory modality. In other words, sequencing difficulties and the language deficits thought to be associated with them are seen as the effects of this auditory processing impairment.

There are some grounds for raising doubts, not only about this conclusion, but about the other theories which, by contrast, attach a central causative role to sequencing disabilities. First, is the defect in these children specifically auditory as Tallal and Piercy claim it is? Secondly, when considering theories of sequencing disabilities in dysphasic children, are such disabilities a primary cause of the dysphasia, as most of these theories seem to hold, or are they merely an effect? Thirdly, do any of these theories really explain the difficulties which are observed in dysphasic children? We can examine these three questions in turn.

Is the sequencing deficit specifically auditory? A number of researchers have suggested that dysphasic children suffer from a general sequencing disability which is not limited to the auditory modality. Withrow (1964) studied immediate memory for sequentially presented visual stimuli in dysphasic, deaf and normally hearing children. He reported that both the deaf and the dysphasic children performed significantly worse than the normal children. Poppen et al. (1969), in an experiment mentioned earlier, asked six dysphasic children (aged 5 years 8 months to 9 years 3 months) to press three frosted panels in the same order as they had seen them lighted. Although they performed better on this visual task than on auditory sequencing tasks, they still only achieved a 75 per cent success rate. In another part of their paper, these authors reported the correlations among several different sequencing tasks, which included both auditory and visual modalities, in the dysphasic and normal groups. They felt that the high intercorrelations (Kendall's coefficient of concordance for five sequencing tasks being 0.716) lent support to the notion that there is a general sequencing ability and that dysphasic children are deficient in that ability.

The evidence for visual sequencing deficits in dysphasic children is not as strong as that for auditory sequencing deficits, and, whereas in some experiments a trend towards impairment appears, it does not quite reach significance. For example, Furth (1964) tested the ability to learn visual sequences in dysphasic, normal and deaf children. The task consisted in learning to associate two-term sequences of shapes with a number. These nonsense shapes were presented sometimes simultaneously (thus requiring the learning of a left–right ordering) and sometimes successively. As these conditions did not differ in any of the three groups, the scores for both types of sequencing were combined. The overall task scores showed a great overlap among the groups, with the hearing children scoring the fewest errors (mean errors = 34.5), followed by the deaf with a score of 41.3. The dysphasic children scored the greatest number of errors (56.5). The mean number of errors by the deaf children did not differ significantly from that for either the normal or the dysphasic children, and the difference between the normals and the dysphasics was only significant at the 0.10 level. Furth points out, however, that the sequences consisted of only two elements and that all of the dysphasic children in his group had been receiving sequencing training for a number of years. These factors in fact may have prevented him from obtaining a clear-cut result in his experiment; however, a strong trend towards poorer sequencing ability in this visual task was shown by the dysphasic children. Stark (1967) tested 30 dysphasic children (aged 4 years 6 months to 8 years 2 months, mean IQ 76.8 on the Stanford–Binet), with three sequencing tasks. These three tests were the Knox Cube-Tapping Task, in which the subject must imitate the order of a series of taps which are graded in difficulty, and two subtests from the Illinois Test of Psycholinguistic Abilities (ITPA) (one auditory and one a visual sequencing task). Stark found that the dysphasic children scored significantly below their age level on all three tasks. On the other hand, Olson (1961) found no differences between deaf and dysphasic children on the same two subtests of the ITPA. Since neither of these experiments used normal control groups, it is difficult to interpret the results. In Olson's experiment, the deaf and the dysphasics performed similarly; but it is not clear whether both groups were average or below average on the sequencing tasks. In Stark's study, dysphasic children performed below their age level on sequencing; but in his particular group a low score was not unexpected as their mean IQ was only 76.8 (although it is important to note that the mean was 95.9 on an adaptation of the non-verbal Leiter International Performance Scale).

Some other experiments, while not concerned with sequencing, have shown a possible involvement of some aspects of the visual cognitive function. Wilson, Doehring and Hirsh (1960), for example, attempted to teach a group of dysphasic children to identify sounds. Their original hypothesis was that certain kinds of perceptual discrimination are difficult for dysphasic children. The stimuli they used consisted of sounds varying in two values (long and short) on two dimensions (duration and quality). Thus, the child had to learn four stimuli (a long tone, a short tone, a long noise and a short noise) and to associate these with four randomly selected letters of the alphabet. 14 children with receptive dysphasia (mean age 8 years 1 month, mean IQ 114) were compared to 13 non-dysphasic children (mean age 8 years 5 months, mean IQ 120). The group of non-dysphasic children was from the same clinic as the dysphasic group, and 10 of these non-dysphasics suffered from hearing loss. The task was to point to the correct letter of the four, each mounted on a 7 in. × 8 in. card, in response to the particular sound. The criterion of learning was six consecutive correct responses, and training was discontinued if learning was not achieved in 80 trials. The results showed that the dysphasic children were not a homogeneous group. Thus, out of the 14, six never achieved criterion, while all 13 non-dysphasic children achieved criterion with 50 trials. On the other hand, the three dysphasic children with the best scores equalled the three best scores of the deaf children. An analysis of errors showed that dysphasic children generally made more errors for short stimuli and had more difficulty discriminating the quality of short sounds. While this may appear to support a hypothesis concerning the specific auditory nature of the deficit, further observations by Wilson et al. lead to a different conclusion. The dysphasic children who had been unable to learn the task were given post-training sessions. It was found that the task was made easier if only a single card was shown and the auditory stimulus repeated several times. With this kind of training, all the children were able to form the correct associations. There was also greater success when all the individual cards were visible; whilst, when all four letters were on one card, only one child was successful. Wilson et al. conclude that the inability to learn shown in the main experiment most likely resulted from 'the complexity of the associative process' rather than from a deficit on the perceptual discrimination of the four acoustic stimuli. One could, of course, argue the opposite; the informal procedure in which the stimuli were repeated several times provided better opportunities to learn the auditory discrimination. But Wilson et al. present still further informal evidence. Two dysphasic and two non-dysphasic children were given a task of discriminating a tone and white noise of different duration. The results showed that all four children could correctly discriminate tone from noise on all trials even when the stimulus duration was reduced to

0.02 second. They could learn to say 'long tone', 'short tone', 'long noise', 'short noise' to the same stimuli used in the original experiment even after a single demonstration. Therefore, their failure could not originate from a difficulty in discriminating sounds. Indeed, repeating the original learning task still took one subject 37 trials. Wilson et al. conclude that the failure appears to be specific to the association between visually presented letters and auditory stimuli, and not because of any special difficulty of auditory discrimination.

Doehring (1960) carried out a visual task in groups of dysphasic, deaf and normal hearing children, divided into two age ranges: 7 years 8 months to 9 years 7 months, and 9 years 8 months to 11 years 7 months. The task was to draw an X exactly where a spot of light, 5 mm in diameter, had been flashed. The experimental design included variations in exposure time (0.25 up to 3.5 seconds) and variations in the time between presentation and response (one and eight seconds). Doehring also studied the effect of interference and no interference with visual-fixation conditions. Errors were evaluated by measuring the distance from the X to the place where the light had actually flashed. Results showed that the dysphasic children performed significantly worse on this task than the normal or deaf children. The deaf were worse than the normal children, but not significantly so. There were significant effects of delay and of interference but these were almost identical for the three groups. There were significantly more errors made by the younger children than by the older children, and the older of the two dysphasic groups performed similarly to the younger of the two deaf and normal groups. Thus, in respect to accuracy on this task, dysphasic children might be supposed to be retarded by about two years. The delay of eight seconds before being allowed to respond did not disrupt dysphasic children any more than deaf or normal children, and so one could assume that these dysphasic children are not retarded in that aspect of visual memory. Doehring (1960) concludes that dysphasic children appear to be normal in the visual symbolic processes associated with delayed response, but they are retarded in the accuracy of their visual memory for spatial location.

Tzortzis and Albert (1974) studied sequencing behaviour in three adults with conduction dysphasia. Such patients are often said to be deficient in memory for the specific sequential order of items. Tzortzis and Albert set out to find whether this defect was specifically one of auditory–verbal short-term memory or whether it was a general deficit in memory for sequences. They administered a battery of 27 tests, among them repetition tests which varied both input (auditory or visual) and response (oral or pointing); matching tests in which strings of one to four letters, words or numbers were followed by a similar or different sequence (requiring the subject to give a same/different judgement); tests of serial speech; and a rhythm test. The three patients with conduction dysphasia were compared with a patient recovering from Wernicke's dysphasia, and with one recovering from Broca's dysphasia; they also tested three normal subjects. The conduction dysphasics were found to have an impaired memory for sequences, and this was true whether the material was verbal or non-verbal, whether the modality of input was auditory or visual, and whether the response was oral or by pointing. It was observed that these dysphasics could often produce all the items in a sequence correctly, but not the sequence itself. Tzortzis and Albert emphasize that the deficit could not have been purely auditory, since these three dysphasics performed poorly even when the input was visual – although their performance was better than that for auditory stimuli. So the basic disorder in these patients with conduction dysphasia seems to lie in their inability to order elements in a sequence, even when they can remember the items that make up the sequence. It was also found that these same subjects had very poor scores on the rhythmic tapping task, and Tzortzis and Albert point out that this is consistent with the clinical observation that patients with conduction dysphasia have great difficulty in maintaining rhythms.

This report on adult dysphasics is included because it deals with the condition in which sequencing is considered the primary difficulty, and Tzortzis and Albert appear to have shown that a sequencing difficulty is not limited to the auditory system. This is contrary to the findings of Tallal and Piercy, who claim to have shown that children with developmental dysphasia do not have difficulty with visual sequences. On an admittedly very different group of subjects, but in contrast to some of the other studies in children with developmental dysphasia (e.g. Furth, 1964; Poppen et al., 1969; Stark, 1967; and Withrow, 1964) Tallal and Piercy (1973b) claim that sequencing difficulty is found only in the auditory modality. They studied the performance of 12 dysphasic children (aged 6 years 9 months to 9 years 3 months) on two types of serial memory – one composed of two different tones and the other composed of two different lights (different shades of green). In this task, the child was trained to press a panel on the right for one tone (or light), and a panel on the left for the other. Serial patterns of three, four and five elements were actually made up of only the two stimuli. In other tasks, in which only two-element patterns were used, the duration of the tone (or light) was varied as was the inter-stimulus interval. Both of these were kept constant in the longer serial memory task, although in one condition the duration of the stimuli was 75 milliseconds and in the other 250 milliseconds. Compared to 12 normal children matched for age, sex and non-verbal intelligence, the dysphasics performed significantly worse on the 75 millisecond tones for three-, four- and five-element patterns. Whereas all of the normal children reached criterion ($p < 0.001$, binomial test) for all lengths, only two of 12 dysphasics reached criterion for strings of three elements, and only one of 12 on any longer pattern. When the tones were of 250 milliseconds duration, however, the dysphasic children improved; 10 of the 12 reached criterion on three-element patterns. But with four- and five-element patterns, only seven and two respectively reached criterion, and this was significantly worse than the normal children, who all reached criterion on all the patterns. On the perceptual tasks (two elements) dysphasic subjects were significantly impaired both when the inter-stimulus intervals and the durations of the tones were decreased. By contrast, when visual stimuli were used no difference appeared between the dysphasic and normal children on any task, whether perceptual or serial memory.

It is not clear why some experiments show deficits of visual sequencing in dysphasic children whilst others do not. The argument is important because, if visual sequencing is disturbed, theories of developmental dysphasia which place the underlying cause in an auditory deficit will, at the very least, have to be elaborated to explain such visual defects. Tallal and Piercy (1973b), in fact, tentatively do just that. They point out that in the experiments in which some visual deficit has been observed the visual sequences were presented spatially, whereas their own presentations were in fact temporal sequences presented in one location. Another difference was that Tallal and Piercy's procedure allowed the child to respond as soon as the stimuli were completed, whereas in some of the other experiments there was a delay before the children were allowed to respond. Tallal and Piercy speculate that these factors may have made some verbal mediation necessary, thus placing the dysphasic children at a disadvantage on the visual tasks. Precisely why verbal mediation would be made necessary was not made clear in their discussion, and in this respect it is important to note that rats and pigeons are capable of delayed responses. It is true that the tasks in the various experiments have been different, and one could argue, for example, that Tallal and Piercy's serial memory task is not a sequencing or temporal order task at all. Indeed, Tallal and Piercy carefully avoid using the term 'sequencing' for their test, as it consisted of ordering serially two elements into longer strings. The other experimenters used either pictures, nonsense shapes or spatial positions, with each element in the sequence being different from all others. Given the wide differences that exist in the various experimental designs, the debate over whether developmentally dysphasic children suffer from a broad sequencing defect or from a specifically auditory one is likely to continue. But there are other reasons for asking whether sequencing deficits of any type are in fact the cause of developmental dysphasia.

Is the sequencing disability a primary cause of the dysphasia? Most of the work on sequencing and temporal-order difficulties assumes that a dysfunction in this area is responsible for the child being unable to comprehend language. The early findings of Efron (1963) on dysphasic adults and of Lowe and Campbell (1965) on 'aphasoid' children, for example, were taken as evidence that the auditory input of phonemes was too rapid for the individual to be able to sort out the order of occurrence; language would sound all jumbled up. But, although a number of the above-mentioned experiments seem to support the conclusion that auditory sequencing is disturbed in dysphasic children (whether as a primary dysfunction or as the result of a deficit in the rate of auditory processing) it is open to question whether this disability is really the *cause* of the dysphasic condition.

An experiment by Furth (1964), cited earlier, showed that dysphasic children responded poorly in a sequencing task, but their scores, while much lower than those of the normal and deaf groups, did not reach statistical significance. Furth speculated that one possible reason for this was that the dysphasic children had been receiving sequencing training in a special school for a number of years. Stark (1967) uses the same argument when discussing both the results of Furth and those of Olson (1961), who had found no differences between deaf and dysphasic children. Stark argues that the dysphasic children who participated in both experiments had received a number of years of training in sequence-learning. But such an argument surely undermines the claimed causal nature of this disability. If children are capable of being successfully trained in sequence-learning, then this ability cannot be basically impaired. Furthermore, there is no evidence that successful sequence-training alleviated their dysphasia.

It may be noted that dysphasic children are often compared not only with normal but also with deaf children in sequencing experiments. One of the reasons for this is that the deaf too are often thought to be deficient in temporal-sequencing abilities. It should also be noted, however, that, when experimentation has shown the deaf to be poorer than normal children in sequencing, no one supposes their inability to sequence to be a *cause* of the deafness! The experiments with dysphasic children are of an identical logical status, but this does not appear to prevent some theorists from adopting the position that a sequencing disability is the cause of the dysphasia. In fact the direction of causation may be reversed; it may be that lack of experience with the auditory information of language, in these children, may result in their seldom relying on temporal order to encode or understand the world. O'Connor and Hermelin have been conducting a number of interesting experiments on deaf children and their ability to deal with temporally ordered phenomena. In one experiment (Hermelin and O'Connor, 1973), they used an ingenious technique in which various short strings of numbers were presented in a manner compatible with both spatial (left-to-right) and with temporal (first-to-last) coding. The apparatus consisted of three small windows arranged horizontally, and a fourth window, on its own, below them. In one situation three numbers appeared in the upper windows one after the other, but in such a way as not to occur in a left-to-right order. For example, if three numbers occurred in the temporal order, 3, 9, 7, the spatial order might have 7 in the left-hand window, 3 in the central window, and 9 in the right-hand window. Thus the temporal order 397 would have appeared spatially as 739. After a one-second pause, a recognition display was exposed in the window below. It showed the same numbers exposed one after another, and this recognition display could show the numbers as they had appeared in temporal order (397), spatial order (739) or else randomly (e.g. 973). In a second condition, the initial presentation was successive, in the lower window, and the recognition task was based on the subsequent three-window display. Again, the three-window display could be presented temporally (but not spatially), spatially (but not temporally) or randomly. In both conditions, the child's task was to judge whether the order of the two presentations was the same or different. Hermelin and O'Connor found that normal hearing children generally gave temporally ordered recognition responses. Indeed, only three out of 40 hearing children (7.5 per cent) recognized the left-to-right but not the first-to-last order of the digits. By contrast, 31 out of 57 deaf children (54.4 per cent) recognized the spatially ordered display but not the temporally ordered one. In other words, even when the spatial-display element was eliminated, from either the initial input or from the recognition display, more than half of the deaf children failed to recognize the previously presented temporal sequence. Such results appear to show an inability by many deaf children to deal with temporally ordered information, and many researchers would have been satisfied with such a conclusion. O'Connor and Hermelin (1973a, 1973b), however, carried out additional experiments. In one of these (1973a), 20 hearing and 20 congenitally deaf children viewed sets of either five photographs of faces or five nonsense syllables presented in five windows. As in their first experimental technique mentioned above, the sequential (temporal, first-to-last) order of the items was incongruent with a spatial (left-to-right) order. In another condition 40 deaf and 40 hearing children saw similar items presented successively at the same location. In both conditions, the task was the same. After viewing the material, the children were shown two temporally adjacent members of the set of five, and they had to tell the experimenter which one had come first. Thus, in this experiment, the children were clearly instructed to retain only temporal-order information. The results showed that in general there were no differences between the hearing and the deaf children on this task. The deaf performed better on the photographs than on the nonsense syllables, and their performance on the photographs was better than that of the normal children. The normally hearing children were better on the nonsense syllables than on the photographs, and achieved better results on the nonsense syllables than did the deaf children. What is significant here is that, when the deaf are instructed to retain only temporally ordered information, they are as efficient as hearing children. In the experiments mentioned previously, most deaf children, when given an option, 'preferred' to remember the left-to-right rather than the first-to-last temporal order. But according to O'Connor and Hermelin the later experiment shows that in deaf children this is an elective strategy rather than an incapacity to appreciate temporal order.

In the deaf children, then, lack of auditory input does not prevent them from being able to appreciate temporal order, but it makes these children unlikely to use that mode of ordering. In children with developmental dysphasia, a temporal-order disability has been observed, but it remains to be shown whether this is 'elective' or not. The notion that such a disability 'causes' the dysphasia, however, should be subjected to greater scrutiny than it has been in the past. Indeed, if a temporal-ordering disability does underlie the dysphasic condition in these children, one would expect it to affect language in a defined and predictable manner. But this also appears not to be the case.

Does the sequencing disability explain the observed language difficulties? This chapter began with the assertion that recent work on the processes underlying childhood dysphasia was subject to difficulty in two areas. The first of these concerned the common assumption that language is serially structured, and it was suggested that this view has exerted an influence on the underlying processes which are thought to be defective in dysphasic children. This section is exploring the hypothesis, which directly reflects such an assumption, that some sort of sequencing disability is the cause of developmental dysphasia. The second problem was said to be the danger of losing sight of the behaviour which was to be explained. If a sequencing disability is responsible for childhood dysphasia, effects of this disability should be at least partly reflected in the language behaviour of these children. If individuals cannot process the incoming auditory signal rapidly enough to determine the relative ordering of the elements, language would presumably appear to be jumbled and disordered. As mentioned in an earlier section, however, Efron (1963) reported, from his work with adult dysphasics, that no relation could be found between the severity of the dysphasia and the degree of difficulty with sequencing. He had noticed that some patients who were profoundly dysphasic scored near-normal results on sequencing tasks. More significantly, a number of patients whom he described as 'hopeless' on sequencing tasks could nevertheless understand speech reasonably well. Geschwind (1967) also reported that some adult dysphasic patients with good auditory comprehension were defective in temporal-ordering abilities. Furthermore, there were some dysphasic patients with impaired comprehension who nevertheless showed the ability to repeat perfectly. Geschwind concluded that in these cases the disturbance could not possibly be due to a defect in auditory temporal-ordering ability. In these patients, for example, the sounds had to be perceived in the correct order to make exact repetition possible. In developmental dysphasia there is also no evidence that speech sounds appear jumbled to the child, nor indeed are there reports that these children produce temporally displaced phonological elements when attempting to speak. Rosenthal (1972), whose research has been reviewed in the sections on auditory imperception and auditory storage, reports problems similar to those encountered in the adult dysphasic research. For example, he states that all of the older children who were subjects in his experiments possessed usable language in spite of the fact that most of them were found to have impaired auditory processing abilities. Although he suggests that such a disorder in dysphasic children may interfere with the establishment of a phonological base for language, he admits that the language systems of these children also show phonological, syntactic and semantic deviations. One suggestion is that auditory dysfunction does not adequately account for developmental dysphasia. Similarly, the notion of impaired sequencing abilities does not appear to explain adequately the observed syntactic deviations in these children. For example, if the sequencing difficulty is conceived as purely auditory in nature and is at the level of the phoneme or stop consonant, one would expect dysphasic children to exhibit jumbled words, not jumbled grammar. Furthermore, if the problem is one of sequencing in the auditory modality alone, then one might expect dysphasic children to be able to acquire language easily by lip-reading or to acquire written language through a visual medium. As will be pointed out, this does not appear to be the case and the errors made in language behaviour in other modalities are not, in the main, errors attributable to ordering difficulties which a broader sequencing-impairment theory might predict. Psychologists often seem peculiarly reluctant to explore the hypothesis which most directly reflects dysphasic language difficulties – that the disorder might be due to a specific linguistic-system impairment which transcends the particular modality of linguistic input.

Specific linguistic-system impairment

One theoretical position which has not been explored adequately is that the dysphasic child suffers from some kind of basic linguistic impairment. According to this hypothesis, the child is unable to process those basic grammatical relations similar to the type suggested to exist as part of some kind of 'language-acquisition device'. Chomsky (1965) has speculated that the ability to perceive and acquire certain linguistic relations is innate in the child. This speculation is based on a number of observations, including the rapidity with which children in all cultures and subcultures acquire language, with or without emphasis on language tuition; the similar ages, worldwide, at which children become proficient in their various native languages; and the hypothesis that there are broad similarities, for all languages, in the children's use of early linguistic productions, even when these do not match in many instances the adult model. From the psychologist's point of view, it is not easy to specify what such a language-acquisition device might contain, and it is therefore difficult to design experiments or make observations which would elucidate its content or structure. It would seem that there are several possibilities as to the nature of this species-specific, language-directed behaviour. One could argue, for example, that there may exist certain, pre-set, specifically linguistic strategies for the acquisition of language structures. A study of the acquisition of certain features of a particular linguistic structure by using new forms containing nonsense words has recently been reported (Cromer, 1975a). The study was made on normal and educationally subnormal children, and also on normal adults. One particular strategy used by the normal children in dealing with the new instances of this structure appeared to coincide with the kind of behaviour which would be predicted if answers were given in accordance with some universally observed language patterns. Educationally subnormal children behaved not like the normal children, but like normal adults. The explanation for this finding was thought to be related to the fact that the subnormal children had been matched with the normal children on the basis of their mental age; they were, therefore, chronologically older and beyond a critical period for language-learning when such strategies were likely to be employed. That is, neither the educationally subnormal children nor normal adults made use of the language-related strategy which was observed in many of the normal children. There is very little experimental work on other possible specifically linguistic strategies for language acquisition.

A slightly different approach might be to consider the 'content' of the language-acquisition device. In this hypothesis, the child is believed to possess certain linguistic structures to which he attempts to match linguistic input. A related possibility is that certain linguistic structures are 'natural' and are easily acquired; they are structures which are found universally or near-universally in the languages of the world. The brain, in other words, is thought to be 'pre-wired' to deal with certain types of specifically linguistic input. If there is any truth in these claims, the study of the linguistic structures of people suffering from damage to the language areas of the brain might provide clues to the nature of the intact language-acquisition device. A few recent studies have begun to look at the language of adult dysphasic patients in terms of more modern linguistic theory, some with the intention of examining the way in which the grammar is actually represented in a speaker's brain. Myerson and Goodglass (1972) attempted to describe the language output of three patients with Broca's dysphasia by the methods of transformational grammar. The three patients were differentially impaired. Myerson and Goodglass found an inverse correlation between the severity of the dysphasia and the number of specific types of distinction that could be made in the base component, as well as in the number and types of rules which were used to generate surface structures. In some cases (e.g. negation, and number of base-generated constituents which could actually be expressed in any utterance) the limitations seemed to parallel the order of acquisition by the child.

Schnitzer (1974) used methods of modern linguistic analysis in studying the language and grammatical judgements of a dysphasic patient. English sentences and non-sentences were read to the patient, and his task was to judge whether they were grammatical or not. His judgements generally agreed with those of normal individuals, but he did make several systematic errors. Overall, he judged certain exceptionally long, embedded or conjoined grammatical sentences to be ungrammatical. In terms of specific structures, almost all of his incorrect judgements were related to three linguistic features: the absence of copula verbs, the absence of the subjects of sentences, and the absence of determiners. Some examples will make each category clear. The absence of the copula verb *to be* was noted in such sentences in his spontaneous speech as 'He mad', 'I scared', and 'They not fast.' In addition, sentences which were read to him with the copula omitted, such as 'The dog sick' and 'The pen coloured green', were judged by him to be grammatically correct. Similarly, he omitted subjects in his spontaneous speech ('Getting hungry', 'Got a good sleep last night') and judged sentences lacking subjects ('Kicked and punched', 'Walked about fifteen miles') to be grammatical. The same pattern occurred with determiners. Thus, he often omitted *a* or *the* ('Population is getting big', 'Almost lost game') in his own speech, and judged sentences without them ('Dog ate grass', 'Dog is in yard') to be grammatical. Schnitzer noted, however, that these forms were only omitted when the sentences did not carry new semantic information or where new information was marked by elements found elsewhere in the sentence. In sentences where the information was of a purely grammatical kind, Schnitzer's patient ignored the grammatical elements. For example, a series of relative clauses such as 'The man who went to the store' and 'The pig that lives in the pen' were judged by him to be fully grammatical sentences. Notice that they are also grammatical when the relative pronoun is omitted. The information which the relative pronoun conveys is syntactic – that this structure is a relative clause embedded on the noun which begins it. Schnitzer concludes that linguists have much to learn from such an analysis. In this case, for example, he claims that grammars ought to provide a way of representing the distinction between syntax and semantics. He feels that the grammars proposed by linguists should be conditioned by knowledge of the actual way in which grammar is represented in speakers' brains. Looked at the other way round, however, it may help to explain the linguistic disorders observed in dysphasic patients.

The problem is that the 'grammars' of adult dysphasic patients are many and varied. Instead of providing clues to the nature of the 'cause' of the language disorder, they merely reflect what occurs when a specified area of the brain is damaged. Language, by whatever means it is acquired, may be predominantly organized in particular areas of the brain. Lesions in these areas produce various kinds of dysphasia. By contrast, the study of developmental dysphasia, of children who possess normal cognitive capacities but who do not easily acquire language, may provide clues to the nature of the language-acquisition device by providing evidence of the types of linguistic structures these children find difficult or impossible to master regardless of the mode of input.

Some 'Language-System' Experiments on Dysphasic Children

There has been a great deal of interest, in the past few years, in the supposed uniqueness of language in human beings. Obviously other animals have their own cognitive systems and display various types of intelligent behaviour. But many theorists have argued that only humans have the capacity for 'true language'. What is meant by 'true language' is not, however, entirely clear. Furthermore, the difficulty of studying 'language' in other species has often been compounded by the problem of choosing means of communication which the animal can handle. Since language functions should transcend particular modalities, it is possible to design systems which other animals may adequately use, but which still give evidence for the possession of these functions. There are really two issues involved here. One is whether non-human animals are capable of using linguistic functions, and the other is the extent to which linguistic functions can be shown in a non-auditory modality. The first issue is outside the scope of this chapter and it will be mentioned only peripherally. It only becomes important in so far as the techniques developed for studying communication in other species may be of use in helping to throw light on the abilities and deficiencies of children with developmental dysphasia. One important point must be emphasized: language functions and cognitive meanings are not identical. To state that an individual possesses a certain type of intelligence and is capable of understanding and making use of symbols for various contents and relations in the world cannot tell us whether or how he is capable of expressing or understanding those meanings in a linguistic system. This point has been discussed elsewhere (see Cromer, 1974a, 1976a). Indeed, as we will later discover, dysphasic children and adults are capable of many types of complicated thought processes while being unable to understand or express them in a language system.

On the basis of the work of David Premack (see pp. 202–3 above), some writers have concluded that chimpanzees have been able to learn subject–verb–object strings, and indeed in Premack's experiment they appear to have done so. But again caution must be used in making such an interpretation. The terms *subject, verb* and *object* are linguistic, and are often used to express the meanings 'actor', 'action' and 'object', but they need not do so, and may not do so in the majority of sentences actually used by speakers. For example, although the subject of a sentence may be an actor or agent as in 'John hit the ball', subjects may serve a variety of other functions as well. In 'The key opened the door', the subject, *key*, is an instrument, not an actor or agent. In 'John received a blow on the head', the subject, *John*, is a patient. In 'John received a gift', *John* is a recipient. In 'London is windy', the subject, *London*, is a location. Indeed, this is the whole point of case grammar. Case-grammatical conceptions express certain meanings more directly. Notions like 'subject', however, express a different level of generalization, and one which is more purely grammatical. It has been argued by some researchers (e.g. Bowerman, 1973) that very young children's grammars are more adequately described in terms of a case grammar. Bowerman also notes, however, that at some point in development it appears necessary to invoke grammatical notions such as 'subject' and 'object' in order to account for the more purely linguistic transformations which are observed. It is not necessary to examine the merits of opposing theories of grammar merely in order to re-emphasize that, at least in some theories, grammatical meanings (such as 'subject') are not identical with specific cognitive meanings (such as 'actor'). It may be that the systems taught to chimpanzees are communication systems encoding the linkage of meanings rather than of linguistic elements. That is, it may be more accurate to describe some of the chimpanzee sentences in terms such as *actor, action, acted upon* rather than *subject, verb, object*. And this may be a crucial distinction when one considers dysphasia, in which cognitive meanings may be preserved whilst the more purely linguistic structures in which these are usually encoded break down. One possibility is that such artificial 'languages' can be learned by dysphasics precisely because they are not 'linguistic'.

Glass, Gazzaniga and Premack (1973) demonstrated that a communication system based on Premack's system for the chimpanzee could be learned by patients with global dysphasia resulting from cerebral vascular accidents. Seven patients were trained in the use of a system employing cut-out paper symbols for words. The paper symbols varied in colour, size and shape, were functionally equivalent to words, and were arranged in a left–right direction on a table. Glass et al. reported that all seven patients, taking on average one month of training, successfully learned same/different and interrogative constructions. In addition, two of the patients were able to learn simple sentences consisting of what were described as 'subject–verb–direct-object' strings. They were able to produce and comprehend such sentences at an approximate level of accuracy of 80 per cent. There was evidence that the other five patients would also have progressed to that level had training been continued, but for administrative reasons this was not possible (e.g. some patients were discharged from the hospital). Glass et al. concluded that global aphasics may not suffer a cognitive impairment which is in direct proportion to their linguistic impairment, and that rather sophisticated and abstract symbolic thought can be carried out by patients with severe language deficits. What is the case of children with developmental or early acquired dysphasia? Might it be that they have the cognitive ability to learn such a communication system despite their deficient or almost non-existent language? The teachers and staff at schools for dysphasic children have no doubts that their children are capable of extremely sophisticated symbolic thought. As we shall show, the teachers are correct in their assessment.

Hughes (1972, 1974–5) carried out a study (following a suggestion of Dr B. M. Hermelin) designed to discover whether children diagnosed as dysphasic could acquire the type of communication system that Premack had used with chimpanzees. The four children she studied were cases of developmental or early acquired dysphasia. These subjects were part of a special group of children with normal or above-normal intelligence as measured on non-verbal tests, but were unable to comprehend or produce language. Hughes trained the four children individually in half-hour sessions twice weekly for about nine weeks, using materials similar to those Premack had employed – i.e. plastic shapes with a metal backing which were placed on a magnetic board. She reported that the dysphasic children rapidly acquired all of the functions taught. These included the names of various objects and persons, verbs such as *give* and *point to*, direct and indirect objects, negatives, modifiers and questions. Thus, like the global aphasics mentioned earlier, these children were able to acquire a fairly sophisticated communication system without difficulty. The crucial question now becomes: why are children without language able to acquire Premack's system? There are a number of possibilities. One is that this system, although a communication system, is not a 'language' in the sense in which linguists would define language. This argument, however, contains a logical fallacy which becomes particularly obvious when applied as a criticism to the research on communication systems in chimpanzees. The argument usually begins with the assertion that only human beings have language. When chimpanzees are shown to be able to acquire one or another analogue of language, it is then argued that the system under consideration is not really 'language' since, by definition, chimpanzees are not capable of language. On the other hand, in the experiments just reviewed, various human groups were trained on just such a communication system. In one group, the known language ability of a group of adults had been impaired as a consequence of a stroke. That they could acquire 'Premackese' in spite of their linguistic impairment is certainly significant. Similarly, the dysphasic children had either never developed language or lost what language abilities they had at an early age. They too were able to acquire the Premack system easily. This in fact could also suggest that the argument put forward by the linguists is after all correct; it may be that Premackese, while encoding some of the functions that language encodes, is, nevertheless, not really the same as a linguistic system, even when it adequately serves as a communication system. That is, it bears little resemblance to natural language; it utilizes only simple ordering rules, and has no transformations; and it does not really constitute a generative system.

There is another possibility, however, which needs consideration. It may be that the impairment in dysphasics is purely auditory in nature. This argument would hold that the Premack system presents little difficulty to dysphasic individuals because it is a visual system. In order to test this possibility, we designed a study (Barna, 1975) in which children with early acquired dysphasia were given instruction in a system analogous to that of Premack, but which was presented in the auditory modality. In order to carry out this study, an apparatus was built which consisted of 15 tape recorders operated by two keyboards, one controlled by the researcher and the other controlled by the dysphasic child. Each keyboard had 15 buttons arranged in three rows of five. Pressing a key operated a particular recorder. Each recorder had a special looped tape with a repeating sound or noise, so that pressing one of the buttons immediately produced that particular sound. With the two keyboards, either the child or the researcher could produce a series of sounds by successively pressing a series of buttons. The original intention was to examine both production and comprehension. After training in the acquisition of particular sounds to stand for particular objects and actions (establishment of 'words'), sequences such as 'Sara point-to car' and 'Monkey insert car dish' could be produced. For example, the experimenter might point to the car, and the child would be expected to encode this action into the appropriate sequences of noises which stood for this, 'Sara point-to car.' In a comprehension task, the researcher would produce the series of noises, and the child would carry out the actions, thereby indicating his understanding of the series. For example, the child hearing the sequence of signals 'Monkey insert car dish' would have to show the monkey inserting the car into the dish. In practice, however, it was virtually impossible to elicit any productive responses by the dysphasic children since they were unwilling to manipulate the control panel. Indeed, they could not be induced to construct a sequence of even two sounds. Consequently, the experimental training developed primarily into the comprehension task, rather than using both comprehension and production as Premack, and later Hughes, had done.

Four children, all with acquired dysphasia, took part in the training programme. These children had IQs within the normal range, only minimal hearing loss, but had either no verbal language or language at a rudimentary level. Their ages at the time of onset of the disability, which occurred in all of them without known traumatic injury, were $2\frac{1}{2}$, $4\frac{1}{2}$, $4\frac{1}{2}$ and 7 years. At the time of the study, three of the children were between 9 and 10 years old, and the fourth was 13.

Experiments by Eimas (see Eimas, 1974b) have shown that perception of speech differs from the perception of non-speech acoustic signals as early as 1 month of age. Since these appear to be processed in different ways, it was decided that two types of signal should be used on the tapes. Thus, two of the children heard only noises for their signals, while the other two heard only speech-like sounds. The noises were produced by various instruments, including bells, rattles, squeakers and two musical instruments – a recorder and a xylophone. The speech-like sounds were chosen in consultation with the children's speech therapist and were based on a set of phonemes which the child could actually say.

Due to scheduling difficulties, we were unable to extend the learning situations to nine weeks in order to parallel the length of time used by Hughes with the visual material. Therefore, many of the more advanced structures were not attempted, since these relied on the knowledge of simpler structures which were just being acquired by the end of the five-week period of the study. The children in Hughes's study were given between 11 and 15 half-hour training sessions; in the Barna study they had 8–10 half-hour sessions. Despite the fact that only simpler structures were eventually attempted with most of the children, the results offer some interesting clues as to the possible nature of the disorder. The first function that it is necessary to establish is that of the 'word'. This was initially done by giving the child a toy to play with, and then taking it back and holding it up while producing the corresponding sound which was to be its name. After a short time the researcher would produce the sound and the child had to hold up the appropriate toy, out of a set of toys. In a similar fashion the children were trained with 'words' for actions such as *give* and *point-to*. In each session, there were specific blocks of testing. The criterion for rating a language function as having been acquired was for the child to have demonstrated at least 70 per cent correct usage in the block of testing. All four children learned the symbols for at least six nouns and four verbs. In addition, three of the four subjects learned the symbols for their own name and that of the researcher. It is clear, then, that for all four children it was possible to establish the 'word' function. These particular dysphasic children were clearly capable of forming links between sound and meaning despite the fact that two of the children had been labelled as having 'auditory agnosia'. The findings of this study do not support a theory of a generalized or global word deafness. On the other hand, Barna (1975) reported that all four children showed some perceptual difficulty. The children appeared to have more trouble in discriminating the sounds than one would expect from normal listeners; they also appeared to need to concentrate their attention all the time. One child had an apparent inability to discriminate between different sounds of the same type. For example, he was unable to discriminate between the sounds of two toy horns even though they varied greatly in pitch. Similarly, he could not discriminate between a high and low recorder note. The children appeared to try to make use of visual cues whenever possible, so that performance was better when actual noise-makers were used or else when the sounds were uttered (offering the possibility of lip-reading) than when the same noises or sounds were presented on the tape equipment. In addition, three of the subjects displayed great variability in their responses both during and between sessions. This was seen not only for the 'word' function, but for other functions as well. Nevertheless, in spite of these difficulties, all four children were able to establish a vocabulary of at least 10 'words'.

Attempts were made to teach the children simple sentences of the so-called subject–verb–object type. The aim was to build up the sentences word by word, beginning with two-element strings such as 'Give doll' and 'Point-to cat.' Eventually three-element strings such as 'Monkey point-to cat' would be attempted. In fact, the two-element stage constituted the ceiling of learning for three of the four children. Only the child who mastered three-element strings was given any training on longer structures and on more complex functions. This child acquired not only three-element strings, but went on to acquire four-element (subject–verb–direct object–indirect object) strings. In a final session in which normal speech rather than the experimental procedure was used, this same child also acquired the functions of class concepts, and questions. Negation was also taught to this child and, while she displayed some acquisition, her performance on this function did not reach the required criterion.

What can we conclude from these preliminary results? Our main purpose was to see whether the Premack-type language functions which Hughes had been able to establish with dysphasic children could also be acquired by four other dysphasic children at the same school, when the material was presented in the auditory rather than the visual modality. There were large discrepancies between the results of the Barna study and that carried out by Hughes. On the other hand, in the Hughes study the average number of sessions per child was 12, whereas in the Barna study it was only nine. Thus, one can only speculate as to the possible outcome had the degree of training been equal. One child was clearly close to acquiring the complete set of functions that Hughes had previously taught. Barna reports that a second child was also showing distinct progress when training was terminated. But the other two subjects showed little improvement from session to session, and Barna claimed that it was quite unlikely that their performance would have reached beyond the results obtained. Examination of these limited accomplishments, however, may nevertheless provide some clues.

It is important to note that the four children who were studied did not constitute a homogeneous group. They differed greatly in their ability to acquire the structures on which training was attempted; but there was no indication that any differences between the subjects was attributable to their training with noises or speech-like sounds. Despite this problem, however, some conclusions can be drawn. First, all of the children were able to link sound with meaning; all four children acquired a vocabulary of at least 10 'words'. Secondly, three of the four children were able to acquire two-element strings. This might be taken as evidence that neither their memory for auditory information nor their ability to sequence sounds was as impaired as some theories would appear to suggest. But the fact that they performed worse on this task than the children in Hughes's study using visual symbols leaves the question unanswered.

There is yet another way to approach the problem. Children with developmental and acquired dysphasia are given instruction in reading and writing in their schools. Although these children are essentially without language in that they do not produce or comprehend *spoken* language, they do acquire writing skills and are able, after a great deal of instruction, to write letters to their parents, and to produce written descriptions and stories. As might be expected, these productions usually contain many grammatical errors. On the other hand, the early written productions by deaf children, who are also learning language 'through the eye' also contain many grammatical errors. An analysis of written material gathered in controlled conditions from dysphasic and from deaf children may reveal whether these two groups differ in the kinds of errors they make. If the underlying deficit in dysphasic children is specifically auditory in nature, then their errors should be similar to those made by the deaf. If these errors differ, however, their analysis may provide clues as to the nature of the dysphasic deficit.

A Study of the Writings of Dysphasic and Deaf Children

In order to study errors in written materials, it is necessary to know what the writer is attempting to communicate. Without this knowledge, sentences which appear to be well formed may in fact be quite disordered. If we merely read the sentence 'The boy talked to the girl and went upstairs', it appears perfectly grammatical. But, if we know that it was the girl who went upstairs, then we are dealing with a sentence in which the writer does not know how to construct the complex sentence involving a change of subject and substitution of pronoun to convey the precise information, i.e. 'The boy talked to the girl and she went upstairs.' In the writings of dysphasic children it is not always possible to know what the child is attempting to communicate. In a preliminary analysis of letters written to their parents, it was virtually impossible to analyse the structure of the sentences since the intended meaning was often unknown and unclear. It was therefore necessary to set up controlled situations for the children to describe. In addition, with situations experimentally controlled, it is possible to design specific stories which could encourage various types of sentence production.

To this end, stories were designed and presented as puppet shows or were acted out with small toy animals (my thanks to Maria Black for her help with the presentation). Here, only the story for which the writings have been analysed will be described. Four hand puppets were employed – a wolf, a monkey, and two ducks. Having two animals of the same type introduced the possibility of plurals; and having those two characters in conflict made it necessary somehow to differentiate between them, by means of adjectives, relative clauses and other linguistic entities. In addition, the materials were chosen with a view to eliciting the largest possible differentiation. Two wire containers were used, one tall and narrow, the other low and wide. The size of the containers was such that they could hold table-tennis (ping-pong) balls, and they were modelled to look like oversize versions of the beakers used in typical Piagetian conservation experiments. The action of the puppet show must be described in order for the writings produced by the children to be understood.

At the beginning of the presentation, the low, wide container holds eight balls, while the tall, narrow container is empty. The wolf, alone in view, looks at the two containers and then grasps one of the balls in his mouth and transfers it to the tall container. He transfers a second ball in this way and then stands back and looks at the two containers again. Next he successively places two more balls in the tall container. At this point the monkey comes into view, bites the wolf on the ear and generally creates a nuisance; finally the wolf chases the monkey away. A duck then appears on the scene and decides to undo what the wolf has done by tipping all the balls back from the tall container into the low one. The duck then leaves. The wolf returns and, with movements meant to imply exasperation, goes through the same sequence as before: moving one ball at a time into the tall container, pausing in between to view the beakers. Again, just as he finishes transferring the fourth ball, the monkey reappears and again annoys the wolf and bites him on the ear, and once again the wolf chases the monkey off-stage. (The repetition was designed to bring out adverbial phrases such as *again, a second time*, and to force the child to explain a repeating sequence of actions.) The duck again returns and again tips the balls from the tall into the low container, but this time is interrupted by a second duck, of somewhat different appearance. This second duck takes the side of the wolf and tries to prevent the first duck from pouring the balls back into the wide container. They fight. The wolf returns and, mistaking the two ducks as being against him, chases them away. (The story was designed to elicit some degree of differentiation, not only in terms of physical appearance – for instance, of the two containers and the two ducks – but also in terms of motivations.)

Children were tested in their classrooms in groups of six to 10. Their own classroom teacher carefully explained to them that they were going to see a puppet show and that they should first just watch it. Then, they would write down what they had seen. The teacher was able to communicate with the dysphasic children through a mixture of repetition and gesture. The puppets were introduced with 'Here is a wolf. Here is a monkey. Here is a duck. Here is another duck.' This was the only verbal interaction during the whole of the show. At the same time, the teacher listed, on the blackboard: 'a wolf, a monkey, a duck, a duck'. Thus, in addition to the four names, the children were provided with the indefinite article *a*, and in the oral introduction they heard the frame 'Here is . . .' and the quantifier adjective *another*. The children were allowed to write for as long as they liked; this was generally for about half an hour to 45 minutes. During this period, children would sometimes ask their teacher for help, usually with the spelling of words, which was communicated to the dysphasic group by means of finger spelling against the palm of the hand. The teacher provided only the spelling of the word asked for, in the grammatical form requested by the child.

The main aim was to compare the writings of dysphasic children with those of deaf children. In this preliminary analysis, the results from a group of receptive–expressive dysphasic children will be compared with the writings obtained, using the same story, from profoundly, congenitally deaf children. The medical records indicated that four of the group of the 10 dysphasic children had never possessed language, and they will be referred to here as the developmental aphasic group. The remaining six children had developed some language function, but this deteriorated in later years. The ages of onset of language deterioration in these six children were 2 years 6 months, 2 years 9 months, 4 years, 4 years 6 months, 5 years, and 7 years. The ages of the 10 children at the time of testing ranged from 7 years 6 months to 16 years, with a median age of 13 years 6 months. Their non-verbal IQs on the Collins–Drever test were in the normal range, with the exception of one child whose IQ was 75, and another with an IQ of 135. The range of the remaining IQs was 93 to 116, and the overall median IQ of the group was 99.5.

Of the 10 children, two merely drew pictures or copied the names of the animals from the blackboard. These were the two youngest children (7 years 6 months and 10 years), and one was in the developmental group whilst the other was in the group of acquired dysphasia. Two other children produced written samples which were so severely disordered that a grammatical analysis cannot be attempted. Again, one of the writings was by a child with developmental dysphasia, and the other by a child with acquired dysphasia. The story one of the children wrote will serve as an example of the difficulty in interpretation or analysis. Several children used the word 'basket' to refer to the low container and the word 'tube' to refer to the tall, narrow one. Punctuation and capitalization are the child's:

> table tennis ball tube putting
>> basket bite in a wolf down.
> the buck [probably reversed letter, intending *duck*] tube
>> look and fritened the to you cause over basket.
> In monkey sad CDMD here you no?
> In duck no over duck two tennis ball down on happy
> In to wolf see look duck duck angry wolf bad
>> quck good duck happy two on over no wolf you

Elimination of the two severely disorganized samples left a total of six to analyse – two from children with developmental dysphasia and four from children with acquired dysphasia at ages 2 years 6 months, 2 years 9 months, 4 years and 7 years.

For a preliminary analysis, the productions of a class of six congenitally profoundly deaf children were chosen for comparison. The range of ages of these six children was 9 years 11 months to 10 years 8 months with a median age of between 10 years 5 months and 10 years 6 months. The range of IQs was 80–123, with a median IQ of 101.5. Hearing loss varied from 90 to 120 dBs. All six children produced material that could be analysed. A few children in other classrooms produced drawings or a list of the animal names as two of the dysphasic children had done, but these were all younger children. None of the deaf children produced the severely disorganized language similar to that quoted above.

At first glance, the productions of the six dysphasic children and the six deaf children do not appear to differ in any distinct way. Indeed, by only reading a story produced by either a deaf or a dysphasic child, it would be difficult to identify the group to which the child belonged. Below there are two stories, one by a deaf and one by a dysphasic child, and the reader is invited to consider which is which.

I

The wolf picked up ball to put the basket. The monkey bite the woof ear. The woof said, 'Woof! wog!' The wolf chased the monkey. Suddenly coming the duck to pick up the basket and dropped the ball. Suddenly the wolf coming but the wolf surprised. The wolf was very angry because the ball is gone. The wolf picked up the ball again. Suddenly the monkey coming and to bite the wolf's ear again. The wolf chased the monkey again. Coming the two ducks to picked up the basket dropped the ball to a small basket but the two duck are frighted. The wolf was very angry the monkey but the poor monkey the wolf bite the monkey. The monkey died.

II

The wolf is taking his table tennis ball. he is putting in the tube. The monkey is bitting the wolf's ear.

          chasing

The wolf is running the monkey. [The word *chasing* was written above the word *running*, as if the child had had second thoughts and changed the latter for the former.] The duck is taking round the tube. The ball is in the basket. The wolf is saying oh gone the ball. again the wolf is taking his table tennis ball in the tube. The monkey is bitting the wolf's ear. The wolf is chasing him.

The duck is saying oh again ball in the tube. The duck is bitting the duck's ear.

There are clearly a great number of grammatical errors in both of these productions; and not many readers would be able to identify with confidence that (I) was written by a deaf child and (II) by a dysphasic. Closer analysis, however, reveals some important differences.

It is not possible to make a transformational analysis on the basis of so small a sample of sentences. It is impossible to see which structures might be interrelated unless one is able to survey a very large number of sentences. In addition, there is the problem that children may be capable of producing other grammatical structures, although these were not present in this story.

The views relative to the omissions of certain grammatical structures can therefore only be tentative until further research is carried out. On the other hand, grammatical errors – errors of commission – may reveal those aspects of language with which the child encounters specific difficulty. That is to say, at this point it is not possible to delineate what are the difficulties of the dysphasic child in encoding particular meanings in the linguistic code. One can note, however, the types of sentences, the types of meanings and of structural types which were attempted, and also those types which were not attempted by the children. The writings were analysed in several different ways, and the results cited here are a summary of the significant differences observed between the deaf and dysphasic productions.

It was not difficult in most cases to divide the structures into sentence units. Usually the child himself has provided the punctuation which indicates his divisions. In only one case were a large number of arbitrary decisions required. This was a deaf child who connected his entire production with a series of *ands*. The deaf, in general, wrote slightly longer stories than the dysphasics, but, when a count was made of the mean number of words per sentence, the deaf and the dysphasics performed similarly, the deaf with an average of 7.76 words per sentence and the dysphasics with 7.61. The language of the dysphasic children, however, under close analysis, is in fact quite different. In terms of word counts this difference is reflected not in the number of words per sentence, which was the same in the two groups, but in the number of categories per sentence. By categories is meant entities such as noun phrases, verb phrases, adverbial phrases, etc. In these terms, the dysphasic language shows itself to be less complex than that produced by the deaf. The deaf, on average, produced 4.51 categories per sentence, whilst the dysphasics produced only 3.73, a difference which was statistically significant ($p < 0.01$).

What linguistic structures are affected by this lack of complexity? One obvious difference between the groups was that a few dysphasic children seemed to repeat a single sentence type with which they were familiar. One child, for example, simply produced a list of ten sentences, nine of which used the present progressive: 'The wolf is getting the balls. The duck is looking at the balls. The wolf is catching the monkey. The monkey is catching the wolf', etc. The deaf, by contrast, appeared to try a number of different sentence types and these included different categories of verb tense. One possible count is therefore the number of different verb types used by each child. Verbs were categorized into seven traditional categories: present, past, future, copulas, progressives, perfects and infinitives. A child was credited with attempting a category even if he made errors in doing so. The children in the dysphasic group never attempted verbs in the present, future (i.e. verb with the auxiliary *will* or *'ll*), or any of the perfect tenses; but each of the above categories was attempted by at least one deaf child. The fact that no dysphasic child attempted those verb types in his story could be accounted for, however, by the small size of the sample. It is nevertheless possible to compare the variety of verb types used by each child. Deaf children attempted an average of 3.33 different verb types in their sentences. Dysphasic children only had an average of 2.16 different verb types. This difference was again statistically significant ($p < 0.02$).

Not only did the use of verb tenses differ, but there was a difference in the use of certain traditional linguistic structure types. Numbers are too small to carry out the usual tests of significance, but it was noted that no dysphasic child produced sentences with negatives; no questions were used; and there were virtually no complement-clause structures (although one child attempted one such sentence). In addition, the dysphasic children never used a qualifying adjective. By contrast, three of the six deaf children used negatives, two used questions, and four used complement clauses. Four deaf children also used a total of 11 qualifying adjectives. It must be emphasized again that these differences are only tentative. In the story which was quoted earlier, and which could not be analysed, the question-mark symbol was used by this particular dysphasic child, although it is impossible to tell with certainty whether any kind of question was intended. Also, it would be surprising if negatives were not present in other writings of the dysphasic children, even if they have trouble forming negative sentences without errors.

In spite of these apparent differences in some of the categories used, the real interest lies not here, but in the analysis of errors. In fact, error analysis on most sentence types revealed that the deaf usually made a greater number of errors, because they attempted more sentence types. The dysphasic writings, on the other hand, had fewer errors, but this was due to the fact that the children did not attempt a variety of structures. The question one can reasonably ask in this respect is, what determines the nature of the omissions? We have already seen that the sentences produced by dysphasic children, although of identical length to those of the deaf, contain fewer grammatical categories. Furthermore, dysphasic children generally wrote only simple sentences – often the various kinds of simple sentences they had been taught. Deaf children seemed far more able to combine sentence types which include additional transformations. A count was carried out of the total number of sentences which included one or more embedded or conjoined structures as opposed to sentences without these. A few examples will make these counts clearer. Sentences rated as having one conjoined structure would include: 'Suddenly the wolf coming but the wolf surprised' and 'The wolf was very angry because the ball is gone.' An example with two embedded or conjoined elements would be 'Suddenly coming the duck to picked up the basket and dropped the ball.' Only 12.0 per cent of the sentences produced by dysphasic children had embedded or conjoined structures, as compared to 35.9 per cent of the sentences produced by the deaf children. This difference was highly significant ($p < 0.001$). It was also noticed that the rare sentences with an embedded or conjoined structure produced by dysphasic children often omitted the second verb, as in 'The monkey is frightened because a wolf bad.' No dysphasic child attempted sentences with more than one embedding or conjoining. The deaf, in contrast, produced sentences of which 10.9 per cent had two or more embedded or conjoined elements. This difference between the two groups was again significant ($p < 0.01$).

The simplicity of the dysphasic children's writings was not restricted to the omission of complex sentences. It was also reflected in the lack of transformational structure within simple sentences; thus they never linked two adjectives (e.g. 'the big, tall one'; 'He is big and strong') whereas adjective-linking occurred in some of the deaf children's stories. The dysphasics never produced adverb–adjective strings (such as 'the very big ball'); again, these occurred in some of the samples of the deaf children. Conjunctions were rarely used by the dysphasic children even internally, as for instance in the linking of two noun phrases within a simple sentence, and they virtually never used them to combine two independent clauses. The deaf by contrast produced many conjunctions, some of these linking two independent clauses.

It is of interest to turn back to the two samples printed earlier. My guess is that, at first glance, most readers will have found difficulty in deciding which story was written by the deaf child and which by the dysphasic child. But now, in the light of the statistical analyses which have just been given, it should be fairly easy to see how those two written productions differ. The first, that written by a profoundly deaf child, contains a variety of verb tenses, although he doesn't attempt to use the simple present tense. (*Bite* was not considered as a present tense since analysis revealed that many children who clearly use past tenses in other situations spelled *bit* – past tense – with a final *e*.) The deaf child uses copula verbs in both present and past (*are frighted, is gone, was very angry*), simple past-tense forms (*chased, dropped, picked up, died, said*), progressive forms (*coming*), and infinitives (*to bite, to pick up*). The dysphasic child (story ii) uses only progressives with the present-tense auxiliary (*is taking, is putting, is bitting, is running, is saying, is chasing*) and one copula verb in the present tense (*is*). The deaf child uses several types of co-ordinate structure, with the subject either remaining the same ('the wolf coming but the wolf surprised', 'Coming the two ducks to picked up the basket dropped the ball but the two duck are frighted') or changing ('The wolf was very angry because the ball is gone'). The dysphasic child uses no co-ordinate constructions. Furthermore he wrote two sentences in which there is one embedded or conjoined structure, but omitted the second verb in both cases ('The wolf is saying oh gone the ball', 'The duck is saying oh again ball in the tube)'; also there are no examples of sentences with two or more embedded or conjoined structures. By contrast, the deaf child's story contains six sentences which have one embedded or conjoined structure, and two which have two or more ('Suddenly coming the duck to pick up the basket and dropped the ball', 'Coming the two ducks to picked up the basket dropped the ball to a small basket but the two duck are frighted'). The deaf child also uses complement verbs ('picked up ball to put . . .', 'coming the duck to pick up . . .', etc.), which are lacking in the dysphasic child's production. Overall, the deaf child has an average of 5.15 categories per sentence, compared to 3.5 for the dysphasic. In these particular samples, the deaf child also has longer sentences (an average of 8.6 words per sentence compared to the dysphasic child's 7.4), although for the group as a whole the mean sentence lengths did not differ. Additional complexity in sentence structure is shown by the deaf child in that he uses nine adjectives including two qualifying adjectives (*small, poor*) (totally lacking in any of the dysphasic writings) and predicate adjectives (e.g. *is gone, are frighted, surprised, angry*). There were also seven uses of adverbs (*suddenly, again, very*), and even an adverb–adjective string (*very angry*). The dysphasic child used three adverbs (*gone, again*), but no adjectives, and consequently no adjective–adjective or adverb–adjective combinations. The two written productions, which appeared on the surface to be similar, are, in fact, quite different in terms of the dimensions described. But what is different about the dysphasic writing? Is it merely less complex, or is it a special kind of complexity that is lacking? If so, could this latter give a clue to the nature of the underlying disability?

The Hypothesis of a Hierarchical-Structuring Deficit

In an overall assessment of the written language abilities of the group of dysphasic children that were studied, varying degrees of disorder were noted. Thus, when the story was presented visually, there was a grammatical disorganization in the output of these children. This disorganization was at the level not of orthography but of the elements and categories of the sentence. This observation, however, also applies to the writing of congenitally deaf children who, like the dysphasic children, are learning language 'by eye'. On the other hand, this preliminary analysis of writings of the deaf and dysphasic children shows that their difficulties are indeed quite different. The deaf children made more errors, but these were errors of commission. They tried a variety of structures, including many which relied on complex transformations; in contrast, the dysphasic children wrote simpler sentences and failed to use the kinds of structure that would involve a true hierarchical organization of the overall sentence.

One reason for the difference could be that the children were from different schools, and had not been exposed to the same teaching methods. (For instance, the dysphasic children had experience with Lea's colour-pattern scheme, 1970, which is especially designed to help children with language disorders.) There are reasons, however, which suggest that the differences between the dysphasic and deaf groups were not related to particular differences in teaching materials. First, dysphasic children are exposed to a type of language which is as complex in structure as the one used with deaf children; secondly, and more important, language samples collected from a group of children labelled as 'phonologically disabled' appear to be quite different from those of the receptive–expressive dysphasic children, even though they were from the same school and were exposed to the same teaching methods.

It might have been expected that the dysphasic children's writings would show difficulties with particular grammatical devices – e.g. the formation of plurals, possessives, etc. In fact this was not the case. It had already been shown, in Hughes's extension of Premack's work, that dysphasic children possessed the cognitive functions encoded in language, and were able to use these with the token symbol system. It is not surprising then, that they should attempt to encode these same functions in written language. What is interesting is that they did not make a significantly greater number of errors than the deaf on those grammatical entities which they attempted.

Another possible expectation was that the dysphasic children's writings would display difficulties with word order, especially in view of the emphasis given to possible sequencing difficulties from which these children are said to suffer. These results, however, do not entirely invalidate the sequencing hypothesis. It should be recalled that two productions were so disorganized that analysis of grammatical constituents could not be attempted. Yet the kind of difficulty in the sequential ordering of words is in fact quite different from that predicted by the experimental results usually cited in support of sequential-deficit hypotheses. The difficulty displayed by the dysphasic children, even in the two disordered samples, is not at the phoneme or orthographical level, and it is also possible that their difficulties may result from a 'hierarchical' disability.

The productions of the remaining six dysphasic children lend support to the view that their problem with language lies in its hierarchical organization. The dysphasic children's problem does not appear to be solely attributable to the increased difficulty found in the transformations involved in complex sentences. They also lacked the kinds of devices that allow any interruptions – e.g. the transformations required for the production of relative clauses, conjunctions joining two nouns or joining two verbs with the same subject, etc. But this conjecture, like those that have been criticized earlier, is also based on a current assumption – namely, that language is hierarchically organized. This assumption stems, in part, from Lashley's early paper (1951) in which he points out the problems and limitations that exist in conceiving several specific types of behaviour as sequentially ordered. His views have been echoed in the modern linguistic approach, proposed by Chomsky (1959, 1965, 1975), and basically supported by even those linguists who criticize other aspects of Chomsky's theory. One fundamental problem is to determine what is meant by *hierarchical ordering*. This terminology is now in common use, although it seems to have different connotations.

The most common use of the term refers to descriptions of behaviour, organized simultaneously at several levels of complexity. I am not referring here, however, to this use of the term *hierarchical*. In the present context, *hierarchical* refers to a type of process which must be assumed to exist if sequential behaviour is to be explained as organized, purposeful and meaningful. Pure sequential ordering and mere associative links between adjacent elements (including higher-order associations) have been shown to be inadequate in explaining grammatical structures. The kind of hierarchical complexity that is meant here involves, for example, the analysis of a complex behaviour into its component parts in which the performance of some parts is postponed while performance of other parts takes priority; in the words of Miller and Chomsky (1963), 'One natural criterion might be the ability to interrupt one part of the performance until some other part has been completed.' Neisser (1967) has written about hierarchical complexity in terms of organized entities in which the individual parts derive their meaning from the whole structure. Sentence elements are interdependent and not all their interrelationships are equally strong. Such a view, applied to language behaviour, calls for the use of transformational devices which allow the reordering and interruption of surface-structure features. This type of analysis is now often applied to the simple sentences which are produced by young children. But the written sentences which were produced by the dysphasic children included simple structures they had learnt. Thus, one major obstacle for the proponent of the hypothesis that dysphasic children suffer from a hierarchical-ordering deficit is the presence in their writing of these simple sentences. It may be, however, that dysphasic children are actually using simple grammatical rules based on adjacent elements. That is, simple sentences written by normal children may, in fact, be evidence of hierarchically organized structures, but in dysphasic children they may merely be sequentially ordered. How might one determine this? One possibility would be to study dysphasic children in an attempt to find evidence of an inability to deal with certain transformations of an understood structure. Another possibility would be to determine whether, in their productions, they are unable to make sentence changes which require 'planning' of the utterance, so that tense or person agreement fails when the sequence is interrupted by other intervening material. A third approach would be to note whether grammatical structures which require hierarchical ordering are lacking in these children. One such structure would be the relative clause which requires interruption of one sequence by another – for example, 'The boy who was hurt was crying.' In their written productions, dysphasic children did not produce relative clauses. Even categories which seem to be merely sequential, such as the ordering of adjective sequences, may in fact be ordered in terms of a hierarchical principle. For example, it is more natural to speak of 'the two large black cats' than of 'the two black large cats', or of 'the black large two cats'. It was interesting to note that the children in the dysphasic group avoided using any qualifying adjectives. But, as has been emphasized, this study was merely a preliminary investigation of written sentence production and it is possible that the dysphasic children had the ability to produce some of these structures but merely failed to do so in the particular samples collected. The fact that their written-language productions omitted the kinds of structure which are dependent on hierarchical organization, whereas these occurred in the language samples from the deaf children, is thus merely suggestive. The hypothesis of a hierarchical-ordering disability, however, is supported by a very different kind of evidence.

It may be recalled that, when reviewing the studies of the disabilities of dysphasic children, there was general agreement that these children lacked all sense of rhythm. They are unable to march in step, to clap to tunes, or to reproduce rhythmic sequences by tapping. Whereas many people might assume that rhythmic behaviour requires solely a serial chain of successive elements, Lashley (1951) has pointed out that a rhythmic pattern is in fact a single structural unit. Neisser (1967) elaborated this idea and claimed that rhythms provide sets of reference points to which digits and words can be attached. He claims that the limit of memory span may be determined by the capacity to organize extended rhythmic sequences. Neisser claims that, if rhythm is viewed as a basic ability, it would help to explain such phenomena as the ability of subjects to know, when recalling a string of digits, the position of a specific digit in the series. It would also help to explain the difficulty of backward recall. According to Neisser, backward reproductions are difficult because they demand rearrangement of a rhythmic pattern. For example, I have often noticed that most people have trouble in working out mentally the name *Franklin* if it is spelt backwards – *N i l k n a r f. Nilknarf*, when pronounced, induces a four–four letter pattern, and even when the letters are rearranged and are put in place it seems difficult to change to the five–three pattern required by Franklin. Neisser speculates that the processes of spoken language are continuous with those of active, verbal memory, both of them involving the synthesis of rhythmic patterns.

Martin (1972) presents the strongest case for the conceptualization of rhythms as hierarchically structured units. It is a misconception, he claims, to believe that rhythms imply only periodic, repetitive behaviour. Rhythmic sequences possess, in fact, hierarchical organization. The alternative – a series of elements that are successive or concatenated in time – cannot have a structured internal organization. Martin suggests that such a view has important implications for the production of rhythmic sequences and spoken language. Indeed it would have important implications in the analysis of perceptual processes. For example, this hierarchical ability would allow input sounds to be temporally patterned. Furthermore, rhythmically patterned sounds have a time trajectory that allows them to be tracked without the necessity for continuous monitoring. That is, the perception of initial or early elements in the pattern would allow later-occurring elements to be anticipated. This would give rise to efficient perceptual strategies. Martin claims that the alternative, the perception of merely concatenated sounds, would require continuous attention; and Kracke (1975) noted in her rhythm experiments that the dysphasic children attempted precisely that. In her experiment, mentioned previously, the children compared rhythmic sequences and were required to give same/different judgements. She reported that the normal and the deaf children used what she termed 'a Gestalt strategy': they appeared to try to perceive the patterns in a direct, unreflective way without concentrating on the individual elements. By contrast, the dysphasic children used what Kracke called an 'element-by-element' strategy; that is to say, they attempted to repeat the elements to themselves, one by one, before giving a judgement. She reports also that some children even tried to capture the rhythm by verbal labelling, as in 'lonn-lonn-shor' (i.e. long–long–short). In direct contrast to the usual view that dysphasic children have a sequencing disability, it may be possible to claim that they can cope with sequencing tasks, but it is important to bear in mind that, unless the elements can be arranged in a rhythmic pattern, nobody can in fact reproduce a sequence. Perkins (1974) has shown that normal adults use rhythmic hierarchies to code sequential positions, and Dooling (1974) demonstrated the importance of rhythm in the perception of speech. There are also observations derived from neurological studies suggesting the important role of rhythm in the language process. Robinson and Solomon (1974) claim that rhythmic patterns, unlike other non-speech auditory entities, are processed better by the same hemisphere as is dominant for speech. Dennis and Whitaker (1976), basing their conclusion on a study of left and right hemidecorticate children, reported that different configurations of language skill develop in the two isolated hemispheres; the right hemisphere showing a deficit, not in the conceptual or semantic features of language, but rather in the 'organisational, analytic, syntactic and hierarchic aspects'.

Summary

At the beginning of this chapter, it was claimed that all research is based on certain assumptions about the nature of the process to be studied; and it was suggested that up to now it has frequently been assumed that language is sequentially organized – despite the large number of recent and compelling arguments to the contrary. Secondly, it was pointed out that any theory concerning an underlying disability must be able to account for the observed behaviour. It was therefore suggested that the hypothesis of a sequential deficit in dysphasic children did not explain adequately many of the observed facts related to their language production. Using current assumptions about the hierarchical organization of language structure in conjunction with a preliminary study of the writings of dysphasic children, it was concluded that the deficit in these children *may* be some kind of hierarchical-structuring disability. This hypothesis received some additional support from observations and studies reporting deficits of rhythmic abilities in these children. There are many questions, as well as objections, that can be raised by this hypothesis – for example, the question of whether the impairment is an inability to deal with hierarchically ordered material, or whether the deficit stems from a basic impairment of rhythm, especially as rhythmic ability has been shown to be a basic element in the comprehension and production of language. A further question raised by this view is whether the deficit extends beyond the inability to deal with hierarchically ordered language structure; that is to say, whether it is specific to language and to rhythm or is present in other types of behaviour. If this latter view is correct, then why is the impairment not displayed in motor or other types of sequential ability? The hypothesis of a hierarchical-ordering disability in dysphasic children raises a great number of questions, but by opening up a new direction in research it may well prove to be of service.

Bibliography

Adams P. (ed.) 1972: *Language in Thinking*. Harmondsworth, Middx: Penguin.

Ammon M. S. and Slobin D. I. 1979: A cross-linguistic study of the processing of causative sentences. *Cognition*, 7: 3–17.

Anderson E. M. and Spain B. 1977: *The Child with Spina Bifida*. London: Methuen.

Anderson M. 1986a: Inspection time and IQ in young children. *Personality and Individual Differences*, 7 (5): 677–86.

——1986b: Understanding the cognitive deficit in mental retardation. *Journal of Child Psychology and Psychiatry*, 27 (3): 297–306.

——1988: Inspection time, information processing and the development of intelligence. *British Journal of Developmental Psychology*, 6: 43–57.

——forthcoming: *Intelligence and Development: a cognitive theory*. Oxford: Basil Blackwell.

Au T. K. 1983: Chinese and English counterfactuals: the Sapir–Whorf hypothesis revisited. *Cognition*, 15: 155–87.

——1984: Counterfactuals: in reply to Alfred Bloom. *Cognition*, 17: 289–302.

Aurnhammer-Frith U. 1969: Emphasis and meaning in recall in normal and autistic children. *Language and Speech*, 12: 29–38.

Baddeley A. D. 1976: *The Psychology of Memory*. New York and London: Harper and Row.

Baddeley A. D., Thomson N. and Buchanan M. 1975: Word length and the structure of short-term memory. *Journal of Verbal Learning and Verbal Behavior*, 14: 575–89.

Baillargéon R. 1986: Representing the existence and the location of hidden objects: object permanence in 6- and 8-month-old infants. *Cognition*, 23: 21–41.

——1987a: Young infants' reasoning about the physical and spatial properties of a hidden object. *Cognitive Development*, 2: 179–200.

——1987b: Object permanence in 3.5- and 4.5-month-old infants. *Developmental Psychology*, 23: 655–64.

Baillargéon R., Spelke E. S. and Wasserman S. 1985: Object permanence in five-month-old infants. *Cognition*, 20: 191–208.

Barna S. 1975: Childhood aphasia: a preliminary investigation of some auditory and linguistic variables. Brunel University: unpublished Bachelor of Technology thesis.

Bartak L. and Rutter M. 1975: Language and cognition in autistic and 'dysphasic' children. In N. O'Connor (ed.), *Language, Cognitive Deficits and Retardation*, London: Butterworth.

Bartak L., Rutter M. and Cox A. 1975: A comparative study of infantile autism and specific developmental receptive language disorder. 1: The children. *British Journal of Psychiatry*, 126: 127–45.

Bartlett E. J. 1978: The acquisition of the meaning of colour terms: a study of lexical development. In R. N. Campbell and P. T. Smith (eds), *Recent Advances in the Psychology of Language: language development and mother-child interaction*, New York: Plenum Press.

Bartlett F. C. 1932: *Remembering: a study of experimental and social psychology*. Cambridge: Cambridge University Press.

Bates E. 1976: *Language and Context: the acquisition of pragmatics*. New York: Academic Press.

——1979: *The Emergence of Symbols: cognition and communication in infancy*. New York: Academic Press.

Beilin H. 1975: *Studies in the Cognitive Basis of Language Development*. New York: Academic Press.

Bellugi U. 1967: The acquisition of the system of negation in children's speech. Harvard University: unpublished doctoral dissertation.

——1971: Simplification in children's language. In R. Huxley and E. Ingram (eds), *Language Acquisition: models and methods*, New York: Academic Press.

Bellugi-Klima U. 1969: Language acquisition. Paper presented at the Wenner-Gren Foundation for Anthropological Research in the Symposium on Cognitive Studies and Artificial Intelligence Research, Chicago.

Benton A. L. 1964: Developmental aphasia and brain damage. *Cortex*, 1: 40–52.

——1965: *Visual Retention Test: multiple choice forms*. Paris: Centre de Psychologie Appliqué.

——1978: The cognitive functioning of children with developmental dysphasia. In M. A. Wyke (ed.), *Developmental Dysphasia*, London and New York: Academic Press.

Berlin B. and Kay P. 1969: *Basic Color Terms: their universality and evolution*. Berkeley, Calif.: University of California Press.

Bernstein B. 1961: Social structure, language and learning. *Educational Research*, 3: 163–76.

Bever T. G. 1970: The cognitive basis for linguistic structures. In J. R. Hayes (ed.), *Cognition and the Development of Language*, New York: Wiley.

——1971: The nature of cerebral dominance in speech behaviour of the child and adult. In R. Huxley and E. Ingram (eds), *Language Acquisition: models and methods*, London and New York: Academic Press.

Bever T. G., Fodor J. A. and Garrett M. 1966: The psychological segmentation of speech. Paper delivered at the International Congress of Psychology, Moscow.

Bever T. G., Fodor J. A. and Weksel W. 1965a: Is linguistics empirical? *Psychological Review*, 72: 493–500.

——1965b: Theoretical notes on the acquisition of syntax: a critique of 'context generalization'. *Psychological Review*, 72: 467–82.

Bever T. G., Lackner J. and Kirk R. 1969: The underlying structure sentence as the primary unit of speech. *Perception and Psychophysics*, 5: 225–34.

Bever T. G., Mehler J. and Valian V. V. 1968: Linguistic capacity of very young children. Mimeographed paper.

Blakemore C. 1974: Developmental factors in the formation of feature extracting neurons. In F. O. Schmitt and F. G. Worden (eds), *The Neurosciences: Third Study Program*, Cambridge, Mass.: MIT Press.

Blakemore C. and Cooper G. F. 1970: Development of the brain depends on the visual environment. *Nature*, 228: 477–8.

Blank M. and Allen D. A. 1976: Understanding 'why': its significance in early intelligence. In M. Lewis (ed.), *Origins of Intelligence: infancy and early childhood*, New York: Wiley.

Bloom A. H. 1981: *The Linguistic Shaping of Thought: a study in the impact of language on thinking in China and the West*. Hillsdale, NJ: Lawrence Erlbaum Associates.

——1984: Caution – the words you use may affect what you say: a response to Au. *Cognition*, 17: 275–87.

Bloom L. 1967: A comment on Lee's 'Developmental sentence scoring: a method for comparing normal and deviant syntactic development'. *Journal of Speech and Hearing Disorders*, 32: 294–6.

——1970: *Language Development: form and function in emerging grammars*. Cambridge, Mass.: MIT Press.

——1971: Why not pivot grammar? *Journal of Speech and Hearing Disorders*, 36: 40–50.

——1973: *One Word at a Time*. The Hague: Mouton.

Borer H. and Wexler K. 1987: The maturation of syntax. In T. Roeper and E. Williams (eds), *Parameter Setting*, Dordrecht: D. Reidel.

Bornstein M. H. 1975: Qualities of color vision in infancy. *Journal of Experimental Child Psychology*, 19: 401–19.

——1981: Psychological studies of color perception in human infants: habituation, discrimination and categorization, recognition, and conceptualization. In L. P. Lipsitt and C. K. Rovee-Collier (eds), *Advances in Infancy Research*, vol. 1, Norwood, NY: Ablex.

——1985: On the development of color naming in young children: data and theory. *Brain and Language*, 26: 72–93.

Bornstein M. H., Kessen W. and Weiskopf S. 1976: Color vision and hue categorization in young human infants. *Journal of Experimental Psychology: human perception and performance*, 2 (1): 115–29.

Bornstein M. H. and Monroe M. D. 1980: Chromatic information processing: rate depends on stimulus location in the category and psychological complexity. *Psychological Research*, 42: 213–25.

Bower T. G. R. 1966: Slant perception and shape constancy in infants. *Science*, 151: 832–4.

Bowerman M. 1973: *Early Syntactic Development*. Cambridge: Cambridge University Press.

——1976: Semantic factors in the acquisition of rules for word use and sentence construction. In D. M. and A. E. Morehead (eds), *Normal and Deficient Child Language*, Baltimore: University Park Press.

——1977: The acquisition of word meaning: an investigation of some current concepts. In P. N. Johnson-Laird and P. C. Wason (eds), *Thinking: readings in cognitive science*, Cambridge: Cambridge University Press.

——1978: Semantic and syntactic development: a review of what, when, and how in language acquisition. In R. L. Schiefelbusch (ed.), *Bases of Language Intervention*, Baltimore: University Park Press.

——1980: The structure and origin of semantic categories in the language-learning child. In M. Foster and S. H. Brandes (eds), *Symbol as Sense: new approaches to the analysis of meaning*, New York: Academic Press.

——1982: Reorganizational processes in lexical and syntactic development. In E. Wanner and L. R. Gleitman (eds), *Language Acquisition: the state of the art*, Cambridge: Cambridge University Press.

Braine M. D. S. 1963a: On learning the grammatical order of words. *Psychological Review*, 70: 323–48.

——1963b: The ontogeny of English phrase structure: the first phase. *Language*, 39: 1–13.

Brown R. 1956: Language and categories. In J. S. Bruner, J. J. Goodnow and G. A. Austin (eds), *A Study of Thinking*, New York: Wiley.

——1970a: The first sentences of child and chimpanzee. In R. Brown, *Psycholinguistics: selected papers by Roger Brown*, New York: Free Press.

——1970b: *Psycholinguistics: selected papers by Roger Brown*. New York: Free Press.

——1973: *A First Language*. Cambridge, Mass.: Harvard University Press.

——1976: Reference: in memorial tribute to Eric Lenneberg. *Cognition*, 4: 125–53.

——1977: Introduction. In C. E. Snow and C. A. Ferguson (eds), *Talking to Children: language input and acquisition*, Cambridge: Cambridge University Press.

Brown R. and Bellugi U. 1964: Three processes in the child's acquisition of syntax. *Harvard Education Review*, 34: 133–51.

Brown R., Cazden C. and Bellugi-Klima U. 1969: The child's grammar from I to III. In J. P. Hill (ed.), *Minnesota Symposia on Child Psychology*, vol. 2, Minneapolis: University of Minnesota Press, 28–73.

Brown R. and Fraser C. 1964: The acquisition of syntax. In U. Bellugi and R. Brown (eds), *The Acquisition of Language*, Monographs of the Society for Research in Child Development, 29 (92): 43–79.

Brown R., Fraser C. and Bellugi U. 1964: Explorations in grammar evaluation. In U. Bellugi and R. Brown (eds), *The Acquisition of Language*, Monographs of the Society for Research in Child Development, 29 (92): 79–92.

Brown R. and Hanlon C. 1970: Derivational complexity and the order of acquisition in child speech. In J. R. Hayes (ed.), *Cognition and the Development of Language*, New York: Wiley.

Brown R. and Lenneberg E. H. 1954: A study in language and cognition. *Journal of Abnormal Social Psychology*, 49: 454–62.

——1958: Studies in linguistic relativity. In E. E. Maccoby, T. M. Newcomb and E. L. Hartley (eds), *Readings in Social Psychology*, 3rd edn, New York: Holt, Rinehart and Winston.

Bruner J. S. 1964: The course of cognitive growth. *American Psychologist*, 19: 1–15.

——1974–5: From communication to language: a psychological perspective. *Cognition*, 3: 225–87.

——1975: The ontogenesis of speech acts. *Journal of Child Language*, 2: 1–19.

Bruner J. S., Goodnow J. J. and Austin G. A. 1956: *A Study of Thinking*. New York: Wiley.

Bruner J. S., Olver R. R. and Greenfield P. M. 1966: *Studies in Cognitive Growth*. New York: Wiley.

Bryant P. E. and Trabasso T. 1971: Transitive inferences and memory in young children. *Nature*, 232: 456–8.

Burling R. 1959: Language development of a Garo and English speaking child. *Word*, 15: 45–68.

Burnham R. W. and Clark J. E. 1955: A test of hue memory. *Journal of Applied Psychology*, 39: 164–72.

Carey S. 1978: The child as word learner. In M. Halle, J. Bresnan and G. A. Miller (eds), *Linguistic Theory and Psychological Reality*, Cambridge, Mass.: MIT Press.

Carmichael L., Hogan H. P. and Walter A. A. 1932: The experimental study of the effect of language on the reproduction of visually perceived form. *Journal of Experimental Psychology*, 15: 73–86.

Carroll J. B. (ed.) 1956: *Language, Thought and Reality: selected writings of Benjamin Lee Whorf*. Cambridge, Mass.: MIT Press; and New York: Wiley.

Carroll J. B. and Casagrande J. B. 1958: The function of language classifications in behaviour. In E. E. Maccoby, T. M. Newcomb and E. L. Hartley (eds), *Readings in Social Psychology*, 3rd edn, New York: Holt, Rinehart and Winston.

Caskey-Sirmons L. A. and Hickerson N. P. 1977: Semantic shift and bilingualism: variation in the color terms of five languages. *Anthropological Linguistics*, Nov.: 358–67.

Catlin J. 1978: Discussion of the chapters by Stolzenberg and Chomsky. In G. A. Miller and E. Lenneberg (eds), *Psychology and Biology of Language and Thought*, New York: Academic Press.

Chafe W. 1970: *Meaning and the Structure of Language*. Chicago: University of Chicago Press.

Chomsky C. 1969: *The Acquisition of Syntax in Children from 5 to 10*. Cambridge, Mass.: MIT Press.

Chomsky N. 1957: *Syntactic Structures*. The Hague: Mouton.

——1959: A review of B. F. Skinner's *Verbal Behavior*. *Language*, 35, pp. 26–58.

——1962: Explanatory models in linguistics. In E. Nagel, P. Suppes and A. Tarski (eds), *Logic, Methodology, and Philosophy of Science*, Stanford, Calif.: Stanford University Press.

——1965: *Aspects of the Theory of Syntax*. Cambridge, Mass.: MIT Press.

——1966: *Cartesian Linguistics*. New York: Harper and Row.

——1967: The formal nature of language. Appendix to E. H. Lenneberg,

Biological Foundations of Language, New York: Wiley.

——1968: *Language and Mind*. New York: Harcourt Brace Jovanovich.

——1969: *The Acquisition of Syntax in Children from 5 to 10*. Cambridge, Mass.: MIT Press.

——1972: *Studies on Semantics in Generative Grammar*. The Hague: Mouton.

——1975: *Reflections on Language*. New York: Pantheon Books.

——1986: *Knowledge of Language: its nature, origin and use*. New York: Praeger.

——1987: Nature, use, and acquisition of language. Invited lecture to the Open University Psychological Society, London, 9 Apr.

——1988: Language and problems of knowledge. *The Managua Lectures*, Cambridge, Mass.: MIT Press.

Chomsky N. and Halle M. 1968: *The Sound Pattern of English*. New York: Harper and Row.

Clark E. V. 1970: How young children describe events in time. In G. B. Flores d'Arcais and W. J. M. Levelt (eds), *Advances in Psycholinguistics*, Amsterdam: North Holland.

——1971: On the acquisition of the meaning of before and after. *Journal of Verbal Learning and Verbal Behavior*, 10: 266–75.

——1973a: How children describe time and order. In C. A. Ferguson and D. I. Slobin (eds), *Studies of Child Language Development*, New York: Holt, Rinehart and Winston.

——1973b: Non-linguistic strategies and the acquisition of word meanings. *Cognition*, 2: 161–82.

——1973c: What's in a word? On the child's acquisition of semantics in his first language. In T. E. Moore (ed.), *Cognitive Development and the Acquisition of Language*, New York: Academic Press.

Clark H. H. and E. V. 1968: Semantic distinctions and memory for complex sentences. *Quarterly Journal of Experimental Psychology*, 20: 129–38.

Cole M. and S. R. 1989: *The Development of Children*. New York and London: Scientific American Books.

Conrad R. 1972: The developmental role of vocalizing in short-term memory. *Journal of Verbal Learning and Verbal Behavior*, 11: 521–33.

Cook V. J. 1973: The comparison of language development in native children and foreign adults. *International Review of Applied Linguistics*, 11: 13–28.

——1974: The acquisition of indirect object constructions. Mimeographed paper.

Cooper J. M. and Griffiths P. 1978: Treatment and prognosis. In M. A. Wyke (ed.), *Developmental Dysphasia*, London and New York: Academic Press.

Corrigan R. 1978: Language development as related to stage 6 object permanence development. *Journal of Child Language*, 5: 173–89.

——1979: Cognitive correlates of language: differential criteria yield differential results. *Child Development*, 50: 617–31.

Crain S. 1987: On performability: structure and process in language understanding. *Clinical Linguistics and Phonetics*, 1 (2): 127–45.

Critchley M. 1953: *The Parietal Lobes*. London: Edward Arnold.

Cromer R. F. 1968: The development of temporal reference during the acquisition of language. Harvard University: unpublished doctoral dissertation.

——1970a: Children are nice to understand: surface structure clues for the recovery of deep structure. *British Journal of Psychology*, 61: 397–408.

——1970b: In defence of the empirical method: a reply to Broadbent concerning psycholinguistics. *Bulletin of the British Psychological Society*, 23: 271–9.

——1972a: The learning of surface structure clues to deep structure by a puppet show technique. *Quarterly Journal of Experimental Psychology*, 24: 66–76.

——1972b: The learning of surface feature clues to deep structure by educationally subnormal children. *American Journal of Mental Deficiency*, 77: 346–53.

——1973: Conservation by the congenitally blind. *British Journal of Psychology*, 64: 241–50.

——1974a: The development of language and cognition: the cognition hypothesis. In B. Foss (ed.), *New Perspectives in Child Development*, Harmondsworth, Middx: Penguin. [Reprinted in this book as chapter 1.]

——1974b: Child and adult learning of surface structure clues to deep structure using a picture card techinque. *Journal of Psycholinguistic Research*, 3: 1–14.

——1975a: Are subnormals linguistic adults? In N. O'Connor (ed.), *Language, Cognitive Deficits and Retardation*, London: Butterworth.

——1975b: An experimental investigation of a putative linguistic universal: marking and the indirect object. *Journal of Experimental Child Psychology*, 20: 73–80.

——1976a: The cognitive hypothesis of language acquisition and its implications for child language deficiency. In D. M. and A. E. Morehead (eds), *Normal and Deficient Child Language*, Baltimore: University Park Press.

——1976b: Developmental strategies for language. In V. Hamilton and M. D. Vernon (eds), *The Development of Cognitive Processes*, London and New York: Academic Press. [Reprinted in this book as chapter 3.]

——1978a: The basis of childhood dysphasia: a linguistic approach. In M. A. Wyke (ed.), *Developmental Dysphasia*, London and New York: Academic Press. [Reprinted in this book as chapter 5.]

——1978b: Hierarchical disability in the syntax of aphasic children. *International Journal of Behavioral Development*, 391–402.

——1978c: Hierarchical ordering disability and aphasic children. Paper presented at the First International Congress for the Study of Child Language, Tokyo, 7–12 Aug.

——1979: The strengths of the weak form of the cognition hypothesis for language acquisition. In V. Lee (ed.), *Language Development*, London: Croom Helm.

——1980: Normal language development: recent progress. In L. A. Hersov, M. Berger and A. R. Nicol (eds), *Language and Language Disorders in Childhood*, Oxford: Pergamon.

——1983: Hierarchical planning disability in the drawings and constructions of a special group of severely aphasic children. *Brain and Cognition*, 2: 144–64.

——1988: The Cognition Hypothesis Revisited. In F. S. Kessel (ed.), *The Development of Language and Language Researchers: Essays in Honor of Roger Brown*. Hillsdale, NJ: LEA.

——forthcoming: A case study of dissociations between language and cognition. In H. Tager-Flusberg (ed.), *Constraints on Language Acquisition: studies of atypical children*, Hillsdale, NJ: Lawrence Erlbaum Associates.

Cross T. G. 1975: Some relationships between motherese and linguistic level in accelerated children. *Papers and Reports on Child Language Development* (Stanford University), 10: 117–35.

——1977: Mothers' speech adjustments: the contributions of selected child listener variables. In C. E. Snow and C. A. Ferguson (eds), *Talking to Children: language input and acquisition*, Cambridge: Cambridge University Press.

Curtiss S., Fromkin V. and Yamada J. E. 1978: The independence of language as a cognitive system. Paper presented at the First International Congress for the Study of Child Language, Tokyo, 7–12 Aug.

Curtiss S. and Yamada J. E. 1981: Selectively intact grammatical development in a retarded child. *UCLA Working Papers in Cognitive Linguistics*, 3: 61–91.

Davenport R. K. and Rogers C. M. 1970: Intermodal equivalence of stimuli in apes. *Science*, 168: 279–80.

Davis J. and Blasdell R. 1975: Perceptual strategies employed by normal-hearing and hearing-impaired children in the comprehension of sentences containing relative clauses. *Journal of Speech and Hearing Research*, 18: 281–95.

Day R. S. 1970: Temporal order perception of a reversible phoneme cluster. Status report on speech research, Haskins Laboratories, SR24: 47–56.

De Laguna G. A. 1963: *Speech: its function and development*. Bloomington: Indiana University Press. (First published 1927.)

Dennis M. and Whitaker H. A. 1976: Language acquisition following hemidecortication: linguistic superiority of the left over the right hemisphere. *Brain and Language*, 3: 404–33.

Dewart M. H. 1972: Social class and children's understanding of deep structure in sentences. *British Journal of Educational Psychology*, 42: 198–203.

——1975: A psychological investigation of sentence comprehension by children. University College, London: unpublished doctoral dissertation.

Dodd B. 1972: Effects of social and vocal stimulation on infant babbling. *Developmental Psychology*, 7: 80–3.

——1976a: A comparison of the phonological systems of mental age matched normals, severely subnormals, and Down's Syndrome children. *British Journal of Disorders of Communication*, 11: 27–42.

——1976b: The phonological systems of deaf children. *Journal of Speech and Hearing Disorders*, 41: 185–98.

Doehring D. G. 1960: Visual spatial memory in aphasic children. *Journal of Verbal Learning and Verbal Behavior*, 3: 404–33.

Donaldson M. and Balfour G. 1968: Less is more: a study of language comprehension in children. *British Journal of Psychology*, 59: 461–72.

Donaldson M. and McGarrigle J. 1974: Some clues to the nature of semantic development. *Journal of Child Language*, 1: 185–94.

Donaldson M. and Wales R. J. 1970: On the acquisition of some relational terms. In J. R. Hayes (ed.), *Cognition and the Development of Language*, New York: Wiley.

Dooling J. D. 1974: Rhythm and syntax in sentence perception. *Journal of Verbal Learning and Verbal Behavior*, 13: 255–64.

Dore J. 1974: A pragmatic description of early language development. *Journal of Psycholinguistic Research*, 3: 343–50.

Dulay H. and Burt M. 1974: A new perspective on the creative construction process in child second language acquisition. *Language Learning*, 24: 253–78.

Edwards D. 1973: Sensory-motor intelligence and semantic relations in early childhood grammar. *Cognition*, 2: 395–434.

Efron R. 1963: Temporal perception, aphasia, and déjà vu. *Brain*, 86: 403–24.

Eibl-Eibesfeldt I. 1970: *Ethology: the biology of behavior*. New York: Holt, Rinehart and Winston.

Eimas P. D. 1974a: Auditory and linguistic processing of clues for place of articulation by infants. *Perception and Psychophysics*, 16: 513–21.

——1974b: Linguistic processing of speech by young infants. In R. L. Schiefelbusch and L. L. Lloyd (eds), *Language Perspectives – Acquisition, Retardation and Intervention*, Baltimore: University Park Press.

Eisenson J. 1968: Developmental aphasia: a speculative view with therapeutic implications. *Journal of Speech and Hearing Disorders*, 33: 3–13.

Ellis N. C. and Hennelly R. A. 1980: A bilingual word-length effect: implications for intelligence testing and the relative ease of mental calculation in Welsh and English. *British Journal of Psychology*, 71: 43–51.

Ervin S. M. 1961: Semantic shift in bilingualism. *American Journal of Psychology*, 74: 233–41.

Ervin-Tripp S. 1966: Language development. In M. and L. Hoffman (eds), *Review of Child Development Research*, vol. 1, Ann Arbor, Mich.: University of Michigan Press.

——1971: An overview of theories of grammatical development. In D. I. Slobin (ed.), *The Ontogenesis of Grammar: a theoretical symposium*, New York: Academic Press.

——1973: Some strategies for the first two years. In T. E. Moore (ed.), *Cognitive Development and the Acquisition of Language*, New York and London: Academic Press.

Faulkner W. 1970: *As I Lay Dying*. Harmondsworth, Middx: Penguin. (First published 1929.)

Ferguson C. A. 1977: Baby talk as a simplified register. In C. E. Snow and C. A. Ferguson (eds), *Talking to Children: language input and acquisition*, Cambridge: Cambridge University Press.

Ferguson C. A. and Farwell C. B. 1975: Words and sounds in early language acquisition. *Language*, 51: 419–39.

Ferreiro E. 1971: Les relations temporelles dans le languauge de l'enfant. Geneva: Librarie Droz.

Ferreiro E. and Sinclair H. 1971: Temporal relations in language. *International Journal of Psychology*, 6: 39–47.

Fillmore C. J. 1968: The case for case. In E. Bach and R. T. Harms (eds), *Universals in Linguistic Theory*, New York: Holt, Rinehart and Winston.

Flavell J. H. 1963: *The Developmental Psychology of Jean Piaget*. New York: Van Nostrand.

Fletcher P. 1981: Description and explanation in the acquisition of verb forms. *Journal of Child Language*, 8: 93–108.

Fodor J. A. 1975: *The Language of Thought*. New York: Thomas Y. Crowell.

——1983: *The Modularity of Mind*. Cambridge, Mass.: MIT Press.

Fodor J. A. and Bever T. G. 1965: The psychological reality of linguistic segments. *Journal of Verbal Learning and Verbal Behavior*, 4: 414–21.

Fodor J. A. and Garrett M. 1967: Some syntactic determinants of sentential complexity. *Perception and Psychophysics*, 2: 289–96.

Fodor J. A., Garrett M. and Bever T. G. 1968: Some syntactic determinants of sentential complexity. II: Verb structure. *Perception and Psychophysics*, 3: 453–61.

Fry D. B., Abramson A. S., Eimas P. D. and Liberman A. M. 1962: The identification and discrimination of synthetic vowels. *Language and Speech*, 5: 171–88.

Furth H. G. 1964: Sequence learning in aphasic and deaf children. *Journal of Speech and Hearing Disorders*, 29: 171–7.

——1966: *Thinking without Language: psychological implications of deafness*. New York: Free Press.

——1969: *Piaget and Knowledge*. Englewood Cliffs, NJ: Prentice-Hall.

Furth H. G. and Youniss J. 1971: Formal operations and language: a comparison of deaf and hearing adolescents. *International Journal of Psychology*, 6: 49–64.

Fyffe C. and Prior M. 1978: Evidence for language recoding in autistic, retarded and normal children: a re-examination. *British Journal of Psychology*, 69: 393–402.

Gardner B. T. and R. A. 1975: Evidence for sentence constituents in the early utterances of child and chimpanzee. *Journal of Experimental Psychology* General, 104: 244–67.

Gardner R. A. and B. T. 1969: Teaching sign language to a chimpanzee. *Science*, 165: 664–72.

Garnica O. K. 1977: Some prosodic and paralinguistic features of speech to young children. In C. E. Snow and C. A. Ferguson (eds), *Talking to Children: language input and acquisition*, Cambridge: Cambridge University Press.

Garrett, M., Bever T. G. and Fodor J. A. 1966: The active use of grammar in speech perception. *Perception and Psychophysics*, 1: 30–2.

Gathercole V. C. 1985: 'He has too much hard questions': the acquisition of the linguistic mass–count distinction in *much* and *many*. *Journal of Child Language*, 12: 395–415.

——1986a: The acquisition of the present perfect: explaining differences in the speech of Scottish and American children. *Journal of Child Language*, 13: 537–60.

——1986b: Evaluating competing linguistic theories with child language data: the case of the mass–count distinction. *Linguistics and Philosophy*, 9: 151–90.

Geschwind N. 1967: The varieties of naming errors. *Cortex*, 3: 97–112.

Gibson E. J. and Walk R. D. 1960: The 'visual cliff'. *Scientific American*, 202 (4): 64–71.

Glass A. V., Gazzaniga M. S. and Premack D. 1973: Artificial language training in global aphasics. *Neuropsychologia*, 11: 95–103.

Gleason J. B. 1977: Talking to children: some notes on feedback. In C. E. Snow and C. A. Ferguson (eds), *Talking to Children: language input and acquisition*, Cambridge: Cambridge University Press.

Gleitman L. R. and Wanner E. 1982: Language acquisition: the state of the state of the art. In E. Wanner and L. R. Gleitman (eds), *Language Acquisition: the state of the art*, Cambridge: Cambridge University Press.

Goodson B. D. and Greenfield P. M. 1975: The search for structural principles in children's manipulative play: a parallel with linguistic development. *Child Development*, 46: 734–46.

Gopnik A. 1984: The acquisition of 'gone' and the development of the object concept. *Journal of Child Language*, 11: 273–92.

Gopnik A. and Meltzoff A. N. 1984: Some specific relationships between cognitive and semantic development: disappearance words and the object concept and success/failure words and means-ends understanding. Paper presented at the Third International Congress for the Study of Child Language, Austin, Texas, July.

——1985: From people to plans, to objects: changes in the meaning of early words and their relation to cognitive development. *Journal of Pragmatics*, 9: 495–512.

——1986a: Relations between semantic and cognitive development in the one-word stage: the specificity hypothesis. *Child Development*, 57: 1040–13.

——1986b: Words, plans, things, and locations: interactions between semantic and cognitive development in the one-word stage. In S. A. Kuczaj, II, and M. D. Barrett (eds), *The Development of Word Meaning. Progress in Cognitive Development Research*, New York: Springer.

Gordon P. 1985: Evaluating the semantic categories hypothesis: the case of the count/mass distinction. *Cognition*, 20: 209–42.

——1988: Count/mass category acquisition: distributional distinctions in children's speech. *Journal of Child Language*, 15: 109–28.

Graham N. C. 1968: Short term memory and syntactic structure in educationally subnormal children. *Language and Speech*, 11: 209–19.

——1974: Response strategies in the partial comprehension of sentences. *Language and Speech*, 17: 205–21.

Graham N. C. and Gulliford R. A. 1968: A psychological approach to the language deficiencies of educationally subnormal children. *Educational Review*, 200: 136–45.

Greenberg J. H. 1966: Language universals. In T. A. Sebeok (ed.), *Current Trends in Linguistics*, vol. 3, The Hague: Mouton.

Greenfield P. M. 1978: Structural parallels between language and action in development. In A. Lock (ed.), *Action, Gesture, and Symbol: the emergence of language*, London and New York: Academic Press.

Greenfield P. M. and Childs C. 1974: Weaving, colour terms, and pattern representation: cultural influences and cognitive development among the Zinacantecos of Southern Mexico. In J. L. M. Dawson and W. J. Lonner (eds), *Readings in Cross-Cultural Psychology* (proceedings of the inaugural meeting of the International Association for Cross-Cultural Psychology, Hong Kong, Aug.), Hong Kong: Hong Kong University Press, 112–13.

Greenfield P. M., Nelson K. and Saltzman E. 1972: The development of rule-bound strategies for manipulating seriated cups: a parallel between action and grammar. *Cognitive Psychology*, 3: 291–310.

Greenfield P. M. and Schneider L. 1977: Building a tree structure: the development of hierarchical complexity and interrupted strategies in children's construction activity. *Developmental Psychology*, 13: 299–313.

Griffiths P. 1972: *Developmental Aphasia: an introduction*. London: Invalid Children's Aid Association.

Hadenius A. M., Hagberg B., Hyttnäs-Bensch K. and Sjögren I. 1962: The natural prognosis of infantile hydrocephalus. *Acta Paediatrica*, 51: 117–18.

Halford G. and Galloway W. 1977: Children who fail to make transitive inferences can remember comparisons. *Australian Journal of Psychology*, 29: 1–5.

Halpern E., Corrigan R. and Aviezer O. 1981: Two types of 'under'? Implications for the relationship between cognition and language. *International Journal of Psycholinguistics*, 8: 37–56.

Harris M. 1976: The influence of reversibility and truncation on the interpretation of the passive voice by young children. *British Journal of Psychology*, 67: 419–27.

Hatwell Y. 1966: *Privation sensorielle et intelligence*. Paris: Presses Universitaires de France.

Heider E. R. 1971: 'Focal' color areas and the development of color names. *Developmental Psychology*, 4: 447–55.

——1972: Universals in color naming and memory. *Journal of Experimental Psychology*, 93: 10–20.

Heider E. R. and Olivier D. C. 1972: The structure of the color space in naming and memory for two languages. *Cognitive Psychology*, 3: 337–54.

Henle P. (ed) 1958: *Language, Thought, and Culture*. Ann Arbor: University of Michigan Press.

Hermelin B. and O'Connor N. 1964: Crossmodal transfer in normal, subnormal, and autistic children. *Neuropsychologia*, 2: 229–35.

——1967: Remembering of words by psychotic and subnormal children. *British Journal of Psychology*, 58: 213–18.

——1973: Ordering in recognition memory after ambiguous initial or recognition displays. *Canadian Journal of Psychology*, 27: 191–9.

Hickerson N. P. 1971: Review of 'Basic Color Terms', *International Journal of American Linguistics*, 37: 257–70.

Hirsch H. V. B. and Spinelli D. N. 1971: Modification of the distribution of receptive field orientation in cats by selective visual exposure during development. *Experimental Brain Research*, 12: 509–27.

Hirsh I. J. 1959: Auditory perception of temporal order. *Journal of the Acoustical Society of America*, 31: 759–67.

Hoijer H. (ed.) 1954: *Language in Culture*. Chicago: University of Chicago Press.

Hoosain R. 1986: Language, orthography and cognitive processes: Chinese perspectives for the Sapir–Whorf hypothesis. *International Journal of Behavioral Development*, 9 (4): 507–25.

Houston S. H. 1970: A reexamination of some assumptions about the language of the disadvantaged child. *Child Development*, 41: 947–63.

Hubel D. H. and Wiesel T. N. 1959: Receptive fields of single neurones in the cat's striate cortex. *Journal of Physiology*, 148: 574–91.

——1962: Receptive fields, binocular interaction, and functional architecture in the cat's visual cortex. *Journal of Physiology*, 160: 106–54.

Hughes J. 1972: Language and communication: acquisition of a non-vocal 'language' by previously languageless children. Brunel University: unpublished Bachelor of Technology thesis.

——1974–5: Acquisition of a non-vocal 'language' by aphasic children. *Cognition*, 3: 41–55.

Hughlings-Jackson J. 1888: On a particular variety of epilepsy ('intellectual aura'), one case with symptoms of organic brain disease. *Brain*, 11: 179–207.

Huttenlocher J., Eisenberg K. and Strauss S. 1968: Comprehension: relation between perceived actor and logical subject. *Journal of Verbal Learning and Verbal Behavior*, 7: 419–27.

Huttenlocher J. and Strauss S. 1968: Comprehension and a statement's relations to the situation it describes. *Journal of Verbal Learning and Verbal Behavior*, 7: 300–4.

Ingram T. T. S. and Naughton J. A. 1962: Pediatric and psychological aspects of cerebral palsy associated with hydrocephalus. *Developmental Medicine and Child Neurology*, 4: 287–92.

Inhelder B. 1969: Memory and intelligence in the child. In D. Elkind and J. H. Flavell (eds), *Studies in Cognitive Development*, Oxford: Oxford University Press.

——1980: Language and knowledge in a constructivist framework. In M. Piattelli-Palmarini (ed.), *Language and Learning: the debate between Jean Piaget and Noam Chomsky*, London: Routledge and Kegan Paul.

Inhelder B. and Piaget J. 1958: *The Growth of Logical Thinking from Childhood to Adolescence*, New York: Basic Books. (First published 1955.)

——1964: *The Early Growth in Logic in the Child*. New York: Harper and Row. (First published 1959.)

Jackendoff R. S. 1972: *Semantic Interpretation in Generative Grammar*. Cambridge, Mass.: MIT Press.

——1983: *Semantics and Cognition*. Cambridge, Mass.: MIT Press.

Jacobs R. A. and Rosenbaum P. S. 1968: *English Transformational Grammar*. Waltham, Mass.: Blaisdell.

Jakobson R. 1968: *Child Language Aphasia and Phonological Universals*. The Hague: Mouton. (First published 1941.)

Jakobson R., Fant C. G. M. and Halle M. 1952: *Preliminaries to Speech Analysis: the distinctive features and their correlates*, Cambridge, Mass.: MIT Press.

Jakobson R. and Halle M. 1956: *Fundamentals of Language*. The Hague: Mouton.

James W. 1950: *The Principles of Psychology*, vol. 1, authorized, unabridged edn. New York: Dover. (First published 1890.)

Jenkins J. J. and Palermo D. S. 1964: Mediation processes and the acquisition of linguistic structure. In U. Bellugi and R. Brown (eds), *The Acquisition of Language*, Monographs of the Society for Research in Child Development, 29 (92).

Johnston J. R. 1979: A study of spatial thought and expression: in back and in front. University of California, Berkeley: unpublished doctoral dissertation.

——1985: Cognitive prerequisites: the evidence from children learning English. In D. I. Slobin (ed.), *The Crosslinguistic Study of Language Acquisition*, vol. 2:

Theoretical Issues, Hillsdale, NJ: Lawrence Erlbaum Associates.

Jorm A. F. 1979: The cognitive and neurological basis of developmental dyslexia: a theoretical framework and review. *Cognition*, 7: 19–33.

Jung C. G. 1959: The Archetypes and the Collective Unconscious. Bollingen Series XX: *The Collected Works of C. G. Jung*, vol. 9, pt 1, New York: Pantheon Books.

Kaplan E. and G. 1971: The prelinguistic child. In J. Eliot (ed.), *Human Development and Cognitive Processes*, New York: Holt, Rinehart and Winston.

Karmiloff-Smith A. 1977a: The child's construction of a system of plurifunctional markers. Paper presented to the Language Development Symposium at the biennial conference of the International Society for the Study of Behavioural Development, Pavia, Sep.

——1977b: More about the same: children's understanding of post-particles. *Journal of Child Language*, 4: 377–94.

——1978: The interplay between syntax, semantics, and phonology in language acquisition processes. In R. N. Campbell and P. T. Smith (eds), *Recent Advances in the Psychology of Language: language development and mother-child interaction*, New York: Plenum.

——1979a: *A Functional Approach to Child Language: a study of determiners and reference*. Cambridge: Cambridge University Press.

——1979b: Metaprocedural behaviour as an explanatory notion in child language acquisition. Paper presented at the Child Language Seminar, Reading, 2 Apr.

Katz J. J. and Bever T. G. 1974: The rise and fall of empiricism. Paper reproduced by the Indiana University Linguistics Club, Bloomington, Ind.

Kay P. and Kempton W. 1984: What is the Sapir–Whorf hypothesis? *American Anthropologist*, 86: 65–79.

Kay P. and McDaniel C. K. 1978: The linguistic significance of the meanings of basic color terms. *Language*, 54: 610–46.

Keenan E. L. and Comrie B. 1977: Noun phrase accessibility and universal grammar. *Linguistic Inquiry*, 8: 63–99.

Kendler T. S. 1963: Development of mediating responses in children. In J. C. Wright and J. Kagan (eds), *Basic Cognitive Processes in Children*, Monographs of the Society for Research in Child Development, 28 (86).

Kessel F. S. 1970: *The Role of Syntax in Children's Comprehension from Ages Six to Twelve*. Monographs of the Society for Research in Child Development, 35 (139).

Klatzky R. L., Clark E. V. and Macken M. 1973: Asymmetries in the acquisition of polar adjectives: linguistic or conceptual? *Journal of Experimental Child Psychology*, 16: 32–46.

Knox S. 1974: A play scale. In M. Reilly (ed.), *Play as Exploratory Learning*. Beverly Hills, Calif.: Sage.

Koehler O. 1972: Non-verbal thinking. In H. Friedrich (ed.), *Man and Animal*. London: Paladin.

Kracke I. 1975: Perception of rhythmic sequences by receptive aphasic and deaf children. *British Journal of Disorders of Communication*, 10: 43–51.

Lack D. 1943: *The Life of Robin*. Cambridge: Cambridge University Press.

Lakoff G. 1971: Presupposition and relative well-formedness. In D. D. Steinberg and L. A. Jakobovits (eds), *Semantics*, Cambridge: Cambridge University Press.

Landau W. M. and Kleffner F. R. 1957: Syndrome of acquired aphasia with convulsive disorder in children. *Neurology*, 7: 523–30.

Lantz D. and Lenneberg E. H. 1966: Verbal communication and colour memory in the deaf and hearing. *Child Development*, 37 (4): 765–79.

Lantz D. and Stefflre V. 1964: Language and cognition revisited. *Journal of Abnormal Social Psychology*, 69: 472–81.

Lashley K. S. 1951: The problem of serial order in behaviour. In L. A. Jeffress (ed.), *Cerebral Mechanisms in Behaviour*, New York: Wiley.

Lea J. 1970: The colour pattern scheme: a method of remedial language teaching. Mimeographed paper, Moor House School, Oxted, Surrey.

——1975: An investigation into the association between rhythmic ability and language ability in a group of children with severe speech and language disorders. University of London, Guy's Hospital Medical School: unpublished master's thesis.

——1980: The association between rhythmic ability and language ability. In F. M. Jones (ed.), *Language Disability in Children*, Lancaster: MTP Press.

Lee L. L. 1966: Developmental sentence types: a method for comparing normal and deviant syntactic development. *Journal of Speech and Hearing Disorders*, 31: 311–30.

Leiter R. G. 1979: *Leiter International Performance Scale*. Chicago: Stoelting. (First version 1927.)

Lenneberg E. H. 1961: Color naming, color recognition, color discrimination: a reappraisal. *Perceptual and Motor Skills*, 12: 375–82.

——1962: Understanding language without ability to speak. *Journal of Abnormal Social Psychology*, 65: 419–25.

——1964: Speech as a motor skill with special reference to nonaphasic disorders. In U. Bellugi and R. Brown (eds), *The Acquisition of Language*, Monographs of the Society for Research in Child Development, 29 (92).

——1967: *Biological Foundations of Language*. New York: Wiley.

Lenneberg E. H., Nichols I. A. and Rosenberger E. F. 1964: Primitive stages of language development in mongolism. In D. McK. Rioch and E. A. Weinstein (eds), *Disorders of Communication*, Research Publications of the Association for Research in Nervous and Mental Disease, 42, Baltimore: Williams and Wilkins.

Lenneberg E. H., Rebelsky F. G. and Nichols I. A. 1965: The vocalizations of infants born to deaf and hearing parents. *Vita Humana* (Human Development), 8: 23–37.

Lenneberg E. H. and Roberts J. M. 1956: *The Language of Experience*. Indiana University Publications in Anthropology and Linguistics, 13.

Leonard L. B. 1972: What is deviant language? *Journal of Speech and Hearing Disorders*, 37: 427–46.

——1979: Language impairment in children. *Merrill–Palmer Quarterly*, 25: 205–32.

Levine S. C. and Carey S. 1982: Up front: the acquisition of a concept and a word. *Journal of Child Language*, 9: 645–57.

Levy Y. 1983: It's frogs all the way down. *Cognition*, 15: 75–93.

——1988: On the early learning of formal grammatical systems: evidence from studies of the acquisition of gender and countability. *Journal of Child Language*, 15: 179–87.

Liberman A. M. 1970: The grammars of speech and language. *Cognitive Psychology*, 1: 301–23.

Liberman A. M., Cooper F. S., Shankweiler D. P. and Studdert-Kennedy M. 1967: Perception of the speech code. *Psychological Review*, 74: 431–61.

Limber J. 1977: Language in child and chimp. *American Psychologist*, 32: 280–95.

Lind J. (ed.) 1965: Newborn infant cry. *Acta Paediatrica Scandinavia*, suppl. 163.

Linden E. 1975: *Apes, Men and Language*. New York: Dutton.

Liu L. G. 1985: Reasoning counterfactually in Chinese: are there any obstacles? *Cognition*, 21: 239–70.

Liublinskaja A. A. 1957: The development of children's speech and thought. In B. Simon (ed.), *Psychology in the Soviet Union*, London: Routledge and Kegan Paul.

Lowe A. D. and Campbell R. A. 1965: Temporal discrimination in aphasoid and normal children. *Journal of Speech and Hearing Research*, 8: 313–14.

Lucy J. A. 1987: Grammatical categories and cognitive processes: an historical, theoretical, and empirical re-evaluation of the linguistic relativity hypothesis. University of Chicago: unpublished doctoral dissertation.

Lucy J. A. and Shweder R. A. 1979: Whorf and his critics: linguistic and non-linguistic influences on color memory. *American Anthropologist*, 81: 581–615.

Luria A. R. and Yudovich F. I. 1971: *Speech and the Development of Mental Processes in the Child*. Harmondsworth, Middx: Penguin. (First published 1956.)

Lyons J. 1966: General discussion of David McNeill's paper 'The Creation of Language'. In J. Lyons and R. J. Wales (eds), *Psycholinguistic Papers*, Edinburgh: Edinburgh University Press.

——1968: *Introduction to Theoretical Linguistics*. Cambridge: Cambridge University Press.

——1970: *Chomsky*. London: Fontana.

Macnamara J. 1972: Cognitive basis of language learning in infants. *Psychological Review*, 79: 1–13.

——1982: *Names for Things: a study of human learning*. Cambridge, Mass.: MIT Press.

Malone R. L. 1967: Temporal ordering and speech identification abilities. *Journal of Speech and Hearing Research*, 10: 542–48.

Mandelbaum D. G. (ed.) 1949: *Selected Writings of Edward Sapir in Language, Culture, and Personality*. Berkeley, Calif.: University of California Press.

——(ed.) 1961: *Edward Sapir, Culture, Language and Personality. Selected Essays*. Berkeley, Calif.: University of California Press.

Maratsos M. P. 1973a: The effects of stress on the understanding of pronominal co-reference in children. *Journal of Psycholinguistic Research*, 2: 1–8.

——1973b: Decrease in the understanding of the word 'big' in preschool children. *Child Development*, 44: 747–52.

Maratsos M. P. and Chalkley M. A. 1980: The internal language of children's syntax: the ontogenesis and representation of syntactic categories. In K. E. Nelson (ed.), *Children's Language*, vol. 2, New York: Gardner Press.

Mark H. J. and Hardy W. G. 1958: Orienting reflex disturbances in central auditory or language handicapped children. *Journal of Speech and Hearing Disorders*, 23: 237–42.

Marshall J. C. and Newcombe F. 1973: Patterns of paralexia: a psycholinguistic approach. *Journal of Psycholinguistic Research*, 2: 175–99.

——1977: Variability and constraint in acquired dyslexia. In H. and H. A. Whitaker (eds), *Studies in Neurolinguistics*, New York: Academic Press.

Martin J. G. 1972: Rhythmic (hierarchical) versus serial structure in speech and other behaviour. *Psychological Review*, 79: 487–509.

McCawley, J. D. 1968: The role of semantics in a grammar. In E. Bach and R. T. Harms (eds), *Universals in Linguistic Theory*, New York: Holt, Rinehart and Winston.

——1971a: Meaning and the description of languages. In J. F. Rosenberg and C. Travis (eds), *Readings in the Philosophy of Language*, Englewood Cliffs, NJ: Prentice-Hall.

——1971b: Where do noun phrases come from? In D. D. Steinberg and L. A. Jakobovitz (eds), *Semantics*, Cambridge: Cambridge University Press.

——1973: A review of Noam A. Chomsky, *Studies on Semantics in Generative Grammar*. Paper reproduced by the Indiana University Linguistics Club, Bloomington, Ind.

——1975: Lexicography and the count–mass distinction. Paper presented at the first annual conference of the Berkeley Linguistics Society, 314–21.

McCune-Nicolich L. 1981: The cognitive bases of relational words in the single word period. *Journal of Child Language*, 8: 15–34.

McKinney W. and McGreal D. A. 1974: An aphasic syndrome in children. *Canadian Medical Association Journal*, 110: 637–9.

McNeill D. 1966: Developmental psycholinguistics. In F. Smith and G. A. Miller (eds), *The Genesis of Language*, Cambridge, Mass.: MIT Press.

——1970a: The development of language. In P. H. Mussen (ed.), *Carmichael's Manual of Child Psychology*, vol. 1, New York: Wiley.

——1970b: Language before symbols: very early child grammar. *Interchange*, 1: 127–33.

——1970c: *The Acquisition of Language*. New York: Harper and Row.

——1987: *Psycholinguistics: a new approach*. New York: Harper and Row.

McNeill D. and N. B. 1968: What does a child mean when he says 'no'? In E. M. Zale (ed.), *Proceedings of the Conference on Language and Language Behavior*, New York: Appleton-Century-Crofts.

McNeill D., Yukawa R. and McNeill N. B. 1971: The acquisition of direct and indirect objects in Japanese. *Child Development*, 42: 237–49.

McReynolds L. V. 1966: Operant conditioning for investigating speech sound discrimination in aphasic children. *Journal of Speech and Hearing Research*, 9: 519–28.

Mehler J. and Carey P. 1968: The interaction of veracity and syntax in the processing of sentences. *Perception and Psychophysics*, 3: 109–11.

Menyuk P. 1964: Comparison of grammar of children with functionally deviant and normal speech. *Journal of Speech and Hearing Research*, 7: 109–21.
——1969: *Sentences Children Use*. Cambridge, Mass.: MIT Press.
——1975: The language-impaired child: linguistic or cognitive impairment? In D. Aaronson and R. W. Rieber (eds), *Developmental Psycholinguistics and Communication Disorders*, Annals of the New York Academy of Sciences, 263.
——1978: Linguistic problems in children with developmental dysphasia. In M. A. Wyke (ed.), *Developmental Dysphasia*, London and New York: Academic Press.
Mervis C. B., Catlin J. and Rosch E. 1975: Development of the structure of color categories. *Developmental Psychology*, 11: 54–60.
Michaels D. 1977: Linguistic relativity and color terminology. *Language and Speech*, 20 (4): 333–43.
Miller G. A. 1962a: *Psychology: the science of mental life*. Harmondsworth, Middx: Penguin.
——1962b: Some psychological studies of grammar. *American Psychologist*, 17: 748–62.
Miller G. A. and Chomsky N. 1963: Finitary models of language users. In R. D. Luce, R. R. Bush, and E. Galanter (eds), *Handbook of Mathematical Psychology*, vol. 2, New York: Wiley.
Miller G. A. and McNeill D. 1969: Psycholinguistics. In G. Lindzey and E. Aronson (eds), *The Handbook of Social Psychology*, 2nd edn, vol. 2, Reading, Mass.: Addison-Wesley.
Miller J. F. and Chapman R. S. 1984: Disorders of communication: investigating the development of language of mentally retarded children. *American Journal of Mental Deficiency*, 88: 536–45.
Millikan C. H. and Darley F. L. (eds) 1967: *Brain Mechanisms Underlying Speech and Language*, New York and London: Grune and Stratton.
Miura J. T., Kim C. C., Chang C.-H. and Okamoto Y. 1988: Effects of language characteristics on children's cognitive representation of number: cross-national comparisons. *Child Development*, 59: 1445–50.
Moeser S. D., and Bregman A. S. 1972: The role of reference in the acquisition of a miniature artificial language. *Journal of Verbal Learning and Verbal Behavior*, 11: 759–69.
Moeser S. D. and Olson A. J. 1974: The role of reference in children's acquisition of a miniature artificial language. *Journal of Experimental Child Psychology*, 17: 204–18.
Monsees E. K. 1961: Aphasia in children. *Journal of Speech and Hearing Disorders*, 26: 83–6.
Moore T. E. (ed.) 1973: *Cognitive Development and the Acquisition of Language*, New York: Academic Press.
Morehead D. M. and A. 1974: From signal to sign: a Piagetian view of thought and language during the first two years. In R. L. Schiefelbusch and L. L. Lloyd (eds), *Language Perspectives: acquisition, retardation, and intervention*, Baltimore: University Park Press.
Morse P. A. 1974: Infant speech perception: a preliminary model and review of the

literature. In R. L. Schiefelbusch and L. L. Lloyd (eds), *Language Perspectives: acquisition, retardation and intervention*, Baltimore: University Park Press.

Mowrer O. H. 1954: The psychologist looks at language. *American Psychologist*, 9: 660–94.

Myerson R. and Goodglass H. 1972: Transformational grammars of three agrammatic patients. *Language and Speech*, 15: 40–50.

Neisser U. 1967: *Cognitive Psychology*. New York: Appleton-Century-Crofts.

Nelson K. 1973: *Structure and Strategy in Learning to Talk*, Monographs of the Society for Research in Child Development, 38, 1–2 (149).

Nelson K. and Bonvillian J. 1973: Concepts and words in the 18-month-old: acquiring concept names under controlled conditions. *Cognition*, 2: 435–50.

Newmeyer F. 1980: *Linguistic Theory in America*. New York: Academic Press.

Newport E. L., Gleitman H. and L. R. 1977: Mother I'd rather do it myself: some effects and non-effects of maternal speech style. In C. E. Snow and C. A. Ferguson (eds), *Talking to Children: language input and acquisition*, Cambridge: Cambridge University Press.

O'Connor N. and Frith U. 1973: Cognitive development and the concept of set. In A. Prangishvili (ed.), *Psychological Investigations: a commemorative volume dedicated to the 85th anniversary of the birth of D. Uznadze*. Tbilisi: Metsniereba.

O'Connor N. and Hermelin B. 1971: Inter- and intra-modal transfer in children with modality specific and general handicaps. *British Journal of Social and Clinical Psychology*, 10: 346–54.

——1973a: Short-term memory for the order of pictures and syllables by deaf and hearing children. *Neuropsychologia*, 11: 437–42.

——1973b: The spatial or temporal organization of short-term memory. *Quarterly Journal of Experimental Psychology*, 25: 335–43.

Olson J. L. 1961: Differential diagnosis: deaf and sensory aphasic children. *Exceptional Children*, 28: 422–4.

Parisi D. and Antinucci F. 1970: Lexical competence. In G. B. Flores d'Arcais and W. J. M Levelt (eds), *Advances in Psycholinguistics*, Amsterdam: North Holland.

Patterson K. E. and Marcel A. J. 1977: Aphasia, dyslexia and the phonological coding of written words. *Quarterly Journal of Experimental Psychology*, 29: 307–18.

Paul R., Chapman R. S. and Wanska S. 1980: The development of complex sentence use. Paper presented at the annual meeting of the American Speech and Hearing Association, Detroit.

Perkins D. N. 1974: Coding position in a sequence by rhythmic grouping. *Memory and Cognition*, 2: 219–23.

Petrie T. 1975: Characteristics and progress of a group of language disordered children with severe receptive difficulties. *British Journal of Disorders of Communication*, 10: 123–33.

Piaget J. 1970a: *Genetic Epistemology*. New York: Columbia University Press.

——1970b: Piaget's theory. In P. H. Mussen (ed.), *Carmichael's Manual for Child Psychology*, vol. 1, New York: Wiley.

Piaget J. and Inhelder B. 1956: *The Child's Conception of Space*. London:

Routledge and Kegan Paul. (First published 1948.)

——1969a: The gaps in empiricism. In A. Koestler and J. R. Smythies (eds), *Beyond Reductionism*, London: Hutchinson.

——1969b: *The Psychology of the Child*. London: Routledge and Kegan Paul. (First published 1966.)

Piaget J., Inhelder B. and Szeminska A. 1960: *The Child's Conception of Geometry*. New York: Basic Books.

Piattelli-Palmarini M. (ed.) 1980: *Language and Learning: the debate between Jean Piaget and Noam Chomsky*. London: Routledge and Kegan Paul.

Pinker S. 1989: *Learnability and Cognition: the acquisition of argument structure*. Cambridge, Mass.: MIT Press.

Poppen R., Stark J., Eisenson J., Forrest T. and Wertheim G. 1969: Visual sequencing performance of aphasic children. *Journal of Speech and Hearing Research*, 12: 288–300.

Premack A. J. and D. 1972: Teaching language to an ape. *Scientific American*, 227 (4): 92–9.

Premack D. 1969: A functional analysis of language. Invited address before the American Psychological Association, Washington, DC.

Premack D. and Schwartz A. 1966: Preparations for discussing behaviorism with chimpanzee. In F. Smith and G. A. Miller (eds), *The Genesis of Language*, Cambridge, Mass.: MIT Press.

Rapin I. and Wilson B. C. 1978: Children with developmental language disability: neurological aspects and assessment. In M. A. Wyke (ed.), *Developmental Dysphasia*, London and New York: Academic Press.

Rees N. S. 1973: Auditory processing factors in language disorders: the view from Procrustes' bed. *Journal of Speech and Hearing Disorders*, 38: 304–15.

Reese H. W. and Lipsitt L. P. 1970: *Experimental Child Psychology*. London and New York: Academic Press.

Reynolds A. G. and Flagg P. W. 1977: *Cognitive Psychology*. Cambridge, Mass.: Winthrop.

Rice M. L. and Kemper S. 1984: *Child Language and Cognition*. Baltimore: University Park Press.

Ricks D. M. 1972: The beginnings of vocal communication in infants and autistic children. University of London: unpublished doctoral thesis.

——1975: Vocal communication in pre-verbal normal and autistic children. In N. O'Connor (ed.), *Language, Cognitive Deficits, and Retardation*, London: Butterworth.

Riley C. A. and Trabasso T. 1974: Comparatives, logical structures, and encoding in a transitive inference task. *Journal of Experimental Child Psychology*, 17: 187–203.

Robinson G. M. and Solomon D. J. 1974: Rhythm is processed by the speech hemisphere. *Journal of Experimental Psychology*, 102: 508–11.

Rosch E. 1973: On the internal structure of perceptual and semantic categories. In T. E. Moore (ed.), *Cognitive Development and the Acquisition of Language*, New York: Academic Press.

——1974: Linguistic relativity. In A. Silverstein (ed.), *Human Communication: theoretical explorations*, Hillsdale, NJ: Lawrence Erlbaum Associates.

——1975: Cognitive reference points. *Cognitive Psychology*, 7: 532–47.

——1977a: Human categorization. In N. Warren (ed.), *Studies in Cross-Cultural Psychology*, London: Academic Press.

——1977b: Linguistic relativity. In P. N. Johnson-Laird and P. C. Wason (eds), *Thinking: readings in cognitive science*, Cambridge: Cambridge University Press.

Rosenstein J. 1957: Tactile perception of rhythmic patterns by normal, blind, deaf, and aphasic children. *American Annals of the Deaf*, 102: 399–403.

Rosenthal W. S. 1971: Auditory threshold-duration functions in aphasic subjects: implications for the interaction of linguistic and auditory processing in aphasia. Paper delivered at the 47th annual convention of the American Speech and Hearing Association, Chicago, Nov.

——1972: Auditory and linguistic interaction in developmental aphasia: evidence from two studies of auditory processing. In D. Ingram (ed.), *Papers and Reports on Child Language Development*, special issue: *Language Disorders in Children*, 4: 19–34.

Rosenthal W. S. and Eisenson J. 1970: Auditory temporal order in aphasic children as a function of selected stimulus features. Paper delivered at the 46th annual convention of the American Speech and Hearing Association, New York, Nov.

Rumbaugh D. M. (ed.), 1977: *Language Learning by a Chimpanzee: the LANA Project*. New York: Academic Press.

Rumbaugh D. M. and Gill T. V. 1976: The mastery of language-type skills by the chimpanzee (Pan). In S. R. Harnard, H. D. Steklis and J. Lancaster (eds), *Origins and Evolution of Language and Speech*, Annals of the New York Academy of Sciences, 280: 562–78.

Sachs J. 1971: The status of developmental studies of language. In J. Eliot (ed.), *Human Development and Cognitive Processes*, New York: Holt, Rinehart and Winston.

——1977: The adaptive significance of linguistic input to prelinguistic infants. In C. E. Snow and C. A. Ferguson (eds), *Talking to Children: language input and acquisition*, Cambridge: Cambridge University Press.

Sapir E. 1949: see Mandelbaum, 1949.

Schlesinger I. M. 1971a: Learning grammar: from pivot to realization rule. In R. Huxley and E. Ingram (eds), *Language Acquisition: models and methods*, New York: Academic Press.

——1971b: Production of utterances and language acquisition. In D. I. Slobin (ed.), *The Ontogenesis of Grammar: a theoretical symposium*, New York: Academic Press.

——1977a: The role of cognitive development and linguistic input in language acquisition. *Journal of Child Language*, 4: 153–69.

——1977b: *Production and Comprehension of Utterances*, Hillsdale, NJ: Lawrence Erlbaum Associates.

Schnitzer M. L. 1974: Aphasiological evidence for five linguistic hypotheses. *Language*, 50: 300–15.

Scribner S. and Cole M. 1981: *The Psychology of Literacy*. Cambridge, Mass.: Harvard University Press.

Sebeok T. A. and Umiker-Sebeok D. J. (eds) 1980: *Speaking of Apes: a critical anthology of two-way communication with man.* New York: Plenum.

Seidenberg M. S. and Petitto L. A. 1979: Signing behavior in apes: a critical review, *Cognition,* 7: 177–215.

Seiler T. B. 1979: Cognitive differentiation as a model of development and its application to a theory of personality. *Archives of Psychology,* 47: 151–64.

Seitz A. and Stewart C. 1975: Imitations and expansions: some developmental aspects of mother–child communications. *Developmental Psychology,* 11: 763–8.

Semenza C., Denes G., D'Urso V., Romano O. and Montorsi T. 1978: Analytic and global strategies in copying designs by unilaterally brain-damaged patients. *Cortex,* 14: 404–10.

Seuren P. A. M. (ed.) 1974: *Semantic Syntax.* London: Oxford University Press.

Shallice T. 1988: *From Neuropsychology to Mental Structure.* Cambridge: Cambridge University Press.

Shallice T. and Warrington E. K. 1975: Word recognition in a phonemic dyslexic patient. *Quarterly Journal of Experimental Psychology,* 27: 187–99.

Shatz M. 1984: Bootstrap operations in child language. Plenary address, Third International Congress for the Study of Child Language, Austin, Texas, 9–13 July.

——1987: Bootstrapping operations in child language. In K. E. Nelson and A. V. Kleeck (eds), *Children's Language,* vol. 6, Hillsdale, NJ: Lawrence Erlbaum Associates.

Sheehan J. G., Aseltine S. and Edwards A. E. 1973: Aphasic comprehension of time spacing. *Journal of Speech and Hearing Research,* 17: 650–7.

Sheldon A. 1974: The role of parallel function in the acquisition of relative clauses in English. *Journal of Verbal Learning and Verbal Behavior,* 13: 272–81.

Siegel G. M. and Spradlin J. E. 1978: Programming for language and communication therapy. In R. L. Schiefelbusch (ed.), *Language Intervention Strategies,* Baltimore: University Park Press.

Siegel I. E. and Hooper F. H. 1968: *Logical Thinking in Children.* New York: Holt, Rinehart and Winston.

Siegel L. S. 1978: The relationships of language and thought in the preoperational child: a reconsideration of nonverbal alternatives to Piagetian tasks. In L. S. Siegel and A. J. Brainerd (eds), *Alternatives to Piaget, Critical Essays on the Theory,* New York: Academic Press.

Sinclair H. 1970: The transition from sensory-motor behaviour to symbolic activity. *Interchange,* 1: 119–26.

——1971: Sensorimotor action patterns as a condition for the acquisition of syntax. In R. Huxley and E. Ingram (eds), *Language Acquisition: models and methods,* London and New York: Academic Press.

Sinclair-de-Zwart H. 1969: Developmental psycholinguistics. In D. Elkind and J. H. Flavell (eds), *Studies in Cognitive Development,* New York: Oxford University Press.

——1973: Language acquisition and cognitive development. In T. E. Moore (ed.), *Cognitive Development and the Acquisition of Language,* New York: Academic Press.

Skinner B. F. 1957: *Verbal Behavior*. New York: Appleton-Century-Crofts.

Slobin D. I. 1966: The acquisition of Russian as a native language. In F. Smith and G. A. Miller (eds), *The Genesis of Language*, Cambridge, Mass.: MIT Press.

——(ed.) 1971a: *The Ontogenesis of Grammar: a theoretical symposium*, New York: Academic Press.

——1971b: *Psycholinguistics*, Glenview, Ill.: Scott, Foresman.

——1973: Cognitive prerequisites for the development of grammar. In C. A. Ferguson and D. I. Slobin (eds), *Studies of Child Language Development*, New York: Holt, Rinehart and Winston.

——1978: Universal and particular in the acquisition of language. Paper presented at the workshop–conference 'Language Acquisition: state of the art', University of Pennsylvania, 19–22 May.

Smedslund J. 1961: The acquisition of conservation of substance and weight in children. III: Extinction of conservation of weight acquired 'normally' and by means of empirical controls on a balance. *Scandanavian Journal of Psychology*, 2: 85–7.

——1963: Development of concrete transitivity of length in children. *Child Development*, 34: 389–405.

——1965: The development of transitivity of length: a comment on Braine's reply. *Child Development*, 36: 577–80.

Smith N. V. 1971: How children learn to speak. *Listener*, 2 Dec.

——1973: *The Acquisition of Phonology*, Cambridge: Cambridge University Press.

Smith S. M., Brown H. O., Toman J. E. P. and Goodman L. S. 1947: The lack of cerebral effects of d-tubocurarine. *Anesthesiology*, 8: 1–14.

Smolak L. and Levine M. P. 1984: The effects of differential criteria on the assessment of cognitive-linguistic relationships. *Child Development*, 55: 973–80.

Snow C. E. 1977: Mothers' speech research: from input to interaction. In C. E. Snow and C. A. Ferguson (eds), *Talking to Children: language input and acquisition*, Cambridge: Cambridge University Press.

Snow C. E. and Ferguson C. A. (eds) 1977: *Talking to Children: language input and acquisition*, Cambridge: Cambridge University Press.

Snowling M. J. 1980: The development of grapheme–phoneme correspondence in normal and dyslexic readers. *Journal of Experimental Child Psychology*, 29: 294–305.

Spelke E. S. 1987: Where perceiving ends and thinking begins: the apprehension of objects in infancy. In A. Yonas (ed.), *Perceptual Development in Infancy*, Minnesota Symposia on Child Psychology, Hillsdale, NJ: Lawrence Erlbaum Associates.

——1988: The origins of physical knowledge. In L. Weiskrantz (ed.), *Thought without Language*, Oxford: Oxford University Press.

Spiker C. C. 1963: Verbal factors in the discrimination learning of children. In J. C. Wright and J. Kagan (eds), *Basic Cognitive Processes in Children*, Monographs of the Society for Research in Child Development, 28 (86).

Stark J. 1967: A comparison of the performance of aphasic children on three sequencing tasks. *Journal of Communication Disorders*, 1: 31–4.

Stark J., Poppen R. and May M. Z. 1967: Effects of the alterations of prosodic features on the sequencing performance of aphasic children. *Journal of Speech and Hearing Research*, 10: 849–55.

Starr S. 1975: The relationship of single words to two-word sentences. *Child Development*, 46: 701–8.

Stefflre V., Castillo Vales V. and Morley L. 1966: Language and cognition in Yucatan: a cross-cultural replication. *Journal of Personality and Social Psychology*, 4: 112–15.

Stigler J. W., Lee S. and Stevenson H. W. 1986: Digit memory in Chinese and English: evidence for a temporally limited store. *Cognition*, 23 (1): 1–20.

Strohner H. and Nelson K. E. 1974: The young child's development of sentence comprehension: influence of event probability, non-verbal context, syntactic form and strategies. *Child Development*, 45: 567–76.

Studdert-Kennedy M. 1974: The perception of speech. In T. A. Sebeok (ed.), *Current Trends in Linguistics*, vol. 12, The Hague: Mouton.

Suci G. J. and Hamacher J. H. 1972: Psychological dimensions of case in sentence processing: action role and animateness. *International Journal of Linguistics*, 1: 34–48.

Swisher L. P. and Pinsker E. J. 1971: The language characteristics of hyperverbal, hydrocephalic children. *Developmental Medicine and Child Neurology*, 13: 746–55.

Tallal P. and Piercy M. 1973a: Defects of non-verbal auditory perception in children with developmental aphasia. *Nature*, 241: 468–9.

——1973b: Developmental aphasia: impaired rate of non-verbal processing as a function of sensory modality. *Neuropsychologia*, 11: 389–98.

——1974: Developmental aphasia: rate of auditory processing and selective impairment of consonant perception. *Neuropsychologia*, 12: 83–93.

——1975: Developmental aphasia: the perception of brief vowels and extended stop consonants. *Neuropsychologia*, 13: 69–74.

——1978: Defects of auditory perception in children with developmental dysphasia. In M. A. Wyke (ed.), *Developmental Dysphasia*, London and New York: Academic Press.

Taylor E. M. 1959: *Psychological Appraisal of Children with Cerebral Defects*. Cambridge, Mass.: Harvard University Press.

Terrace H. S. 1979: *Nim: a chimpanzee who learned sign language*. New York: Alfred A. Knopf.

Tew B. 1979: The 'cocktail party syndrome' in children with hydrocephalus and spina bifida. *British Journal of Disorders of Communication*, 14: 89–101.

Tomasello M. and Farrar M. J. 1984: Cognitive bases of lexical development: object permanence and relational words. *Journal of Child Language*, 11: 477–93.

——1986: Object permanence and relational words: a lexical training study. *Journal of Child Language*, 13: 495–505.

Turnage T. W. and McGinnies E. 1973: A cross-cultural comparison of the effects of presentation mode and meaningfulness in short-term recall. *American Journal of Psychology*, 86: 369–81.

Tzeng O. and Hung D. 1981: Linguistic determinism: a written language perspective. In O. Tzeng and H. Singer (eds), *Perception of Print*, Hillsdale, NJ: Lawrence Erlbaum Associates.

Tzortzis C. and Albert M. L. 1974: Impairment of memory for sequences in conduction aphasia. *Neuropsychologia*, 12: 355–66.

Uzgiris I. C. and Hunt J. M. 1975: *Assessment in Infancy: ordinal scales of psychological development*. Urbana: University of Illinois Press.

Van Harskamp F., Van Dongen H. R. and Loonen M. C. B. 1978: Acquired aphasia with convulsive disorders in children: a case study with a seven-year follow-up. *Brain and Language*, 6: 141–8.

Vetter H. J. and Howell R. W. 1971: Theories of language acquisition. *Journal of Psycholinguistic Research*, 1: 31–64.

Vygotsky L. S. 1962: *Thought and Language*. Cambridge, Mass.: MIT Press. (First published 1934.)

Wales R. and Campbell R. 1970: On the development of comparison and the comparison of development. In G. B. Flores d'Arcais and W. J. M. Levelt (eds), *Advances in Psycholinguistics*, Amsterdam: North Holland.

Warrington E. K., Logue V. and Pratt R. T. C. 1971: The anatomical localization of selective impairment of auditory verbal short-term memory. *Neuropsychologia*, 9: 377–87.

Waryas C. L. and Ruder K. 1973: Children's sentence processing strategies: the double-object construction. Parsons Research Center Working Paper 296.

Waryas C. L. and Stremel K. 1974: On the preferred form of the double-object construction. *Journal of Psycholinguistic Research*, 3: 271–80.

Waryas C. L. and Stremel-Campbell K. 1978: Grammatical training for the language-delayed child. In R. L. Schiefelbusch (ed.), *Language Intervention Strategies*, Baltimore: University Park Press.

Wechsler D. 1967: *Wechsler Preschool and Primary Scale of Intelligence*. New York: Psychological Corporation.

Weist R. M. 1986: Tense and aspect. In P. Fletcher and M. Garman (eds), *Language Acquisition: studies in first language development*, 2nd edn, Cambridge: Cambridge University Press.

Wells G. 1979: Learning and using the auxiliary verb in English. In V. Lee (ed.), *Language Development*, London: Croom Helm.

Wescott R. W. 1970: Bini color terms. *Anthropological Linguistics*, 12: 349–60.

Wetstone H. S. and Friedlander B. Z. 1973: The effect of word order on young children's responses to simple questions and commands. *Child Development*, 44: 734–40.

Whorf B. L. 1952: *Collected Papers on Metalinguistics*. Washington, DC: Department of State, Foreign Service Institute.

——1956: see Carroll, 1956.

——1958: Science and linguistics. In E. E. Maccoby, T. M. Newcomb and E. L. Hartley (eds), *Readings in Social Psychology*, 3rd edn, New York: Holt, Rinehart and Winston.

Wilcox S. and Palermo D. S. 1975: 'In', 'on', and 'under' revisited. *Cognition*, 3: 245–54.

Wills D. D. 1977: Participant deixis in English and baby talk. In C. E. Snow and

C. A. Ferguson (eds), *Talking to Children: language input and acquisition*, Cambridge: Cambridge University Press.

Wilson L. F., Doehring D. G. and Hirsh I. J. 1960: Auditory discrimination learning by aphasic and nonaphasic children. *Journal of Speech and Hearing Research*, 3: 130–7.

Wishart J. G. and Bower T. G. R. 1985: A longitudinal study of the development of the object concept. *British Journal of Developmental Psychology*, 3: 243–58.

Withrow F. B. Jr 1964: Immediate recall by aphasic, deaf and normal children for visual forms presented simultaneously or sequentially. *American Speech and Hearing Association*, 6: 386.

Wolff P. H. 1969: The natural history of crying and other vocalizations in early infancy. In B. M. Foss (ed.), *Determinants of Infant Behaviour*, vol 4, London: Methuen.

Worster-Drought C. 1971: An unusual form of acquired aphasia in children. *Developmental Medicine and Child Neurology*, 13: 563–71.

Worster-Drought C. and Allen I. M. 1929: Congenital auditory imperception: report of a case with cogenital word deafness. *Journal of Neurology and Psychopathology*, 9: 193–208.

Wyke M. A. (ed.) 1978: *Developmental Dysphasia*. London and New York: Academic Press.

Yamada J. 1981: Evidence for the independence of language and cognition: case study of a 'hyperlinguistic' adolescent. *UCLA Working Papers in Cognitive Linguistics*, 3: 121–60.

Yamada J. and Curtiss S. 1981: The relation between language and cognition in a case of Turner's syndrome, *UCLA Working Papers in Cognitive Linguistics*, 3: 93–115.

Index

Index compiled by Meg Davies (Society of Indexers)